Your Official America Online® Membership Kit

2nd Edition

by Jennifer Watson and David Marx

Foreword by Steve Case

AOL Press

Dulles, VA

Your Official America Online® Membership Kit, 2nd Edition

Published by

AOL Press

An imprint of IDG Books Worldwide, Inc.

An International Data Group Company

919 E. Hillsdale Blvd., Suite 300

Foster City, CA 94404

www.aol.com (America Online Web site)

Copyright © 2001 America Online, Inc. All rights reserved. No part of this book, including interior design, cover design, and icons, may be reproduced or transmitted in any form, by any means (electronic, photocopying, recording, or otherwise) without the prior written permission of the publisher.

Library of Congress Control Number: 00-107572

ISBN: 0-7645-3553-6

Printed in the United States of America

10 9 8 7 6 5 4 3 2 1

1B/TQ/RR/QQ/IN

Distributed in the United States by IDG Books Worldwide, Inc. and America Online, Inc.

For general information on IDG Books Worldwide's books in the U.S., please call our Consumer Customer Service department at 800-762-2974. For reseller information, including discounts and premium sales, please call our Reseller Customer Service department at 800-434-3422.

Trademarks: All brand names and product names used in this book are trade names, service marks, trademarks, or registered trademarks of their respective owners. IDG Books Worldwide is not associated with any product or vendor mentioned in this book.

 is a trademark of America Online, Inc.

 is a registered trademark or trademark under exclusive license to IDG Books Worldwide, Inc. from International Data Group, Inc. in the United States and/or other countries.

Welcome to AOL Press™

AOL Press books provide timely guides to getting the most out of your online life. AOL Press was formed as part of the AOL family to create a complete series of official references for using America Online as well as the entire Internet — all designed to help you enjoy a fun, easy, and rewarding online experience.

AOL Press is an exciting partnership between two companies at the forefront of the knowledge and communications revolution — AOL and IDG Books Worldwide, Inc. AOL is committed to quality, ease of use, and value, and IDG Books excels at helping people understand technology.

To meet these high standards, all our books are authored by experts with the full participation of and exhaustive review by AOL's own development, technical, managerial, and marketing staff. Together, AOL and IDG Books have implemented an ambitious publishing program to develop new publications that serve every aspect of your online life.

We hope you enjoy reading this AOL Press title and find it useful. We welcome your feedback at AOL Keyword: **Contact Shop Direct** so we can keep providing information the way you want it.

About the Authors

Jennifer Watson is one of the foremost experts on America Online, authoring over ten books on learning and mastering AOL. Jennifer also authored the previous edition of *Your Official America Online Membership Kit* with her partner Dave Marx, and co-authored three editions of *The Official America Online Tour Guide* with Tom Lichty, her friend and mentor. Her invaluable compilation of keywords prepared and shared with America Online's membership became the bestselling *AOL Keywords* (now in its third edition). Jennifer followed that up with the popular *AOL Companion,* a collection of AOL tips and tricks now in its second edition, and *AOL E-Mail,* a guide to making the most of e-mail on AOL. In addition to her writing, Jennifer had the privilege of teaching America Online members and staff how to use AOL effectively and efficiently in her roles as a community leader and founder of an online training academy. Jennifer received her undergraduate degree in social psychology from the University of Michigan, a field that serves her well in understanding and explaining the new social climate on AOL and the Internet. Jennifer lives in Ann Arbor, Michigan with her dog Kippi, an adorable Alaskan Malamute.

Dave Marx is the co-author of *AOL E-Mail* and a major contributor to Jennifer Watson's *AOL Keywords* and *AOL Companion* titles. Dave's early journalism training led to a career in broadcasting and music production, and he's zigzagged from technical titles to writing, producing, and back again. After many years as a broadcast engineering supervisor and recording engineer, Dave found a new world of communications on America Online. Initially applying his background in computers, technical communications, and end-user education, he spent over a year and a half as a Tech Live Advisor, helping members use AOL's features and software. For three years, he held leadership positions as a course developer and instructor in Jennifer's training academy. He is now working full-time as a writer and editor in the worlds of print and online publishing.

Credits

America Online

Technical Editors
Ann Burkhart
Jim Callahan
John Crotty
Kerstin Crutchfield
Kristie Cunningham
Caroline Curtin
Keith Fleming
Todd Forest
Marta Grutka
Pam Irvine
Sandra Jackson
Jeff Kimball
Jane Lennon
Debra Llavoy
Mary-Sara Ortutay
Dan Pacheco
Mark Pilipczuk
Lisa Pittman
Bruce Stimpson
Ginny Wydler
Blair Zervos

Cover Design
DKG Design, Inc.

IDG Books Worldwide

Senior Project Editor
Paul Levesque

Acquisitions Editor
Kathy Yankton

Senior Copy Editor
Kim Darosett

Proof Editor
Jill Mazurczyk

Technical Editor
Susan Glinert

Permissions Editor
Carmen Krikorian

Publishing Director
Andy Cummings

Editorial Manager
Leah Cameron

Media Development Manager
Heather Dismore

Editorial Assistants
Candace Nicholson, Seth Kerney

Project Coordinator
Regina Snyder

Layout and Graphics
LeAndra Johnson, Brian Torwelle, Erin Zeltner

Proofreaders
Laura Albert, Arielle Carole Mennelle, Susan Moritz, Angel Perez, Marianne Santy, Charles Spencer

Indexer
Ann Norcross

Acknowledgments

First and foremost, we thank you, the members of America Online. You are why we joined AOL, why we became involved, and why we're writing this book. You've created a special community to be proud of.

Thank you to George Louie, who has offered support to Jennifer throughout every book she's ever written. George is also the original co-author of the glossary that appears at the back of the book. Thank you, George!

Thank you to the fine folks at IDG Books Worldwide, who continue to impress us with their professionalism and excellence: Andy Cummings, Paul Levesque, Leah Cameron, Kathy Yankton, and Kim Darosett.

Lastly, thank you to the folks at America Online who helped us with our questions: Marta Grutka, Kathy Harper, Kristi Cunningham, and Jane Lennon.

Contents at a Glance

About the Authors vi
Acknowledgments. vii
Foreword. xxiii
Introduction 1
Quick Start 7

Part I: Starting Your Online Journey with AOL 15
Chapter 1: Discovering the Welcome Screen 17
Chapter 2: Getting Around AOL 31
Chapter 3: Finding Help 45
Chapter 4: Online Safety 61

Part II: Communicating with the World 85
Chapter 5: Using E-Mail 87
Chapter 6: Advanced E-Mail 121
Chapter 7: Instant Messaging 147
Chapter 8: The Buddy List Feature 163
Chapter 9: Chat Rooms and Other Online Forums 173
Chapter 10: Downloading Files 209
Chapter 11: "You've Got Pictures" 225

Part III: Customizing Your AOL 241
Chapter 12: AOL Anywhere and Preference Settings 243
Chapter 13: My Calendar 281
Chapter 14: Favorite Places 291
Chapter 15: Shopping Preferences 301
Chapter 16: AOL Hometown 313

Part IV: Searching on AOL & the Internet 329
Chapter 17: AOL Search Tools 331
Chapter 18: People Search 343
Chapter 19: Internet Shopping 355
Chapter 20: Business and Information Channels 363
Chapter 21: Personal Enrichment and Information Channels 387

Part V: AOL Member Benefits and Premium Services 413
Chapter 22: AOLTV 415
Chapter 23: Long Distance and Paging 423
Chapter 24: Shopping and Reward Programs 431

Part VI: Appendixes 439
Appendix A: How to Get the Most Out of AOL 441
Appendix B: Broadband Opportunities 453
Appendix C: Glossary 459

Index 477

Table of Contents

About the Authors . . . . **vi**

Author's Acknowledgements . . . . **vii**

Foreword . . . . **xxiii**

Introduction **1**
    Who Should Read This Book? 2
    What Hardware and Software Do You Need? 2
    How This Book Is Organized 2
        Part I: Starting Your Online Journey with AOL 2
        Part II: Communicating with the World 3
        Part III: Customizing Your AOL 3
        Part IV: Searching on AOL & the Internet 3
        Part V: AOL Member Benefits and Premium Services 3
    Conventions Used in This Book 3
        Windows and Macintosh Conventions 4
        Key Combinations 4
        Arrow Combinations 4
        Typographical Conventions 4
    Navigating Through This Book 4

Quick Start **7**
    AOL and the Internet 7
    The AOL Mission 8
    What You Can Expect to See and Do 8
        Learn New Things and Explore Your Interests 8
        Meet New People and Strengthen Old Ties 8
        Manage Your Finances and Spend Money Wisely 10
        Keep Up-to-Date 11
        Contribute Something 12

Part I: Starting Your Online Journey with AOL — 15

Chapter 1: Discovering the Welcome Screen — 17

Welcome Screen — 19
    Icons — 19
    Links — 20
    My Places — 20

Menus — 21
    File — 21
    Edit — 23
    Print — 24
    Window — 24
    Sign Off — 25
    Help — 26

Toolbar — 26

Navigation Bar — 27

Chapter 2: Getting Around AOL — 31

Mouse Clicks and Keyboard Shortcuts — 32

Buttons, Icons, and Hyperlinks — 35

Windows and Scroll Bars — 37

Close, Maximize, Restore, Minimize, Resize, and Move — 39

List Boxes, Menus, and Drop-Down Lists — 40
    List Boxes — 41
    Drop-Down Menus and Drop-Down Lists — 42

Text Boxes — 42

Keywords and URLs — 43

Chapter 3: Finding Help — 45

Offline Help — 47
    Software Help — 47
    Phone Support — 49
    More Books — 49

Online Help (When Connected to the AOL Service) — 49
    Welcome to AOL — 49
    QuickStart — 50

| Table of Contents | xi |

AOL Help 51
Live One-on-One Help 54
AOL Help Community 55
Help Classes 57
Computing Help 58

Chapter 4: Online Safety 61

AOL Neighborhood Watch 62
Terms of Service 64
Notify AOL 66
Parental Controls 68
Creating Your Child's Screen Name 68
Selecting a Parental Controls Age Category 69
Online Timer 72
E-Mail Control 73
Chat Control 75
Instant Message Control 76
Web Control 77
Additional Master Screen Names Control 78
Download Control 78
Newsgroup Control 79
Premium Services Control 80
Categories 81
Kids Only 81

Part II: Communicating with the World   85

Chapter 5: Using E-Mail 87

What Is E-Mail? 88
Reading Your First E-Mail 89
Scanning Your Online Mailbox 90
Reading New E-Mail 90
Accessing Old Mail 94
Dealing with Junk Mail 95
Sorting Your Online Mailbox 97
Downloading Attached Files 98

E-Mail Addresses on AOL and the Internet 101
The Address Book 102
The Mail Menu 105
The Mail Center 107
Sending Your First E-Mail 107
    Courtesy Copies 110
    Blind Courtesy Copies 110
Replying to E-Mail 111
    Replying to All 112
    Quoting 112
Forwarding E-Mail 113
Checking the Status of Sent Mail 114
Unsending Mail 115
Attaching Files 116

Chapter 6: Advanced E-Mail 121

Saving and Organizing Your E-Mail in the Filing Cabinet 122
    Automatically Saving E-Mail in the Filing Cabinet 123
    Using the Filing Cabinet 123
    Searching the Filing Cabinet 126
    Organizing the Filing Cabinet 127
Offline Mail 128
Spell Checking 130
Greetings and Mail Extras 131
Mail Controls 133
Styled Text 136
Signatures 137
Inserting Pictures and Graphics 139
Picture Finder 142
AOL Mail (On the Web) 143

Chapter 7: Instant Messaging 147

What Is an Instant Message? 149
Sending and Receiving Instant Messages 149
    Timestamping 154
    Emoticons 156
    Icons 156

Table of Contents

Turning Off Instant Messages	157
Away Messages	159
AOL Instant Messenger	161

Chapter 8: The Buddy List Feature 163

Who Are Your Buddies?	165
Setting Up Your Buddy List	165
Using Your Buddy List	167
Getting Information at a Glance	169
Setting Up an Away Message	169

Chapter 9: Chat Rooms and Other Online Forums 173

Chat and Conferences	174
Finding Communities	175
Anatomy of a Chat	177
Chatting	180
Creating Your Own Chat Room	180
Logging a Chat	182
Auditoriums	183
Message Boards	185
Finding Communities	186
Reading Messages	188
Finding Messages	191
Setting Message Board Preferences	192
Viewing	*193*
Posting	*194*
Filtering	*194*
Posting Messages	195
Replying to Messages	197
Newsgroups	198
Finding Communities	198
Subscribing to Newsgroups	200
Reading Newsgroup Messages	201
Setting Newsgroup Preferences	203
Finding Newsgroup Messages	205
Posting Messages	206
Downloading Messages	206

Chapter 10: Downloading Files 209

Downloading Files 210
How to Download 211
File Libraries 214
Download Center 216
    Searching for Files 216
    Browsing Files 218
Viruses and Trojan Horses 218
Download Manager 220
Automatic AOL 222

Chapter 11: "You've Got Pictures" 225

Dropping Off Your Pictures 227
Viewing Your Pictures Online 227
    Viewing a Roll 229
    Renaming a Roll 231
    Finding a Missing Roll 231
Saving Pictures and Rolls 232
Creating an Album 233
Downloading Pictures to Your Computer 235
Sharing Your Pictures 237
    E-Mail a Picture 237
    Buddy Albums 238
    Prints and Photo Merchandise 238
Safety Considerations 239
    Parental Concerns 239
    Secure Commerce 240

Part III: Customizing Your AOL   241

Chapter 12: AOL Anywhere and Preference Settings 243

Screen Names and Passwords 244
    Choosing Screen Names 245
    Choosing Passwords 247
    Creating, Deleting, and Restoring Screen Names 247
    Changing Passwords 250

AOL Anywhere 251
AOL Preferences 253
   Marketing 254
   Passwords 255
   Privacy 256
   Association 258
   Mail 258
   Automatic AOL 261
   Spelling 263
   Font, Text, and Graphics 264
   Chat Preferences 266
   Filing Cabinet 267
   Toolbar & Sound 268
   Download 270
   Internet Options (Web Preferences) 272
      General Web Preferences 272
      Security 274
      Content 275
      Web Graphics 277
      Shopping Assistant 277
   Multimedia 277
Connection and Setup Preferences 278

Chapter 13: My Calendar 281

Getting Started 283
My Calendar Settings 285
My Calendar View 286
Adding New Appointments to My Calendar 286
Idea List 288
Event Directory 289

Chapter 14: Favorite Places 291

Finding and Adding Favorite Places 293
Favorite Places Window 295
Editing and Organizing Your Favorite Places List 296
Sharing Favorite Places 298
My Places 299

Chapter 15: Shopping Preferences 301

Ringing Up the Sale with Quick Checkout 302
Using the Reminder Service 305
Getting Good Customer Service 307
Shopping with Confidence with the AOL Shopping Guarantee 308
Getting Help from the AOL Shopping Assistant 309
Surfing Safety 311

Chapter 16: AOL Hometown 313

The Hometown Community 315
1-2-3 Publish 316
Easy Designer 320
Advanced Authoring 324
Groups@AOL 325
AOL Invitations 327

Part IV: Searching on AOL & the Internet 329

Chapter 17: AOL Search Tools 331

AOL Search 332
Special Searches 335
Channel Searches 338
Local Searches 339
Keyword Searches 340

Chapter 18: People Search 343

People Directory 344
Yellow Pages 348
White Pages 350
E-Mail Finder 351

Chapter 19: Internet Shopping 355

Browsing the Categories 356
Shopping Search 359
Shopping AOL Shop Direct 361

Chapter 20: Business and Information Channels 363

- The Channels 364
- News Channel 366
- International Channel 369
- Personal Finance Channel 373
  - Quotes, Charts, News & Research 373
  - Departments 374
  - Financial and Brokerage Centers 375
- Careers & Work Channel 376
  - Job Search 376
  - Career Resources 377
- Computer Center 377
  - CNET 378
  - Download Center 378
  - Help and Education 379
  - Communities 380
- Research & Learn Channel 380
  - Explore a Subject 381
  - References 381
  - Ask-a-Teacher 382
  - Education and Courses 383
- Local Guide Channel (Digital City) 384

Chapter 21: Personal Enrichment and Information Channels 387

- Sports Channel 388
  - Scoreboard 389
  - Grandstand 390
- Travel Channel 391
  - Fares & Reservations 392
  - The Independent Traveler 393
- Entertainment Channel 394
- Games Channel 397
  - The Game Parlor 398
  - Xtreme Games 398
  - Game Shows Online 399
- Autos Channel 399

House & Home Channel 400
Women Channel 401
Shopping Channel 402
Health Channel 402
   allHealth.com 402
   Thrive Online 404
Parenting Channel 404
   Parent Soup 405
   Moms Online 405
   The Genealogy Forum 406
Kids Only Channel 407
Teens Channel 408
People Connection 409
   Ages & Stages 409
   Gay & Lesbian 410

Part V: AOL Member Benefits and Premium Services   413

Chapter 22: AOLTV 415
What Is AOLTV? 416
What You Can Do With AOLTV 417
What You Need For AOLTV 421

Chapter 23: Long Distance and Paging 423
AOL Long Distance 424
Paging 425
AOL Anywhere 426
The AOL Household: Get "Connected" to Match Your Lifestyle 426
AOL at Work or on the Road: Stay Connected to Fit Your Schedule 427
AOL Plus 429
   AOL Plus Broadband Services 429
   AOL Plus Content 429

Chapter 24: Shopping and Reward Programs 431
AOL Rewards 432
AOL Visa 433

AOL Insider Savings Club 434
AOL Netmarket 435
AOL Travelers Advantage and AutoVantage 436
Blockbuster Movie 436

Part VI: Appendixes   439

Appendix A: How to Get the Most Out of AOL 441
Basic System Requirements 441
    AOL 6.0 for Windows 95 441
    AOL 6.0 for Windows 98 442
    AOL 6.0 for Windows NT/2000 442
    Macintosh 442
    The Software 443
    The Money 444
    The Screen Name 444
Upgrading Your Software 445
Guest Access 450

Appendix B: Broadband Opportunities 453
DSL 455
AOL Plus Broadband Service 456
Satellite 456
Cable 457

Appendix C: Glossary 459

Index 477

Foreword

When we founded America Online, Inc., our objectives were simple. First, we wanted to make going online easy and convenient. Second, we wanted to make it something that would be central to people's lives.

It's clear that we've succeeded. Our focus on improving people's everyday lives is undoubtedly the main reason that AOL continues to be the world's leading online service, with a worldwide community of more than 24 million users.

More important, AOL has gone beyond a place at the center of these members' lives to become a powerful tool for managing those lives. Every day, millions of AOL users communicate by e-mail and Instant Messages. They check hundreds of millions of stock quotes, spend millions of dollars shopping online, book travel, order tickets, find restaurants, choose a movie, get directions, read the news, get help on homework, do their banking, get loans, access information about their health, play games, download music and run their businesses.

Now, AOL is about to move even further into the core of your daily life as we enter the second interactive revolution. Our combination with Time Warner will create the defining company of the Internet Century, offering users a range of exciting new products and services. AOL is leading the way as the Internet goes anywhere through AOL TV, our new kitchen appliance, and our availability over cell phones and palmtop devices.

And AOL's new 6.0 software, driven by members' suggestions, is once again redefining ease and convenience online ... with great new features that make it easier to get to the content and services you want, manage your e-mail and file cabinets, make the most of broadband connections, share digital photos online, download and play music, and open the door to AOL Anywhere services.

But even all these opportunities don't begin to scratch the surface of what you can do on AOL. That's why Jennifer Watson — the author of *AOL Companion* and *AOL Keywords* and co-author of 2 previous editions of this book — has joined with Dave Marx, the co-author of the previous edition of this book and *AOL E-mail,* to turn out yet another edition of the AOL Membership Kit. Jennifer's a longtime AOL community leader and currently coordinates AOL's online training center for community leaders and content providers, and Dave's a former AOL Tech Live adviser.

They know their way around the AOL service — including the 6.0 version. And they draw on that experience to offer you a virtual guided tour of the best that AOL can offer: the unique and feature-rich communications opportunities, the many convenience features, the unmatched range and quality of shopping partners, the extensive range of first-class financial services, the multitude of news and information sources, the entertainment guides — and most important, the living, breathing community of members.

My hope is that with the new *AOL Membership Kit* you'll too find AOL offers more and more of what you need to manage your daily life — bringing you new value, convenience . . . and fun.

Steve Case
Chairman and CEO, America Online, Inc.

Introduction

We can still remember our first timid moves into the world of America Online. A poke here in search of a stock quotation, a jab there for some computer/tech knowledge. It didn't take long to find out there was something else afoot here. There were people. Real people who were reaching out in every direction, straining to make contact. You could feel the tendrils of emotion hidden behind simple black-on-white text, and sense the hurt and frustration when our first clumsy attempts at communication failed to convey our intended meaning. It was all so ephemeral, yet more real than many of our face-to-face interactions. We just *had* to master it and become full-fledged members of this brave new community.

Of course, there was information, and news. We learned our way around search engines and into Gopher and FTP space while the World Wide Web was first being spun. We tried every resource and a ridiculous number of free programs before we had any reason to fear viruses. And we searched. If it was a research library, it was the noisiest library around. We could chat with our friends, pass notes under the table, shout questions at the top of our lungs, all while our electronic desktops were cluttered with search tools and buried under page after page of information.

And we loved it, and nurtured it, and championed it to the world. And as we labored to make our chat rooms and forums friendlier and more comprehensive and easier to navigate, the folks back in Virginia were creating better and better software and systems and finding more and more ways to make the online experience rewarding for members. And despite the technical glitches and growing pains, we saw AOL grow from 200,000 members to 1 million, 5 million, and 20 million.

It's hard to believe how mature, confident, and polished AOL has become over the years, but it has. We know that the America Online you are now first discovering will be as exciting for you as it has been for us. If the past is any measure of the future, you, too, will look back in a few years and marvel at how far you and AOL have come together.

Who Should Read This Book?

Are you an AOL member, or are you considering a membership? Then this book is for you! We present a broad overview of the many features and areas that make up AOL's software and services. We know it will be valuable to everyone, but it will be most valuable to new members. In the space allotted, we can't possibly explore the richness and depth of AOL in the kind of detail that we would like. Even so, we hope to paint a picture that will leave you eager to dive in and make AOL your home, or open your eyes to new possibilities and understanding.

What Hardware and Software Do You Need?

This edition is written about America Online software version 6.0 for Windows 95/98/NT/2000. The software requires a PC-compatible Pentium-class computer with at least 16MB RAM (at least 64MB for Windows NT/2000); 70–190MB available hard drive space; 640 x 480, 256 color or better display (optimized for 800 x 600); and a 14.4 Kbps modem. (See Appendix A for more details about hardware and software requirements.)

How This Book Is Organized

Your Official America Online Tour Guide, 6th Edition, takes you on a step-by-step journey, loosely modeled on a travel guide. It is organized into five parts: the preparations and information needed for AOL; communicating with others through e-mail, IMs, chats, and boards; customizing AOL through preferences, tools, and forums; searching AOL and the Internet; and a brief look at member benefits and perks. Two appendixes and a glossary follow the main text to provide detailed background information on upgrading to AOL 6.0, high-speed connection options, and online terms.

Part I: Starting Your Online Journey with AOL

Part I begins with a tour of the AOL Welcome screen, along with the menu bar, toolbar, and navigation bar. Attention is also given to the basics of common Windows features, which are essential for navigating the AOL service. You also learn of the many ways you can find additional help and information, both offline and online. And because your online travels will bring you in contact with people of all descriptions, online safety, Parental Controls, and online etiquette complete the tour.

Part II: Communicating with the World

This part is dedicated solely to the many ways you can communicate with others through AOL. It begins with two chapters on e-mail, the first mode of online communication most members will use. Mastery of e-mail and its many features empowers you for the journey yet to come. You will also explore the many other modes of online communication — Chat, instant messages, message boards, and Internet newsgroups.

Part III: Customizing Your AOL

The third part shows you how to personalize the AOL software for your needs. It begins with a tour of the settings and services of "AOL Anywhere"℠, along with a rundown of your AOL software preferences. Next is "My Calendar"℠ for planning ahead, followed by Favorite Places to help you find your way. We also discuss shopping preferences for safe and enjoyable shopping online. The part concludes with an introduction to creating your own Web page in AOL Hometown.

Part IV: Searching on AOL and the Internet

Learn how to search and explore with AOL's search tools, from AOL Search to channel and local searches. You also find out how to search outside AOL with Netscape and other search engines. Next you explore the methods of searching for e-mail addresses and street addresses. That is followed by a primer on shopping online, with a tour of shopping destinations. Finally, you go on a grand tour of AOL's channels, from News and Personal Finance to Games and Interests.

Part V: AOL Member Benefits and Premium Services

The guide concludes with a peek at the many, many AOL member benefits and perks. We turn you on to AOLTV, get you connected with AOL Long Distance and Paging, show you how to access AOL anywhere, and explore the various shopping and reward programs.

Conventions Used in This Book

Throughout this book, we use a number of conventions to help explain concepts or directions. Here is an explanation of each of these conventions.

Windows and Macintosh Conventions

This book covers the Windows AOL version 6.0 software; the Mac AOL version 6.0 software was not yet available for evaluation when this book was written. If pertinent information for other versions or for the Mac is available, we clearly communicate this in the text. If you don't see a notation regarding other versions, please assume we're discussing Windows AOL version 6.0.

Key Combinations

AOL offers many keyboard shortcuts for quicker, easier use. Whenever possible, we give relevant key combinations for various features in the text. For instance, Ctrl+M is the keyboard shortcut to open a new Write Mail window. In this example, *Ctrl* refers to the key labeled Ctrl (or Control) on your keyboard (usually located in the lower-left corner). The + symbol indicates you should hold down the Ctrl key while typing the following letter, which is M in this case. Chapter 2 presents a list of all key combinations available with the AOL software.

Arrow Combinations

When we give directions on what menus and menu items to use, we use an arrow in between the steps. For example, when you see the command "choose File⇨Print," this means to open the File menu and choose Print.

Typographical Conventions

AOL keywords (shortcuts to AOL features and forums) always appear in bold — for instance, AOL Keyword: **Help** (in this example, *Help* is the keyword). The bold formatting helps to distinguish a keyword from the text surrounding it. You do not need to type a keyword in all capital letters to use it. In fact, keywords are neither case- nor space-sensitive. So typing **HELP** or **help** into the Address box on the AOL toolbar or in the Keyword window does the same thing: It takes you to AOL Help.

Navigating Through This Book

Every chapter begins with a Quick Look, a list of key points covered in the text, and a brief introduction. The chapters conclude with "Putting Your Knowledge to Work," a signpost suggesting further travels. Within each chapter, we will call your attention to important concepts and information through the use of the following icons:

Introduction

Tips provide you with extra knowledge that separates the novice from the pro.

Notes provide additional or critical information and technical data on the current topic.

Definitions explain important terms and concepts.

Cross-Reference icons indicate places where you can find more information on a particular topic.

Find It Online icons direct you to a location on AOL or the Internet.

Caution icons warn you of potential problems or pitfalls to avoid.

Quick Start

Welcome! We're delighted you've chosen to join us for your tour of the America Online service.

In this guide, we show you how to find your way around the service and find a helping hand, how to keep yourself and your family safe online, and how to use e-mail. We also show you how to interact with fellow AOL members in chat rooms, on message boards, and by using the instant message feature. You find out how to download and exchange computer files and photos, shop in an electronic mall, and maintain a stock portfolio. We also take you on a grand tour of AOL's channels, from Computing to Games, Health News to Personal Finance, Sports, and Travel, and more than a few others in between. And just when you think we're done, we also show you how to search for people and information throughout the AOL service and the Internet.

AOL and the Internet

America Online means many things to many people. By itself, the AOL service is a community of over 23 million members — individuals, families, and companies. Even if you never pass beyond its limits, AOL is the kind of diverse, thriving metropolis that can be a home to people of all interests and sensibilities. You can meet and interact with groups of fellow AOL members in chat rooms; on public message boards; in live, one-on-one conversations using the instant message feature, and, of course, through e-mail. AOL's community is so large and its offerings so diverse that you might never be tempted to stray beyond its comforting borders.

America Online is also part of a much wider world, the international computer network known as the Internet. Although AOL is by far the largest "city" on the Internet, it is still only a small part of that world. All the wonders and riches of the Internet are available to AOL's members at no additional charge. You can exchange e-mail and view Web sites anywhere on the globe. Indeed, AOL and the Internet make up a global community where nearly any need for information and interaction can be quickly satisfied.

The AOL Mission

AOL's mission is to build a global medium as central to people's lives as the telephone or television ... and even more valuable.

What You Can Expect to See and Do

The AOL service is overflowing with information on an incredible array of topics, from business and finance to health and hobbies. Whether you are looking for formal lessons, want to browse around on your own, or join a community dedicated to your favorite pastime, the AOL service has something for you.

Learn New Things and Explore Your Interests

Your search can start right at the top with AOL's Welcome Screen (shown in Figure Q-1), where you can access your e-mail, pictures, and chat, as well as links to the latest content and features.

Meet New People and Strengthen Old Ties

Can you really make new friends on AOL? *Community* is an important word around AOL. It means that online areas not only deliver information and services, but also create places where people can meet, get to know each other, and share their knowledge and interests.

Quick Start

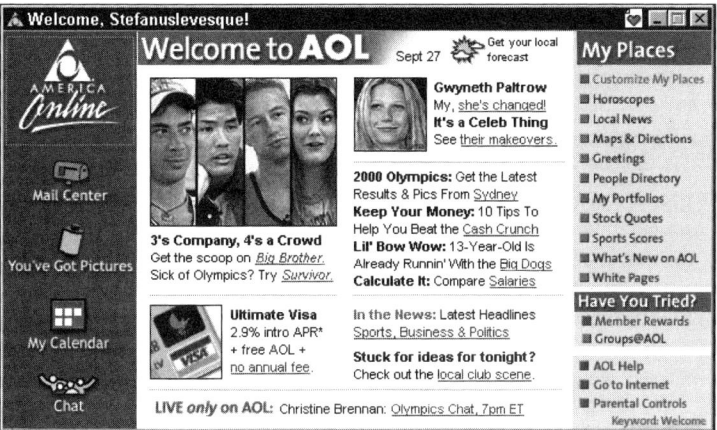

Figure Q-1. The AOL Welcome Screen.

Community is not just about chance encounters in chat rooms (although chat rooms are a great way to meet people from all over the world). Message boards on topics of every description give people a chance to share their questions, answers, and thoughts with people who have similar interests. Live events bring thousands of people together for interviews with movers, shakers, and movie stars — you can ask the guests questions and share the experience with a small group of friends or other AOL members. Once you've created ties, the instant message and Buddy List® features help strengthen those ties.

The instant message feature (shown in Figure Q-2) offers the ability to exchange private real-time messages, and the Buddy List feature indicates which of your friends are online at the moment. Together, these features give you a sense of always being connected to your friends and loved ones. When you see that a friend has signed on to the AOL service, just send that person a quick instant message. Before you know it, you'll both be caught up on the latest news, and the two of you can keep sharing thoughts and ideas for as long as you're both online. What's more, this conversation costs much, much less than a phone call because it's all included in your monthly AOL membership!

Finally, there's AOL e-mail. More than 67 million e-mail messages are exchanged over AOL every day. E-mail can tie together far-flung families, friends, and business associates in a way the telephone or post office never could. You can address one

You must use AOL software to make use of the AOL service. This allows AOL to seam-lessly integrate its many features so that you can chat, exchange e-mail, surf the Web, download files, check your stock portfolio, and much more.

The instant message feature is discussed in Chapter 7, and the Buddy List feature is discussed in Chapter 8.

See Chapters 5 and 6 for details on AOL e-mail.

message to dozens or even hundreds of people and instantly share news, views, and even photos with relations all over the world, at absolutely no extra charge.

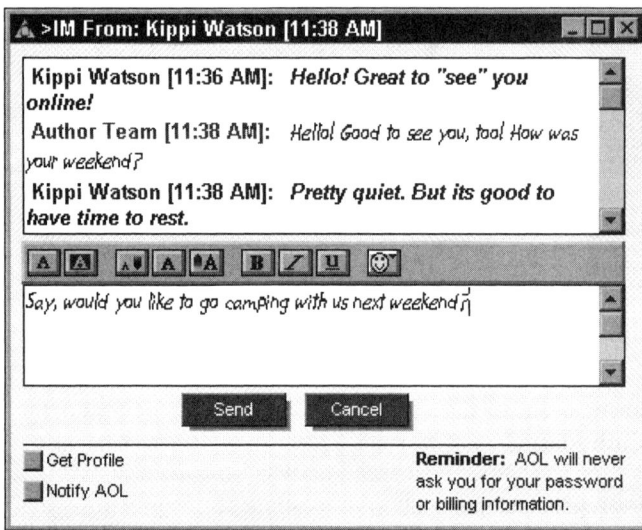

Figure Q-2. The instant message feature brings a far-off relative a whole lot closer.

Manage Your Finances and Spend Money Wisely

Everyone has a nest egg to build and bills to pay, and those jobs get more complicated with each passing day. AOL can make your life a little easier. With AOL, you can trade stocks, manage your bank accounts, pay bills, shop for a home, apply for a mortgage, obtain insurance quotes, and get help with financial aid for your college-age children, all without leaving the comfort of your home!

AOL's Personal Finance Channel, the center for all these activities, is where you find relevant financial information. Track your investments with an online stock portfolio, open an online brokerage account, calculate interest on a loan, or find lessons in nearly every aspect of home finance — all through AOL.

Now that AOL has shown you the tools that might help make you richer, it can help you save time by shopping online. Shop@AOL is the biggest shopping destination on the Internet (see Figure Q-3).

Quick Start

Shop for everything for your home, from appliances for the kitchen to a Zip drive for your computer. For that matter, let AOL help you shop for your next home, too! From clothing to chocolates, flowers to furniture, and toys to televisions, there's little you can't buy or comparison-shop for online. Are you going places? Through your AOL connection, you can get airline tickets, theater tickets, movie tickets, and concert tickets, and, if you do your banking online, you can even pay for parking tickets.

AOL and its retailing partners go to great lengths to gain and maintain your trust. Your credit card information is carefully protected, AOL's Certified Merchants Program promises the highest standards of customer service and quality, and AOL stands directly behind those merchants with its own money-back guarantee.

See Chapter 20 for more about the Personal Finance Channel.

Shopping preferences are detailed in Chapter 15, and shopping sites are discussed in Chapter 19.

Figure Q-3. Shop@AOL — shop 'til you drop, 24 hours a day, without leaving home.

Keep Up-to-Date

How does the AOL service help keep you up-to-date? It starts with the Welcome Screen. Do you have e-mail? What's happening on AOL today, how's the local weather, and what's the top news story? The Welcome Screen has the answers to all these questions.

The My Calendar service, shown in Figure Q-4, is an electronic appointment book that you tailor to your needs and interests. My Calendar's Event Directory has lists of online events, concerts, TV shows, and sporting events. Just click the items

Get to know the Welcome Screen in Chapter 1.

You can find more details on My Calendar in Chapter 13.

you want to appear on your calendar, and the AOL 6.0 software adds them automatically. You can also schedule events for yourself, your friends, and your family. Create recurring entries for birthdays, weekly softball games, or your carpool schedule. Not only can you keep up-to-date with events, but you can also share them with anyone else who uses My Calendar.

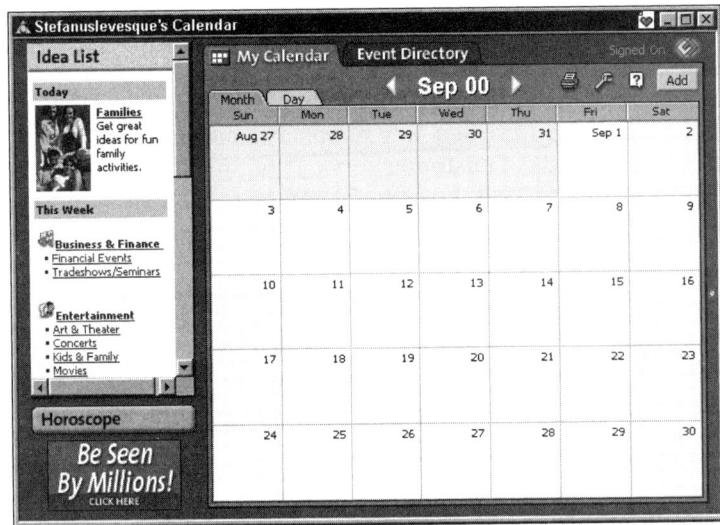

Figure Q-4. My Calendar works online or off, and is available from the AOL service or the Internet.

From the moment you sign on to the moment you sign off, a world of news and information swirls around you. Monitor the news ticker at AOL News, keep abreast of the financial markets, and keep your eyes on the sports scoreboard, all at the same time. The current weather report is just a click away. Leave every one of these items up on your screen while you chat online, shop, or plan your next vacation.

Contribute Something

Learn about AOL News in Chapter 20.

The online world is a two-way street where you can share your expertise, interests, and passions with others. Exchange files and pictures in libraries, voice your opinions and experiences on message boards and newsgroups, organize a chat in People Connection, and even publish to the Web — AOL provides the means. Every AOL member (in fact, each one of the seven screen names on a member's account) can create a home page on the Web at no extra cost (see Figure Q-5).

Create your own Web page in Chapter 16.

Figure Q-5. AOL Hometown lets you create your very own Web page.

What's New in AOL 6.0

America Online introduces many new features and improvements in AOL 6.0. Here are some highlights:

- A redesigned Welcome Screen helps you get where you're going even faster — with more news that matters to you.

- My Places now lets you store up to ten favorite places on the Welcome Screen.

- The "My Calendar"^{sm} service is now accessible from anywhere, AOL or the Internet, online or offline.

- Mailbox and Filing Cabinet sorting let you sort all your e-mail.

- Auto-completion of e-mail addresses means less typing.

- HTML-formatted mail is now supported.

- Attached files can now be decompressed automatically at download.

- The Filing Cabinet can be backed up and restored manually and automatically.

Continued

What's New in AOL 6.0 *(continued)*

- An enhanced Address Book feature has expanded data fields and enables you to print records.
- The Address Book now travels with you, regardless of what computer you're using.
- You can personalize your instant messages with new Buddy Icons. And a new Insert Smile preference automatically converts a :) text smile — or other popular emoticons — to a yellow smiley face graphic.
- You can also set a customized "do not disturb" message while online, and receive notice of what instant messages you received while busy and the time each message was sent.
- New Groups@AOL lets you set up personalized *groups* on the Web, where you can get together with friends, family, and other social groups to plan events and parties, post quick notes to each other, share photos, hold discussions, and more.
- The new AOL Shopping Assistant[sm] delivers contextual store and product information while you shop.
- AOL Invitations allows you to create a personalized online invitation and send it to friends and family who can conveniently RSVP and get directions.
- A built-in AOL Media Player lets you play music and videos with the click of a button.

Putting Your Knowledge to Work

AOL wants to be sure your experience as a new member is satisfying. As you may have already noticed, AOL recommends this book to every new member and extends an invitation to take a new member tour of AOL and its features. If you haven't already taken the tour, why not check it out? We even guide you through this tour in Chapter 3.

Before we go much further, we'd like to get back to where everything begins: the AOL Welcome Screen. Join us in Chapter 1 as we explore the Welcome Screen, menu bar, toolbar, and navigation bar.

PART I

STARTING YOUR ONLINE JOURNEY WITH AOL

Chapter 1
Discovering the Welcome Screen

Chapter 2
Getting Around AOL

Chapter 3
Finding Help

Chapter 4
Online Safety

CHAPTER

1

DISCOVERING THE WELCOME SCREEN

Quick Look

▶ Welcome Screen   page 19
Get started in the right direction with the Welcome Screen, which appears as soon as you sign on to the AOL service. You can use it to collect your e-mail, keep up on the news, and access your Favorite Places on AOL.

▶ AOL Toolbar   page 26
The bar of menus, icons, and buttons at the top of your AOL window is the AOL toolbar. Use the toolbar to navigate and perform a variety of actions on AOL.

▶ AOL Navigation Bar   page 27
You can zip around AOL with the help of the AOL navigation bar, situated directly below your toolbar. Use it to move forward and backward between pages, go to AOL keywords and Internet addresses, and search for the information you want online.

Chapter 1

Discovering the Welcome Screen

IN THIS CHAPTER

Starting your online day with AOL's Welcome Screen

Saving files, copying text, and rearranging windows with the menu bar

Accessing e-mail, chat, settings, and Favorite Places with the AOL toolbar

Browsing AOL and the Web with the navigation bar

"Welcome! You've got mail! You've got pictures!" The Welcome Screen is a great way to explore America Online and the perfect start to a busy day. From the Welcome Screen, you can check the news and weather, read your e-mail, and review your appointment calendar — it delivers everything but a cup of coffee. After you've finished with that warm welcome, we show you all the basic navigation tools at the top of your screen, which we refer to throughout this book.

Welcome Screen

From the moment you sign on to the moment you sign off, AOL's Welcome Screen, shown in Figure 1-1, stays with you. You can minimize it to a small box at the bottom of your AOL window, but it's never far from your reach.

Figure 1-1. The AOL Welcome Screen.

Have you forgotten which screen name you're currently using? Just look at the top of the Welcome Screen!

Don't worry if you're unfamiliar with computing terms like click, window, icon, menu, and button. We cover these words and much more in Chapter 2.

The Welcome Screen offers a wide variety of useful information and services intended to make your AOL experience as enjoyable and productive as possible. Like the front page of your daily newspaper, it offers a combination of indispensable daily features, late-breaking news, and information to help you make the most of your day.

Icons

Along the left-hand side of the Welcome Screen is a row of large icons for e-mail, "You've Got Pictures," My Calendar, and Chat:

▶ **E-mail:** You know if you have new e-mail because the red mail flag is raised on the mail icon. One click of the mouse opens your online mailbox.

See Chapter 5 to find out how to make the most of your e-mail.

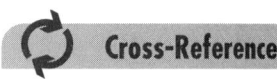

See Chapter 11 to learn more about "You've Got Pictures."

Learn how to use the My Calendar service in Chapter 13.

Learn about AOL's online chats in Chapter 9.

See Chapter 14 to learn how to customize My Places.

Visit Chapter 4 to learn more about Parental Controls.

- ▶ **"You've Got Pictures":** AOL and Kodak's film processing service delivers pictures to your AOL account. Click here when the film canister icon changes to show exposed film, indicating your pictures are available for viewing.
- ▶ **My Calendar:** Click the calendar grid icon to display your personal online calendar.
- ▶ **Chat:** The Chat button takes you to People Connection, AOL's center for person-to-person interaction.

Even the big AOL triangle logo in the upper-left-hand corner is a button. Click it whenever you want to find out What's New on AOL.

Links

The center of the Welcome Screen is packed with pictures, hyperlinks, and buttons that lead to useful information features and the day's hot topics, including your local weather forecast. Click the blue hyperlinks to explore the topics and stories that catch your interest. This center part of the Welcome Screen is constantly updated with news and timely topics, so keep checking back throughout the day.

My Places

On the right-hand side of the screen is the My Places feature. My Places lets you customize your Welcome Screen with links to the areas you use most often. Below My Places is the Have You Tried? area, which highlights some of AOL's most useful features. Finally, in the bottom right-hand corner, you find handy buttons for Parental Controls (which help parents tailor their children's AOL experience), the Web, and AOL Help.

To customize My Places, follow these steps:

1. Click the Customize My Places button in the Welcome Screen.
2. Use the drop-down menus to select the places you want to see on your Welcome Screen. You can choose from areas like the Computing Channel's Daily Download or the Entertainment Channel's Horoscopes (see Figure 1-2).

3. Click Save My Changes. The Welcome Screen automatically updates to display your places.

You can choose up to 10 places and change them at anytime.

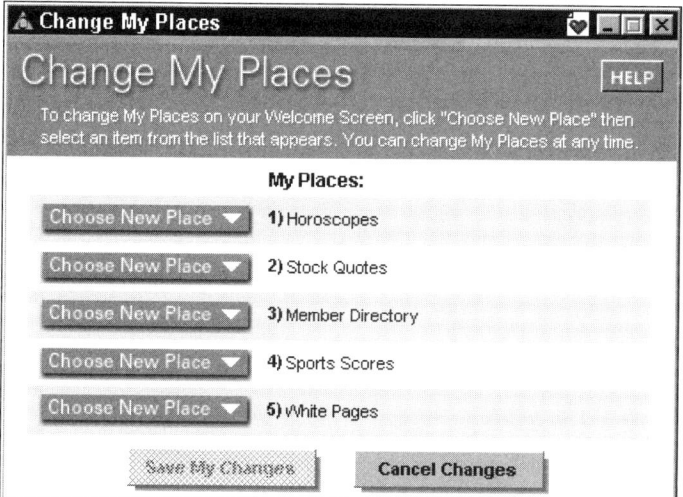

Figure 1-2. Customizing My Places for the Welcome Screen.

Menus

The six quiet little phrases that stretch across the top of the AOL window — File, Edit, Print, Window, Sign Off, and Help — comprise the AOL menu bar, shown in Figure 1-3. Each one represents a drop-down menu full of useful functions and features. Click any one of them to open its menu and then click the desired menu item. Here's what those menus offer.

Figure 1-3. The AOL menu bar, located at the top of the AOL screen.

File

The File menu, shown in Figure 1-4, has selections familiar to any experienced computer user, including New, Open, Save, Save As, Print, Print Setup, and Exit.

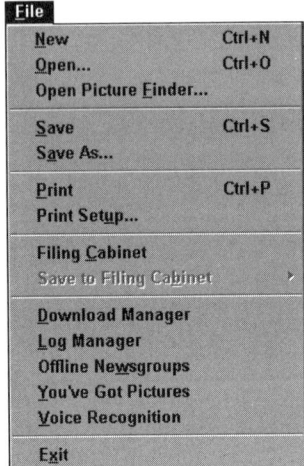

Figure 1-4. The File menu.

Table 1-1 lists the menu options and what they do.

Table 1-1. File Menu Options

File Menu Option	What It Does
New	Opens a blank text document that you can use for word processing
Open	Opens many kinds of text, graphic, audio, and HTML documents stored on your hard drive
Open Picture Finder	Helps you quickly find one of the many images that you've saved
Save and Save As	Saves the e-mail, graphics, and contents of articles and Web pages you're currently viewing to your hard drive
Print and Print Setup	Helps you set up and print to the printer that is attached to your computer
Filing Cabinet	Opens your Filing Cabinet (which is designed for storing e-mail)
Save to Filing Cabinet	Saves the e-mail you are currently reading to your Filing Cabinet

File Menu Option	What It Does
Download Manager	Keeps track of files downloaded from AOL
Log Manager	Can automatically record your chats and save information you view on AOL
Music Player	Takes you to AOL Keyword: **Music**, where you can listen to MP3 and Online Radio by using AOL's built-in Music Player software.
Offline Newsgroups	Part of your Filing Cabinet that holds Internet Newsgroup discussions saved by Auto AOL
You've Got Pictures	Takes you to the AOL Keyword: **You've Got Pictures** service
Voice Recognition	Activates AOL Speaks, optional software that comes free on AOL 6.0 CDs and lets you compose e-mail messages and chat with your voice
Exit	Closes the AOL software (and signs you off if you are signed on).

Edit

The Edit menu, shown in Figure 1-5, is your helper whenever you're writing or viewing text and images on AOL.

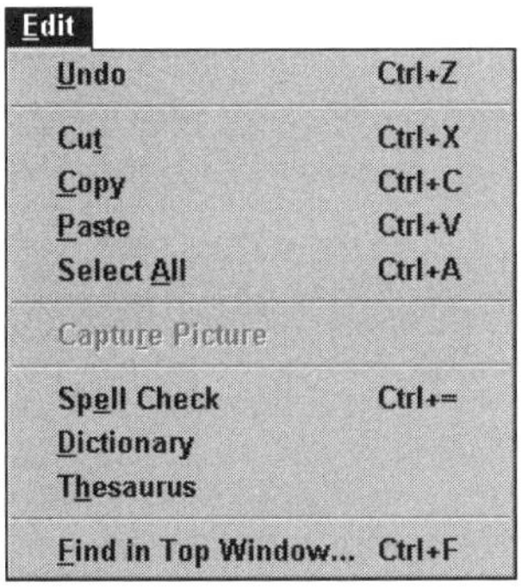

Figure 1-5. The Edit menu.

With the Edit menu, you can copy and paste text into an e-mail message, spell check your e-mail, and so on. Find in Top Window is very handy for locating text in a large online document, and Dictionary and Thesaurus are shortcuts to AOL's online versions of these writer's tools. Capture Picture comes into play if you have a scanner connected to your computer.

Print

The Print menu, shown in Figure 1-6, includes the same Print and Print Setup features found in the File menu and includes handy links to online areas offering useful printing-related information and services.

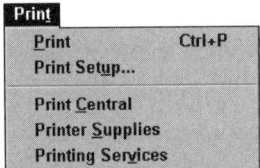

Figure 1-6. The Print menu.

Window

The Window menu, shown in Figure 1-7, helps you organize, modify, and find the windows that tend to fill your AOL screen.

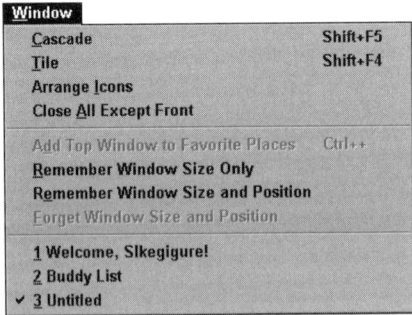

Figure 1-7. The Window menu.

The following table shows some of the Window menu options and what they do.

Chapter 1 ▲ Discovering the Welcome Screen

Table 1-2. Windows Menu Options

Window Menu Option	What It Does
Cascade	Arranges all open windows like a stack of playing cards
Tile	Arranges open windows side by side, like a mosaic floor
Arrange Icons	Organizes any minimized windows
Close All Except Front	Closes all but the frontmost window
Add Top Window to Favorite Places	Creates a shortcut to whatever the top window happens to be (see Chapter 14 for more details)

If you have modified the dimensions of a window and/or moved it to a new position on the screen, you may find the options Remember Window Size, Remember Window Size and Position, and Forget Window Size and Position to be quite useful. At the bottom of the Window menu is a listing of all currently open windows. Just click the window's name to bring it to the front for easy viewing.

 **Cross-Reference**

You can find out how to organize and work with your windows in Chapter 2.

Sign Off

The Sign Off menu, shown in Figure 1-8, offers two powerful choices:

Figure 1-8. The Sign Off menu.

- ▶ **Switch Screen Name** lets you switch to another screen name on your account without signing off.
- ▶ **Sign Off** is a bit different from Exit: It signs you off from AOL without closing the AOL software. If you sign on and off of AOL frequently, this is a huge time-saver.

 **Note**

When you're offline, the Sign Off menu becomes the Sign On menu.

Help

Need we say more? The Help menu, shown in Figure 1-9, is your lifesaver in times of trouble.

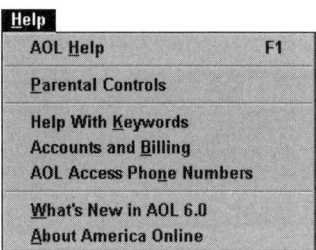

Figure 1-9. The Help menu.

We cover AOL's help features in depth in Chapter 3.

You can choose the options AOL Help and AOL Access Phone Numbers, regardless of whether you're signed on to AOL. When you're offline, you receive the Help instructions and access numbers that came with your software. When you're online, you're connected to AOL Keyword: **Help** or AOL Keyword: **Access**, both of which are constantly updated. When you're online, you can also get Help with AOL Keywords, connect to AOL Billing, and learn What's New in AOL 6.0. About America Online provides information about your AOL software that the folks at AOL Technical Support may want to know, should you have to ask them for assistance.

Toolbar

Right below the AOL menu bar is the AOL toolbar (shown in Figure 1-10), a color-coded row of drop-down menus and icons offering access to many of AOL's most popular features.

Figure 1-10. The toolbar is located at the top of your screen, below the menu bar.

The toolbar is a very powerful feature of AOL, and you'll be moving your mouse in its direction often as you explore all the AOL service has to offer. Each section of the toolbar contains a drop-down menu listing major features related to that category, plus one or more buttons leading to the most popular features below each menu:

- **Mail** offers more than a dozen e-mail-related menu choices including Read mail and Write mail.
- **People** is where you can access the many ways you can interact online with friends, relatives, and AOL members.
- **AOL Services** is a very useful list of online tools that make your life easier, including Shop@AOL, My Calendar, Homework Help, Maps & Directions, Online Greetings, Sports Scores, Stock Portfolio, and Travel Reservations.
- **Settings** gathers together the many ways you can personalize AOL software and features to meet you and your family's needs.
- **Favorites** collects shortcuts to your Favorite Places on AOL and the Web.
- The **AOL Progress icon** appears when you're loading an AOL page or Web page. The icon "swirls" to show you that the requested page is on its way. When the page has finished loading, the icon stops its animated motion.

Learn how to customize your Favorites in Chapter 14.

Navigation Bar

The navigation bar, shown in Figure 1-11, is located right below the toolbar and contains some useful features for getting around AOL and the Web.

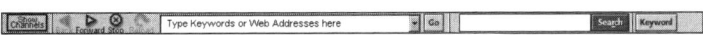

Figure 1-11. A typical view of the navigation bar.

The basic features of the navigation bar will already be familiar to those who know how to use a Web browser, but AOL has gone one step further by extending its functions to areas within AOL as well as those on the Web. Features of the navigation bar, from left to right, include the following:

If you want to stop a window while it's still loading, press the Esc (escape) key on your keyboard.

See Chapter 17 for more information on searching AOL.

In Chapter 12, we show you how to customize your navigation options.

▶ **Hide/Show Channels:** This toggle button controls the presence of the Channels window. The small Channels window makes navigation between AOL's channels very simple and convenient by putting the information you want just a click away.

▶ **Back, Forward, Stop, and Reload buttons:** Click the Back button to go back through AOL windows or Web pages you've previously viewed. After you've gone backward a bit, the Forward button can take you in the other direction. Click the Stop button to stop the loading process (primarily for Web pages), which can be a real time-saver if you know you don't want to view a page. You can click the Reload button to reload a Web page (in case it gets stuck during the loading process). The Reload button also refreshes (retrieves the information again) the browser window, in case you think something has changed.

▶ **Address text box/History List:** The wide white text box that says Type AOL Keywords and Web addresses here (shown in Figure 1-11) serves several purposes. Type AOL keywords or Web addresses in the text box and then either click the Go button or press the Enter key. AOL then opens the desired AOL area or Web page. If you click the small down arrow icon to the immediate right of the box, you reveal the history trail, a list of the last 25 AOL areas or Web pages you visited, as shown in Figure 1-12. To return to any item on the list, just click the item you want.

Figure 1-12. The history trail revealed.

- **Search box and Search button:** Type a search word or phrase in the Search box — the text box to the right of the Go button — and click the Search button to start AOL Search, which can find areas of interest on AOL and the Internet.
- **Keyword button:** Click this button to open AOL's Keyword window, an alternative to typing in the Address text box.

AOL keywords are words or phrases that provide shortcuts to many areas on America Online. We discuss keywords in depth in Chapter 2.

To receive more search options (such as searching specific sections or categories) before you start your search, leave the Search box empty. Click the Search button first to open the AOL Search window.

Putting Your Knowledge to Work

Sign on to AOL and explore every button and feature of the Welcome Screen. When you're done, take another look, to see if anything has changed while you've been busy exploring. Peek at your history trail to see where you've been and then try selecting an item from your history trail to revisit it.

If you get turned around, don't worry — the next chapter gets you acquainted with the many navigational tools available on the AOL service. We show you how to use buttons, icons, menus, list boxes, and AOL Keywords to move about online with confidence and ease.

CHAPTER 2

GETTING AROUND AOL

Quick Look

▶ Keyboard Shortcuts   page 32
Keyboard shortcuts let you speed up common actions, such as opening e-mail or sending instant messages. Most keyboard shortcuts are displayed to the right of an item in a menu. We include a complete list of keyboard shortcuts in this chapter.

▶ Hyperlinks   page 35
Hyperlinks are the blue, underlined words that you see frequently around the AOL service and the Internet. Clicking a hyperlink takes you to a site, such as to a new page or just to new information within the same page. Beware of clicking hyperlinks in e-mail from strangers, however.

▶ Keywords   page 43
Keywords are shortcuts to AOL channels, forums, and areas online. Type a keyword into the text box on the navigation bar and click the Go button to activate it. You must be online to use keywords.

Chapter 2
Getting Around AOL

IN THIS CHAPTER

Mastering the skill of using keyboard shortcuts

Understanding windows, buttons, and icons

Speeding up your sessions with AOL keywords

Navigating the Internet with URLs

To get around a service as large as AOL, you need to know some of the basics of online navigation. This chapter tells you how to get the most out of your mouse; travel swiftly from place to place with hyperlinks, keywords, and URLs; and use the many windows, buttons, icons, and other controls you'll find on AOL.

Mouse Clicks and Keyboard Shortcuts

The mouse attached to your computer is an indispensable part of your AOL experience. Your mouse pointer (the arrow that moves around the screen in step with your mouse) has many functions on AOL. Sometimes it's an arrow, but other times it changes shape or offers "hints" to you. We discuss how it changes in the upcoming sections of this chapter.

Every mouse on a Windows-compatible computer has at least two buttons. If you press and release the left button, we call it a *click* (or single-click). If you click the left button twice in quick succession, it's a *double-click*. You probably already know how to do both kinds of clicks. If you place your mouse pointer over an object on the screen, press and hold down the left button, move the mouse to another location, and release the mouse button, that's a *drag and drop* (also known as *click and drag*). "Click, drag, and drop" is probably the best way to describe it.

Now, what about that second button, the one on the right? Every so often (mostly when you're working with text or graphics) a click of the right button (called a *right-click*) opens a small menu, called a *context menu*. Context menus contain the options you're most likely to need at that particular moment.

Many things that you can do with your mouse can also be done without your mouse. These things are called *keyboard shortcuts,* and you may find a few that you adopt as your very own. As you open various menus on your menu bar and toolbar, you'll see that certain selections have an extra notation next to the name, such as Ctrl+S or Ctrl+C (you can also use ⌘+S or ⌘+C on the Mac). These are shortcuts. Hold down the Ctrl key and press a letter key, such as S or C (if you're curious, those letters stand for *save* and *copy*). There are many shortcut combinations, and it's unlikely you'll want to memorize them all, but you may find a few of them quite handy at those times when both of your hands are already on the keyboard. See Table 2-1 for a complete list.

You can also open and navigate through menus by using just your keyboard. Hold down the Alt key and press the key corresponding to the underlined letter in the menu's name. For example, *Alt+F* opens the File menu, shown in Figure 2-1.

Figure 2-1. The underlined letter is the keyboard shortcut key (in this case, Alt+F opens the File menu).

You can also move from menu to menu by using the left and right arrow keys, move within a menu by using the up and down arrow keys, and press the Enter key to make a selection. The Esc key closes the menu.

Table 2-1. Keyboard Shortcuts

Function	Windows	Macintosh
New	Ctrl+N	⌘+N
Open	Ctrl+O	⌘+O
Close	Ctrl+F4	⌘+W
Save	Ctrl+S	⌘+S
Print	Ctrl+P	⌘+P
Exit (Quit)	Alt+F4	⌘+Q
Undo	Ctrl+Z	⌘+Z
Cut	Ctrl+X	⌘+X
Copy	Ctrl+C	⌘+C
Paste	Ctrl+V	⌘+V
Select All	Ctrl+A	⌘+A
Spell Check	Ctrl+=	⌘+=

Function	Windows	Macintosh
Exit Free Area	Ctrl+E	⌘+E
Read Mail	Ctrl+R	⌘+R
Write Mail	Ctrl+M	⌘+M
Send Mail	Ctrl+Enter	Enter
Add to Favorite Places	Ctrl++ (plus sign)	⌘++ (plus sign)
Go to Keyword	Ctrl+K	⌘+K
New Instant Message	Ctrl+I	⌘+I
Send an Instant Message	Ctrl+Enter	Enter
Locate AOL Member Online	Ctrl+L	⌘+L
Get AOL Member Profile	Ctrl+G	⌘+G
Find	Alt+D	⌘+F
Help	Alt+H	⌘+/ (slash)
Abort Incoming Text	Esc	⌘+. (period)

Buttons, Icons, and Hyperlinks

As you navigate through AOL, much of what you do involves buttons, icons, and hypertext links (or *hyperlinks*).

Buttons are used to perform all sorts of actions — send information to AOL, open and close menus and windows, or take you to another online area (see Figure 2-2). You can often determine that an on-screen item is a button if you move your mouse pointer over the item and the mouse pointer turns into a little hand, with one pointing finger (although this isn't true for all buttons). If that test doesn't work, click the suspected button and hold down the mouse button: You'll see the button appear to go in. If you'd rather not perform the action associated with the button, keep holding down the mouse button and slide the mouse pointer to the side, away from the button, before you release the mouse button. The button will bounce back, and nothing will have happened.

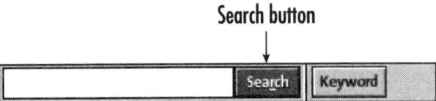

Figure 2-2. The Search button is a good example of a typical AOL button.

Icons are symbols or pictures that represent some important feature or function. If you click or double-click most icons, some action will be performed. For example, a single click of the mailbox icon in the upper-left corner of your AOL screen (see Figure 2-3) opens your AOL mailbox.

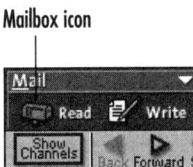

Figure 2-3. The famous mailbox picture is an icon.

Again, your mouse pointer usually turns into a pointing hand if it is moved over a functioning icon.

Hypertext links (or *hyperlinks*) are a wondrous thing, because they're one of the features that made the World Wide Web the wonder that it is today. Hypertext links are words that work like buttons. They can perform actions, such as opening new windows or Web pages. You can identify a hyperlink in several ways. First, hyperlinks are almost always colored bright blue, and the text is underlined (see Figure 2-4).

If you move the mouse pointer over a hyperlink, it should turn into the familiar pointing hand. One click on a hyperlink takes you wherever the hyperlink leads, and after you've clicked a hyperlink, it changes color to show that you've already clicked it.

Tip

Because hyperlinks can lead almost anywhere (good or bad), it pays to look before you click. To see where a particular hyperlink leads, move the mouse pointer over the hyperlink or button on the Web page. A small caption may appear telling you the destination of the link. If you don't see a caption, look at the bottom border of the page. It may display the address or description of that button or hyperlink.

Chapter 2 ▲ Getting Around AOL

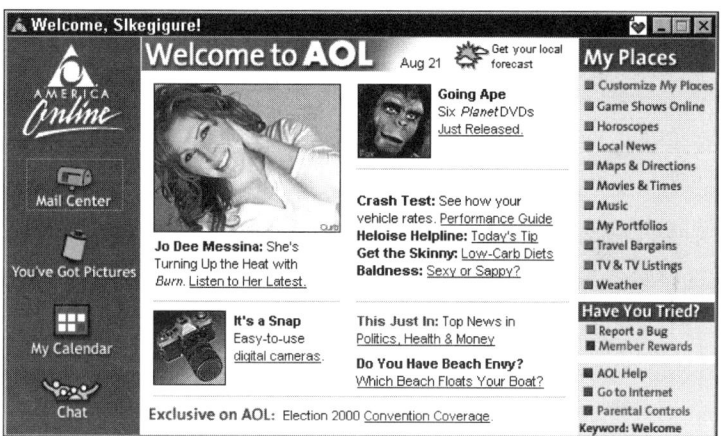

Figure 2-4. All the underlined words in the Welcome Screen are hyperlinks.

Windows and Scroll Bars

Windows are so important that an entire computer operating system was named after them. In fact, one of AOL's old advertising slogans was, "The more windows you open, the cooler it gets!" AOL itself is one large window, within which you can open many other windows. You can have many windows open at one time, some of which you may be reading while you write or chat in others. See Figure 2-5 for an example of a typical window on AOL.

At the top of each window is a *title bar,* which contains text that describes the contents of the window. To the left of that title is a triangular *AOL icon* that hides a control menu. On the right may be a *heart icon* (more about this icon, also known as the *Favorite Places icon*, discussed in Chapter 14) and three little square buttons. We describe what each of the three *control boxes* does in just a bit. Each window also has a *frame* around it, a thin border that holds things within the window.

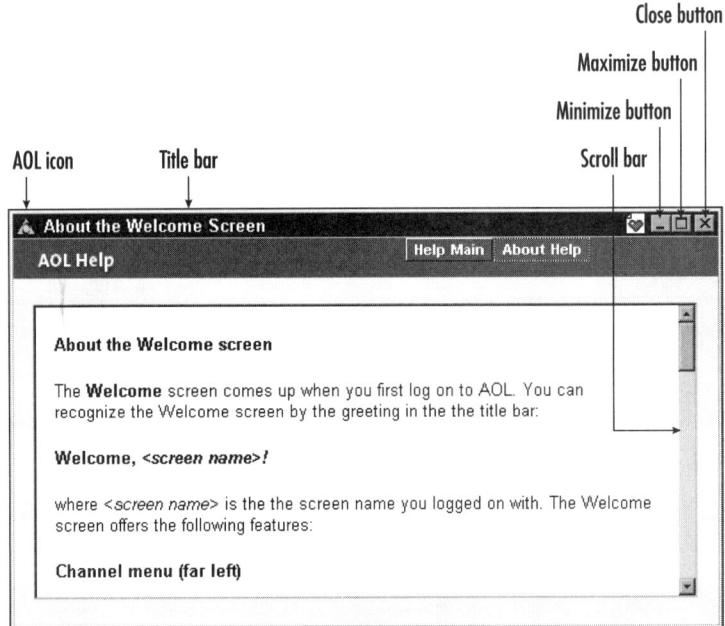

Figure 2-5. An AOL Help article. Note the title bar at the top of the window, with its buttons and control boxes, and the scroll bar at the right.

In some cases, the window will also have *scroll bars* — broad gray ribbons running along the right-hand border of the window (as shown in Figure 2-5) and perhaps across the bottom, too. Imagine that there's a broader vista hidden behind the window's frame. The scroll bars let you move that vista up and down, left and right, so that you can see another portion of the view.

Each scroll bar has several buttons. There is a button with an *up arrow* (or *left arrow*), another with a *down arrow* (or *right arrow*), and a square box called a *slider* in the middle. Click the various arrow buttons to scroll the contents of the window. Click once to make a small move, or hold down the mouse button to keep scrolling. The slider has two purposes. It shows which part of the view you're seeing (when it's in the center you're viewing the middle of the window's contents), and you can click and drag the slider box to scroll the contents of the window to a new position. You can also scroll in larger steps by clicking the gray *ribbon* above or below the slider.

The title bar may have a dark background color, such as navy blue, or it may be gray. In fact, that color changes, depending on whether the window is *in front* (or on top). You can have many windows open at one time, but only one window can be in active use. That's the window that's in front, and no other window will obscure your view of that window. To bring a window to the front, just click your mouse anywhere within its borders, and note that the title bar changes from gray to blue (or some other color).

Close, Maximize, Restore, Minimize, Resize, and Move

As you move around on AOL, there will be some windows you want to keep open, some you need to move out of the way, and others you'll want to close out.

To close a window, click the Close button — the small button with the X on the far right of the window's title bar (refer to Figure 2-5).

You can make a window fill the entire AOL window by clicking the Maximize button. That's the button on the right of the title bar labeled with a square (refer to Figure 2-5). After a window is maximized, its control boxes appear in the upper-right corner of the main AOL window, right below the main AOL window's own control boxes.

You'll note that after you've maximized a window, the Maximize button has changed. It now has a symbol that looks like two overlapping boxes. It has become a Restore button. The next time you click this box, the window is restored to its original size. You can also shrink most windows down to an icon. (Click the Minimize button — the one with the minus sign (-) on it — and the window shrinks down and moves to the bottom of the AOL window. You can have more than a dozen minimized windows at the bottom of your screen. If you look at that little title bar, you'll see that the Minimize button has been converted to a Restore button (with the overlapping squares). To restore a minimized window, you can either double-click its title bar or click the Restore button.

Tip

After you resize and/or move a window, you can make the change permanent by choosing the options Remember Window Size Only or Remember Window Size and Position from the Windows menu at the top of your AOL screen.

Many windows (but not all) can also be resized. Resizing is a great way to make text easier to read or to make room on your screen for more windows. You can make a window wider, narrower, taller, or shorter. You can even change the window's height and width at the same time. To resize a window, move your mouse pointer over one of the borders of that window. If the mouse pointer changes to a double-headed arrow, you're free to resize the window. Click and drag the mouse until the window is the size you want. If you move the mouse pointer over one of the corners of the window, you can drag the mouse diagonally and change the width and height at the same time.

You can also *move* a window around on the screen. All you have to do is a bit of dragging and dropping — click the title bar, hold down the mouse button, move the mouse (and window) to the desired position, and release the mouse button.

Finally, we return to the small AOL icon on the left side of the title bar. A single click on this icon opens a small *control menu* that performs many of the tricks we've discussed in this section.

List Boxes, Menus, and Drop-Down Lists

The top of the main AOL window is lined with menus. Each word — File, Edit, Window, Sign On, and Help — is a menu. Just click one of these words to open the corresponding menu (see Figure 2-6). We discuss the function of each of these menus in Chapter 1.

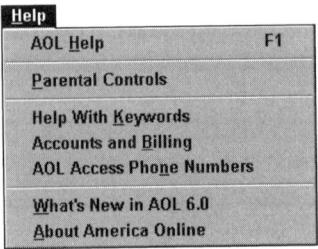

Figure 2-6. The Help menu.

Move your mouse pointer down through the menu, and note how each item is highlighted in a contrasting color when the pointer hovers over it. Click the mouse to select the highlighted item. Some menu items are followed by an ellipsis (...); if you click such an item, another window opens, offering you a variety of choices. Menu items followed by a little right-pointing triangle lead to additional *submenus*. Just slide your mouse pointer sideways to make selections from a submenu.

List Boxes

Wherever you go on AOL, you encounter list boxes. Each list box is another kind of menu that may offer a wide choice of items — forums to visit, articles to read, files to download, message boards and chat rooms to visit, and Web sites to see. Most list boxes come equipped with scroll bars so you can see the entire list. To access an item, simply double-click it. See Figure 2-7 for an example of a window with a list box.

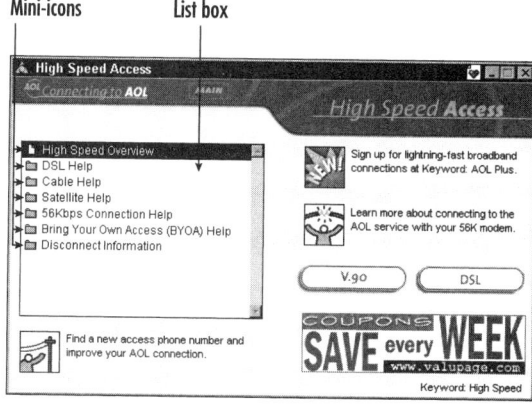

Figure 2-7. The High Speed Access window, complete with list box and mini-icons.

AOL tries to make your choices easier by providing *mini-icons* to help describe the items being offered in a list box (refer to Figure 2-7). Text articles are often accompanied by a small sheet-of-paper icon, forums by a file folder, Web sites by a blue globe, and chat rooms by two people in profile. There are many other mini-icons, too.

> **All Grayed Out**
>
> As you explore menus, note that some items are in black, and others are merely gray shadows. Such grayed-out selections are choices that aren't working at the moment. For example, you cannot choose Help With Keywords from the Help menu unless you're signed on to AOL. Menu items aren't the only things that may be grayed out. You'll occasionally encounter buttons and icons that are similarly "off duty," waiting for the right conditions before they become useful again.

Drop-Down Menus and Drop-Down Lists

Drop-down menus and drop-down lists are variations on menus and list boxes. Typically, you'll see an icon and/or a line of text flanked by a small down-pointing arrow. If you click the arrow, a complete list box or menu appears. The AOL toolbar (described later in the chapter) has many drop-down menus.

Text Boxes

The four arrow keys, usually located between your character keys and the number pad, are useful in moving through lists and menus.

You can move around some windows, such as the Write Mail window, by pressing the Tab key to hop from field to field.

Whether you're entering your password in the Sign On screen, composing e-mail, looking up a word in the online dictionary, or participating in a freewheeling chat, you'll be using a *text box* (or field). Text boxes are pretty easy to recognize and just as easy to use. If you see an empty white box within a window, you can be fairly sure you've found one. Sometimes the flashing, vertical text *insertion mark* is already waiting for your first word. Other times the box will be completely empty. Just click your mouse anywhere within the box, and that flashing insertion mark should appear. If it doesn't, AOL doesn't want your text (for example, you can't type in the AOL toolbar when you're signed off). The Write Mail window has four good examples of text boxes (see numbers 1–4 in Figure 2-8).

Chapter 2 ▲ Getting Around AOL   43

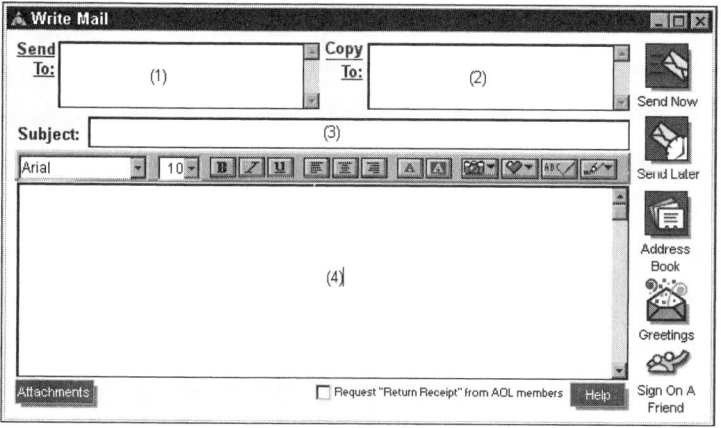

Figure 2-8. The Write Mail window has four text boxes. (To see this window, click the Write icon on the toolbar.)

Keywords and URLs

The shortest route between two points is a straight line, and when you want to go somewhere on AOL, no line is straighter than a *keyword*. When you know an online area's keyword, you can stop clicking link after link after link in order to get there — just type the keyword. You can type the keyword into the Address box on the AOL navigation bar and press the Enter key. Alternatively, you can click the Keyword button on the navigation bar, type the keyword into the keyword window, and click the Go button (see Figure 2-9). Your next stop will be your desired destination.

 **Note**

If the word(s) you enter is not an AOL keyword, AOL automatically initiates an AOL Search (see Chapter 17).

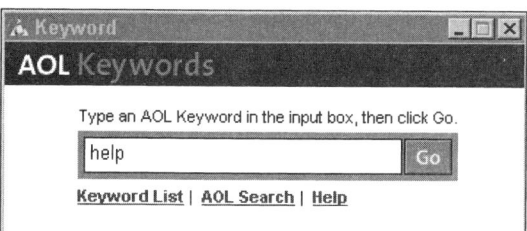

Figure 2-9. The Keyword window — just type the keyword and click Go.

At last count, there were over 20,000 AOL keywords providing shortcuts to everything from AA (American Airlines) to ZOO.

How do you find keywords? When you arrive at an AOL online area you like, look to see if a keyword is listed on the window. Another way is to visit AOL Keyword: **Keyword** (or click the Keyword List button in the Keyword window or just type it in).

Although most World Wide Web URLs officially start with `http://www`, companies often drop that part and just say `netscape.com` or `blockbuster.com` (for example). You can enter that abbreviated name successfully in the text box on the navigation bar or in the Keyword window.

URLs are addresses on the World Wide Web. You see them everywhere these days, in advertisements, on business cards, and embroidered on people's shirtsleeves. URL stands for *Universal Resource Locator,* and it looks like this: `http://www.aol.com` (which is the URL to AOL's home page on the World Wide Web). You can use a URL just like you use a keyword. Type it into the Address box on the navigation bar (see Figure 2-10) or enter it in the Keyword window. In moments, the corresponding Web page should open right before your eyes.

Type a URL here.

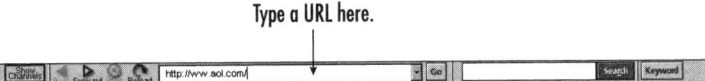

Figure 2-10. Just type a URL into the Address box on the navigation bar and click the Go button.

Putting Your Knowledge to Work

When it comes to learning how all these features work, there's no substitute for trying them out yourself. Go back through this chapter and try every feature you can.

Open a bunch of windows on your screen and then try reorganizing them. Drag them around the screen, resize some, minimize others, and give your mouse a workout. While you have all those windows open, experiment with the features offered on the Window menu (see Chapter 1 for details).

If you get turned around and lost, don't worry — the next chapter discusses finding and using Help on America Online.

CHAPTER

3

FINDING HELP

Quick Look

▶ **Offline Help**   **page 47**
Your AOL software comes with an entire database of help articles, which you can access when you're offline (not connected). Just choose Help➪AOL Help or press the F1 key.

▶ **Phone Support**   **page 49**
Can't find the online or offline help you need? Give AOL a ring. Member Services representatives are on hand to help you with general, technical, and billing questions. Call toll-free at 800-827-6364.

▶ **QuickStart**   **page 50**
Get off to a great start on AOL with help from QuickStart, an online guide for new members. Use AOL Keyword: **QuickStart** and take an online tour, get AOL facts, and tips, and more!

▶ **AOL Help**   **page 51**
Your first stop for online support is AOL Help, available in the Help menu. Here you can search help articles, get live online tech support, and update your account information.

Chapter 3
Finding Help

IN THIS CHAPTER

Finding help before you get online

Learning about the new features of AOL 6.0

Getting answers from fellow members and AOL representatives

Registering for a live, interactive class

Looking for help with something? This chapter describes the many help resources available to you. If you're offline (not signed on to America Online) or unable to connect to America Online, we recommend that you start with the "Offline Help" section. If you're able to get online, make a beeline for the "Online Help" section. Here, you'll find directions to the many help resources available online.

Offline Help

We feel that the book you're holding is one of the best offline help sources available. Before you spend valuable time in pursuit of help elsewhere, make sure that we haven't already answered your questions in the pages of this book. Use the table of contents, Quick Looks, chapter introductions, glossary, and index as tools to find what you're seeking. If you don't find what you need here, go to the source — America Online itself.

Software Help

Your AOL software comes complete with a set of help databases that you can access when you're not connected to the service. To find them, open the AOL software (but don't sign on) and choose Help⇨AOL Help or just press the F1 key on your keyboard. The introductory window for the offline Help database then appears, as shown in Figure 3-1.

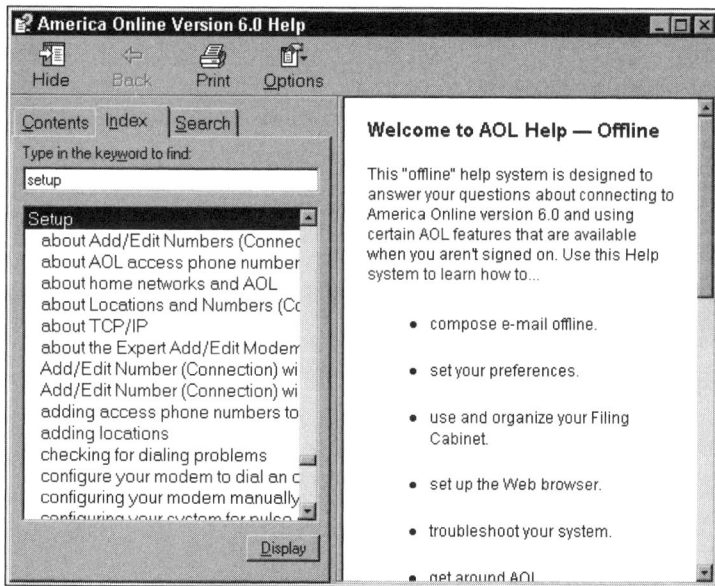

Figure 3-1. The offline AOL Help database in your AOL software.

The three tabs in the upper left of the Help window offer different ways to find the same information. If you prefer to see the help topics organized by category, click the Contents tab. To see a list of every help topic, including nested subtopics, click the Index tab. Click the Search tab to search for whatever has you stumped.

The offline Help database is similar to help features you may have seen in other programs on your computer. Double-click topics and subtopics, which appear in the window's right panel, to open articles with information and step-by-step descriptions (see Figure 3-2).

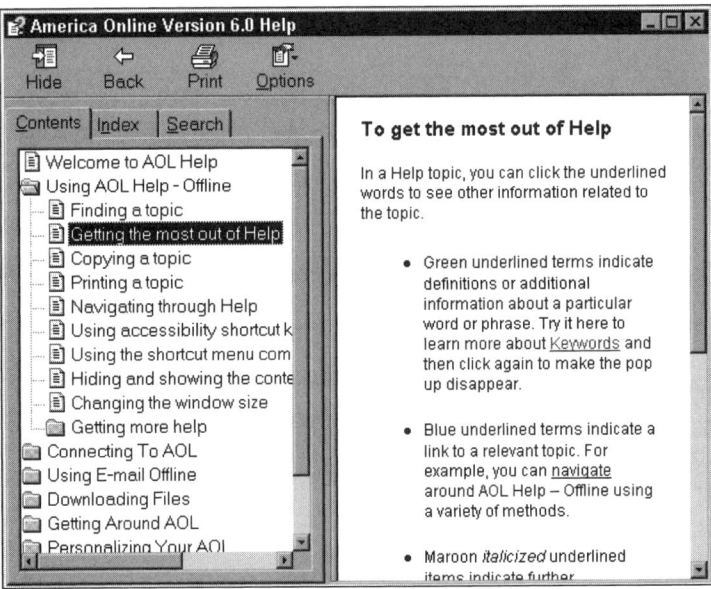

Figure 3-2. The offline Help database has hundreds of help articles.

Words with a dotted line below them lead to further clarification or more information. Also note the four buttons arrayed at the top of the window:

▶ **Hide:** Click to view the article without the list of topics.
▶ **Back:** Click to go to the previous help article.
▶ **Print:** Click to print a copy of the article.
▶ **Options:** Click to access additional navigational and miscellaneous commands.

Watch for the Related Topics button at the bottom of a help article. Clicking this button opens a drop-down menu of more articles on your topic.

Phone Support

AOL also provides around-the-clock toll-free telephone support for general, billing, and technical questions. Before you call, have the following information handy: your AOL screen name, your account address and phone number, and a detailed description of your problem.

Call Member Services at 800-827-6364 for AOL Support. Upon calling either of these numbers, listen to the menu choices and choose those that best apply. Hold times are quite reasonable these days. You can also visit AOL Keyword: **Call AOL** after you're able to sign on to AOL — this keyword leads to the current list of direct AOL telephone support numbers.

More Books

If you're looking for help with a specific topic, you may want to consider other books. For Internet questions, pick up *Your Official America Online Internet Guide,* 4th Edition, by David Peal (AOL Press). For help creating your own Web page in AOL Hometown, try *Your Official America Online Guide to Creating Web Pages,* 2nd Edition, by Ed Willett (AOL Press). Most AOL books are available at AOL Keyword: **Bookstore**.

Online Help (When Connected to the AOL Service)

You'll find numerous articles and message boards on virtually every AOL topic. Still can't find what you're looking for? Real-time interactive help is available with Member Services representatives one-on-one or in help rooms. You can even take a class on how to use AOL.

Welcome to AOL

The first time you sign on, the voice of AOL greets you with a hearty welcome and an offer to learn more about AOL. The Welcome to AOL 6.0 window, shown in Figure 3-3, is visible to all new members and members with newly upgraded software.

TTY Service requires TTY-enabled equipment. Callers are instructed to leave a message for the AOL staff upon calling. A Member Services representative will return the call within 24 hours.

If you find a solution to an unusual problem, share it with the Help Community or on message boards. And in these same places, others may have unique solutions to share with you.

Figure 3-3. Get up to speed on AOL.

Just click the Tell Me About AOL 6.0 button in the center of the window to embark on a quick and easy introduction to AOL 6.0. The button leads to the What's New in AOL 6.0 slide show. Click the New Features button in the slide show window for a quick look at AOL 6.0's newest additions. To return to this area later, use AOL Keyword: **Click and Go**.

QuickStart

QuickStart, shown in Figure 3-4, is a guide for new members, focusing on general features of the AOL service rather than specific features of the AOL 6.0 software. You can find it at AOL Keyword: **QuickStart**. QuickStart offers five features of interest to new members:

If you've already closed this window in a previous session, don't worry. Just choose Help➪What's New in AOL 6.0 to see the same information.

Figure 3-4. QuickStart puts you on the fast track to AOL.

- **Quick Tour of AOL:** A short tutorial on basic AOL features. It helps you learn how to create additional screen names or change your password, send and receive e-mail, get around AOL quickly with keywords and hyperlinks, search AOL, chat with people online, and surf the Web.
- **AOL FastFacts:** A directory of help resources and tools on a variety of topics. This is an excellent resource and one that we suggest you set as a Favorite Place so you can return to it quickly later (or remember the AOL Keyword: **FastFacts**). (See Chapter 14 for more on Favorite Places.)
- **Best of AOL:** A list of the features that members love. You can learn about Buddy Lists, online safety, junk mail, screen names, and more. Use AOL Keyword: **Best of AOL.**
- **AOL Tips:** The AOL Insider Tips collection offers friendly, down-to-earth information on getting the most out of your AOL experience. The tips are organized by topic, such as "Using AOL Like a Pro" and "Tips for Making AOL Faster." You can even sign up to have a tip delivered daily to your mailbox. Use AOL Keyword: **AOL Tips** to get to the area directly.
- **The More Help button:** (Located in the lower-right corner of the QuickStart window.) If you don't find the answers to your questions in any of the previous four features, check out More Help. Help resources include a link to AOL Guide Books, information on help buttons around AOL, and New Member Class information. There's even a link to AOL Help, our next stop.

AOL Help

AOL Help is the main repository of help information online. In fact, we would go so far as to call it an online guide to AOL, authored by AOL itself. AOL Help, shown in Figure 3-5, is accessible in several ways: Click the AOL Help button in the bottom-right corner of the Welcome Screen, or choose Help⇨AOL Help, or use AOL Keyword: **Help**.

Tip

Looking for more help using AOL? FastFacts lists five places to look: AOL Help, AOL Basics, Help Community, AOL Computing, and Online Classrooms. We describe each of these places in this chapter, but the FastFacts list provides convenient links to these areas.

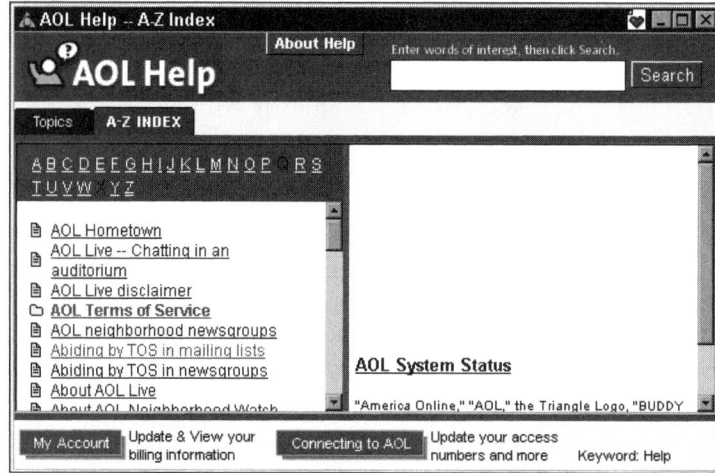

Figure 3-5. AOL Help is always at hand.

Help topics line the left side of the window — click a topic to go to a list of related subjects, each containing a number of subtopics. Clicking a subtopic name displays a list of articles on the right side of the window, as shown in Figure 3-6.

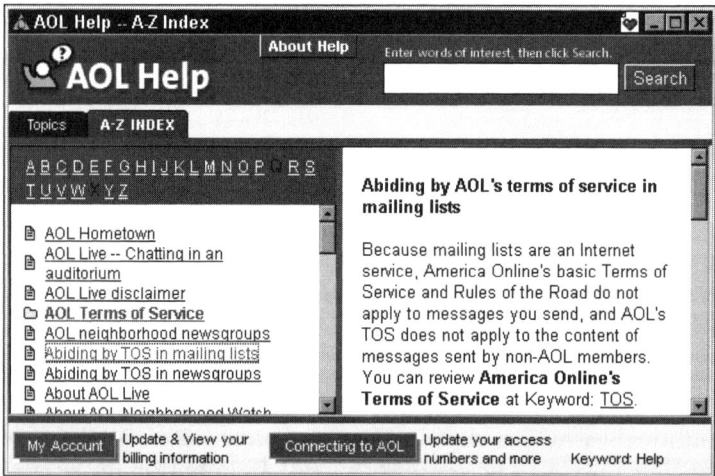

Figure 3-6. AOL Help offers a wealth of information.

If you're not sure which topic or subtopic will answer your question, you can simply search AOL Help. Here's how to perform a search:

1. In the Search box in the top-right corner of the window, type in the word that best describes what you need help with (refer to Figure 3-6).
2. Click the Search button.
3. In the resulting list of related articles, double-click an interesting topic to display an article.

If you don't find the answer to your question within AOL Help, look for the Ask the Staff links scattered throughout the area. Ask the Staff leads to the Customer Service Center, shown in Figure 3-7, which gives you the opportunity to ask your question via e-mail, in a chat room, in a real-time, one-on-one online conversation, or in a post to a message board. You can also reach this area through AOL Keyword: **Customer Service**.

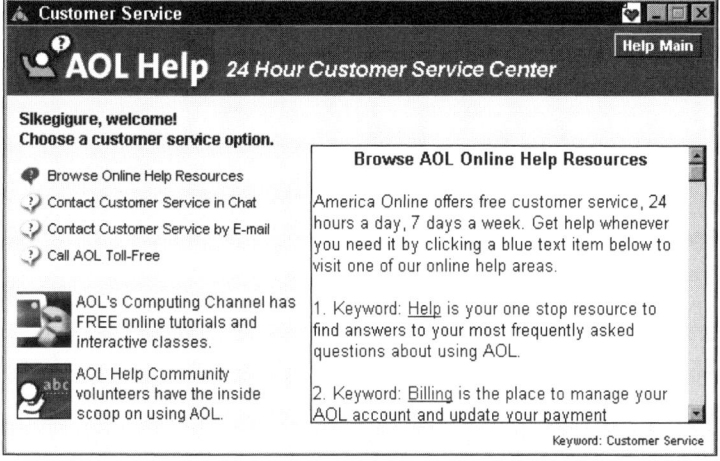

Figure 3-7. Have a question? Ask AOL Customer Service.

Sending your questions to AOL Customer Service via e-mail is simple. Here's how:

1. In the Customer Service Center window, click the Contact Customer Service by E-Mail button.
2. Choose one of the three help types (general, technical, or billing help) by clicking the appropriate link that appears in the box on the right.

3. In the resulting Send a Question to Our Staff window, shown in Figure 3-8, type your question and include as many details as possible.
4. Click the Send button.

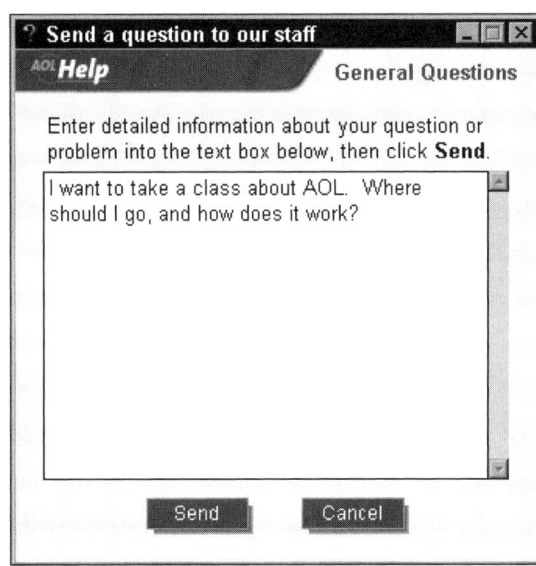

Figure 3-8. Type your detailed question in the text box and click Send.

An AOL Customer Service representative will reply to your question via e-mail within 24 hours. If you need support sooner, we recommend that you click the Contact Customer Service in Chat button in the Customer Service Center window, described next.

Live One-on-One Help

You have two ways of getting live, one-on-one help. One is to call AOL, as we discuss earlier in this chapter. The other is to contact Customer Service in chat, an online feature that puts you in direct contact with someone who can help while you're connected to the AOL service. Unlike the e-mail-based help, assistance is provided only for technical and billing questions. Follow these steps to contact Customer Service in chat:

1. In the Customer Service Center window (AOL Keyword: **Customer Service**), click the Customer Service in Chat button (refer to Figure 3-7).

Chapter 3 ▲ Finding Help

2. Click the appropriate link in the scroll box in the resulting window, and then click the Go There button to connect.

   A new window appears, calculates the estimated time you will need to wait before help arrives, and offers a link in the event you want to search the AOL Help database while you're waiting. Feel free to do other things while you're waiting — you'll keep your place in the virtual queue so long as you stay connected to AOL. When support becomes available, a window appears on your screen along with a greeting from your representative (see Figure 3-9).

While you're waiting for a representative, open a new text window (choose File⇨New) and type your detailed question. Now when the representative appears, you'll know exactly what you want to ask. You can even copy and paste the question into the window to save some time and effort.

Figure 3-9. Communicate in real time with your representative through this window.

AOL Help Community

In the "Offline Help" section, earlier in this chapter, we mention that you can ask your friends, family members, and coworkers for help. Now that you're online, you can also ask other AOL members. The AOL Help Community, shown in Figure 3-10, is a gathering place for members to exchange and share information on AOL. You can get there directly with AOL Keyword: **Help Community**.

56   Part I ▲ Starting Your Online Journey with AOL

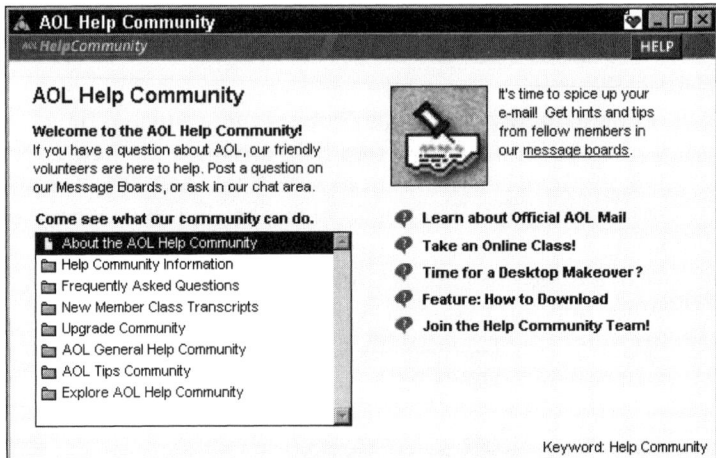

Figure 3-10. The AOL Help Community is one of the best help resources on AOL.

The AOL Help Community offers a network of message boards organized by topic. No AOL employees post in these boards — only members and member volunteers do. To access the message boards, click the Message Boards link in the top right of the AOL Help Community window and then click the appropriate link in the resulting window. The message board topic list appears on your screen, as shown in Figure 3-11.

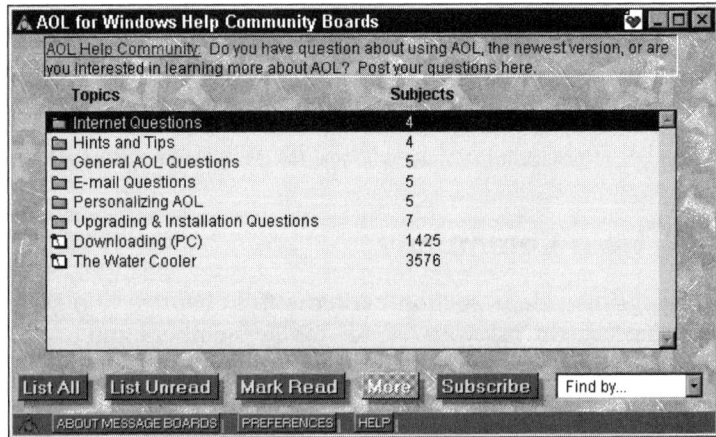

Figure 3-11. Members help members in these popular and active message boards.

Click the message board topic in which you want to ask a question or learn more. Before you ask your question, glance through the posts to see if it has already been answered. If your question hasn't been asked yet, go ahead and post your question, clearly explaining your situation and giving as many details as possible. Replies are often swift, and you may see an answer as soon as a few minutes later, though in most cases it takes an hour or a day. You may receive a reply to your question via e-mail, though we recommend you revisit the message board itself in the event the reply was only posted and not e-mailed.

The AOL Help Community also offers chat rooms in which you can network with other members, a helpful list of frequently asked questions (and their answers), and online help classes (more on that next).

Help Classes

In addition to the various help resources we discuss in this chapter, AOL has free, interactive classes on a variety of AOL-related topics. At the time of writing, available classes included Basic AOL, Intermediate AOL, Advanced AOL, Basic Internet, and even one on finding help. Classes are taught by member volunteers and are held in chat rooms at specific dates and times. Classes are generally offered several times a day and last roughly two hours, though advanced registration is required.

You can get more information, schedules, and the registration form at AOL Keyword: **Help Class**. Registration is simple and easy. Click the Try It Now button at the bottom of the Help Class window, and in the window that appears (see Figure 3-12), fill in the requested information and click the Submit Registration button.

Cross-Reference

We introduce message boards in Chapter 9. You'll benefit from reading the section on message boards before you post a question.

Tip

When you get to the end of this book, you may find that you can answer most of the questions asked by others in the AOL Help Community. If you're interested in sharing your expertise with other members, you're free to dive in and start posting replies to posts in the message board. This is also a great way to make friends online!

We recommend that you read Chapter 9 before you sign on for your class. Knowing how to use chat rooms helps you get the most out of your class.

The member volunteers are also called Community Leaders, and this group consists of members from all walks of life. They generously donate their time and effort to helping make your experience on AOL more enjoyable. You can often recognize them by their screen names, which may start with names like `Guide`, `Host`, or `Ldrs`. If you're interested in learning more about Community Leaders or becoming one yourself, visit AOL Keyword: **Leaders**.

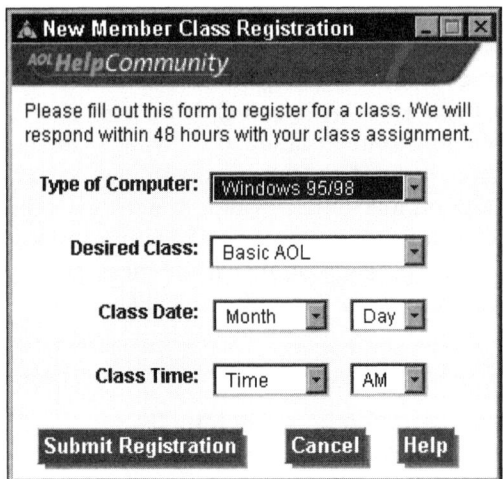

Figure 3-12. Complete the registration form to sign up for a class. You will receive confirmation via e-mail within 48 hours.

Computing Help

If you're pretty well-versed on AOL but need some help with your computer itself, look to the Computer Center Channel for assistance. The Computer Center Channel offers frequently asked questions (and the answers), how-to articles, live help, a dictionary, and links to other help resources. Topics cover both computer-related and AOL-related issues. You can get to the Computer Center Channel's main help area, shown in Figure 3-13, directly with AOL Keyword: **Computing**.

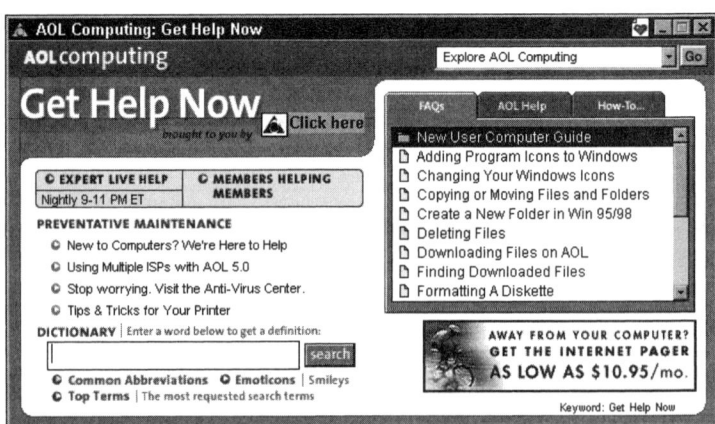

Figure 3-13. Get Help Now offers plenty of assistance . . . now!

Chapter 3 ▲ Finding Help

We recommend the AOL Computing live help sessions, held every night from 9 p.m. to 11 p.m. eastern time. If you need help outside of those hours, message boards are also available for posting questions. Click the Expert Live Help link near the top of the Get Help Now window to reach both the live help sessions and the message boards.

Another excellent resource is the Help Illustrated diagrams under the How-To Tab on the right side of the AOL Computing window. The Computing Channel offers more than 20 figures that show you how to do such things as customize the toolbar and copy and paste (see Figure 3-14).

Don't overlook the tabs in the top-right corner of the Get Help Now window. Clicking one of these tabs updates the list below it with new collections of information and resources.

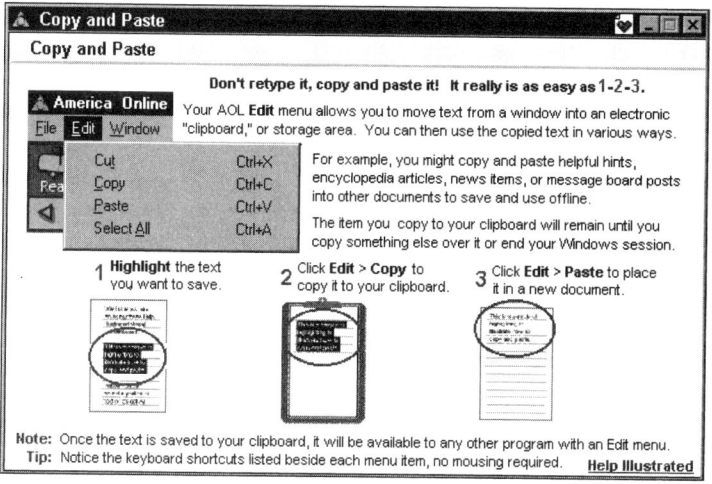

Figure 3-14. Get step-by-step, visual help with Help Illustrated.

Putting Your Knowledge to Work

AOL wants to be sure that your experience as a new member is satisfying. As you may have already noticed, AOL recommends this book to every new member and extends an invitation to take a new member tour of AOL as soon as you sign on. By taking advantage of the many help resources, you can find an answer to virtually every AOL question you may have.

One common question asked by many new members is "how can I stay safe online?" Perhaps you've heard tales of online scams and are worried about how to keep yourself, your family, and your account secure. Online safety is an important issue and one to which we devote an entire chapter, coming up next.

CHAPTER

4

ONLINE SAFETY

Quick Look

▶ AOL Neighborhood Watch page 62
Find out how to keep yourself and your family safe at AOL Neighborhood Watch. Advisories, tools, and resources are available to help you safeguard your account and personal information while you're online. Use AOL Keyword: **Neighborhood Watch** to reach this area quickly.

▶ Terms of Service page 64
The AOL Terms of Service, which you agree to at sign-up, contain your rights and responsibilities as an AOL member. To read the Terms of Service in their entirety, visit AOL Keyword: **TOS**.

▶ Notify AOL page 66
If you observe another member violate the Terms of Service, you may report the violation at Notify AOL. Use AOL Keyword: **Notify AOL** to report inappropriate activity witnessed in chat, e-mail, files, instant messages, message boards, Web pages, screen names, or profiles.

▶ Parental Controls page 68
Take control of your family's online experience with Parental Controls. You can block e-mail, instant messages, chat rooms, file downloads, Premium Services, and more at AOL Keyword: **Parental Controls**.

Chapter 4
Online Safety

IN THIS CHAPTER

Protecting your family and personal information online

Understanding AOL's community standards: the Terms of Service

Using Parental Controls to help keep kids safe

Respecting others with online etiquette

Whenever you think about visiting new places, your mind is likely to drift toward safety considerations. Can you drink the water? Is it safe to walk the streets? How can you protect your family? Can you call for help in a foreign language? So before you venture far out into America Online, we tell you what the folks at AOL are doing to make sure your online sessions are safe and enjoyable.

AOL Neighborhood Watch

America Online has over 24 million members, making it the size of a very large metropolis. In fact, according to U.S. Census estimates, it is larger than the New York/Northern New Jersey metropolitan area! Knowing this, you can probably surmise the importance of safety online. AOL recognizes the need for community safety and offers the Neighborhood Watch area, shown in Figure 4-1, to help safeguard its membership. Use AOL Keyword: **Neighborhood Watch** for access to safety resources, tools, information, and tips.

Figure 4-1. Learn how to stay safe online at AOL Neighborhood Watch.

Without knowing more about the features and services on AOL (most of which we've yet to cover), many of the topics at Neighborhood Watch simply won't make sense yet. So in the following list, we go through each one, introduce it, and explain it or point you to the chapter where you can find more details:

You can find out how to use keywords in Chapter 2.

- **Parental Controls** are tools that let you manage your child's online experience. You can control how much time your child spends online each day, prevent unwanted e-mail, and limit your child's Internet access to age appropriate sites. Use AOL Keyword: **Parental Controls** to go directly to the Parental Controls area, which we discuss in detail later in this chapter.
- **E-Mail Safety** gives you control over your e-mail, ways to control unsolicited mail, methods of avoiding objectionable e-mail, and tips for avoiding computer viruses. We discuss e-mail in detail in Chapters 5 and 6.

Note

You cannot contract a computer virus simply by opening a piece of AOL e-mail. If you want to protect your AOL account and your computer, do not download files, click on hyperlinks, or visit Web sites in an e-mail from someone you do not know — no matter how enticing the e-mail may appear!

Note

The AOL staff will never ask you for your password or credit card information. Individuals intent on doing harm may pose as AOL employees in instant messages, e-mails, and chat rooms. If someone asks you for your password or credit card, use AOL Keyword: **Notify AOL** to report it.

Tip

Don't use the same password for your AOL account that you use with your ATM card, home security alarm, or other Web sites. If a key is lost or stolen, it's better if it can open only one door.

▶ **Computer Safety** offers help and information on safeguarding your computer from viruses and Trojan Horses. We discuss viruses and Trojan Horses in detail in Chapter 9.

▶ **Suggested Safeguards** recommends password protection tips, describes online scams and schemes, details Privacy Preferences settings, and discusses online etiquette, kids' online safety, and Internet safety resources. We discuss password creation and protection in Chapter 11 and Appendix A, privacy preferences in Chapter 11, and the remaining topics in this chapter.

Along the bottom of the Neighborhood Watch window are two buttons: Notify AOL and Shopping & Banking. Notify AOL is a way to let AOL know when you encounter inappropriate behavior or activities online, and we discuss it in the next section of this chapter. Shopping & Banking offers reassurances on the safety of shopping and banking online, which are covered in Chapter 14.

Are you eager to begin your adventures online, even before you continue through the book? If so, use our quick list of top ten safeguards to protect you and secure your account (see the sidebar, "Top Ten Safeguards"). Read them, live them, love them, and share them with family members also using AOL.

Terms of Service

AOL is a community, and the guidelines for what goes on in this community are called the *Terms of Service* or *TOS*. All members agree to abide by these terms when they sign up for their accounts with AOL. The Terms of Service explains what members can expect from AOL, what AOL expects from its members, and what members should expect from each other. Do you know what the terms entail? If not, take a moment now to visit AOL Keyword: **TOS** and read the terms in their entirety (see Figure 4-2).

Chapter 4 ▲ Online Safety

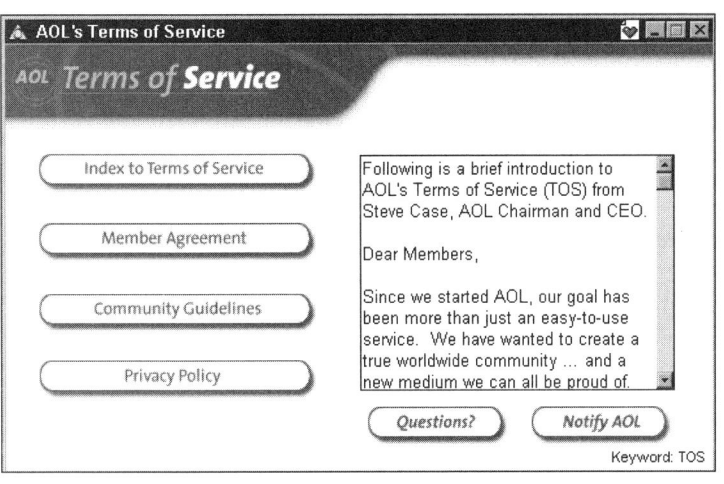

Figure 4-2. America Online's Terms of Service applies to every member online.

> **Tip**
>
> Looking for a specific reference in the Terms of Service? Click the Index to Terms of Service button at the top of the Terms of Service window. In the index, click any of the blue underlined words to jump to that reference.

AOL organizes its Terms of Service into three parts: the Member Agreement, the Community Guidelines, and the Privacy Policy. AOL prides itself for offering all three in straightforward language, which you can read and understand easily.

Although we don't reprint the Terms of Service in this book (it does change from time to time, we do strongly encourage you to read it. Here's a brief summary of each of the three parts of AOL's Terms of Service:

▶ The **Member Agreement** contains the basic legal terms of an AOL Membership. The agreement covers things like AOL's cancellation policy, the reponsibilities of the master account holder, and AOL's procedures relating to billing and surcharges.

▶ The **Community Guidelines** explain the common-sense principles for how all members should behave online. To ensure everybody's right to enjoy this medium, the guidelines cover items such as observing all laws, showing basic manners, using good judgment, and not sending unsolicited bulk e-mail or *spam*.

▶ The **Privacy Policy** sets out the priples that AOL believes are necessary to protect your privacy as an AOL member.

Treat others with respect and common courtesy. Hate speech is unacceptable anywhere on the service. Do not post, transmit, promote, distribute, or facilitate distribution of content intended to victimize, harass, degrade, or intimidate an individual or group of individuals on the basis of age, disability, ethnicity, gender, race, religion, or sexual orientation.

If you have questions about TOS, click the Questions button at the bottom of the Terms of Service window. A list of frequently asked questions appears, as shown in Figure 4-3; double-click any question to read its answer. If your question doesn't appear, click the Ask the Staff button to send your question to AOL's staff.

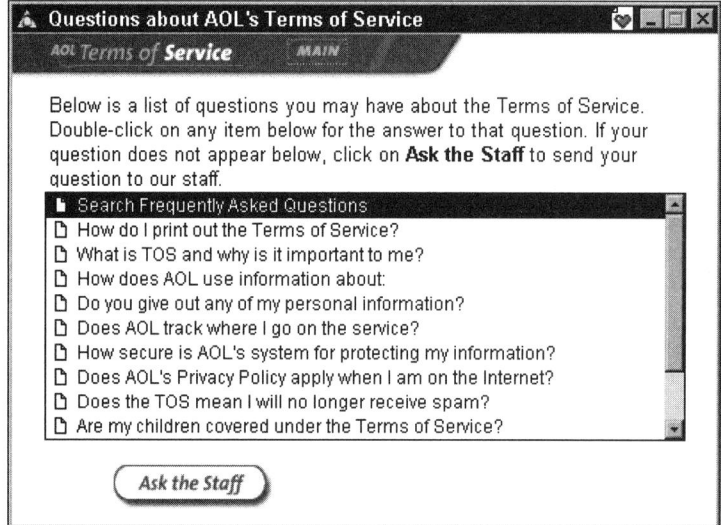

Figure 4-3. Get your TOS questions answered here!

Notify AOL

After you know what *is* acceptable and unacceptable behavior online, you are in a better position to notice inappropriate behavior by someone else. If you're confronted with such behavior, you can report a problem at Notify AOL (shown in Figure 4-4), which is accessible by clicking the Notify AOL button in the Terms of Service window or by using AOL Keyword: **Notify AOL**.

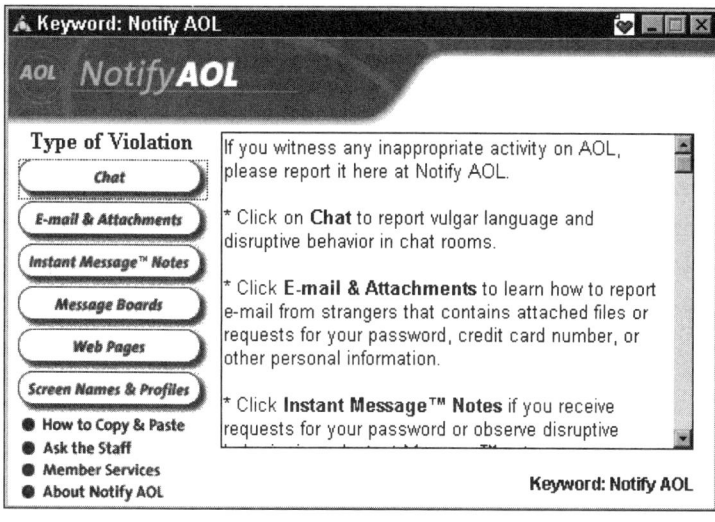

Figure 4-4. File a report with AOL at Notify AOL.

Notify AOL lets you report violations that occur in chat, e-mail (and attachments), instant messages, message boards, Web pages, and screen names/profiles. Just click the appropriate button on the left-hand side of the screen to open the report form. Fill in the information as requested (the more information you provide, the more likely that action can be taken). In most cases, you need to demonstrate the problem, and that often requires pasting a copy of the violation into the Notify AOL window. If you're unfamiliar with this technique, read the sidebar "Copying and Pasting" or just click the How to Copy & Paste link in the lower-left corner of the Notify AOL window.

Note

Don't reply to people that you don't know just to reprimand them for inappropriate behavior. Let AOL handle it.

All reports are sent to AOL's Community Action Team, which reviews the reports and takes appropriate action whenever possible. Members who violate the Terms of Service may receive warnings or even have their accounts terminated. AOL takes its Terms of Service very seriously. If you send a notice to Notify AOL, you don't find out what action is taken, but in most cases, you do receive confirmation from the Community Action Team that your report was received and reviewed.

If you receive an e-mail warning that you violated the Terms of Service, and you feel the warning is in error, read the letter carefully before proceeding. The e-mail should advise you what to do if you feel the warning is unwarranted. A recent online scam involved sending fake warnings to members, and the hyperlinks lead to Web pages that asked for personal information. We recommend that you call America Online to verify and discuss any warnings you may receive.

Parental Controls

Parents are concerned about the safety of their children when they go online. Will they receive inappropriate e-mail? Download files from people they don't know? Fall prey to scams in instant messages? Or venture into dangers on the Internet? AOL recognizes that children deserve special protection. That's why AOL created easy-to-use Parental Controls.

Parental Controls aren't just for use on your child's screen name. You can also use Parental Controls to tailor an online experience for anyone else who accesses AOL through your account, such as another adult family member, friend, or coworker. You can even use Parental Controls for yourself!

Parental Controls are a set of tools that enable parents to participate in deciding what types of experiences their children have online. While Parental Controls don't eliminate the need for parents to sit down with their children and experience AOL and the rest of the Internet together, they do give children the security for independent explorations. And they can give parents peace of mind! You can access Parental Controls by going to AOL Keyword: **Parental Controls**.

After you open the Parental Controls window located at AOL Keyword: **Parental Controls**, shown in Figure 4-5, AOL presents you with an array of choices. Before you get started, we recommend that you take a moment to watch the slideshow highlighting the features and benefits of Parental Controls. To view, just click the View Slideshow button on the right side of the window.

Creating Your Child's Screen Name

To get started with Parental Controls, you need a screen name to control. Parental Controls are tied to individual screen names. If your child doesn't yet have his or her own screen name, you can create one by clicking the Create Screen Names button in the lower-left corner of the Parental Controls window (refer to Figure 4-5). Remember that you need to be signed on with a master screen name to create a new screen name.

Chapter 4 ▲ Online Safety

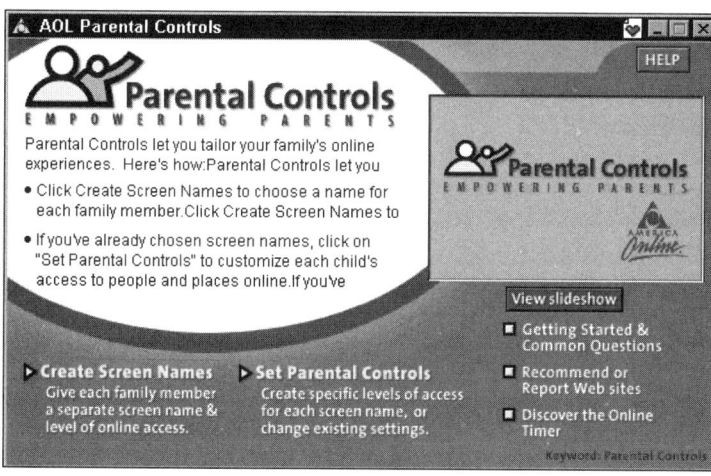

Figure 4-5. Parents are empowered with Parental Controls.

You are prompted with a question asking you if you are creating the screen name for a child. If you answer Yes, you will see AOL's Important Note to Parents, which provides information about AOL's practices regarding children's online privacy. Please take the time to read this note before creating your child's screen name.

Selecting a Parental Controls Age Category

After you create a screen name for your child, you are prompted to select a basic age category, as shown in Figure 4-6. AOL gives you the following choices:

▶ Kids Only (recommended for ages 12 and under)
▶ Young Teen (recommended for ages 13 to 15)
▶ Mature Teen (recommended for ages 16 to 17)
▶ General Access (for ages 18+)

Go ahead and select the appropriate category for your child's new screen name.

When creating a screen name for a child, keep in mind that screen names are visible to others on the AOL service. As a result, we recommend that you do not use your child's full name as his or her screen name. And don't use any other personal information that someone could use to locate your child. You can find more details on creating screen names (and good ones at that) in Chapter 11 and by going to AOL Keyword: **Note to Parents**.

You can read more about master screen names in Chapter 11.

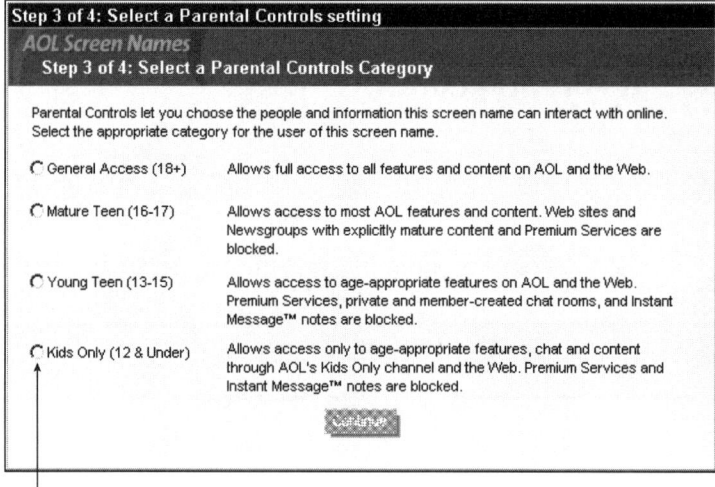

Select a basic age category for your child's screen name

Figure 4-6. You can customize control settings within the category you choose.

Each age category has default settings that you can either accept or choose to customize. After you accept the settings, you return to the AOL Screen Names window, as shown in Figure 4-7. You can still customize the Parental Controls settings by clicking Edit Parental Controls Settings on the bottom-right side of the AOL Screen Names window.

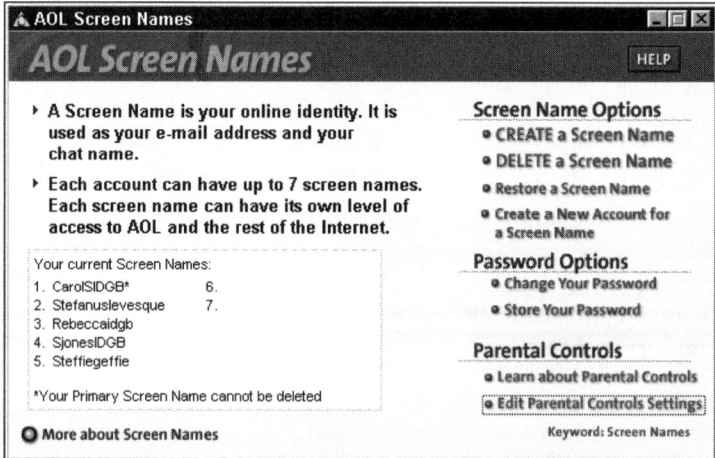

Figure 4-7. After you choose your child's age category, you are taken to the AOL Screen Names window.

If you want to edit controls for a screen name that already exists, you do not need to go through the process of creating a new screen name. You can go directly to AOL Keyword: **Parental Controls** and click the Set Parental Controls button at the bottom of the Parental Controls window (Refer to Figure 4-5). Either method opens the Edit Parental Controls Settings window, shown in Figure 4-8.

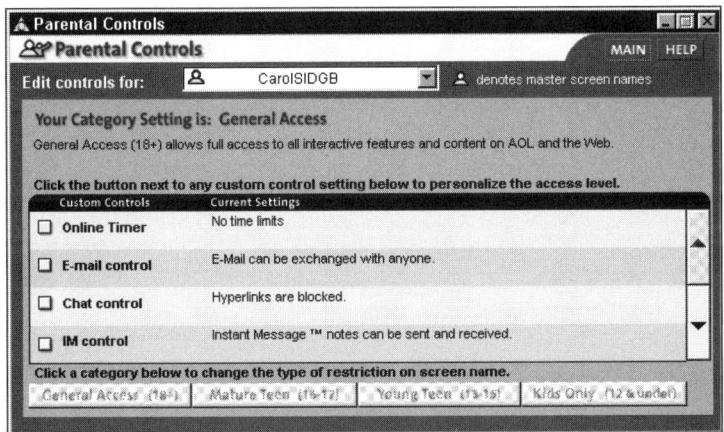

Figure 4-8. The Edit Parental Controls Settings window.

Begin by choosing the screen name you want to edit. Just click the arrow to the right of the screen name drop-down list at the top of the window, move your pointer down to the appropriate screen name on the list, and click the name to select it. A small person icon next to a screen name denotes that the name is designated as a master screen name. As long as you are using a master screen name, you can edit the controls for any of the screen names on your account.

After selecting a screen name for editing, the Age Category setting and Custom Controls update to display the current settings for the screen name you selected from the menu. For example, we created the screen name Steffiegeffie to represent a child under 13 years old. When we selected the screen name for editing, the category changed to Kids Only, and the Custom Controls changed to display the current settings, as shown in Figure 4-9.

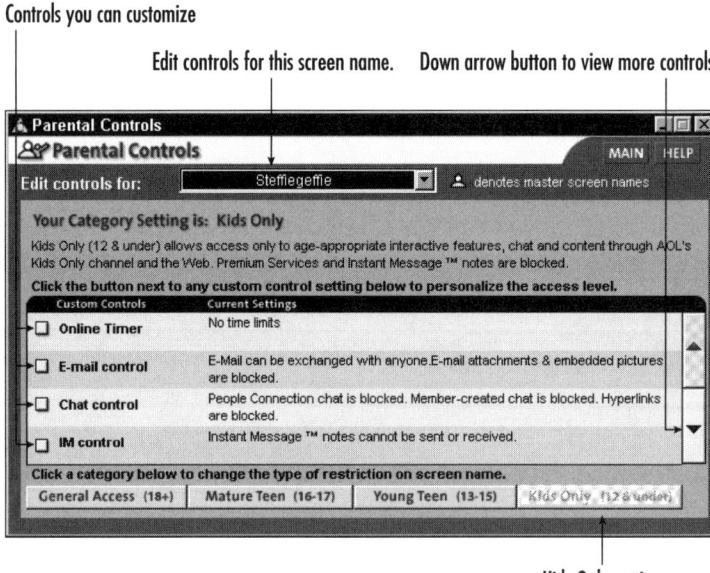

Figure 4-9. The Kids Only settings in the Edit Parental Controls Settings window.

To see all Custom Controls, use the down arrow button on the right side of the window.

Note that AOL displays the screen name you're currently editing in the upper-right corner of the window.

If you want to make changes to Parental Controls, you have a variety of options. You can customize any of the Custom Controls in the middle of the window. Just click the green button to the left of the Custom Control that you want to change to open the customization window. We discuss each of the Custom Controls in turn.

Online Timer

The Online Timer lets you decide when and for how long your child (or anyone else using your account) may use AOL during the course of a day and during the course of the week. You can set different limits for individual days of the week, have separate rules for weekdays and the weekend, or have no restrictions at all. Your children are able to sign on when permitted, and when the time's up, they'll automatically be signed off after receiving a 10-minute warning.

To begin setting time limits, click the Online Timer button in the Edit Controls window. The resulting window, shown in Figure 4-10, shows the current settings for that screen name.

Chapter 4 ▲ Online Safety

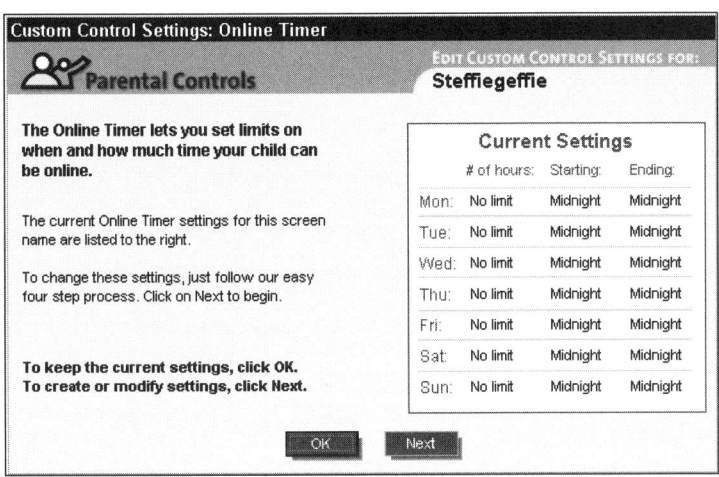

Figure 4-10. The Online Timer's custom daily limits you decide when and for how long a child can use AOL.

To change the settings, click the Next button at the bottom of the screen. You can then choose to set the *Same Limit Daily,* have separate *Weekday/Weekend Limits,* set *Custom Daily Limits,* or allow *Unlimited* access to AOL.

Choose the kind of limits you want and click the Next button. Whichever limits you select, you're able to choose the **# of hours** your child can be online, as well as the **Starting time** and **Ending time,** as shown in Figure 4-11. For example, you can allow access to AOL from 3:00 p.m. to 9:00 p.m. daily, but only permit a total of two hours usage within that time period.

After you set the hours, click Next and then choose your time zone. Click Next again to confirm your settings. If everything looks good, click Save. You can always go back to the previous screen by clicking the Prev button.

E-Mail Control

Mail Controls let you set limits on how a screen name can send and receive e-mail and with whom. The first three settings near the top of the Mail Controls window, shown in Figure 4-12, allow for general, across-the-board control. You can decide whether the screen name can exchange e-mail

Use the Online Timer to reduce fights over access to the family computer.

You cannot set the Online Timer for master screen names.

with all AOL and Internet addresses (Allow All E-Mail), exchange e-mail only with other AOL members, or block all e-mail entirely.

Figure 4-11. The Online Timer's custom daily limits lets you set different usage limits for every day of the week.

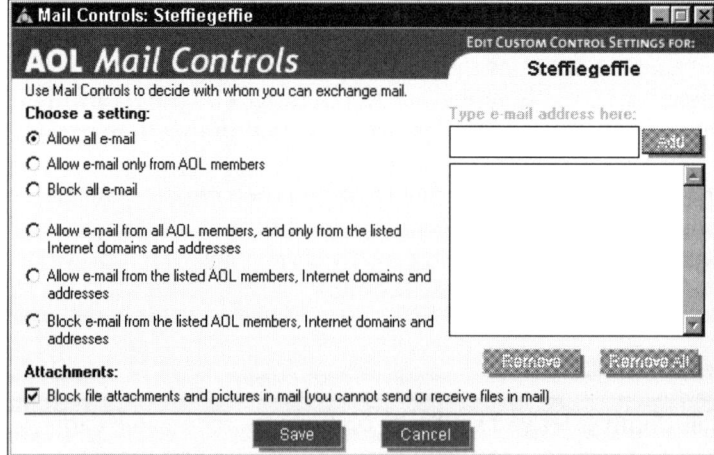

Figure 4-12. Edit Custom Control settings for e-mail.

The next three settings let you allow (or block) specific e-mail domains and addresses. Here are your options:

- ▶ Allow e-mail only from AOL members and the specific domains and addresses you select
- ▶ Allow e-mail only from listed AOL members, Internet domains, and addresses
- ▶ Block e-mail from listed AOL members, Internet domains, and addresses

You can list the specific domains and addresses you want to allow or block by typing them in the text box on the right and clicking the Add button.

At the bottom of the Mail Controls window is the file attachments setting. If you don't want the screen name to receive e-mail with attached files or pictures, be sure that you select this check box. Note that by selecting this check box, any e-mail containing file attachments or pictures will be returned to the sender, and the member with that screen name will be unaware that any e-mail was sent to him or her.

Chat Control

Chat is an online feature that enables participants to "talk" by typing messages that everyone in a particular chat room can read at the same time. Conversations often happen quickly in a chat room and your child may likely be "conversing" with others they know only through the online world. AOL offers several settings to empower parents to control access to AOL chat rooms, as shown in Figure 4-13.

Five settings offer various kinds of chat controls:

- ▶ The first setting enables you to block a screen name from all AOL chat.
- ▶ The second setting enables you to block all People Connection chat areas, such as featured chat rooms in People Connection's chat areas and lifestyle forums, AOL Live auditorium events, and member-created chat rooms.

E-mail is discussed in depth in Chapters 5 and 6.

A domain is the location of an e-mail address. For example, in the e-mail address member@netscape.com, the domain is netscape.com. You can learn more about domains and e-mail addresses in Chapter 5.

When you're finished making Mail Control changes, click the Save button to keep your settings.

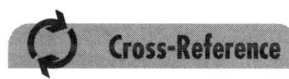

We discuss chat rooms in detail in Chapter 10.

Settings with gray boxes (such as the hyperlink setting at the bottom of Figure 4-13) indicate that they cannot be changed. Settings may be *grayed out* because of the Parental Controls category chosen (as is the case with the hyperlink setting).

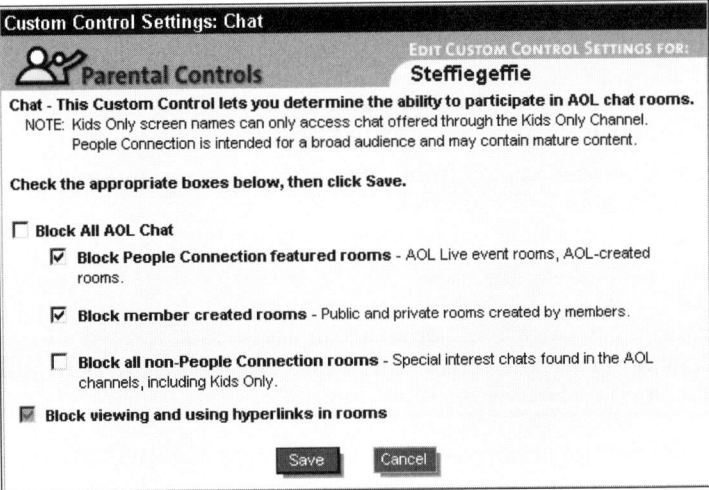

Figure 4-13. Protect your kids from inappropriate chat room activity with Chat Controls.

▶ The third setting lets you block all non-AOL-sanctioned chat areas, such as member-created public and private chat rooms. If you select this option by itself, the screen name can visit AOL-created chat rooms, but not those created by members, whether public or private.

▶ The fourth setting blocks all the rest of the chat areas, such as conference rooms (found in forums) including the Kids Only chats. Many AOL channels have their own chat rooms, including the Kids Only channel. If you select this option, the screen name won't be able to enter those chat rooms.

▶ The last setting at the bottom of the Chat Control window lets you block hyperlinks in chat rooms. Selecting this option keeps links, either to AOL areas or Web sites, from appearing in whichever chat rooms the screen name is able to enter, preventing the screen name from following those links to potentially objectionable destinations.

Instant Message Control

Instant messages are the real-time, one-on-one notes that members can pass back and forth between themselves. The Instant Message Controls, shown in Figure 4-14, are simple: You can either allow instant messages or block them. In addition, any

Learn how to determine the location of a hyperlink before you click it in Chapter 2.

Create a second screen name for your child for chatting. By blocking all e-mails and instant messages to that screen name, your child can chat without receiving unsolicited communications.

screen name with instant messages allowed can control their instant messages by setting their Privacy Preferences within their Buddy List feature. To access your Buddy List Privacy Preferences, click the Setup button on your Buddy List window.

Cross-Reference

We discuss instant messages in detail in Chapter 7.

Figure 4-14. Block or allow instant messages with a simple click of the mouse.

Web Control

The Internet is a worldwide network of computers, offering rich resources for kids, as well as some content intended only for adults. Web Custom Controls, shown in Figure 4-15, enable you to choose which level of access to the Web you feel is appropriate for your child.

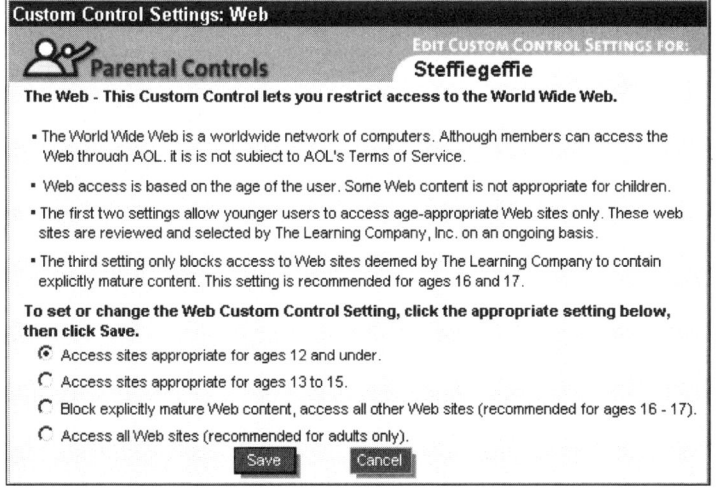

Figure 4-15. Block access to Web sites that may be inappropriate for your child.

The first Web Custom Control setting is intended for children ages 12 and under, and the second setting is recommended for teens ages 13 to 15. If you prefer to give your teen access to all Web sites except ones that are known to contain explicitly mature content, choose the third control (recommended for ages 16–17). The fourth Web control allows access to all Web sites, regardless of content.

Additional Master Screen Names Control

We also discuss master screen name rights in Chapter 11.

You can designate other screen names on your account as master screen names. The users associated with master screen names can create, delete, and restore screen names, change an account's billing options, and edit Parental Controls settings. Only screen names set for the General Access (18+) category can be designated as master screen names. Note the grayed out check box at the bottom of Figure 4-16, which indicates that this screen name cannot be given master screen name status.

Note

Only the original master screen name (the first one you created on your account) can grant or remove the master screen name status to other screen names. Additional master screen names are intended for adult use only.

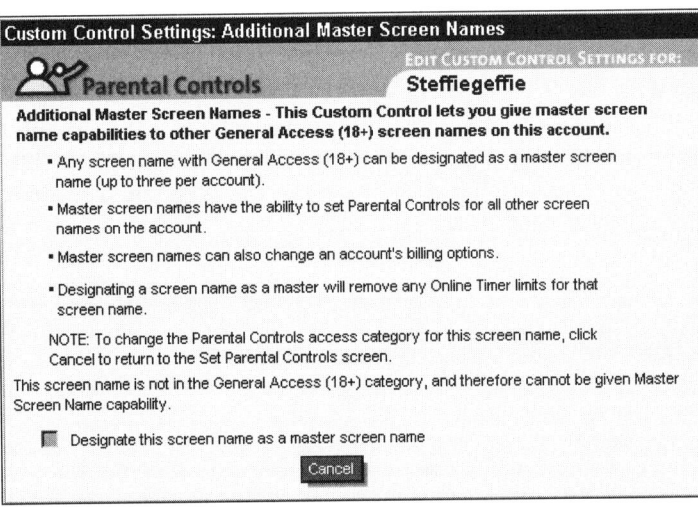

Figure 4-16. Give the privilege of master screen name status to appropriate screen names.

We describe downloading from libraries and FTP sites in Chapter 10.

Download Control

Downloading Files Custom Controls, shown in Figure 4-17, let you block a particular screen name from downloading files from AOL software libraries and/or FTP sites.

Chapter 4 ▲ Online Safety

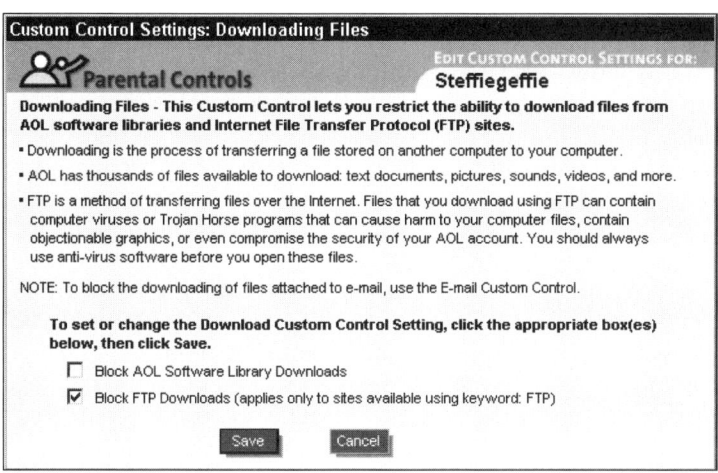

Figure 4-17. Restrict file downloads from libraries and FTP sites.

Newsgroup Control

The Newsgroups Custom Controls, shown in Figure 4-18, let you restrict access to *newsgroups,* which are discussion areas on the Internet. Newsgroups can be adult in nature or may contain inappropriate information for children.

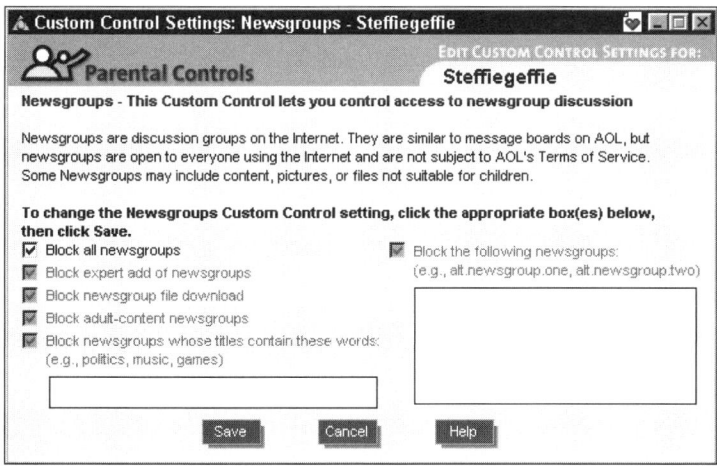

Figure 4-18. Get control of newsgroups with Custom Controls.

The first setting lets you block any and all newsgroups. If you want to allow some newsgroups, choose instead to block expert add of newsgroups (the second setting) to restrict the ability to add a newsgroup by its exact name, which may bypass AOL's menus and possibly other limitations. You may also wish to block file downloads in newsgroups (the third setting), and/or newsgroups with adult content (the fourth setting).

Cross-Reference

Learn more about newsgroups in Chapter 10.

The fifth setting in the bottom-left corner lets you block newsgroups with titles containing specific words (for example, you may want to block any newsgroup with the word *sex* in it). Just type the word(s) that you want blocked in the field below the setting, separating multiple words with commas. You can also block specific newsgroups with the sixth setting, on the right side of the screen. Type the complete newsgroup name and separate multiple newsgroup names with commas.

Premium Services Control

Don't want your little angel playing Air Warrior after school? Block Premium Services and prevent your monthly bill from skyrocketing (see Figure 4-19). If you've choosen the Kids Only or Young Teen category for your child's screen name, Premium Services is blocked by default.

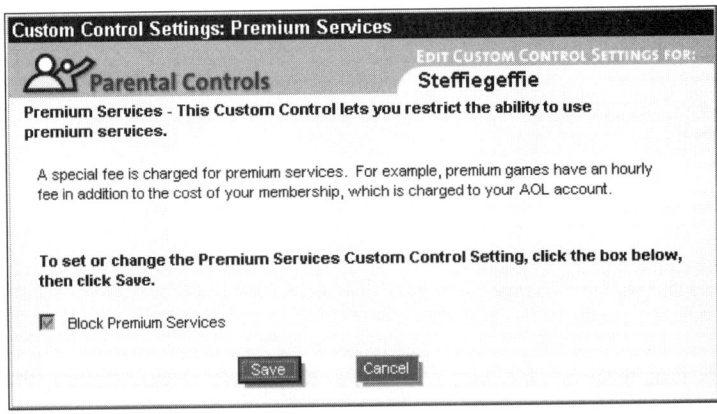

Figure 4-19. Block Premium Services, which incur hourly fees in addition to the cost of your membership.

Categories

Are you wondering what children with screen names set to the Kids Only category see when they sign-on? Why not sign on with the screen name yourself and take a look around? We encourage you to do this for all screen names on your account, just to be sure that the settings work the way you expect. Kids Only screen names do have their own AOL, so to speak. In the next section, we take a look at the world of AOL through the eyes of a child with a Kids Only screen name.

Kids Only

Any screen name set with the Kids Only Parental Controls category is greeted with a unique welcome screen upon signing on to AOL, as shown in Figure 4-20.

Figure 4-20. The pint-sized version of the AOL Welcome Screen.

Cross-Reference

We explore the Kids Only Channel in detail in Chapter 20.

The Kids Only Welcome Screen bears some resemblance to the regular version. Weather, e-mail, and help are all there. Cool Tips replaces the daily features, and a Come On In button leads to the Kids Only Channel. Wait! Did you set your child's e-mail controls to block e-mail? Don't worry. If the screen name is blocked from e-mail, clicking the mailbox only results in a note to that effect.

The Kids Only Help area, shown in Figure 4-21, is a child's version of Neighborhood Watch and Member Services (described in Chapter 3) rolled into one.

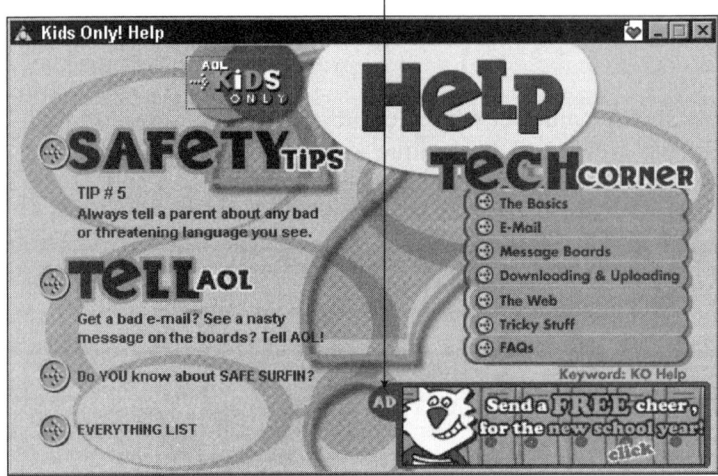

Figure 4-21. Kids have their own Help!

Note

The Kids Only category blocks kids from visiting virtually any AOL areas that aren't within the Kids Only Channel.

We strongly recommend that you introduce your children to the Kids Only Help area. Point out the safety tips and discuss each one with your children. If you feel your children are old enough, you may also want to show them how they can tell AOL if they run into any problems while they are online. The buttons along the right side of the window lead to help articles on using various aspects of the AOL software. We also encourage you to teach your child the difference between features and advertisements. All ads in the Kids Only Channel have the word *Ad* next to them on the left.

AOL's Privacy Policy for Children Under 13

AOL is especially sensitive to the safety and privacy of children, and is always finding ways to provide greater protection to children and comfort for their parents. Look for the Note to Parents button on the main Kids Only screen or go to AOL Keyword: **Note to Parents** to keep up-to-date with AOL's efforts. Among AOL's current initiatives are

▶ **Notifying parents:** If a child enters a Kids Only contest or sweepstakes, AOL sends an e-mail to the child's parents offering the option to prevent the child's participation.

▶ **Limiting personal information collection:** In general, the only information AOL has about a child is his or her screen name. AOL will not collect more information from children than is reasonably necessary for them to participate in activities. AOL will not share any personal information about children with third parties. Should AOL ever want to do so, AOL will get parental permission.

▶ **Partnering only with select outside companies:** A list of AOL's Kids Only partners can be found at AOL Keyword: **Kids Partners**.

Putting Your Knowledge to Work

In truth, nothing in this chapter is too strange or overboard; most of the information is common sense, which we're sure you have in abundance (you bought this book, after all). Now that you've digested the safety guidelines and ground rules, you're ready to start exploring the world of America Online in security and comfort. Your next stop: e-mail!

PART II

COMMUNICATING WITH THE WORLD

Chapter 5
Using E-Mail

Chapter 6
Advanced E-Mail

Chapter 7
Instant Messaging

Chapter 8
The Buddy List Feature

Chapter 9
Chat Rooms and Other Online Forums

Chapter 10
Downloading Files

Chapter 11
You've Got Pictures

CHAPTER

5

USING E-MAIL

Quick Look

▶ **Reading Your Mail**   **page 89**
When the AOL guy announces, "You've Got Mail!" it's time to spring into action. You have e-mail in your online mailbox. Don't you want to see what it says?

▶ **Junk Mail**   **page 95**
As exciting as new e-mail can be, it won't be long before junk e-mail starts finding its way to your online doorstep. You can get some tips for recognizing junk when you see it and how to toss it without reading it.

▶ **Address Book**   **page 102**
You've got a little black book built right into your AOL software. It's simple to save e-mail addresses when your friends and associates correspond with you, and once they're listed in your Address Book, addressing e-mail to them is quick and easy.

▶ **Mail Center**   **page 107**
You've got an electronic postal clerk sitting in your Mail menu. The Mail Center stands ready to help with all your e-mail needs.

▶ **Courtesy Copies**   **page 110**
If you want to send a copy of an e-mail to someone else, just type his or her name in the Copy To field. That person will receive an exact copy of the e-mail. If you'd prefer to send the copy discreetly, put the screen name in parentheses so other recipients won't see that you copied that person.

▶ **Attached Files**   **page 116**
You can send a file along with your e-mail message. Just click the Attachments button, select your file(s), and click OK.

Chapter 5
Using E-Mail

IN THIS CHAPTER

Discovering the world of electronic mail

Accessing, reading, and replying to e-mail

Creating, checking, and formatting e-mail

Saving and organizing your e-mail

You'll never have a problem keeping in touch when you're on AOL. No, it isn't just because you can access AOL from home or work (though that is part of it). It's because AOL offers electronic mail (or *e-mail* for short). E-mail is easy to use and convenient, and it seems like the whole world is using it. Like the man says, "You've got mail!"

What Is E-Mail?

E-mail is a private, electronic communication — similar to a handwritten letter in an envelope. You will definitely receive e-mail as an AOL member and most likely will send it. *E-mail is easy:* No paper, no pens, no stamps, no fuss. *E-mail is convenient:* You can use it wherever you are on AOL. *E-mail is fast:* Your message can go around the world in a matter of seconds. Even better, e-mail costs nothing beyond your normal AOL connect charges.

Every screen name on your AOL account has an online mailbox where the e-mail you've received and sent is temporarily held. And because you can have up to seven screen names on your AOL account, you can also have up to seven mailboxes, each of which can hold up to 1,000 e-mails at a time.

Reading Your First E-Mail

First things first: Do you have e-mail to read? You can find out by turning up your computer's sound volume, signing on to AOL, and listening for the "You've got mail!" announcement immediately after the "Welcome!" greeting. Another way to check for new e-mail is to take a look at one of the Mailbox icons you find either on the left side of the Welcome Screen or at the far left of the AOL toolbar. If you have new e-mail, the red flag is raised on the icon, as shown in Figure 5-1.

Figure 5-1. The red flag on the mailbox icon means that you have new e-mail!

As you can see in Figure 5-2, we have three new e-mails. We suspect that you have new e-mail, too; all new members have e-mail from the moment they sign on. The good folks from America Online, including Steve Case, the CEO, sent you some. To see for yourself, open your mailbox by clicking either of the two mailbox icons or by pressing Ctrl+R.

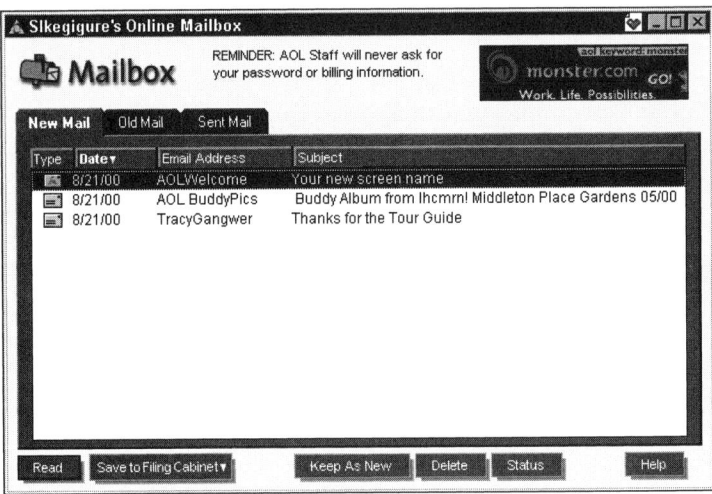

Figure 5-2. Our online mailbox, complete with e-mail from AOL.

Scanning Your Online Mailbox

Note

If you have a new AOL account or created a new screen name, the e-mail you receive from AOL has a blue icon in your mailbox and has a blue border when you read it. That's *Official AOL Mail,* which we explain in greater depth in Chapter 4.

After opening your online mailbox, take a closer look at it. AOL displays all your new e-mail in the list in the center of your Online Mailbox window (refer to Figure 5-2). Each line shows an icon, the date the e-mail was sent, the address (or screen name) of the person who sent the e-mail, and the subject line (the topic of the e-mail). All this information can help you decide whether to read the e-mail immediately, save it for later, delete it without further consideration, or approach it with care.

Across the top of the window are three tabs: New Mail, Old Mail, and Sent Mail. Click these tabs to display, respectively, lists of new e-mail (refer to Figure 5-2), old e-mail (e-mail you read recently), and sent e-mail (e-mail you've sent recently). Across the bottom are six buttons, starting with Read (which opens a piece of e-mail).

Reading New E-Mail

To read an e-mail message, first make sure that the e-mail you want to open is selected (highlighted). If it isn't, select the e-mail and then click the Read button. Alternatively, just double-click the e-mail you want to read. Your e-mail opens in a new window on your screen, as shown in Figure 5-3.

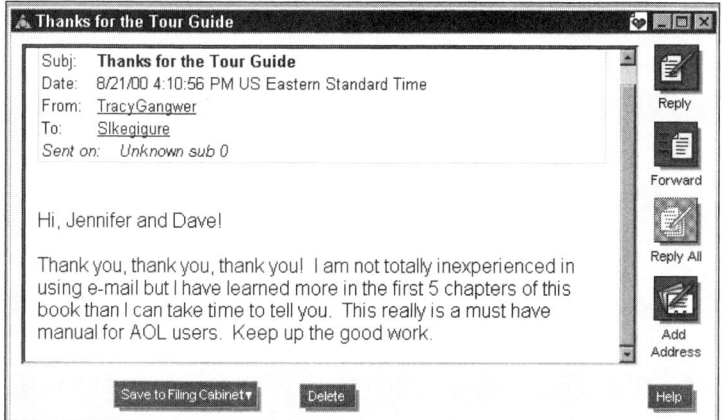

Figure 5-3. Your e-mail appears in a window on your screen.

The e-mail message is in the large box that takes up most of the window. At the top of the message are the *mail headers,* which essentially display the routing information. Headers include the subject line (which you already saw in the mailbox), the date and time the message was sent (including the time zone), the sender's name, and the recipient's name. The body of the message appears below the mail headers and the horizontal line.

E-mail messages can contain styled text (**bold,** *italic,* <u>underlined</u>, colored, big, and small), as well as graphics.

The e-mail window has a bunch of buttons on it, too. The following list explains what these buttons do:

▶ **Save to Filing Cabinet:** Saves this message in an electronic "filing cabinet" (AOL calls it your Filing Cabinet) in your computer (see Chapter 6).

▶ **Delete:** Removes the e-mail from your mailbox.

▶ **Next:** Opens the next e-mail in your mailbox; the numbers to the left of the Next button tell you how much e-mail is in your mailbox.

▶ **Reply:** Lets you send a response to the currently viewed e-mail message.

▶ **Forward:** Lets you forward the e-mail to another person.

▶ **Reply All:** Lets you send a response to all persons who received this e-mail. *Note:* Reply All is not available if no one was copied on the e-mail.

▶ **Add Address:** Lets you add the sender's address to your Address Book.

▶ **Help:** Leads to more help with using e-mail.

You can retrieve deleted mail for up to 24 hours by choosing Mail⇨Recently Deleted from the AOL toolbar, but we don't recommend using the Delete button until you feel more comfortable working with e-mail.

Note

You don't need to use the Save to Filing Cabinet button if you have your Filing Cabinet preferences set to automatically save e-mail (see the sidebar titled "Saving E-Mail in Your Filing Cabinet"). We discuss the Filing Cabinet again in Chapter 6.

Note

The Reply button automatically addresses the message but leaves the message text blank. The Forward button does not address the message, but it sends the body of the original message to the new recipient.

You can do several things with your e-mail from this point:

- **Print the e-mail.** If you have a printer, just choose Print⇨Print from the menu bar (or press Ctrl+P).
- **Save the e-mail to your Filing Cabinet.** Click the Save to PFC button in either the Online Mailbox or e-mail window and then choose Incoming/Saved Mail from the menu that appears.
- **Close the e-mail window without deleting the e-mail.** Click the Close button in the upper-right corner of the window (the one with the X on it).
- **Delete the e-mail.** Click the Delete button if you have no interest in reading this e-mail again or if you have already saved it.
- **Open the next e-mail.** Click the Next button. The current e-mail automatically closes (but is not deleted) when you open the next e-mail.

When you finish reading the last e-mail in your mailbox, close the e-mail, and the mailbox window is once again visible on the screen. It looks a little different now, however, as shown in Figure 5-4.

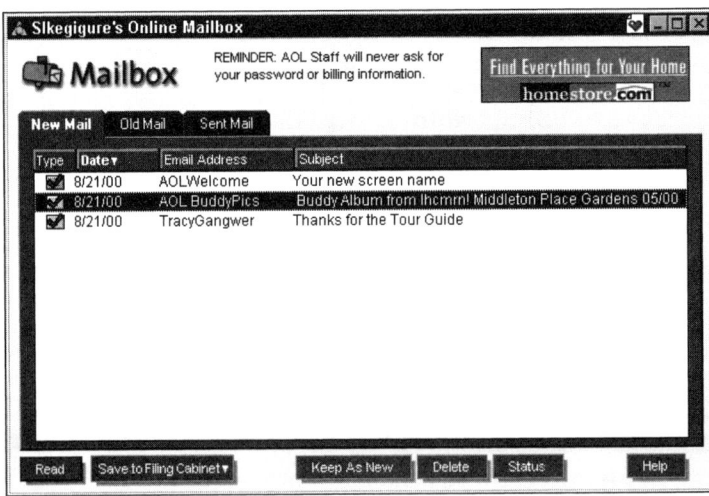

Figure 5-4. The mailbox indicates which pieces of e-mail have already been read.

If you look closely at Figure 5-4, you see that the e-mail icons on each line have check marks on them. The check marks indicate that you've read the e-mails already. If you now close your mailbox and reopen it, all the e-mail with check marks disappears from the New Mail list and moves to the Old Mail list (under the Old Mail tab). If you don't want an e-mail to move to your Old Mail list quite yet, you can control that. Just select the e-mail and click the Keep As New button at the bottom of the mailbox window. Presto! The check mark disappears.

Saving E-Mail in Your Filing Cabinet

E-mail in your online mailbox doesn't hang around forever. If you want to store your e-mail on your computer permanently, follow these steps:

1. Choose Settings➪Preferences from the AOL toolbar.

2. In the Preferences window, click the Filing Cabinet link.

3. In the resulting window, select the Retain All Mail I Send in My Personal Filing Cabinet check box and/or the Retain All Mail I Read in My Personal Filing Cabinet check box. For now, we recommend that you select both check boxes.

4. Click the Save button when you're finished.

These settings save all e-mail you read or send from this point forward. We discuss the Filing Cabinet in Chapter 6, and we cover Filing Cabinet preferences in more depth in Chapter 12.

Before peeking at the Old Mail list, take another look at the buttons along the bottom of the Online Mailbox window. The Read, Save to Filing Cabinet, Keep As New, Delete, and Help buttons are explained earlier in this chapter. The Status button, however, does need a bit of an introduction, because it can be a very useful feature. The Status button tells you when an e-mail was read and when it was sent (see Figure 5-5). The Status button is discussed in more detail in the "Checking the Status of Sent Mail" section, later in this chapter.

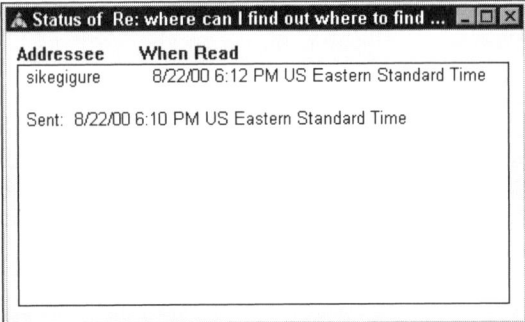

Figure 5-5. The E-Mail Status window.

Accessing Old Mail

Click the Old Mail tab at the top of the mailbox window to access your old e-mail. Any e-mail that you've read (and haven't kept as new) appears in the Old Mail list in reverse chronological order (the most recent stuff is listed first). The two e-mails in Figure 5-6 are listed in the opposite order as they appeared in Figure 5-4. The third e-mail from Figure 5-4 isn't listed because we kept it as new.

If you're online and you have New Mail, you hear the "You've got mail!" announcement, and the red flag raises on your mailbox icons. To see that new e-mail, open your mailbox again or refresh it if it's already open; it doesn't appear in your New Mail list automatically. Just press Ctrl+R, click the Read icon on your toolbar (or the mailbox icon on the Welcome Screen), or choose Mail⇨ Read Mail⇨New Mail from the toolbar to open or refresh your new e-mail list.

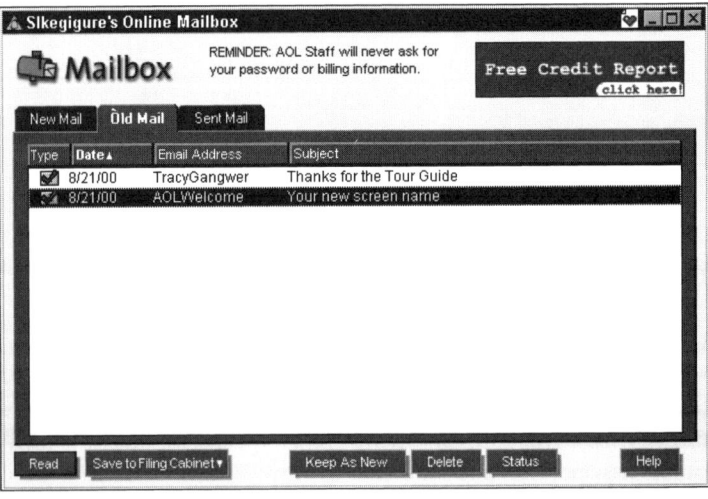

Figure 5-6. An Old Mail list.

Note that the red check mark shows up on the e-mail icons in the Old Mail list as well. If you change your mind and want to keep an e-mail as new, it isn't too late. Select the e-mail in the Old Mail list and click the Keep As New button, just as you would do in the New Mail list. The other buttons along the bottom of the Old Mail list are the same as those in the New Mail list, too.

Now that you know how to read e-mail, you may be wondering how you can get more e-mail to read. Relax — you'll have new e-mail in your mailbox before you know it. In fact, some of the e-mail you receive may be unwelcome, as we describe in the following section.

Dealing with Junk Mail

Advertisements for adult sites, offers for questionable businesses, chain letters, and worse are all common in today's world of e-mail. This unwelcome and unsolicited e-mail is known as *junk e-mail,* or *spam.* It's annoying, offensive, and makes a mess of your mailbox. You could just delete it from your mailbox — this is a good use for the Delete button. If you want to help decrease the amount of spam you get in the future, however, we encourage you to take action against junk e-mail at AOL Keyword: **Junk Mail.** The Junk Mail window is shown in Figure 5-7.

If you do receive junk e-mail, we caution you not to click any hyperlinks in that e-mail; they may lead to undesirable places or infect you with a virus that could compromise your account. Also, never give your password out to anyone; AOL will never request it in an e-mail!

Figure 5-7. Learn how to recognize, report, and block junk mail.

Tip

You can check the location of a hyperlink before actually going to it. Just position your pointer over the hyperlink, wait a moment, and the yellow help bubble will appear. If bubble help tells you that the link is on AOL only, you're probably okay. However, it's better to be safe than sorry and simply not click hyperlinks in e-mail sent to you by strangers.

Tip

Consider setting your Mail Controls to allow or disallow specific kinds of e-mail or e-mail from specific domains. Mail Controls are discussed in Chapter 4.

Here are some tips for recognizing the junk before you click:

- ▶ **Check the sender's address that appears in the mailbox.** Did the e-mail come from someone you know? If not, you know that it is unsolicited and most likely junk mail. Additionally, junk mail often comes from Internet addresses with the @ symbol in them (which we discuss in detail later in this chapter). This includes most addresses that end with @aol.com, because that often indicates Internet e-mail that is disguising itself as AOL e-mail.

- ▶ **Check the subject line.** Any subjects with the words *sex, free, giveaway,* or *hot* are almost invariably subject lines of junk e-mail. Subjects that infer familiarity, such as About last night or The picture I promised to send, are probably also junk e-mail if they come from senders you don't know. E-mail subjects that begin with Fwd: are often chain letters.

- ▶ **Be wary of official-sounding screen names.** Some junk e-mailers will try to trick you into opening e-mail by using addresses that sound legitimate, like MailRep57. Exceptions include AOL screen names with *AOL, Billing, Help, Guide,* or *Host* in them, unless they have @aol.com at the end of their names.

If you don't recognize junk mail and open it anyway, don't worry — you can't catch a virus or give out your password or credit card information by just reading an e-mail. You have to click a hyperlink or download an attached file for anything bad to happen.

So what can you do about junk e-mail? You can forward it to screen name TOSSpam, which will review the e-mail and take any appropriate action against the sender. We discuss forwarding e-mail in more detail later in this chapter, but for now, here's how to forward e-mail in three easy steps:

1. Click the Forward button in the opened junk e-mail.
2. Type **TOSSpam** in the Send To box in the upper-left corner of the resulting window.
3. Click the Send Now button.

If you receive an e-mail that violates AOL's Terms of Service (discussed in Chapter 4), forward the e-mail to screen name

TOSmaill instead. If the e-mail had an attached file, forward it to TOS Files.

Another way to stop junk e-mail in its tracks is to make yourself less of a target. Chatting in People Connection is one of the ways that junk e-mailers find your name. If you want to chat, we recommend that you create a new screen name and block e-mail entirely (or at least for everyone but those you know) for that particular screen name — you can learn how to block e-mail in Chapter 6. Another way junk e-mailers can find you is through your member profile. If you don't create a member profile, junk e-mailers can't find your name in the People Directory.

Sorting Your Online Mailbox

When you open your online mailbox, your e-mail is automatically sorted by date. As your lists of New Mail, Old Mail, and Sent Mail get longer and longer, you may want to temporarily sort that e-mail some other way so you can find a missing item or focus in on a particular e-mail conversation. AOL 6.0 makes this very easy to do.

The column labels in your online mailbox — Type, Date, Email Address, and Subject — are actually buttons, as shown in Figure 5-8. Here's how to use these columns to organize the contents of your online mailbox:

If you ever forget your screen name(s), check the Select Screen Name menu in your Sign On screen when you're offline. Alternatively, you can check the name in the title bar of the Welcome Screen when you're online; AOL always greets you by your screen name when you sign on.

Member profiles are described in Chapter 7.

Chatting is discussed in Chapter 9.

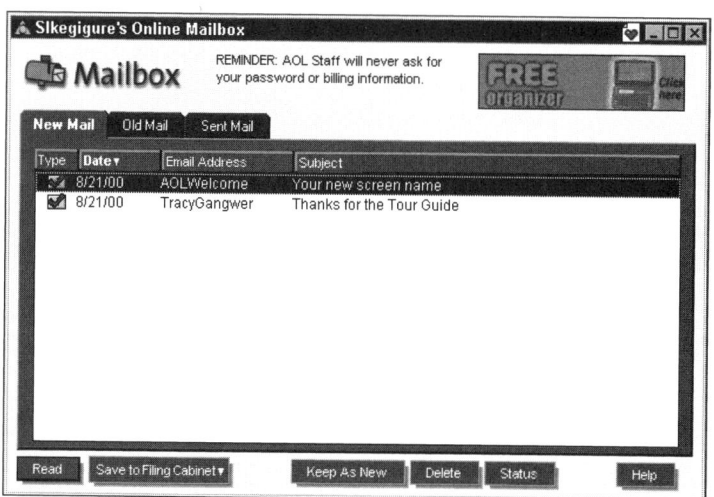

Figure 5-8. The online mailbox columns.

- **Type:** The icons displayed in this column are different, depending on whether the e-mail is Read or Unread, is Official AOL Mail, has an attached file, or contains a photo or graphic.
- **Date:** This column sorts the e-mail right down to the hour, minute, and second that it was sent.
- **Email Address:** This column sorts the e-mail alphabetically by e-mail address *and* by whether the e-mail came from an AOL screen name or an Internet address.
- **Subject:** This column sorts the messages alphabetically by subject, and groups all messages with the same subject together, regardless of whether the e-mails are replies, forwards, or originals.

The column that you sort is labeled in **bold** type. Note also that adjacent to that bold-type label is a small up arrow or down arrow. This arrow indicates whether the list is sorted from top to bottom, or bottom to top. Would you like to reverse the sort order of a column? Just click the same label button a second time.

The next time you open your online mailbox, it will be sorted by date, which is the permanent default setting.

Downloading Attached Files

E-mail can contain more than a simple text message — it can be a package containing one or more computer files. You can receive (and send) computer programs, word processing documents, spreadsheets, photos, databases, and any other kind of computerized information. The e-mail message can be considered a cover letter or packing slip, and if you decide to open the package (see the sidebar "Safe Downloading"), the file (or files — several files can be exchanged in a single message) is transferred from AOL to your computer.

Downloading is the process of transferring information from a centralized *host* computer (such as AOL or an Internet site) to a *client* computer, such as your home computer.

Safe Downloading

Attached files are the single biggest carriers of computer viruses and Trojan horses (programs that secretly find and transmit information stored on your computer). Before you start downloading every file that comes your way, consider these safety tips:

Chapter 5 ▲ Using E-Mail

- ▶ Don't download files from strangers.
- ▶ Invest in a good antivirus program and make sure that you update it frequently.
- ▶ Learn how to recognize suspicious files and much more at AOL Keyword: **Virus**.
- ▶ Consider setting Mail Controls to prevent family members from receiving and downloading attached files (see Chapter 4).
- ▶ Heed the warning message that AOL delivers whenever you open e-mail with an attached file. If you no longer receive that warning, reinstate it by changing your mail preferences (see Chapter 12).
- ▶ Even files sent by your friends may inadvertently contain a virus, so be sure that your antivirus software scans every download you receive.

When you open an e-mail containing an attached file, the e-mail window (shown in Figure 5-9) has a Download button, and the e-mail header includes information on the name of the file, its size (in bytes), and the estimated time it will take to download that file.

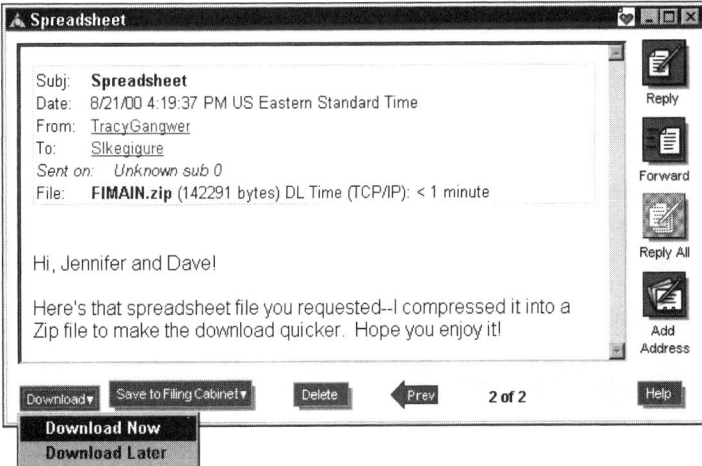

Figure 5-9. This e-mail includes an attached file.

Here are the basic steps for downloading a file, but we cover the topic in greater depth in Chapter 10:

1. Open the e-mail that includes the attached file.
2. Click the Download button in the e-mail window.
3. Select Download Now from the drop-down menu. You may receive an E-Mail Attachment Warning from AOL Neighborhood Watch. If you do, read the warning and click Yes if you still want to download the file.
4. Select a destination folder on your hard drive in the Download Manager dialog box, shown in Figure 5-10. (By default, the file is placed in the Download folder in your AOL software folder.)
5. Change the filename as desired (optional).
6. Change the file directory as desired (also optional).
7. Click Save to start the download.

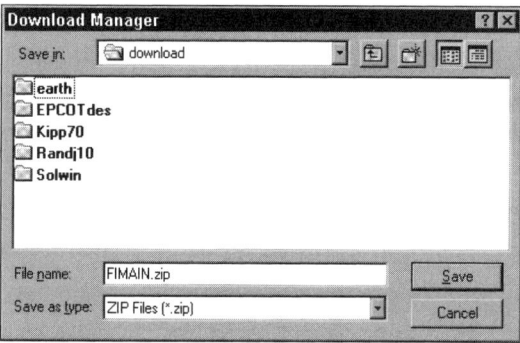

Figure 5-10. The Download Manager dialog box directs your download to the desired folder.

Note

See Chapter 10 to find out how to make use of the Download Later feature, use your Download Manager, and much more.

When the download has finished, the Download Confirmation dialog box appears, with the message `Would you like to locate the file now?` Click the Yes button to open a window displaying the contents of the folder that received the downloaded file. This is a great convenience if you want to open or install that file immediately.

E-Mail Addresses on AOL and the Internet

Just like regular mail — which requires names, street addresses, cities, states, zip codes, and sometimes countries to find its recipients — e-mail needs addresses, too. On AOL, your screen name is your e-mail address.

When you give your e-mail address to other AOL members, you can just give them your screen name. In fact, you may not have to give it to them at all; your screen name is automatically attached to every e-mail you send.

If a non-AOL member asks for your address, you need to add @aol.com to the end of your screen name. For example, our address would be bookauthors@aol.com. When you send e-mail to someone on the Internet or post a message to a newsgroup, AOL automatically attaches this Internet e-mail form of your address.

When you read your e-mail, notice the address of the sender in the e-mail headers above the message. If the address is nothing more than a screen name (no @ symbol is included), you know that the sender is an America Online member. If you see the @ symbol in the address, you can bet that the sender is either elsewhere on the Internet (not on AOL) or used the Internet to send the message (as is the case with some addresses that contain @aol.com).

Every Internet e-mail address has two components: a name and a domain. The name is similar to an AOL screen name. Everything before the @ symbol is the *name*. For example, in the address authorteam@passporter.com, the name is authorteam. The domain is everything after the @ symbol. In this case, the domain is passporter.com. The domain is similar to the street address, city, state, and zip code (but much shorter).

Because the world is a big place, domains come in many different forms. Examples of domain names include aol.com (AOL's domain), usps.gov (the United States Post Office), aclu.org (the American Civil Liberties Union), umich.edu

Note

AOL members can use the Internet e-mail form of your address, too, although they only need your screen name. If someone sends e-mail to authorteam@aol.com, we will receive it in our Author Team mailbox.

You may notice that we list Internet addresses in all lowercase letters. Not only is this practice customary, but it is also often necessary — some servers on the Internet are case-sensitive. Always type an e-mail address as you see it — if it has uppercase letters, use uppercase letters as well.

(the University of Michigan), and so on. The letters after the period at the end of the domain stand for various things: `.com` is for commercial sites, `.net` for networks, `.gov` for the government, `.org` for organizations, `.edu` for educational institutions, and so on. You may also see codes with just two letters; these codes indicate a country, such as `.ca` (Canada), `.uk` (United Kingdom), `.de` (Germany), and `.to` (Tonga).

If you think e-mail addresses are hard to decipher, try memorizing them. Fortunately, that isn't necessary. AOL's Address Book feature is the perfect place to store your addresses so you have them when you need them. Read on to find out more about this handy feature.

The Address Book

The information in your Address Book is stored on AOL's computers, so you can access the same information at home, work, and even when you're using a friend's computer.

Your AOL software comes with a built-in Address Book, shown in Figure 5-11. You can access it online or offline by choosing Mail➪Address Book from the AOL toolbar. Use your AOL Address Book to collect the e-mail addresses of your friends and associates. Later, when you want to send e-mail to them, the Address Book can automatically copy those addresses into a new e-mail message.

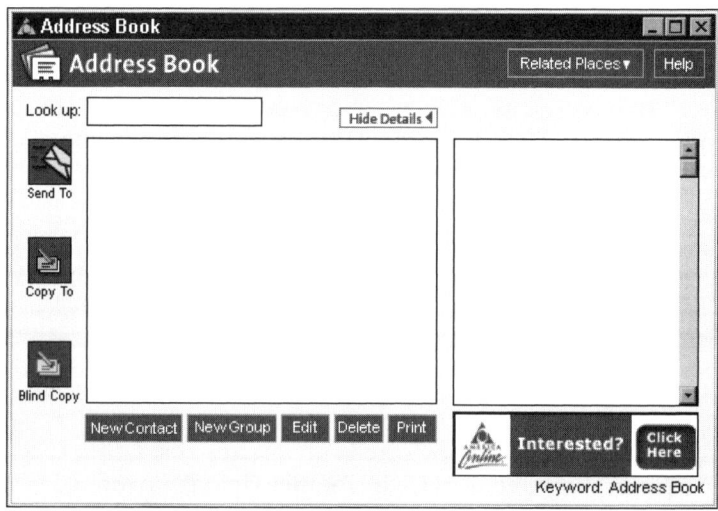

Figure 5-11. The Address Book stands ready to store e-mail addresses.

The empty Address Book shown in Figure 5-11 just begs to be used. The easiest way to add an entry to your Address Book is in an e-mail window. Here's how:

1. Open an e-mail from an address that you want to save.
2. Click the Add Address button on the right side of the window (refer to Figure 5-3). The Contact Details window, shown in Figure 5-12, appears.

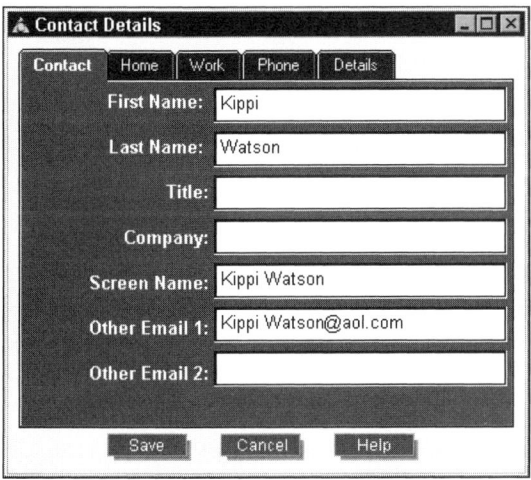

Figure 5-12. Adding a new entry to your Address Book.

> Did you notice how AOL filled in the First Name, Last Name, Screen Name, and Other Email 1 fields in the window? Of course, you can edit any or all of these fields, though we don't recommend that you edit the Other Email 1 field.

3. Click the tabs at the top of the window to record home and work addresses, telephone numbers, and other details, such as a birthday and useful notes.
4. Click Save when you're finished. AOL then adds the entry to your Address Book.

To see the new entry, choose Mail⇨Address Book again from the AOL toolbar (if you closed the Address Book window). The new entry you added appears in alphabetical order in the Address Book, as shown in Figure 5-13.

You can add a second e-mail address for a contact and even decide which one will be used for e-mail by selecting the Primary Email Address radio button in the Contact Details window.

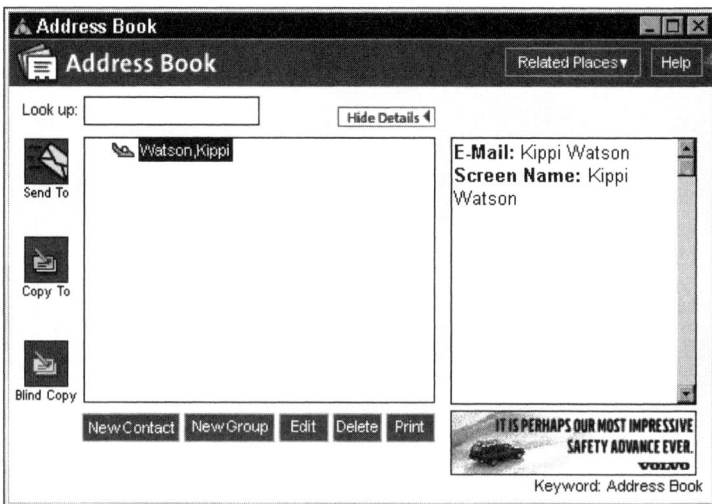

Figure 5-13. An Address Book with its first entry.

Tip

You can select multiple contacts for printing or copying into e-mail. Click the first contact you want to select, hold down the Ctrl key, and click the other contacts; all selected contacts are then highlighted. Release the Ctrl key when you're finished. You can deselect one or more of the highlighted names by clicking them while holding down the Ctrl key. Deselect all contacts by clicking on another contact without holding down the Ctrl key.

Rows of buttons line the top and bottom of the Address Book window. The following list describes when to use these buttons:

▶ **New Contact:** Click this button to add a new entry to the address book.

▶ **New Group:** Click this button to create a group mailing list from the contacts in your Address Book. You can also type in additional addresses (separate the addresses with commas or press the Enter key after entering each address).

▶ **Edit:** Click this button to edit an entry (highlight the entry and then click the Edit button).

▶ **Delete:** Click this button to remove an entry from the Address Book.

▶ **Print:** Click this button to print all contacts, or contacts highlighted in the address list.

▶ **Send To:** Highlight a contact and/or group and then click this button. A Write Mail window then opens, with the addresses of the selected contact or group already listed in the Send To field.

▶ **Copy To:** Highlight a contact and/or group in the Address Book, and then click this button. A Write Mail window opens, containing the addresses of the selected contact and/or group in the Copy To field (see "Courtesy Copies" later in this chapter).

- **Blind Copy:** Highlight a contact and/or group in the Address Book window, and then click this button. A Write Mail window then opens, containing the addresses of the selected contact and/or group in the Copy To field. All addresses are surrounded by the parentheses required for a blind courtesy copy (bcc), which is when you copy someone else on an e-mail without any of the other recipients knowing (see "Blind Courtesy Copies" later in this chapter).

The Look Up field at the top of the Address Book window enables you to search for a contact or group.

Entries in the Address Book are automatically alphabetized, either by e-mail address (if there is no name), by first name (if there is no last name), or by last name. Icons to the right of the entry indicate the type of entry. An individual entry shows an icon of one person waving, whereas a group entry shows an icon of two people waving.

If you participate in Groups@AOL (see Chapter 16), your group mailing list(s) can automatically appear in your Address Book.

If you write a lot of e-mail, keep your Address Book open at all times.

The Mail Menu

The Mail menu on the AOL toolbar, shown in Figure 5-14, offers easy access to the most common e-mail features. Table 5-1 outlines the menu options and what they do.

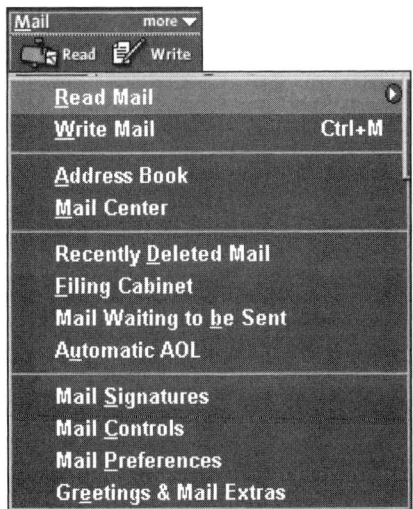

Figure 5-14. The toolbar sports the Mail menu and handy Read and Write e-mail buttons.

Table 5-1. *The Mail Menu*

Mail Menu Option	Function
Read Mail	Opens or refreshes the online mailbox. Choose New Mail, Old Mail, or Sent Mail from the submenu that appears.
Write Mail	Opens a Write Mail window (for composing a new e-mail message).
Address Book	Stores and manages e-mail addresses and contact information.
Mail Center	E-mail help at AOL Keyword: **Mail Center**.
Recently Deleted Mail	Displays all e-mail you deleted in the last 24 hours.
Filing Cabinet	Enables you to read and organize e-mail saved on your computer.
Mail Waiting to be Sent	Enables you to read and edit e-mail marked to be sent later.
Automatic AOL	Retrieves, stores, and sends e-mail automatically (see Chapter 10).
Mail Signatures	Adds a prewritten signature to e-mail you write (signatures are discussed in Chapter 6).
Mail Controls	Helps you stop junk mail and set Parental Controls (see Chapter 4).
Mail Preferences	Helps you set e-mail options (see Chapter 6).
Greetings and Mail Extras	Enables you to send online greeting cards and add pizzazz to your e-mail.

Right below the Mail menu on the toolbar, you find two icons. The Read icon (Ctrl+R) opens or refreshes your online mailbox, and the Write icon (Ctrl+M) opens a Write Mail window for composing a new message.

The Mail Center

When you choose Mail⇨Mail Center, you reach AOL Keyword: **Mail Center**, an online area that helps you get the most out of e-mail. Resources include tools for finding e-mail addresses, tips and tricks for protecting your e-mail and yourself, a tutorial on using e-mail, and cool things you can do with your e-mail, such as keeping up with the news and tracking your investments.

Sending Your First E-Mail

Before you can send e-mail, you must first compose it. Thankfully, AOL makes it easy to get started. You can click the Write button on the toolbar, choose Mail⇨Write Mail from the toolbar, or simply press Ctrl+M. Any of these three methods brings up the Write Mail window, ready to take your e-mail messages (see Figure 5-15).

You don't have to be signed on to AOL to compose e-mail. The Write Mail button works whether you're online or offline.

E-mail addresses can simply be an AOL screen name (for sending e-mail to a fellow AOL member) or an Internet address (for sending e-mail to anyone else).

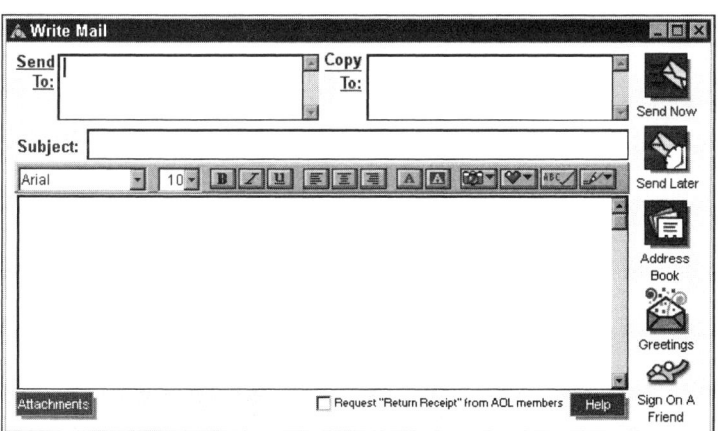

Figure 5-15. Compose your e-mail in the Write Mail window.

Part II ▲ Communicating with the World

If you're not sure how to spell your screen name exactly (and it does need to be spelled exactly to work) try this trick: Open the Window menu on the toolbar, find the item toward the bottom that begins with *Welcome,* and note the name after it — this is your screen name. If you find it confusing to spell, you probably need an easier screen name.

Good subject lines are descriptive, short, attention-getting, and relevant. For example, a subject line like `message` doesn't say much at all, but `My First E-Mail` does.

If you don't type anything in the Subject field before sending your e-mail, your recipient sees `(no subject)` as the subject line.

Use the following steps to compose an e-mail message in the Write Mail window:

1. Click in the Send To field (the first field in the Write Mail window) and type the intended recipient's e-mail address. For your first e-mail, you can use your own screen name to send a practice e-mail to yourself. Then press the Tab key twice on your keyboard to move the cursor to the next field.

2. Type an e-mail address in the Copy To field to send a courtesy copy of your message to that address. You can leave this field blank, if you want. Press the Tab key again to move your cursor to the Subject field.

3. Type the topic of your e-mail in the Subject field. Make your subject line as informative as it can be; otherwise, your recipient may mistake your message for junk e-mail and delete it. Press the Tab key again to reach the last and largest text field, which holds your e-mail message.

4. Type your message into the large text field.

5. After you finish composing your e-mail (see Figure 5-16), check your e-mail carefully. Did you type the screen name exactly as it should be? Did you say everything you wanted? Is your spelling correct?

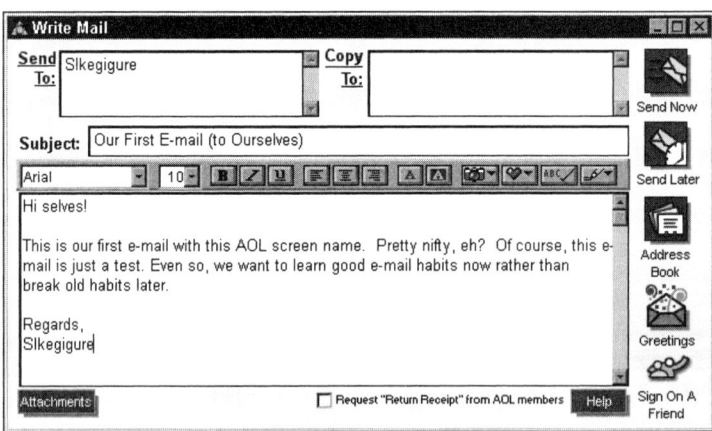

Figure 5-16. This e-mail is ready to go!

6. When your e-mail is ready to go, click the Send Now button in the upper-right corner of the window. AOL responds by instantly sending your e-mail, closing the e-mail window, and confirming that your e-mail was sent (see Figure 5-17).

Figure 5-17. Your e-mail is now winging its way to your recipient. In fact, it is probably already at its destination by the time you see this window.

Congratulations! You just sent your first e-mail.

Are you curious about all those other buttons in the Write Mail window? Here's a description of some of the other buttons you find in the Write Mail window (refer to Figure 5-15):

- ▶ **Send Later:** Saves and queues your e-mail for later.
- ▶ **Address Book:** Opens your Address Book so you can find an address and copy it to your e-mail.
- ▶ **Greetings:** Opens Greetings and Mail Extras, online greetings and a collection of fun tools for use in e-mail. The online greetings offer a fun, easy way to send "electronic cards" to friends and family via e-mail.
- ▶ **Sign on a Friend:** Sends an AOL sign-on kit to a friend.
- ▶ **Attachments:** Attaches a file (or files) to your e-mail when it is sent.
- ▶ **Request Return Receipt:** Sends you e-mail notification when your mail has been read.
- ▶ **Help:** Gives you assistance with using e-mail.

The formatting bar across the center of the Write Mail window contains many more features, which we discuss in Chapter 6.

If you anticipate sending e-mail frequently, we recommend that you create a signature that will be automatically attached to your sent e-mail. See Chapter 6 for more details.

To learn how to use the formatting buttons arrayed across the top of the message field, see Chapter 6.

If you composed your e-mail offline (or want to send it later for any other reason), click the Send Later button instead of the Send Now button. The Send Later button queues the e-mail for later sending. We discuss how to actually tell AOL to send this e-mail in Chapter 6.

Use your Address Book to address your e-mail quickly and accurately.

Courtesy Copies

A *courtesy copy* (cc) is identical to a regular e-mail. The only difference is that when the courtesy-copy recipients open the e-mail you copied them on, they see the letters *CC* in front of their screen names (rather than *To*). Everything else that you send is included: your address, other addresses, the subject line, the message, and any attached files (discussed later) or embedded images (discussed in Chapter 6).

To send a courtesy copy to one address, simply type the address in the Copy To field of your Write Mail window. To send a courtesy copy to more than one address, insert a comma or press the Enter key after each address. Figure 5-18 shows an e-mail with multiple courtesy copies (and multiple addresses).

All the recipients of the e-mail shown in Figure 5-18 will see to whom the e-mail is addressed and copied. Can you send a copy without anyone else knowing? Yes! Use blind courtesy copies, discussed next.

When addressing e-mail to other AOL members, capitalization isn't important. Neither is spacing. (This contradicts what we told you earlier about typing addresses exactly as they appear, but that rule still applies to Internet addresses).

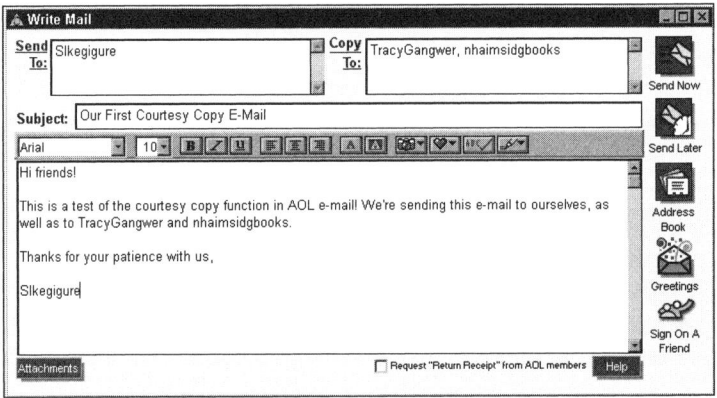

Figure 5-18. This e-mail will be sent to one individual, and several others will get courtesy copies.

Blind Courtesy Copies

You can send blind courtesy copies (bccs) along with regular courtesy copies; however, the only people who will know you sent a blind courtesy copy are you and whomever you blind copied. Just put parentheses around those addresses you want copied in secret, and leave the parentheses off those you

If you open the e-mail you sent later and notice the BCC and the recipient's address that was blind copied, don't be alarmed. *You* can see this information, and so can your recipient, but no one else can.

want copied normally. If you have a group of e-mail addresses that all need to be copied blindly, separate each address with commas and then put the parentheses around the whole set. If you send e-mail to a large group of people (large meaning more than five screen names), we recommend that you blind courtesy copy the group. This protects the privacy of everyone in the group, as some individuals are sensitive to having their e-mail address divulged to others. Blind courtesy copies also make it quicker for your recipients to open your e-mail (no waiting for additional addresses to display). See Figure 5-19 for an example of addressing blind courtesy copies.

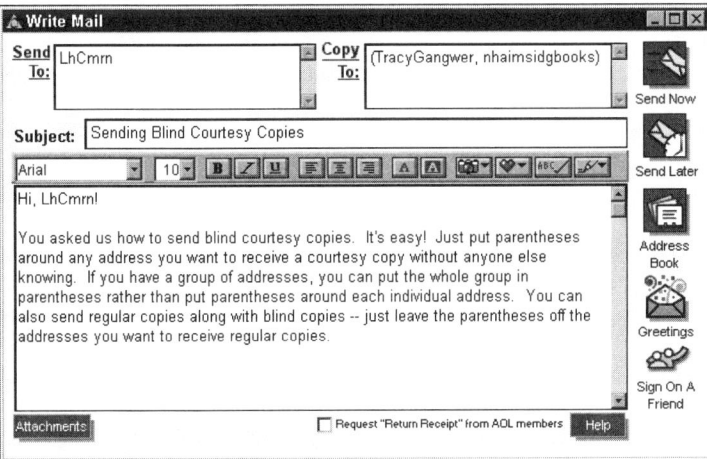

Figure 5-19. Two people will receive blind courtesy copies — look for the parentheses in the Copy To field.

Replying to E-Mail

Except for the times you initiate a correspondence, much of the e-mail you'll send is likely to be *replies* to e-mail that you received. Replying to an e-mail is easy; just follow these steps:

1. Open the e-mail to which you want to reply.
2. Click the Reply button in the top-right corner of the e-mail. A new Write Mail window appears (see Figure 5-20), complete with the sender's address in the Send To field and a subject in the Subject field.

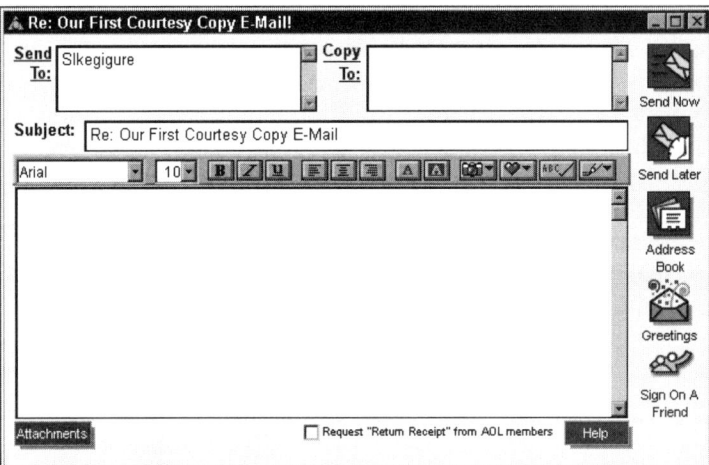

Figure 5-20. The reply e-mail window, with the address and subject line automatically filled in.

3. Type your message in the message field.
4. If you want, you can modify any of the fields before you send the reply, including the Sent To, Copy To, and Subject fields.
5. When you're finished, click the Send button.

Replying to All

Do you want to reply to someone other than the sender? First choose Settings➪Preferences from the AOL toolbar, click the Mail link, and select the Show Addresses as Hyperlinks check box. Now open your mailbox, read an e-mail (new or old), and click the address you want to respond to in the headers. Voilá! A new Write Mail window opens, with that particular address automatically filled in.

From time to time, you'll receive e-mail addressed to other addresses as well as your own. For example, the courtesy copy e-mail in Figure 5-18 is addressed to three addresses. If you want all the other recipients to see your reply, just click the Reply to All button to create an e-mail reply that will be sent to all addresses that received the original e-mail. If you want, you can remove or add any addresses before you send the reply.

Quoting

When you send a reply, it is considered good netiquette to include a reference to the original message. Before you click the Reply button in an e-mail, select (highlight) a passage from the original message that you want to include in your reply. You probably don't need to quote the whole message.

Now click the Reply button. Your reply e-mail window appears, with the recipient's name, the subject line, and the text you selected already filled in, as shown in Figure 5-21. A vertical blue line borders the left-hand side of the quoted text, to distinguish it from the rest of the message you'll write. AOL conveniently includes a line of text above your quote, indicating who wrote it at what time on which day. You can edit or remove this text if you want.

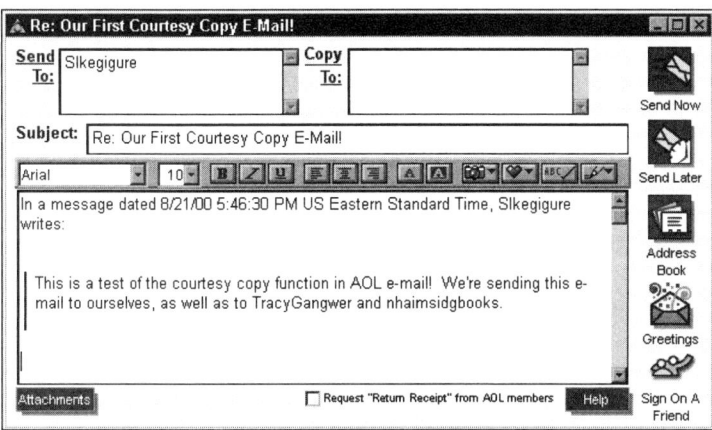

Figure 5-21. AOL automatically quotes any selected text.

If you want to quote the entire e-mail, you may be better off forwarding the e-mail instead. Continue reading to learn how.

Forwarding E-Mail

Forwarding an e-mail is simply sending a complete copy of an e-mail you received to someone else who may or may not be the person who sent it to you originally. If you want to forward an e-mail, follow these steps:

1. Open the e-mail that you want to forward.
2. Click the Forward button on the right side of the window. AOL responds by opening a new e-mail window, shown in Figure 5-22.

Tip

You can forward e-mail you've written, too. Just click the Sent Mail tab in your mailbox, open the e-mail you want to forward, and click the Forward button. Note that if you blind copied anyone in the original e-mail, those names won't be visible to the recipient of the forwarded e-mail (unless, of course, the recipient was one of those who was originally blind copied).

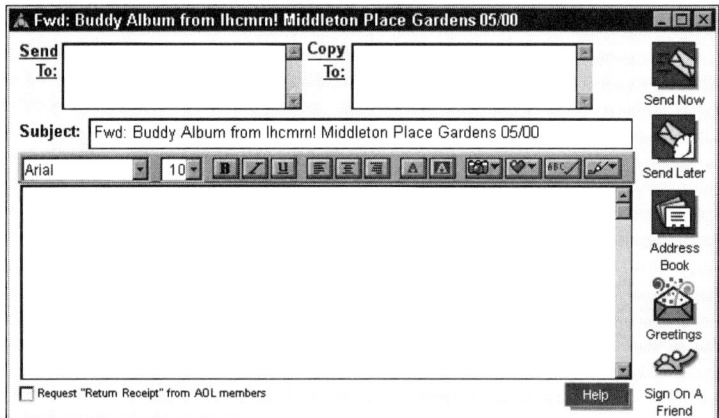

Figure 5-22. A forwarded e-mail window, complete with subject line.

You'll notice that AOL fills in the subject line with Fwd (which stands for Forward). AOL doesn't fill in the address, because it can't assume you want to forward the e-mail back to the person who sent it to you.

3. To complete the forwarding process, type in the appropriate addresses and any message you feel necessary to explain why you're forwarding the e-mail.
4. Click the Send Now button, and off it goes!

When your recipient opens the forwarded e-mail, he or she first sees your message (if you included one) and then a copy of the forwarded e-mail below that, complete with e-mail headers.

Checking the Status of Sent Mail

Did your e-mail reach its destination? To check the status of an e-mail you've sent, choose Mail⇨Read Mail⇨Sent Mail from the AOL toolbar, select the e-mail you want to check, and click the Status button at the bottom of the window.

The Status window, shown in Figure 5-23, lists the address(es) to which your e-mail was sent, along with a status beside each address. If the recipient read your e-mail, a date and time appear to the right of that person's address. If the e-mail hasn't been read, you see the message (not yet read). Other status messages you may see are you cannot check status of Internet mail (which appears for all Internet addresses), deleted (if the recipient deleted the e-mail you sent), and ignored.

To ignore e-mail in your New Mail list, right-click on the e-mail in your mailbox and choose Ignore from the context menu that appears. The e-mail icon changes to display a check mark, indicating the e-mail won't be kept as new when you refresh or reopen your mailbox. Ignored e-mail isn't deleted, but it is sent to your Old Mail list. If you later change your mind, display your Old Mail list, select the e-mail, and click the Keep As New button. Note the other convenient commands in the context menu, such as Read, Status, Keep As New, and Delete.

Figure 5-23. The status of our courtesy-copy test e-mail.

Besides keeping tabs on your addresses, checking the status of an e-mail serves another purpose: It enables you to know when someone hasn't yet read your e-mail. Why is this helpful? Because you can unsend any e-mail you sent to another AOL address if it hasn't already been read.

Unsending Mail

Did you send an e-mail before its time? Change your mind about something? You may be able to unsend what you've sent! To unsend an e-mail, follow these steps:

1. Choose Mail⇨Read Mail⇨Sent Mail from the AOL toolbar.
2. Select the offending e-mail and then click the Unsend button at the bottom of the window.
3. If your e-mail can be unsent, AOL asks you if you're sure you want to unsend the message (and notes that no copy will remain in your mailbox). Click Yes to confirm (or No to cancel). If successful, AOL confirms that the message was unsent.

If you want to unsend an e-mail, we advise you to do so as soon as possible — that way, you're more likely to catch it before it gets read.

Only e-mail that hasn't yet been read can be unsent. If even one person has read the e-mail, you're too late. If you send e-mail to two recipients, one an AOL address and the other an Internet address, you can't unsend it — e-mail to Internet addresses can't be unsent.

Attaching Files

How do you get a spreadsheet into an e-mail? Copying and pasting probably won't work. Instead, attach it! Just follow these steps:

1. Click the Attachments button at the bottom of a Write Mail window. This produces the Attachments window (shown in Figure 5-24) through which you can attach (and detach) one or more files.

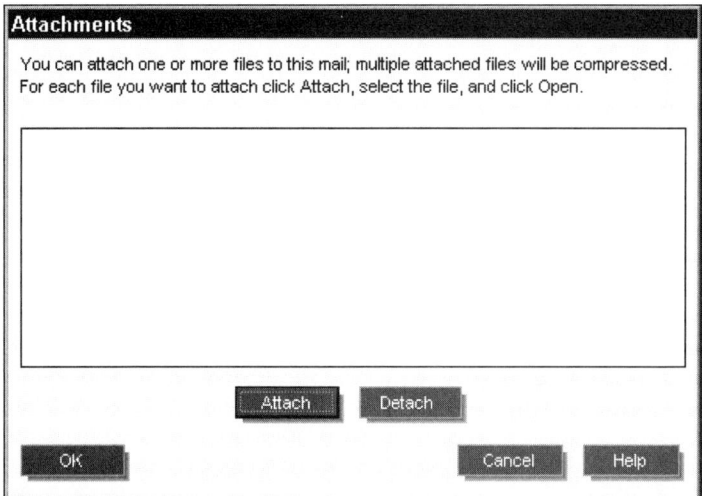

Figure 5-24. The Attachments window.

2. Click the Attach button to open the Attach dialog box.
3. In the Attach dialog box, locate the file by scrolling through your directories. When you find the file you want, click the Open button. The Attach dialog box closes, and your Attachment window now lists the attached file.

4. Repeat Steps 2 through 3 to add another file, if you want. Figure 5-25 shows what an Attachments window with multiple files looks like.

   If you want to Detach files, select the name of the file you want to remove in the Attachments window and click the Detach button.

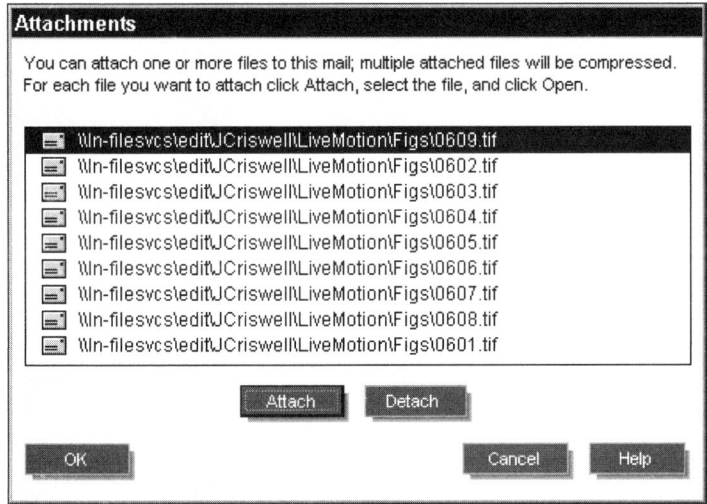

Figure 5-25. Attaching multiple files. In this case, each of these files is a picture.

5. When you're finished attaching files, click the OK button in the lower-left corner of the Attachments window.
6. Complete the e-mail as you normally would. In your message, we recommend that you reference the attached file(s) for your recipients. Let them know what the files contain, any special software they may need to use or view the files, and so on.

   Note that all or part of the filenames appear next to the Attachments button in the Write Mail window, along with a mini-icon of two diskettes (see Figure 5-26). If you need to check your list of attachments before you send the e-mail or edit the attachment list itself, click the Attachments button again.

You can select more than one file at a time. Click a file that you want to attach, hold down the Ctrl key and click additional files, and then release the Ctrl key. Each selected file is then highlighted. If you make a mistake, hold down the Ctrl key again, and click any highlighted file to deselect it, or click others you want to add. You can also lasso several files by dragging your cursor around them.

Although AOL places no practical limit on the number of files you can add (at least that we found), there is a size limit — you can't attach a file or set of files greater than 16MB total.

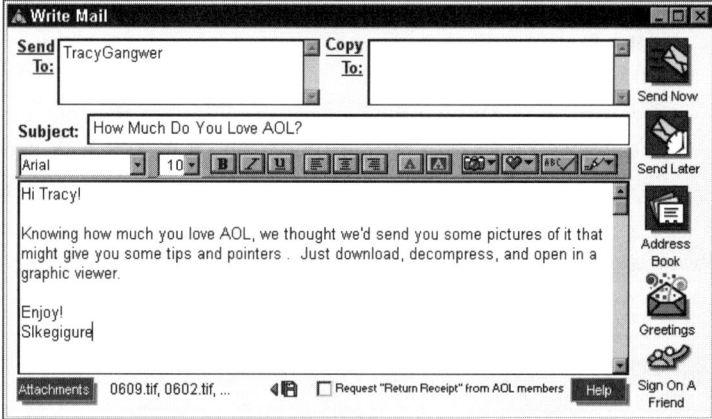

Figure 5-26. Our e-mail with attached files.

7. When your e-mail is ready, click the Send Now button.

If you attached two or more files, AOL responds with a message that it is compressing your attachments (which means it is decreasing the size of the files with ZIP file compression techniques and then archiving them into one file for transfer). If the attached files are any larger than a few kilobytes, AOL displays a File Transfer window that displays the progress of the file transfer, as shown in Figure 5-27.

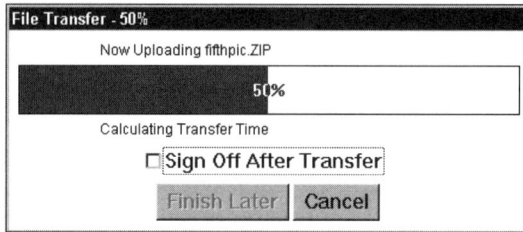

Figure 5-27. AOL is transferring the e-mail and its attached files.

Note the name of the file you're transferring, the percentage completed, the time remaining in the transfer, and the Sign Off After Transfer check box. If you select the Sign Off After Transfer check box, AOL automatically signs you off when the thermometer reaches 100 percent. If you click the Finish Later button, AOL stops the file transfer and queues your e-mail to be sent later. If you let the file transfer complete on its own, AOL informs you when your file transfer is successfully completed.

Here are a few caveats regarding attached files:

- **You can't send attached files to everyone.** Some members choose to block all e-mail with attached files through their Mail Controls (discussed in Chapter 4).
- **Attached-file-size limits to Internet addresses can be even more restrictive.** Some Internet e-mail addresses accept files only up to 1 or 2MB in size, and some block them completely. It pays to check with Internet addressees before sending them attached files.
- **Be considerate of what files you attach and to whom you send them.** Don't send a huge file to someone with a slow connection, or an inappropriate graphic image to a minor. The Terms of Service apply to attached files, too. Additionally, please scan your file(s) for viruses before you send them to someone else (see Chapter 10 for details).
- **AOL compresses file attachments created in Windows AOL into the ZIP compression format, which Mac users may not be familiar with.** Conversely, Mac AOL compresses files in the StuffIt file compression format. For utilities that decompress ZIP archives on the Mac and StuffIt (.SIT) archives on the PC, search the AOL software libraries at AOL Keyword: **File Search**. Note that Mac AOL does decompress ZIP files automatically.

Putting Your Knowledge to Work

If you're eager to receive more e-mail and experiment with your e-mail features, subscribe to a free AOL newsletter at AOL Keyword: **Newsletter**. Choose a newsletter (or two, or three) that you like and follow the subscription directions. Many newsletters send you a confirmation of your subscription via e-mail and then follow with periodic e-mails containing the newsletter itself.

Now that you've mastered the basics of sending e-mail, why not send e-mail to all your friends, family members, and coworkers? You may be surprised at how many people have e-mail addresses these days. Try searching the People Directory (described in Chapter 18) for the screen names of people you know or would like to know better.

Ready to learn how to put the finishing touches on your e-mail? Turn the page to Chapter 6.

CHAPTER

6

ADVANCED E-MAIL

Quick Look

▶ **Filing Cabinet** page 123
Your AOL software comes with a powerful database known as the Filing Cabinet, which you can use to store and organize e-mail you send and receive. You can set your AOL software to automatically save copies of your e-mail in your Filing Cabinet, and then use the built-in search and sorting features to locate e-mail quickly and efficiently. Your Filing Cabinet is accessible under the Mail menu in the AOL toolbar.

▶ **Spell Checker** page 130
You need never worry about sending an e-mail with misspelled words again, thanks to AOL's built-in spell checker. You can use the spell checker to automatically check every e-mail you send or just check your text on command. The Spell Check feature is available under the Edit menu on the menu bar, or you can use the Edit button on the Write Mail Form.

▶ **E-Mail Signatures** page 137
You can automatically add your signature to the end of e-mail you send. You can create and use up to five different signatures. Click the pencil button at the far right of the formatting toolbar in the Write Mail window to set up your signature(s).

▶ **Pictures in E-Mail** page 139
E-mail isn't just for text anymore. You can also add full-color pictures to the e-mail you send to fellow AOL members. To add a picture, click the camera button in the Write Mail window.

Chapter 6
Advanced E-Mail

IN THIS CHAPTER

Safeguarding your e-mail in the Filing Cabinet

Polishing your e-mail with the spell checker and Mail Extras

Using styled text and signatures in your e-mail

Embedding pictures and graphics in your messages

AOL's e-mail system is loaded with features, yet it still manages to stay easy to use. Within the bounds of this book, we lack the space to tell you everything there is to know about AOL e-mail. Most members get by knowing little more than we covered in the previous chapter; however, with just a touch more effort, you can raise your e-mail from the gray, drab basics to a colorful and efficient communications tool.

Saving and Organizing Your E-Mail in the Filing Cabinet

Don't make the mistake of thinking your e-mail will stay in your online mailbox forever. Within a few days, the e-mail you've read disappears, and the e-mail you've sent disappears after about a month. Why? AOL stores that e-mail on its own computers, and space is at a premium. If you want to keep track of your online correspondence, you have to use space on your own hard drive.

The Filing Cabinet is AOL's built-in system for saving, organizing, and searching the e-mail you've read and sent. It's also a part of the offline mail system (which we discuss a little later in this chapter). Auto AOL and the Download Manager (both of which are discussed in Chapter 10) use the Filing Cabinet to store e-mail and message board postings and to record information about files you download. If you're beginning to think that your Filing Cabinet is an important feature, you're right.

Automatically Saving E-Mail in the Filing Cabinet

Although you can save e-mail to the Filing Cabinet on an item-by-item basis, most folks prefer to automatically save all e-mail to the Filing Cabinet. To do this, you have to change some of your AOL Mail Preferences. If you didn't do this in Chapter 5, now is the time to do it. Just follow these steps:

1. Choose Settings⇨Preferences from the AOL toolbar. The Preferences window appears.
2. Click the Filing Cabinet link to open the Filing Cabinet Preferences window, shown in Figure 6-1.
3. Select the Retain All Mail I Send in My Personal Filing Cabinet and the Retain All Mail I Read in My Personal Filing Cabinet check boxes. These preferences affect all screen names on your account, so you only have to do this once.

Using the Filing Cabinet

Your Filing Cabinet will be a bit empty in the beginning. After all, you have to start sending and reading e-mail before any of it can be automatically saved. Eventually, though, there will be something worth seeing, so why not take a look?

Each of the screen names on your account has its own Filing Cabinet.

As we note in Chapter 12, you can password-protect your Filing Cabinet to hide its contents from prying eyes.

AOL 6.0 calls this feature the *Filing Cabinet*, but in earlier versions of AOL software, it was called the *Personal Filing Cabinet*, or PFC. You'll still find the term Personal Filing Cabinet and the PFC abbreviation here and there on AOL. It's all the same thing.

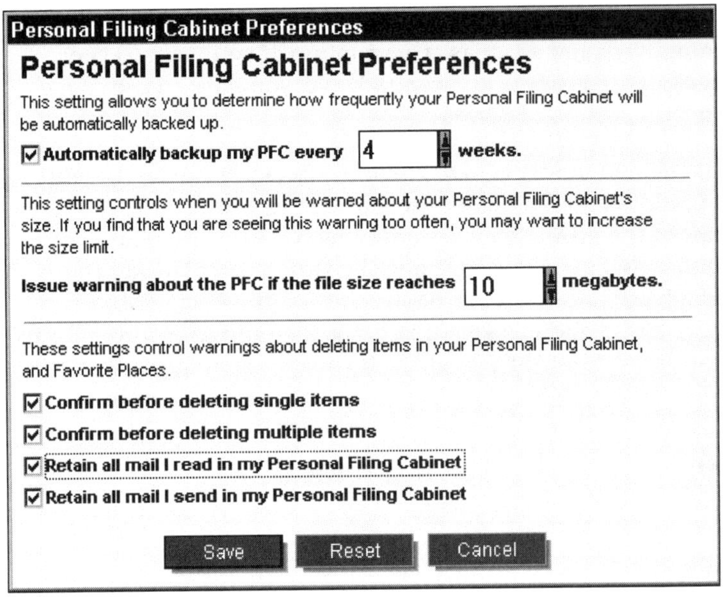

Figure 6-1. Setting your Filing Cabinet preferences to save e-mail you read and send.

You can read what's in your Filing Cabinet whether you're online or offline. Just choose Mail➪Filing Cabinet from the AOL toolbar. This command opens the Filing Cabinet, shown in Figure 6-2.

Figure 6-2. The Filing Cabinet. All the folders are closed in this example. Double-click a folder to see what's inside.

Across the top of the Filing Cabinet are tabs for Mail, Newsgroups, and Downloads. If the Mail tab hasn't already been selected, click it now. Double-click the Incoming/Saved Mail folder, and see what's inside, as shown in Figure 6-3.

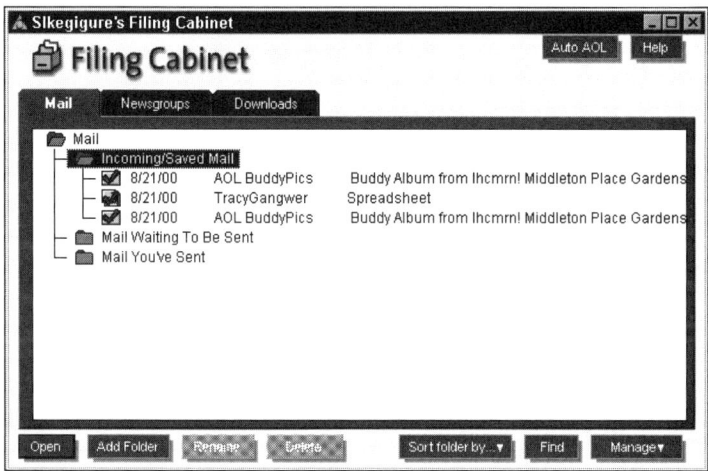

Figure 6-3. The contents of the Incoming/Saved Mail folder.

The Filing Cabinet lists the date, the screen name of the sender, and the subject of every e-mail — the same information you see in your online mailbox. Double-click any item to open it. The e-mail window is just the same here as it is when you read your online mailbox. You can use the Reply, Forward, or Reply All options, or add a name to your Address Book, just as always. The only difference is if you're replying to e-mail while you're offline. In that case, you can only use the Send Later option.

Now take a look at the buttons around the edges of the Filing Cabinet window. The following list lets you know what each button does:

- **Open:** Lets you open the selected e-mail
- **Add Folder:** Lets you add a new folder
- **Rename:** Lets you rename folders you created
- **Delete:** Lets you delete e-mail items and folders you created
- **Sort Folder By:** Sorts the contents of a specific folder by date, subject, mail type, or e-mail address

- **Find:** Searches your Filing Cabinet (see the next section)
- **Manage:** Enables you to back up your Filing Cabinet, restore or install a copy of an existing Filing Cabinet from another computer, or compact your Filing Cabinet file to conserve hard drive space
- **Auto AOL:** Lets you configure and operate *Automatic AOL,* which automatically signs on to AOL, collects and sends your e-mail, and saves it to your Filing Cabinet
- **Help:** Online and offline help with the Filing Cabinet's many features

Read how to use Automatic AOL in Chapter 10.

Searching the Filing Cabinet

One of the joys of the Filing Cabinet, in our opinion, is the Find feature (see Figure 6-4). To use this feature, click the Find button in the Filing Cabinet to open the Search dialog box. Type all or part of a screen name or important words or phrases into the Find What text box. Here are some additional search options in the Search dialog box:

- **Match Case:** Select this dialog box to look for words with capitalization matching the text you entered.
- **Scope of Search:** Select the All Folders radio button to look through every folder in your Filing Cabinet, or select the Open Folders only radio button to search only the open folders. If you only want to search the Mail You've Sent folder, close the Incoming/Saved Mail folder and select the Open Folders Only option.
- **Type of Search:** Select the Full Text radio button to look in the full text of every saved e-mail, or select the Titles Only radio button to look for e-mail with a particular subject or sent by a particular person. A Full Text search can take much longer than a Titles Only search, but it's a lifesaver if you don't remember much about the e-mail other than the information within it.

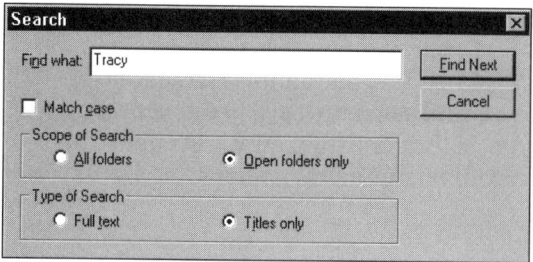

Figure 6-4. Search for an elusive e-mail with your Filing Cabinet's Find search engine.

Organizing the Filing Cabinet

Your Filing Cabinet can get stuffed with e-mail, so at some point you'll want to clean house and organize it. Start by deleting all the junk mail you've received. You may also want to create one or more folders in order to organize the e-mail by topic or sender. To create a folder in your Incoming/Saved Mail folder, follow these steps:

1. Click the Incoming/Saved Mail folder once to highlight it.
2. Click the Add Folder button to open the Create Folder dialog box.
3. Type a name for that folder and then click OK. The new folder then appears inside the Incoming/Saved Mail folder.

Now you can drag and drop e-mail items into that folder. If you like, create more folders, and place folders inside of other folders, until your Filing Cabinet is organized to your satisfaction. You can do the same thing with the Mail You've Sent folder.

Your Filing Cabinet file can take up a good bit of space on your hard drive. No matter how much e-mail you delete, the Filing Cabinet file won't shrink until you click the Manage button, choose Compact from the drop-down menu, and click Compact Now in the resulting window.

If you find you're deleting far more e-mail from your Filing Cabinet than you're keeping, perhaps you should manually save e-mail you've read to your Filing Cabinet, rather than

As you're cleaning house, you can save a step or two by right-clicking on any item you want to delete and choosing Delete from the context menu that appears.

Tip

You can follow this procedure to write as many messages as you want before you sign on. Just open a new Write Mail window for each message.

automatically save it. First, deselect the Retain All Mail I Read in My Personal Filing Cabinet option that we mention in "Automatically Saving E-Mail," earlier in this chapter. Now, when you read your e-mail, click the Save to Filing Cabinet button at the bottom of the e-mail window and choose the appropriate folder from the drop-down menu.

Offline Mail

Offline mail is one of best ways to avoid telephone toll charges, stay within your AOL budget, and prevent conflicts over telephone usage. You can start by writing your next new e-mail while you're offline. These are the basic steps to follow:

1. Select the screen name you want to use from the Sign On screen.
2. Click the Write icon in the AOL toolbar.
3. Write your e-mail as you always do.
4. Sign on to AOL.
5. Click the Send Now button in the Write Mail window.

Note

When you click the Send Later button, a dialog box may appear, to acknowledge that your mail has been placed in your Filing Cabinet and to explain your offline mail options. This dialog can be eliminated or restored by changing a setting in your mail preferences (see Chapter 12).

The Send Later button adds extra convenience and safety to your offline mail writing. To use it, compose a new e-mail offline, following the preceding steps, but click the Send Later button when you're finished writing. One of the big benefits of Send Later is that it saves your e-mail on your hard drive. That way the e-mail won't be lost if someone shuts down the computer or needs to sign on with another screen name before you can sign on yourself. When you're ready to send that e-mail, sign on, open the Mail menu on the AOL toolbar, and choose Mail Waiting to Be Sent. The Mail Waiting to Be Sent window, shown in Figure 6-5, lists any e-mail that you've chosen to send later.

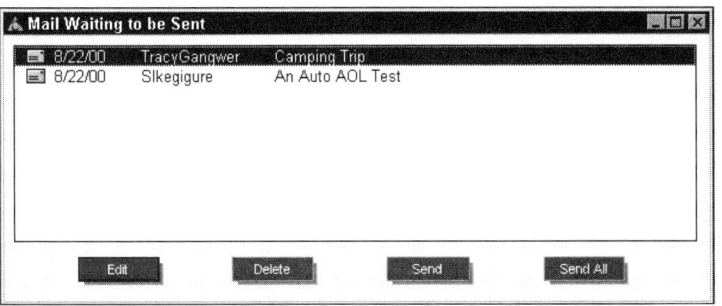

The Mail Waiting to Be Sent window is available offline, too. Use it to review and edit your e-mail before you sign on.

Figure 6-5. The Mail Waiting to Be Sent window saves your works in progress.

Here's what you can do using the buttons in the Mail Waiting to Be Sent window:

- ▶ **Edit:** Open the selected message for review or editing
- ▶ **Delete:** Delete the selected message
- ▶ **Send:** Send the selected e-mail message
- ▶ **Send All:** Send every e-mail message in Mail Waiting to Be Sent

Your Filing Cabinet is essential to reading and replying to e-mail offline. After you select the Retain All Mail I Read in My Personal Filing Cabinet check box (see the section "Automatically Saving E-Mail in the Filing Cabinet"), you can gather your e-mail very quickly while online and then read and reply to it offline. When you're online, just open the first new e-mail in your online mailbox and start clicking the Next button as quickly as you can. Don't bother to stop and read the messages as they flash by. When you sign off, open your Filing Cabinet to start reading and replying to your e-mail.

This is only half of the offline e-mail picture. Auto AOL can totally automate the process of collecting and sending your e-mail, which minimizes the time you spend online. You can read all about Auto AOL in Chapter 10.

If you have mail waiting to be sent when you sign on to AOL, a dialog box may appear, asking whether you want to send that e-mail, review the mail waiting to be sent, or send it later. You can click an option to eliminate that dialog box. This dialog can also be eliminated or restored by changing a setting in your mail preferences (see Chapter 12).

You can also access your off-line e-mail features by opening your Filing Cabinet. Just choose Mail⇨Filing Cabinet from the AOL toolbar and then open the Mail Waiting to Be Sent folder. You can then edit, delete, or send individual messages.

Spell Checking

Not evriwon wood agre, butt spellin and grammer is verry importint two gud komyounicashuns. Fortunately for those of us who are spelling-challenged, a spelling and grammar helper is built right into the AOL software. You can start a spell check several ways. The most obvious way is to click the Spell Check button in the Write Mail window formatting bar (it's the button that has the letters ABC and a check mark on it).

The spell check begins wherever the text insertion mark happens to be, which can just as easily be at the end of a document as at the beginning. The spell checker starts looking for misspelled words, common typographical errors, and common grammatical errors. When it finds one, the Check Spelling window opens to display its findings, as shown in Figure 6-6.

Tip

You can also start a spell check by choosing Edit ⇨ Spell Check from the AOL menu bar, by using the right-click context menu, or by setting your Mail preferences (see Chapter 12) to automatically spell-check every e-mail when you click the Send Now button.

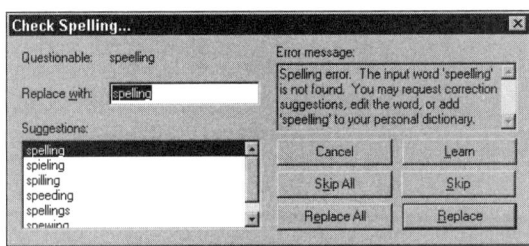

Figure 6-6. The spell checker found a problem. It describes the questionable term, explains why it thinks there's a problem, and proposes a solution.

Here's a feature-by-feature description of all the buttons and boxes in the Check Spelling window:

- ▶ **Questionable:** The questionable term is highlighted in the text and listed in the Check Spelling window.
- ▶ **Error Message:** The spell checker explains why it found the term questionable and describes your options.
- ▶ **Replace With:** The term in this box will replace the questionable term, if you so choose. You can use the solution suggested by the spell checker, select a different term from the Suggestions list box, or type in your own replacement text.

Cross-Reference

See Chapter 12 for a detailed description of your spell check preferences.

- **Suggestions:** This list box contains potential replacements for the questionable term. Click the item of your choice if you disagree with the spell checker's first choice.
- **Cancel:** The Cancel button ends the spell check.
- **Learn:** The Learn button adds the questionable term to your personal spelling dictionary.
- **Skip All:** Click this button to skip all instances of a questionable term in the document being checked. This is useful when unusual names or terms are used correctly and appear often in the text.
- **Skip:** You may want to allow a questionable term just this once, rather than add it to your personal dictionary.
- **Replace All:** Click this button to replace all instances of a questionable term, throughout the document, with the text in the Replace With box. This is especially useful for unusual names.
- **Replace:** This button replaces the current (highlighted) instance of a questionable term with the text in the Replace With box.

Spell-checking software is never perfect. It will find problems where there are none and miss other common problems altogether. However, a spell checker will find all sorts of problems you never would have caught yourself. Save yourself some embarrassment and start spell-checking your e-mail before you click Send Now.

You can spell-check a single word. Just highlight the word with your mouse and click the Spell Check button in the Write Mail window. Cancel the spell check when you're finished.

Greetings and Mail Extras

Have you ever wondered what the Greetings button in the Write Mail window does? Clicking this button opens the Greetings and Mail Extras window, shown in Figure 6-7.

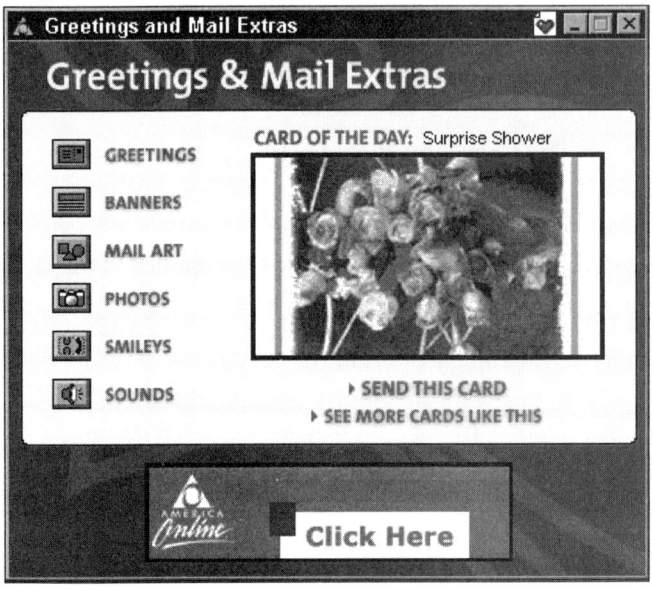

Figure 6-7. Greetings and Mail Extras — dandy ways to jazz-up your e-mail.

Only AOL members can experience the Greetings and Mail Extras feature.

Drag and drop the image onto your AOL desktop. The image will open in an image editing window where you can modify the picture before using it.

The Greetings and Mail Extras feature is an introduction to some of the ways you can go beyond basic e-mail and add some sparkle to your communications. Several buttons in the Greetings and Mail Extras window take you to the American Greetings Online Greetings store. When you buy online greetings for your friends, American Greetings does the e-mailing for you.

Greetings and Mail Extras is a collection of pictures and sounds you can add to your AOL e-mail. Just select the category (Greetings, Banners, Mail Art, Photos, Smileys, or Sounds) and browse the collection for an appropriate or pleasing item. When you find an item you like, click a button to add it to a new Write Mail window or add it to the currently open Write Mail window. If you'd rather, you can also drag and drop the item into an existing Write Mail window.

Here's a run down of what Greetings and Mail Extras has to offer:

- **Greetings:** Visit the American Greetings Online Greetings store.
- **Banners:** Add wide, decorative images to the top of your message.

- **Mail Art:** Jazz up your notes with these lighthearted pictures.
- **Photos:** Add some snap to your e-mail with a selection of greeting card-style photographs.
- **Smileys:** Put a happy (or not-so-happy) face on your e-mails.
- **Sounds:** Make your message speak volumes with hyperlinks to these brief words of greeting.

Greetings and Mail Extras is a great demonstration of inserting images into e-mail, which we discuss in greater detail later in this chapter.

Mail Controls

Are you getting too much junk e-mail? Take control of your online mailbox with Mail Controls! This group of e-mail settings enables you to block (or allow) a wide range of e-mail. To access Mail Controls for every screen name on your account, sign on with a master screen name and then follow these steps:

1. Choose Mail⇨Mail Controls from the AOL toolbar or use AOL Keyword: **Mail Controls**. Either command opens the Mail Controls window, shown in Figure 6-8.

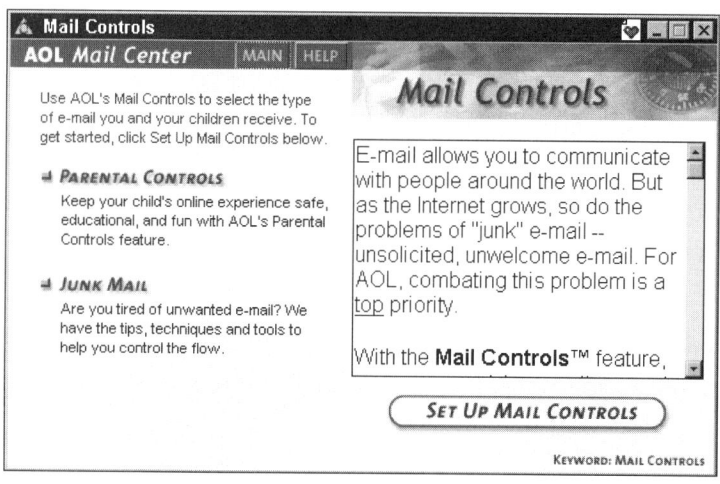

Figure 6-8. Mail Controls are within reach whenever you're online with a master screen name.

Note

You can change Mail Controls only when you're signed on with a master screen name. You can find more information on using and designating master screen names in Chapter 4.

Cross-Reference

If you're not yet familiar with Mail Controls, you can learn the basics back in Chapter 4.

2. Click the Set Up Mail Controls button in the lower-right corner of the window. Assuming you're signed on with a master screen name, the E-Mail Parental Controls window appears, as shown in Figure 6-9.

Figure 6-9. Choose the screen name you want to modify.

3. Select the screen name that you want to modify and then click the Edit button at the bottom of the window. The Mail Controls window for the screen name you chose appears, as shown in Figure 6-10.

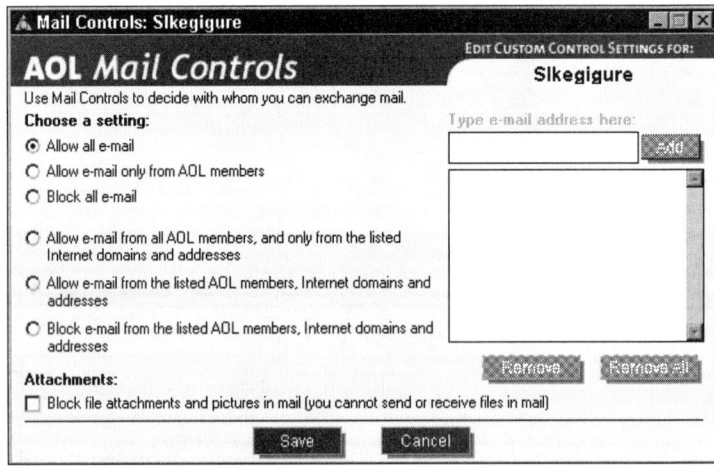

Figure 6-10. The Mail Controls window.

To get the most out of your AOL e-mail, here are some options to consider in the Mail Controls window:

- ▶ **Block a specific address:** When you receive junk e-mail, copy the address in the e-mail and then visit your Mail Controls. In the Mail Controls window, choose the Block E-Mail from the Listed AOL Members, Internet Domains and Addresses check box. Then paste that e-mail address into the text entry box on the right-hand side of the window and click the Add button. The address will be added to the list on the right-hand side of the window. Doing this ensures you won't receive junk e-mail from those addresses ever again.

- ▶ **Block a specific domain:** If you continue to receive junk e-mail from different addresses at the same domain, such as `makemoney@junk.com` and `freeoffer@junk.com`, you can block the entire domain. Just add the domain (such as **junk.com**) to your list. Once you do this (and set your controls to block e-mail from the listed addresses), you'll never receive e-mail from this domain again.

- ▶ **Block all Internet mail:** If most of your junk e-mail is from Internet addresses, consider choosing the Allow E-Mail from AOL Members Only option. This option blocks all Internet e-mail. If you do occasionally get Internet e-mail that you want to continue receiving, choose the Allow E-Mail from AOL Members, and Only from the Listed Internet Domains and Addresses option and then add to your list the domains and/or addresses from which you want to get Internet e-mail.

- ▶ **Create a screen name just for chatting:** If you enjoy chat rooms but hate all the junk e-mail you get as a result, we recommend you create another screen name just for chatting. After creating your new screen name, use Mail Controls to block all e-mail on that name. After you start using your new screen name and making friends, you may want to change your setting to Allow E-Mail from the Listed AOL Members, Internet Domains and Addresses and then add your friends' screen names to your list.

- ▶ **Block attachments and pictures:** If you're concerned about security, seriously consider using the Block File Attachments and Pictures in E-Mail setting at the bottom of the Mail Controls window. If no one is able to send you attached files, you have no risk of downloading a Trojan horse or virus. However, choosing this option also means that you will not be able to attach pictures or files to the e-mails that you send.

Styled Text

Note

Only fellow AOL members can see AOL's styled text features. AOL removes all styled text features before e-mail is sent to Internet addresses.

Styled text is just another way to say *formatting,* a concept that is very familiar to anyone who uses a word processor. The truth is, AOL's e-mail system includes a built-in word processor, so if you've never processed a single word before, here's your chance. The AOL Write Mail window includes a formatting bar, which makes all this styling possible (see Figure 6-11).

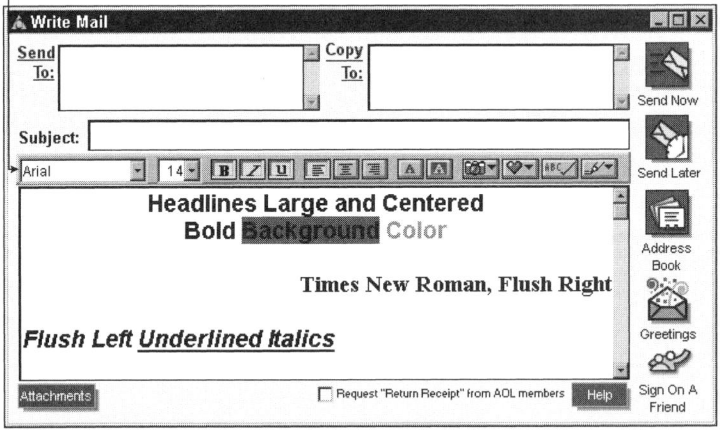

Figure 6-11. The formatting bar in the Write Mail window — choose fonts, text formatting, colors, and more.

As we describe the features in the text that follows, why not experiment as you read along? Open a Write Mail window and type a few sentences of sample text. Highlight a bit of the text and start experimenting.

In the following list, we focus on the features on the left and center of the formatting bar; the buttons on the far right are discussed in other sections:

- **Font Selection:** Select a font (or typeface) from the drop-down list. You can choose from every font installed on your computer. Unfortunately, if the recipients don't have the same fonts on their computers, all they see is their default font (usually Arial).
- **Text Size:** Choose a number from this menu to make the text larger or smaller. The bigger the number, the bigger the text.
- **Bold:** Click this button to make a bold statement.
- **Italics:** Use italics for emphasis.
- **Underline:** Underline important concepts.
- **Align Left:** Click this button for straight margins on the left and ragged text on the right.
- **Align Center:** This button centers text on the page, and both margins are ragged.
- **Align Right:** Click this button for straight margins on the right and ragged text on the left (which is the reverse of what is usually seen).
- **Text Color:** Click this button to change the color of your text for extra impact.
- **Background Color:** Click this button to put a block of color behind your text for extra contrast.

You can change the default font and many other aspects of your e-mail. Check Chapter 12 for a discussion of the font preferences settings.

Now that you've experimented a bit with all these features, start thinking about good taste. Learn to use these effects with subtlety. A little bit of formatting brings clarity and emphasis, whereas a lot simply distracts from your message.

Signatures

E-mail users have a version of pen and ink, called a *sig* (or *signature file*). A sig is more like a letterhead than an actual signature. Sigs usually include a person's full name, e-mail address, and Web page address. After that, some folks go on to add telephone numbers, street addresses, favorite slogans, or a quote of the day. You can create signatures from the formatting bar in the Write Mail window. See Figure 6-12 for a tasteful sig.

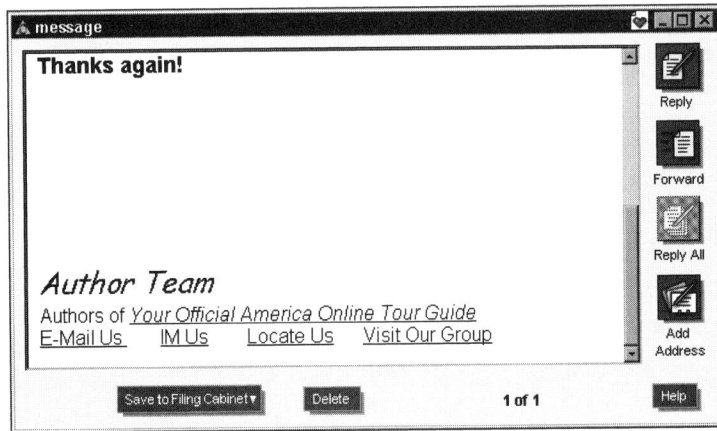

Figure 6-12. One of the authors' signatures.

Sigs can be very plain or very fancy. There's even netiquette for sigs. Quite simply, when communicating with friends or folks who already know you, keep your sig simple and avoid advertisements. If it's pertinent to the conversation, include your professional credentials but don't beat people over the head with them. Unless it's absolutely necessary, do not create a sig that requires folks to scroll the text.

Every screen name on your AOL account can have up to five signature files, which are stored on your hard drive. To install the same sigs on another screen name or another computer, send yourself e-mail containing the sig(s) you need, and then paste it into the Set Up Signatures window, which is described in the following steps.

To create your sigs, follow these steps:

1. Choose Mail⇨Mail Signatures from the AOL toolbar. This opens the Set Up Signatures window.

2. Click the Create button. The Create Signature window then appears, as shown in Figure 6-13. This window enables you to build elegant signatures.

3. Give your signature a name that distinguishes it from the other signatures you may create later, and go to work on the signature itself. The window comes equipped with all the styled text capabilities we discussed earlier, plus the spell checker and the Insert Favorite Place button, which is handy for sharing your favorite URL.

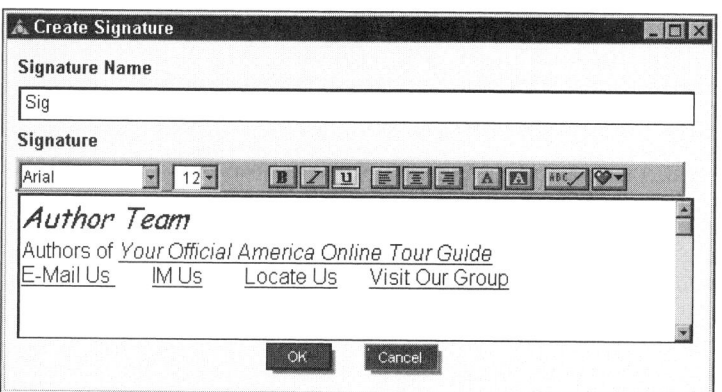

Figure 6-13. The Create Signature window contains a work in progress.

4. When your sig is done, click OK.

When the Set Up Signatures window is open, you have the choice to edit or delete the sig(s) that you created, or declare one of your sigs as a default. Your default sig is automatically added to every e-mail you create with this screen name. Other sigs can be used whenever you desire.

When you're ready to insert a sig, open a Write Mail window, and compose your e-mail. When you're done, click the Insert Signature File button on the far right of the formatting bar and select the sig you want to insert from the drop-down list. Of course, if you've already chosen one of your sigs as a default, you don't even have to do this, because your e-mail already includes that sig. You'll also note that you can select Set Up Signatures from the drop down list when you click that Insert Signature File button.

Tip

Create sigs with styled text for your AOL friends and other sigs that look good without resorting to styled text for your Internet e-mail.

Inserting Pictures and Graphics

Why not send illustrated e-mail that includes a picture? AOL gives you the creative power to exchange fully illustrated e-mail with all your friends and family who use AOL. Create a virtual family photo album or just a snapshot. You can even make greeting cards like the ones you find in gift shops!

Cross-Reference

Learn about "You've Got Pictures" in Chapter 11.

To begin, you need images to work with. You can use photos downloaded from "You've Got Pictures" (choose photos with low resolution), or other images in GIF, JPG, or BMP format stored on your hard drive.

To add a photo to your e-mail, follow these steps:

1. Open a Write Mail window.
2. Click the Insert a Picture button on the formatting bar (it's the one with the camera on it) and choose Insert a Picture from the menu that appears.
3. In the Open dialog box, browse to find the file you're looking for, and then click OK. The photo is then added to your e-mail, as shown in Figure 6-14.

   If the image happens to be large, AOL may ask if you want to resize the image. In most cases, you'll want to choose Yes, but if you don't like the results, you can go back and do it again, without resizing.

Note

AOL treats inserted pictures like files attached to e-mail. If the e-mail recipient can't receive downloaded pictures due to a Parental Controls or Mail Controls setting, the e-mail will not go through.

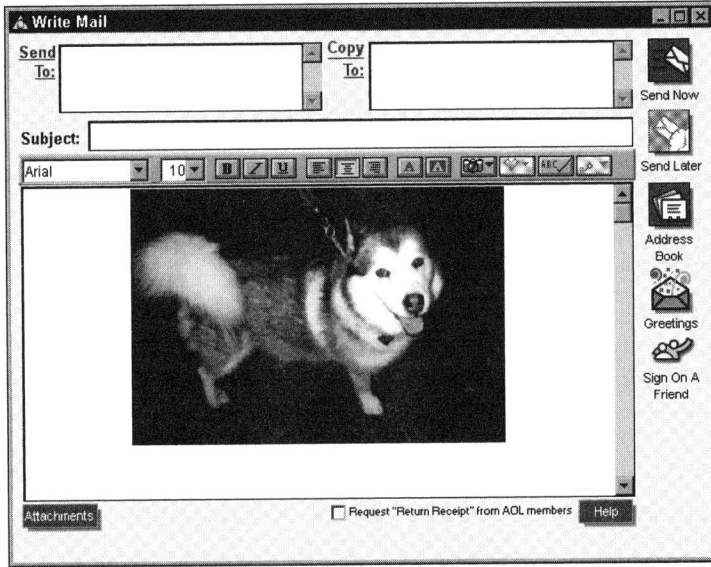

Figure 6-14. A simple e-mail starring Kippi the Malamute.

After the picture has been inserted in your e-mail, you can move it around as if it were a block of text. Highlight the picture with your mouse and try clicking the Center button on the formatting bar. Insert text before or after the picture. Change the background color. Have a blast! Is this easy, or what?

Why not add more pictures? You can click the Insert a Picture button again, or try something different. Choose File➪Open from the menu bar and then open another graphic file. The picture will open in another window, but you can just drag and drop the graphic into the Write Mail window. Do you want to remove that graphic from the e-mail? Just highlight it with your mouse and press the Delete key.

Want to send a colorful e-mail to mark a special occasion? Then put your artistic talents to use by creating your own electronic greeting card. Just click the camera button in the formatting toolbar of a Write Mail window, choose Background Picture, and choose a graphic file from your hard drive. The graphic will completely fill the Write Mail window through a technique called *tiling*. That means the picture is repeated over and over, like a floor tile. Obviously, this may not always be the best effect possible; a half-dozen copies of last month's family reunion photo tiled in the background of your message may confuse rather than delight the card's recipient. However, if your background graphic is a simple colored pattern like the kind created for the backgrounds of Web pages, you're in great shape. You can then insert other pictures over that background, add text in a contrasting color, and before long you'll have something that looks like Figure 6-15.

If you insert images into your e-mails, other AOL members receiving the e-mails will see them, but recipients on the Internet will not see the images.

Respect copyright law when using graphics and photos. Be sure you have permission to use the works of others. Your best bet is to only use photos and artwork you've created yourself.

E-mail with inserted graphics cannot be sent to Internet addresses. If you want to send pictures to your friends on the Internet, send the pictures as attached files instead.

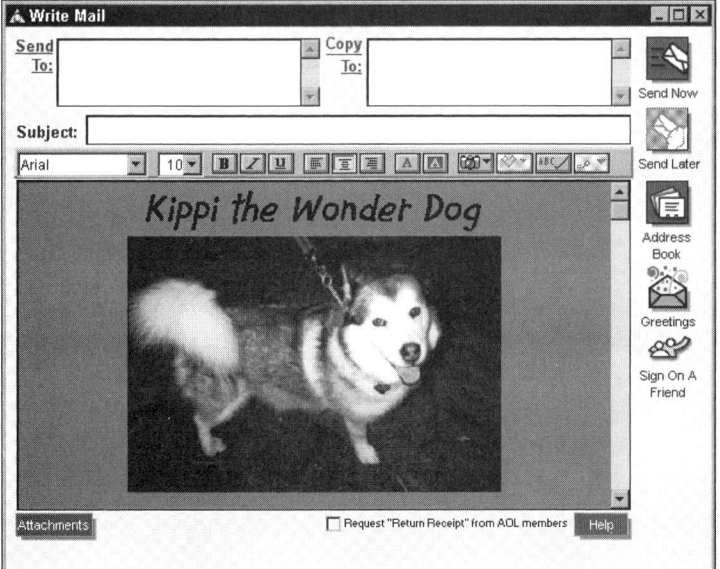

Figure 6-15. Doesn't Kippi look great in this greeting card?

Note

Graphics can take a long time to transfer via e-mail. An e-mail with a dozen pictures can take ten minutes or more to download, and if the original graphics were high resolution, the e-mail could exceed the maximum allowable size.

Picture Finder

The Picture Finder is yet another way to find pictures on your hard drive that you can insert into e-mail. Just choose File⇨ Open Picture Finder from the menu bar and then select a folder on your hard drive that contains the pictures you're interested in. A Picture Gallery window opens, displaying a small *thumbnail image* of every picture in the folder, as shown in Figure 6-16.

You can drag an image directly into e-mail from the Picture Gallery, or you can view it full size and/or edit it by clicking the picture. The picture then opens in an editing window. You can rotate, flip, resize, crop, modify the contrast and brightness, and even turn the picture from negative to positive and from color to black and white. When you're done, you can drag the results into e-mail, or open a new e-mail with the edited image already inserted.

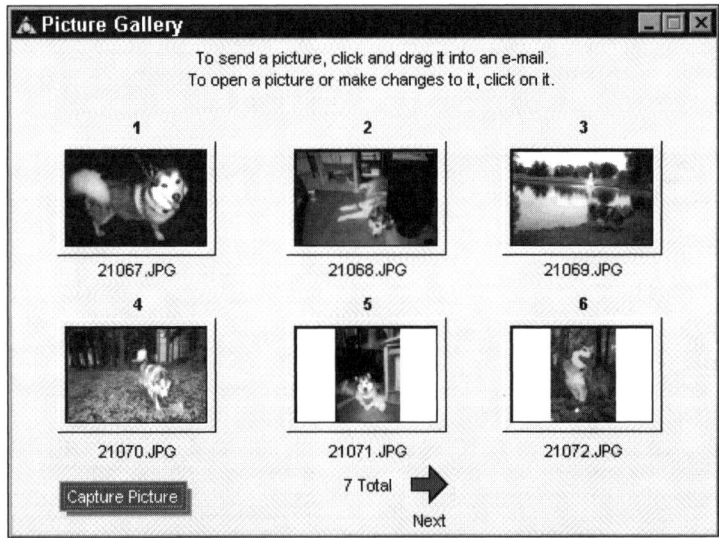

Figure 6-16. The Picture Gallery shows Kippi grinning for the camera.

The Picture Gallery is also a wonderful tool for searching for lost images or for cataloging the contents of your hard drive. It's a very nice feature, indeed!

AOL Mail (On the Web)

You have the power to access your e-mail from almost any computer connected to the Internet with AOL Mail. You could be visiting a public library in Peoria, an Internet café in Istanbul, or a college dorm in Cambridge. If you can browse the Web, you can read your e-mail. This is the perfect solution if your company won't let you install AOL on your Internet-connected office computer. All you have to do is access the AOL Mail Web page, sign on with your regular AOL screen name and password, and start reading your e-mail.

To sign on to AOL Mail on the Web, go to aolmail.aol.com or visit the AOL.com home page at www.aol.com and click the tab for AOL Mail. What you'll see is very much like the regular AOL online mailbox (see Figure 6-17). You can view New Mail, Old Mail, and Sent Mail. Each e-mail item is listed, as usual, but note that the subject of each e-mail item is a hyperlink. Click the hyperlink to open the e-mail.

If you want to check for newly arrived e-mail while you're signed on to AOL Mail, just click the Sent Mail or Old Mail tabs, and then return to the New Mail tab. If you received additional e-mail, it will have been added to the list.

Figure 6-17. AOL Mail's version of your online mailbox, including the New Mail, Old Mail and Sent Mail tabs.

Your e-mail looks remarkably similar to the way it does on AOL (see Figure 6-18). You'll find the familiar AOL e-mail icon and the Download Now (when a file has been attached), Close, Keep As New, Delete, Reply, Reply All, and Forward buttons, and you can step through your e-mail by clicking the same Prev and Next buttons you're accustomed to using.

Figure 6-18. Reading e-mail on AOL Mail — all the comforts of home!

Note

AOL Mail should work on nearly any computer with an Internet connection and a Web browser, but it is optimized for Microsoft Internet Explorer Versions 3.0 and higher and Netscape Navigator 3.02 and higher.

The Write Mail page (as well as the Reply and Forward pages) is a bit simpler than the one you're used to (see Figure 6-19). The Send To, Copy To, and Subject boxes are the same, and you can attach files and request a return receipt. What you don't have are the styled text buttons or other features, such as the Address Book, Filing Cabinet, Insert Picture, Insert Favorite Place, Spell Check, and Insert Signature File.

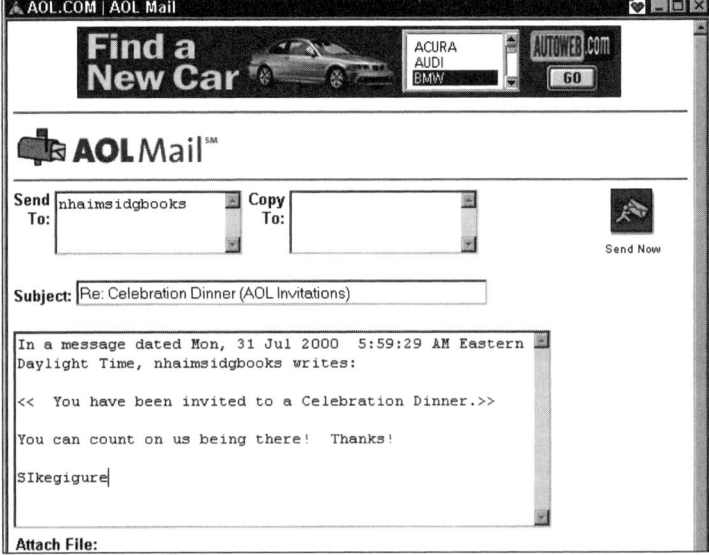

Figure 6-19. Write e-mail on AOL Mail — all the basic features you need.

Because you're away from your regular computer, you won't be able to save e-mail you've read to your Filing Cabinet or hard drive unless you keep the e-mail as new and read it again when you return home. To keep the mail as new, click the Keep As New button as you read each e-mail, or return to the New Mail screen, click the Select check box next to every item you want to preserve, and click the Keep As New button. The same is true of e-mail you compose and send from AOL Mail. Your best bet in this case is to include yourself in the distribution list of the e-mail you send.

Although AOL Mail on the Web doesn't come with all the bells and whistles you're accustomed to, it covers the basics and a bit more with ease, and that's really just what you need when you're on the road.

Putting Your Knowledge to Work

You can do so much with e-mail. We've just barely scratched the surface. We encourage you to use AOL's e-mail features to enhance your communications, but be careful not to let them overpower your message. If your bells and whistles draw more attention than your letter itself, it's time to tone them down a bit.

CHAPTER 7

INSTANT MESSAGING

Quick Look

▶ **Sending and Receiving Instant Messages**   **page 149**
Chat one-on-one with friends, family, and colleagues with instant messages. Each private conversation occupies a compact window, so you can exchange comments no matter what else you may currently be doing online. Even your friends on the Internet can chat with you!

▶ **Timestamping**   **page 154**
AOL 6.0 introduces a new timestamping feature that lets you see when your instant messages are sent and received. After enabling timestamping in your instant message preferences, the time appears to the right of your screen names in an instant message conversation.

▶ **AOL Instant Messenger**   **page 161**
Instant message and Buddy List features are already included with the AOL service. In addition, AOL has extended these popular features with the "AOL Instant Messenger"sm service (AIM), which is available free to anyone on the Internet.

Chapter 7
Instant Messaging

IN THIS CHAPTER

Sending instant messages to family and friends

Expressing yourself through instant messages

Turning off instant messages

Chatting with faraway friends using AOL instant messenger

Do you see your friends and family as often as you'd like? Today's busy schedules can make it hard to keep in touch. Perhaps you find it difficult to talk on the phone due to time zone differences or budget constraints. And who has time for old-fashioned letter writing these days? Hunting for stamps usually takes more time than penning the letter itself.

If all this sounds hopeless, take heart! There is a way to communicate with your friends and family on a daily or weekly basis even if you can't get together, talk on the phone, or send them mail. How? One word: AOL.

With the instant message feature available on the AOL service, you can chat with others in real time and at no additional cost. It's easy, quick, and simple . . . and it can make a real difference in your life. This chapter shows you how to make the most of instant messages.

What Is an Instant Message?

An instant message is a live, totally private, one-on-one chat between two people who are currently online. The instant message window doesn't take up a lot of space on your screen and makes it convenient to converse with others in real time as you check e-mail, explore the Web, and so on. If you're in a chat room, you can chat with specific people in the chat room through instant messages. If you're browsing AOL or the Web, you can share the experience with a friend. Although keeping track of multiple conversations is difficult, we've known people who have kept up to 15 different online conversations via instant messages going at the same time.

Some people start instant messages with their friends as soon as they sign on to the AOL service and exchange occasional comments for the entire time they're online. Instant messages can even be a valuable collaboration tool for coworkers.

Sending and Receiving Instant Messages

Starting an instant message conversation is easy. You can open a Send Instant Message window with any of these methods:

- Click the IM icon (the one that looks like a person running) on the AOL toolbar.
- Choose People⇨Send Instant Message from the AOL toolbar.
- Press Ctrl+I.
- Click the Send IM button in your Buddy List window (Buddy Lists are discussed in Chapter 8).
- Click the IM button in your Address Book (the Address Book feature is discussed in Chapter 5).

Each of these actions produces the Send Instant Message window, shown in Figure 7-1.

By default, instant messages are turned off for screen names that are set to Kids Only or Young Teens (through Parental Controls). Turning off this feature helps protect young people from inappropriate instant messages. Parents, be sure to learn about Parental Controls (AOL Keyword: **Parental Controls**) and apply them appropriately to your children's screen names. We tell you about Parental Controls in Chapter 4.

The easiest way to deal with an unwanted instant message is to totally ignore it or to click Cancel without saying a word in reply.

Figure 7-1. The Send Instant Message window is always close at hand.

After the Send Instant Message window opens on your screen, you can fill it out and send a message. Here's how:

1. In the To box, type the screen name of an AOL member or AOL Instant Messenger user (see "AOL Instant Messenger," later in this chapter).
2. Press Tab to move to the large message box and then type a greeting (see the example shown in Figure 7-2).
3. After you finish composing your message, click Send (or press Ctrl+Enter).

Cross-Reference

The Send Instant Message window has extra buttons that look a lot like those in an e-mail window. You can use these buttons to create styled text — different type sizes, colors, and styles — in your instant messages. See Chapter 6 for more information on styled text.

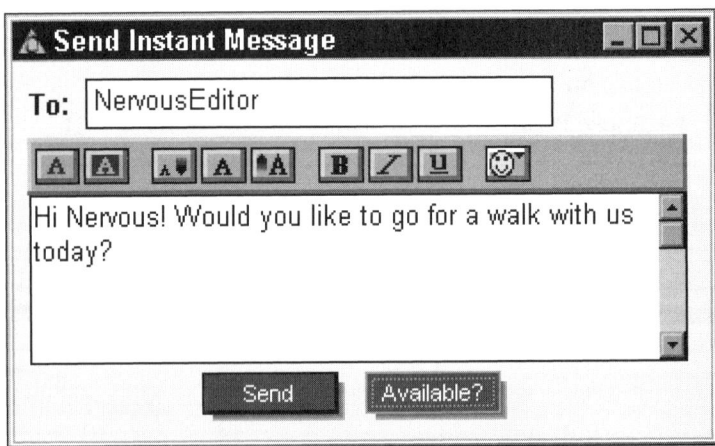

Figure 7-2. An instant message filled out and ready to send.

Protect Your Personal Information

As with unwanted e-mail messages, you may receive an instant message from someone unknown who may ask for important personal information, such as a credit card number or your AOL password. Nobody from AOL will ever ask you for your password or billing information online, and you should never share that information, no matter how official people seem or what threats they make. If you receive such a message, don't close it. Click the Notify AOL button and follow the instructions that appear. If you or another family member did divulge a password, immediately change the password for that screen name at AOL Keyword: **Password**. If your credit card number was divulged, contact your credit card company immediately. Be sure that everyone in your household knows what to do if someone asks for a password or a credit card number.

If your friend is not online or has chosen not to receive instant messages, AOL informs you of this. If your instant message does go through, both you and your friend hear a chime, and a small window opens on each of your screens, displaying your screen name and your message. Note that the window that appears on your screen (see Figure 7-3) differs a bit from the screen that appears on your recipient's screen (see Figure 7-4).

Your friend can do two things after receiving your instant message:

- ▶ Respond to your message by clicking the Respond button.
- ▶ Ignore the message altogether (do nothing or close the instant message window).

Tip

If an instant message can't go through because the intended recipient isn't signed on or has his or her instant messages blocked through Buddy List preferences, a dialog box appears and states that "[screen name] is not signed on." If a person has used the $im_off command (discussed later in the "Turning Off Instant Messages" section) to turn off instant messages, AOL displays a dialog box with this message: "[screen name] cannot currently receive instant messages."

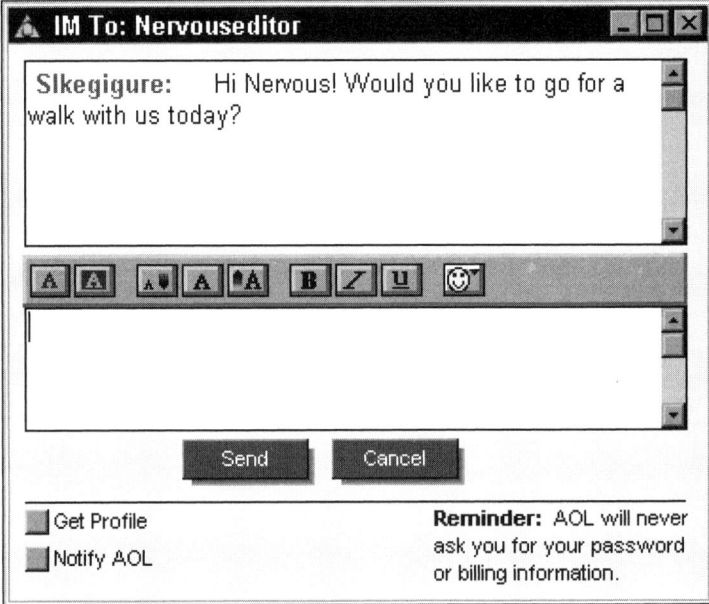

Figure 7-3. What you see when you send an instant message. Note that your screen name appears in red.

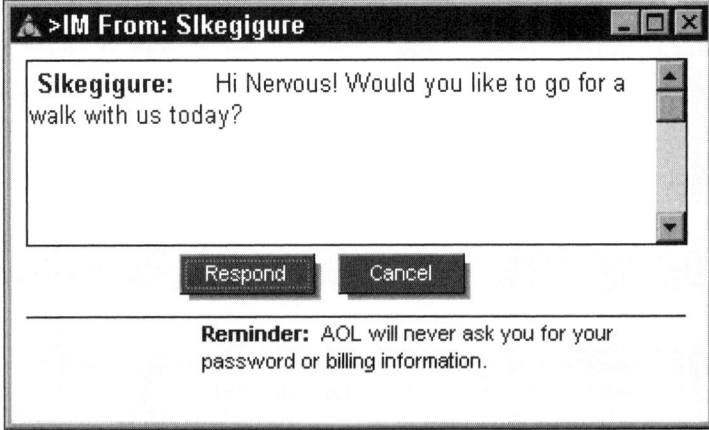

Figure 7-4. What your recipient sees when you send an instant message to him or her. Note that your screen name appears in blue in the recipient's window.

Because we are talking about your friend, we assume that he or she clicked the Respond button. Immediately, the window on his or her screen changes to look more like yours (refer to Figure 7-3) and three more options become available:

Chapter 7 ▲ Instant Messaging

▶ Check the AOL member profile by clicking the Get Profile button.

▶ Report a misdeed to AOL by clicking the Notify AOL button.

▶ Reply to the message by typing a new message in the text box and clicking the Send button.

Your greeting is now displayed in a box at the top of the window, and a text box appears below it, waiting for your friend's reply. After your friend types a message in the text box and clicks the Send button, you hear another chime, and your friend's greeting joins yours at the top of your instant message window, as shown in Figure 7-5.

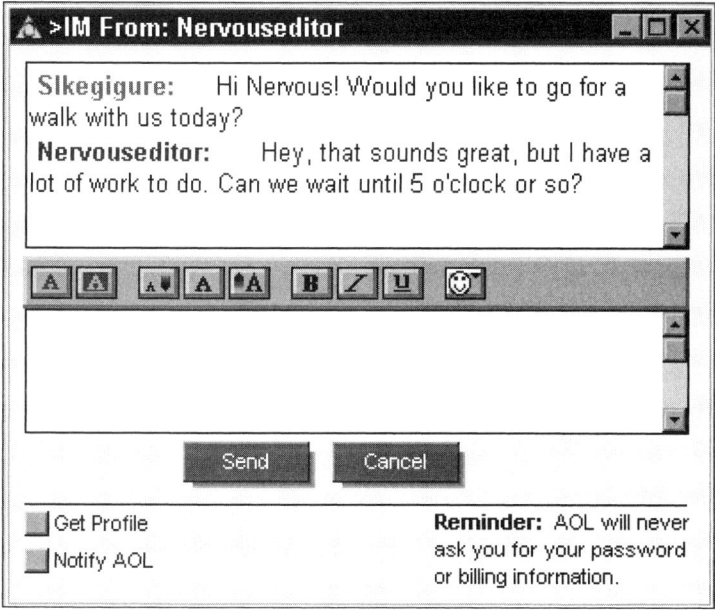

Figure 7-5. A reply to an instant message appears in the same window. Note that the friend's screen name appears in blue.

As the conversation continues, everything you say is preceded by your screen name, and likewise for your friend's responses. The conversation quickly fills the upper window and scrolls up out of sight. Just use the scroll bar on the side of the window to review earlier parts of the conversation.

You can have more than one instant message conversation going at once, too. If you want to initiate another, just press

Ctrl+I to open a new window. Each conversation stays within its own window, and no one but you and the individual you're chatting with can see your conversation.

When you get the hang of instant messages, you can do all sorts of amazing things with them. Here are a few:

▶ Copy and paste (or drag and drop) short excerpts of text.

▶ Drag the Favorite Places heart icon from whatever you're viewing into the instant message window to create a hyperlink you can share with your friend. See Chapter 14 for more details on Favorite Places.

▶ Use different colors, sizes, and styles with the styled text buttons. See Chapter 6 for details on styled text.

▶ Timestamp your messages so you can tell when they were sent and received. See the next section for instructions.

▶ Express your feelings with emoticons, available from the handy smiley face drop-down menu in your instant message window. See the "Emoticons" section, later in this chapter, for more details.

▶ Add some personality to your instant messages with a personal icon. See the "Icons" section, later in this chapter.

The one thing you can't do is invite other friends into the instant message to share in the conversation. For that, you have to open a private chat room, which we discuss in Chapter 9.

Timestamping

A new feature in AOL 6.0 is the ability to timestamp your instant messages. Here's how to turn on this useful tool:

1. Go to AOL Keyword: **Buddy** (or click the Setup button in the Buddy List window).
2. Click the Preferences button. The Buddy List Preferences window appears, as shown in Figure 7-6.
3. Click the IMs tab at the top of the window.
4. Select the Display Timestamp on IM check box.
5. Click the Save button.

When you have two or more instant messages open, determining when someone makes a new comment may be difficult. You hear the familiar chime, but which person sent the message? Look at the title bar of each IM window, where it says IM From:. If a > precedes that phrase, it means that your friend has responded to your previous comment. You may need to reposition the message windows if they appear on top of one another.

Would you like to create a hyperlink, perform a spell check, or change the font for your instant message text? Just right-click your mouse button in the instant message window's text box. The context menu that appears includes those three options and several others.

Chapter 7 ▲ Instant Messaging

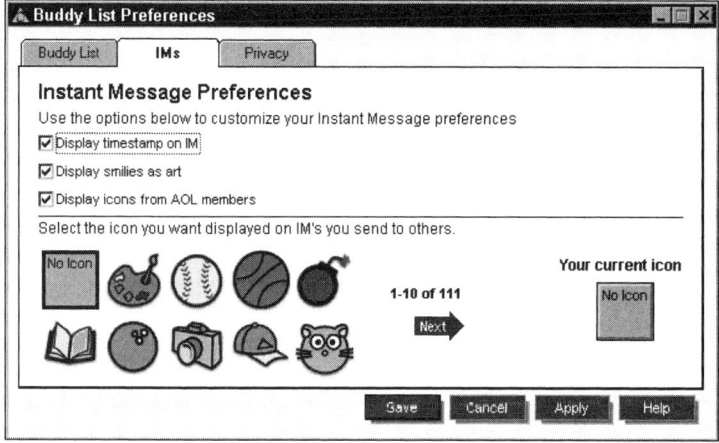

Figure 7-6. Turn on your instant message preferences to get the most of instant messages.

Now when you send and receive messages, the time is displayed to the right of the screen name, as shown in Figure 7-7. This information is wonderfully helpful in determining if a message is recent or if it has been sitting there a while unnoticed.

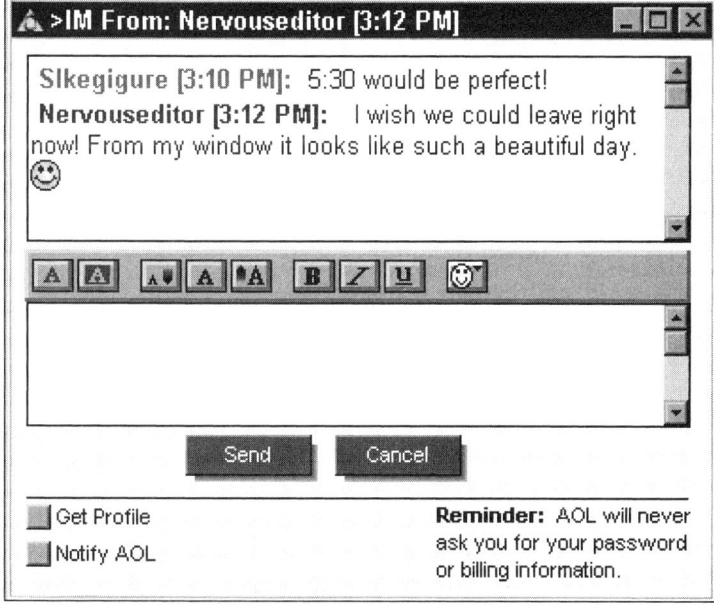

Figure 7-7. An instant message conversation with timestamps.

Emoticons

Another new feature in AOL 6.0 are *emoticons,* also known as smileys. Emoticons are a way of expressing feelings on the computer. You may be familiar with them in their text form, such as :-) (turn your head 90 degrees to the left, and you'll see two eyes, a nose, and a smile).

You can *log* all your instant message conversations if you want to save them. Just choose File⇨Log Manager from the menu bar, click the Open Log button, click Save in the resulting window, and then select the Log Instant Message Conversations check box. When you're done logging, click Close Log in the Log Manager window. You can then view the logs by opening them from the File menu (though if they are lengthy conversations, you may need to use Notepad instead).

The smiley face button in your instant message window lets you easily choose and create emoticons. Clicking this button opens a drop-down menu of emoticons, as shown in Figure 7-8. The emoticons appear as either text or as art in your messages, depending upon your instant message preferences. You can toggle between text and art by using your instant message preferences (as shown in Figure 7-6), which you find by going to AOL Keyword: **Buddy**, clicking Preferences, and then clicking the IMs tab.

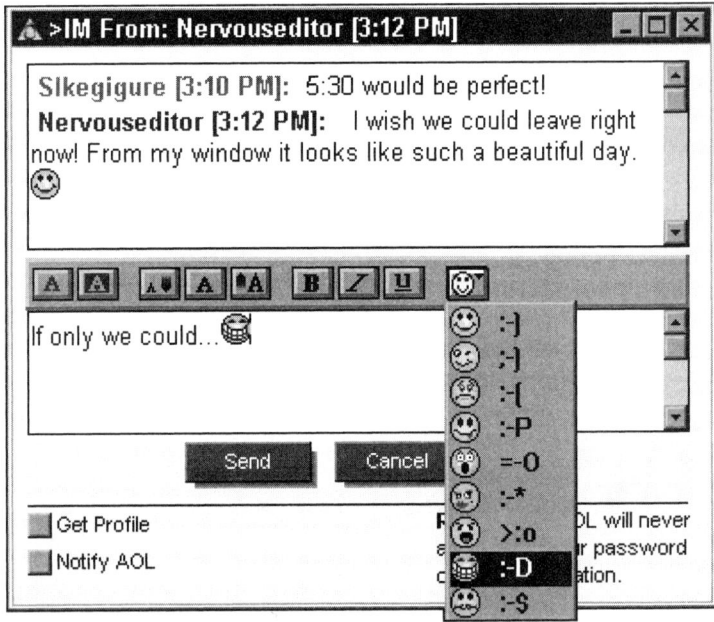

Figure 7-8. Choose from a variety of different emoticons for your messages.

Icons

Show some personality in your instant messages by selecting and displaying a personal icon, another new feature in AOL

6.0. You can enable instant message icons and choose your own in the instant message preferences (as shown in Figure 7-6), which you find by going to AOL Keyword: **Buddy**, clicking Preferences, and then clicking the IMs tab. Your personal icon is visible to anyone with whom you exchange instant messages, presuming the other person has also enabled icons and is using AOL 6.0. And, with your preference enabled, you'll see the personal icons of anyone else who has chosen one (see Figure 7-9).

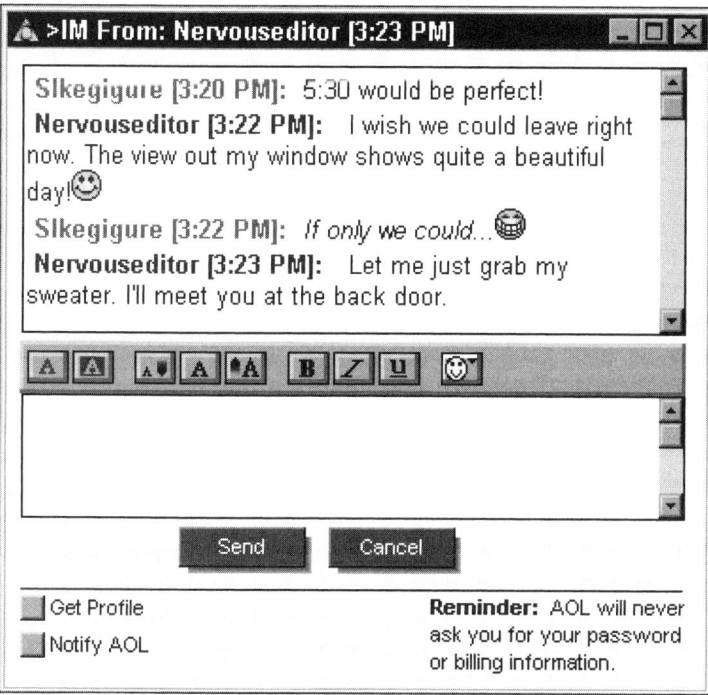

Figure 7-9. Kippi's personal icon appears in her instant message window.

Turning Off Instant Messages

You may want to exercise control over who can and can't send you an instant message. Fortunately, the AOL service gives you a few tools that put you in the driver's seat.

Cross-Reference

If you're looking for AOL members with common interests, consider searching the People Directory. We discuss how to do this in Chapter 18.

Member Profiles

Would you like to know more about someone you just met online? Perhaps that person created a member profile in AOL's People Directory. To view a profile while you're carrying on an instant message conversation, click the Get Profile button at the bottom of the instant message window. You can also choose People⇨Get Directory Listing from the AOL toolbar. In the window that appears, type the person's screen name and click OK. Don't be surprised if AOL tells you that it has no profile for that member. Listings in the People Directory are voluntary. (We tell you more about member profiles in Chapter 19.)

Tip

You can also turn off instant messages for just a specific person and keep talking to everyone else. Just type **$im_off**, press the spacebar, type the person's exact screen name, and then click the Available button. You can turn instant messages back on for that individual by typing **$im_on**.

The simplest thing to do when you want to be alone is to turn off the instant message feature: Just open a new instant message window, type **$im_off** in the To box (as shown in Figure 7-10), and click the Available button. You'll get a message from AOL acknowledging that you've turned off the instant message feature. This feature stays turned off for the length of your online session, or until you turn it on again, whichever comes first. The next time you sign on, your instant message feature is turned on again.

Figure 7-10. Preparing to turn off your instant messages — all you have to do now is click the Available button.

To turn instant messages back on during an online session, follow the same procedure, except this time, type **$im_on** in the To box of that instant message.

Do you want more control over your instant messages? The AOL service has privacy preferences which allow you to restrict who can and cannot see you in their Buddy List and/or send you an instant message. Just choose Settings⇨Preferences from the toolbar and then click Privacy to open the Buddy List Preferences window, shown in Figure 7-11.

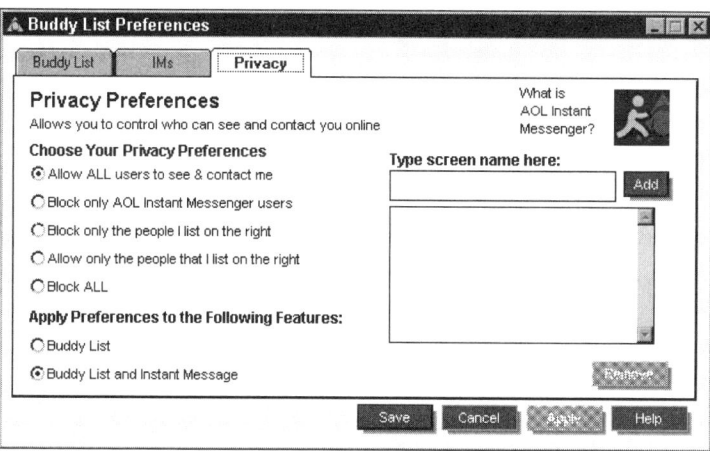

Figure 7-11. Privacy preferences help keep all your instant messages friendly.

Privacy Preferences were added to the AOL service after the introduction of the Buddy List, which we discuss in the next chapter. Whether you use a Buddy List or not, others can use Buddy Lists, the Locate Member Online feature, or even the People Directory to see if you're currently online. Privacy Preferences give you the freedom to conceal yourself in the way that suits you best. See Chapter 12 for details on Privacy Preferences.

Away Messages

A brand new feature for AOL 6.0 is the Away Message, which lets you display a message to anyone who tries to send you an instant message while you're away from your computer or don't want to be disturbed while busy online. Here's how to use this feature:

1. Go to AOL Keyword: **Buddy View** to open the Buddy List window (see Chapter 8 for more details on Buddy Lists).
2. Click the Away Notice button at the bottom of the Buddy List window.
3. Select one of the preset messages in the list box and click OK (see Figure 7-12).

Figure 7-12. Choose a preset Away Message or create your own.

You can create your own personal Away Messages or edit any of the existing messages. Just click the Away Notice button in the Buddy List window, click New (or Edit), and follow the on-screen directions.

When your Away Message is turned on, anyone who tries to send you an instant message is told that you're away and why. You can always determine if your Away Message is turned on because a red note to that effect appears at the top of your Buddy List. When you're ready to turn off the Away Message, open your Buddy List window again by using AOL Keyword: **Buddy View** and click the Away Notice button again.

The AOL service then displays a small window, which shows how long you were away, how many instant messages you received, and who the last instant message was from. Click the OK button in this window to receive any instant messages that came in while you were away.

AOL Instant Messenger

AOL Instant Messenger (AIM) is a free service available to anyone on the Web. AIM allows Internet users to exchange instant messages with other AIM users, as well as with AOL members. It's also handy for AOL members who may be at an Internet-connected computer that doesn't have the AOL software installed on it — such as at work or school.

Just think about the convenience of this type of communication. You can send instant messages to your daughter via her college's computer network or to your husband at home from your office's computer network.

To use AOL Instant Messenger, all potential users (even those who are already AOL members) need to first download and install the free software from the AOL.COM Web site, and then register for the service. To make things easier for your friends and family to use AOL Instant Messenger, visit AOL Keyword: **Instant Messenger** and fill in an e-mail invitation with all the details, which AOL then sends on to your friends. Every AIM user has his or her own screen name, just like an AOL screen name, and if you're already an AOL member, you can use your regular AOL screen name with AIM, too.

Receiving instant messages from AOL members and those using AOL Instant Messenger is different in one distinct way. The first time you receive an instant message from someone using AOL Instant Messenger during an online session, you must specifically accept the message — it doesn't just pop up on your screen. This protects AOL members from unwanted messages originating on the Internet.

You can use AOL Instant Messenger at the same time you're signed on to AOL with your own account. This way, you can send instant messages from AOL Instant Messenger using one screen name while you're signed on to AOL with a different screen name.

Your friends and family members may already have AOL Instant Messenger software, because it is included with the Netscape Navigator browser and comes pre-installed on many new computers.

To learn more about AOL Instant Messenger, visit www.aol.com/aim.

Putting Your Knowledge to Work

Instant messages are among the popular features on America Online. They're easy, convenient, and, thanks to AOL 6.0, full of new features that make real-time communications even better.

You may have noticed how often the Buddy List feature came up in the discussion of instant messages. Buddy Lists go hand-in-hand with instant messages, providing powerful, complimentary features to help you keep in touch with your friends and family. Page ahead to the next chapter to find out more about using the Buddy List feature of the AOL service.

CHAPTER

8

THE BUDDY LIST FEATURE

Quick Look

▶ The Buddy List® Feature   page 165

Find out which of your friends, family members, and colleagues are online at the moment with the AOL Buddy List feature. While you are online, you can personalize the Buddy List feature, and it will keep track of who just came online, who just left, and who's just hanging around. The Buddy List feature also makes sending instant messages even easier and more convenient!

▶ Instant Messages to Buddies   page 167

You can quickly send instant messages to anyone on your Buddy List. Just double-click a person's name, and a new instant message appears on your screen, already filled in with your buddy's screen name and ready for you to type a message.

▶ Away Message   page 169

The new Away Message feature lets your friends and family know when you're away from your computer or just busy online and don't want to be disturbed. Just turn on this feature, and anyone who sends you an instant message or sees you in their Buddy List will know that you're away and unable to talk. Turn it off, and you'll get any messages that came in while you were away!

Chapter 8
The Buddy List Feature

IN THIS CHAPTER

Finding out when your friends, family, and coworkers sign on

Organizing your buddies into groups for easy at-a-glance viewing

Inviting your buddies to a private "Buddy Chat" with a click of your mouse

Seeing which of your buddies are away from their computers

The Buddy List is an essential tool for anyone who communicates online, uses instant messages or chats online, or simply has friends and family who are also online. After customizing your Buddy List with the screen names of people you care about, you'll be able to see whenever friends, family members, and business associates are currently online. The Buddy List even notifies you as soon as they sign on or off. If you see a friend's name, you can send him or her an instant message with the click of your mouse. Click a different button to see if that friend is in a "Buddy Chat" room (and if so, join him or her in that room), or invite a bunch of friends to visit a private room for a group discussion. Because your privacy is important, AOL's Privacy Preferences are available for you to customize the Buddy Lists to control who does and doesn't know you are online and who is able to send you an instant message.

Who Are Your Buddies?

Your buddies are anyone you want them to be. If you have friends who are already members of the AOL service, you can simply add their screen names to your Buddy List. If they aren't members of AOL, anyone on the Internet can use AOL Instant Messenger, a free product, to get a screen name, exchange instant messages, and personalize a Buddy List. (See Chapter 7.) If you know a person's screen name(s) or AOL Instant Messenger (AIM) name, you can add it to your Buddy List. You can also create separate lists for special groups of people, such as family members online, team members, coworkers, college friends, or members of your favorite online communities. To open your Buddy List window, go to AOL Keyword: **BuddyView**.

Setting Up Your Buddy List

Your Buddy List actually starts with three empty lists (or *groups*) called Buddies, Family, and Co-Workers, as shown in Figure 8-1. You can immediately begin adding screen names to any of these three lists. You can also customize additional Group titles if you like. To add someone to your Buddy List, follow these steps:

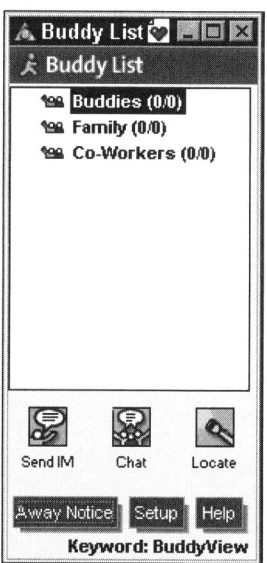

Figure 8-1. The Buddy List window — click the Setup button to get started.

1. Open the Buddy List Setup window, shown in Figure 8-2, by clicking the Setup button in the Buddy List window. Or go to AOL Keyword: **Buddy List**.

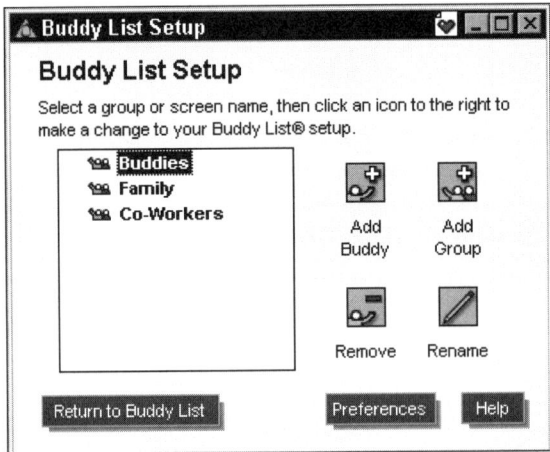

Figure 8-2. The Buddy List Setup window.

2. Select the group name (Buddies, Family, or Co-Workers) by clicking its name or the small people icon to the left of its name.
3. Click the Add Buddy button.
4. In the resulting Add New Buddy window (shown in Figure 8-3), type the exact screen name or AOL Instant Messenger name of the person you want to add. Be sure to include any numbers, if they're part of the screen name.

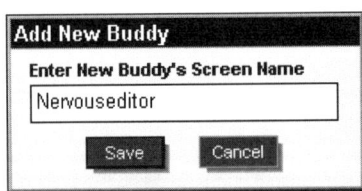

Figure 8-3. Adding a new buddy to the Family group.

5. Click Save in the Add New Buddy window.

Your Buddy List Setup window updates to show the new buddy under the group name, as shown in Figure 8-4. If your buddy is online, his or her name now appears in your Buddy List window as well.

Note

Your Buddy List holds around 160 names. This is the total for your entire AOL account, however; so you'll probably want to limit yourself to 50 buddies per screen name at most.

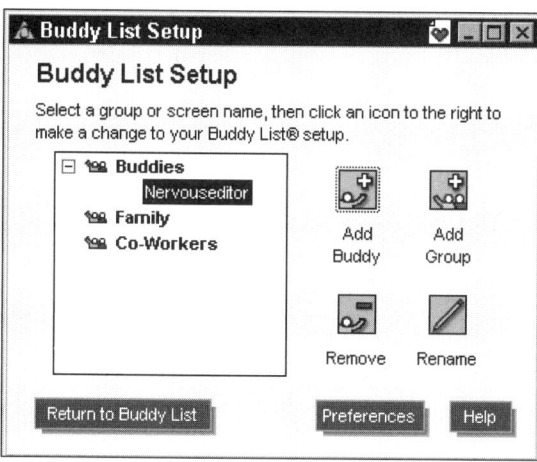

Figure 8-4. A new buddy appears in the Family group.

You can change the name of the group, add new groups, and remove both buddies and groups:

- ▶ To change a group's name, select it, click the Rename button, type a new group name, and click Save.
- ▶ To add a new group, click Add Group, type a new group name, and click Save.
- ▶ To remove a buddy or a group, select it, click the Remove button, and confirm that you want to delete the item.

The Preferences button affects the cosmetic aspects of your Buddy List, such as showing your Buddy List at sign on and playing sounds when buddies sign on and off. Buddy List preferences are detailed in Chapter 12.

 **Cross-Reference**

Want to control who is able to see you in their Buddy Lists when you're online? You can protect your privacy through privacy preferences, as discussed in Chapter 12.

Using Your Buddy List

After your Buddy List is up and running, it's very easy to use. All you have to do is keep your eyes (and ears) open to know when your friends, family members, and coworkers arrive and depart. Here are some tips:

Right-click on a name in the Buddy List window to get a drop-down menu with three handy options: IM, Chat, and Locate.

- To send one of your friends an instant message, just click the Send IM button (or double-click that person's screen name in your Buddy List window) and a preaddressed Instant Message window appears.
- To see if a friend is in a chat room, click that person's name and then click the Locate button. If your friend is chatting, you can click the Go button to join him or her in that room.
- To invite your friends to a private chat room (chat rooms are discussed in Chapter 9), use the Buddy Chat feature. Here's how:
  1. Click the name of the buddy or the entire Buddy Group you want to invite, and then click the Chat button.
  2. In the Buddy Chat window, shown in Figure 8-5, you can edit the list of buddies to invite, type a message that they all will receive, and type in the name of a private room you want them to visit.
  3. When you're done, click Send, and each friend on your list will receive an invitation, which they can accept or decline.

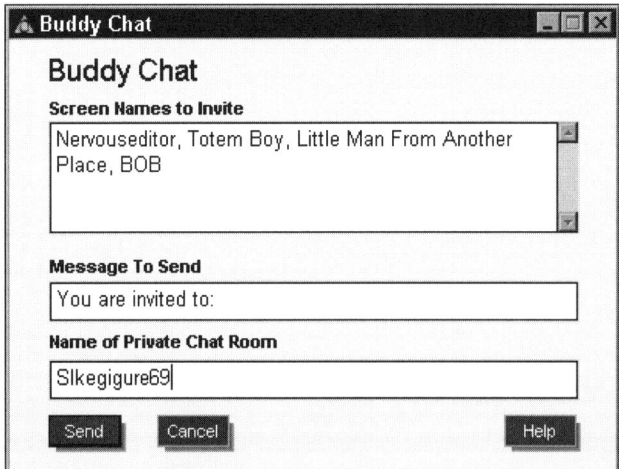

Figure 8-5. The Buddy Chat feature helps you keep several of your friends and family instantly in touch.

Getting Information at a Glance

Your Buddy List has a bit more to tell you, if you know the signs:

- ▶ If a name on your Buddy List has an asterisk (*) next to it, that buddy is the most recent buddy to sign on to AOL. The asterisk disappears when a new buddy signs on (the new buddy then gets the asterisk) or when the last buddy to sign on has been online for a few minutes.
- ▶ If a person's screen name is in parentheses, he or she just signed off.
- ▶ The numbers next to a group name tell you how many group members are currently signed on and how many names are in that group.
- ▶ If you double-click a group name, the names on the list are hidden and a plus (+) symbol appears next to the group name so that you know the names have been hidden. Another double-click reveals the full list.

Setting Up an Away Message

Another Buddy List feature is the Away Message, introduced in AOL 6.0. We discuss how to use the Away Message feature in the Chapter 7, as it relates to the instant message feature. In a nutshell, the Away Message lets you (and others) notify your buddies that you're online but not currently at your computer or otherwise busy.

Even if you don't initiate instant messages yourself, you may have uses for the Away Message feature. A friend or family member may notice that you're away, or you may appreciate knowing who is away from their computer even if you don't wish to send them an instant message. When a buddy turns on the Away Message, a small, yellow note appears to the left of that person's name in your Buddy List, as shown in Figure 8-6.

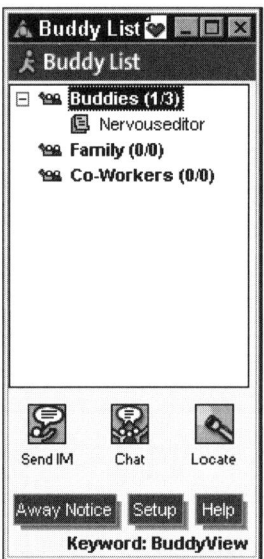

Figure 8-6. In this Buddy List, we can tell that Kippi Watson is away from her computer.

You can send an instant message to someone with the Away Message feature on, and that person will receive the message upon returning. You can, of course, wait until that little yellow note disappears next to that person's name. If you do send an instant message to buddies when they're away, you receive a note to that effect (see Figure 8-7).

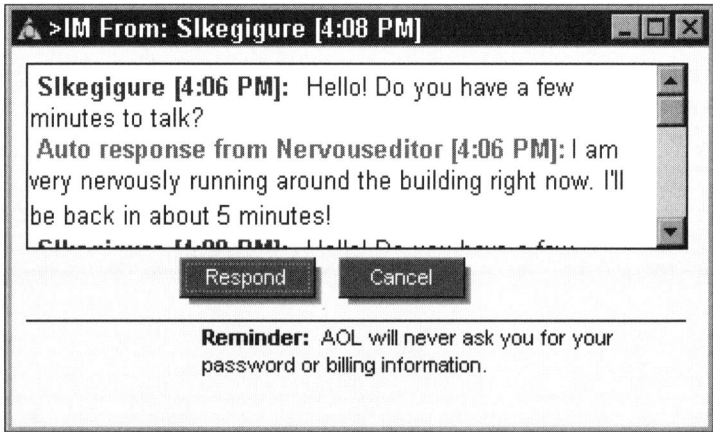

Figure 8-7. You receive a notice if you send an instant message to someone who is away.

Where Are My Buddies?

If you've added people to your Buddy List who never seem to be online, here are a few reasons why this may have occurred:

▶ You may have typed the screen name incorrectly. If you're not sure how to spell a person's screen name, refer to an e-mail sent to you by that person, search the People Directory, or just ask him or her directly.

▶ Your buddy may have his or her privacy preferences enabled so that you and others cannot see him or her in your Buddy List.

▶ Your buddy may never come online (or perhaps has a new screen name).

Putting Your Knowledge to Work

Buddy Lists are invaluable, especially if you communicate online and have many friends, family, and coworkers who are also online. If you don't have many friends online yet, however, the next chapter will have you making friends in no time. You can meet new people and keep in touch with family and friends with chat rooms, message boards, and Groups@AOL, all of which are discussed in the next chapter.

CHAPTER

9

CHAT ROOMS AND OTHER ONLINE FORUMS

Quick Look

▶ Chat Rooms   page 175
Find out what all the talk is about in AOL's popular chat rooms. To enter a chat room fast, just click the Chat button on the AOL toolbar.

▶ Message Boards and Newsgroups   page 185
Message boards and Internet newsgroups are collections of messages, available on virtually every topic. All members are welcome to read the messages and add their own if they want.

▶ Finding Messages   page 191
The AOL service provides a handy search function in every message board. You can search by date, word, or phrase, or construct a custom search. Look for the Find By menu in the bottom-right corner of your favorite message board.

▶ Offline Reading   page 206
You can download the most recent posts on your favorite message boards and newsgroups using the Auto AOL feature. Once downloaded, posts are available in your Filing Cabinet. Choose Automatic AOL from your Mail menu on your AOL toolbar to get started.

Chapter 9
Chat Rooms and Other Online Forums

IN THIS CHAPTER

Chatting in online chat rooms

Hobnobbing with celebrities and newsmakers in AOL Live

Broadening your reach with message boards and Internet newsgroups

Downloading messages for offline reading

People come to the AOL service with all sorts of interests, from purely social to purely professional, and everything in between. You can meet others who share a love for the arts, news, sports, or romance, or even a old colleague or potential client. Where? In chat rooms and other online forums, such as AOL Live, message boards, and newsgroups.

Chat and Conferences

Chatting is the essence of online community, because chat rooms are the place for live group interaction on AOL. Most online areas offer some sort of chat. Some areas host chats around the clock, whereas others present a schedule of chats, classes, or presentations.

Finding Communities

People Connection, shown in Figure 9-1, is the Times Square of the chat world. To enter through its front door, click the Chat button on the AOL toolbar or use AOL Keywords: **PC** or **People Connection**.

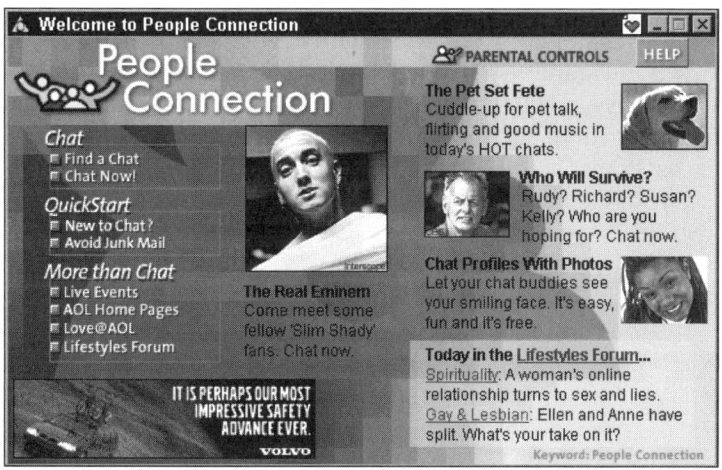

Figure 9-1. The People Connection.

To start chatting in a People Connection chat lobby, just click the Chat Now button in the People Connection window. A chat window opens on your screen, as shown in Figure 9-2.

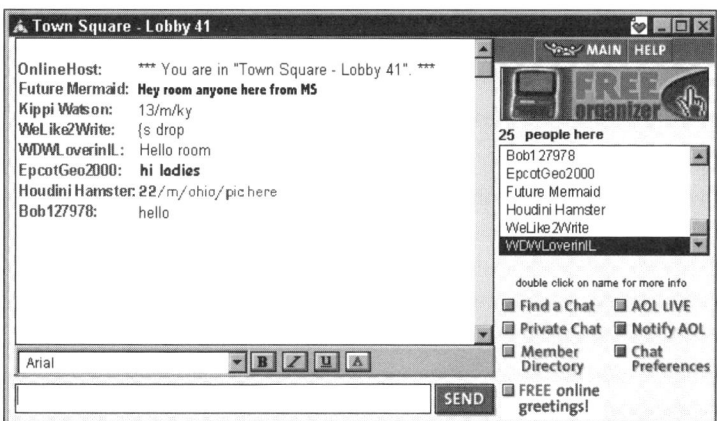

Figure 9-2. Watching the world pass through a People Connection chat lobby.

Chat lobbies aren't the best place to make lasting friends, but they're a quick way to get your feet wet. Just don't be surprised if you feel like you're standing in the middle of downtown traffic.

The chat can be better in a room that is organized around a theme or topic. Choose People⇨Find a Chat on your AOL toolbar, or click the Find a Chat button in the People Connection window. Either command opens the Find a Chat window, shown in Figure 9-3. On the left-hand side of the Find a Chat window is a scroll box with a dozen or so different categories, including Town Square, Arts and Entertainment, Friends, Places, Romance, and Special Interests. At the top of that scroll box, you find two tabs. Click the first tab to select from chats created and operated by People Connection. The other tab lists chats created by AOL members like yourself. In both cases, you see the same list of categories.

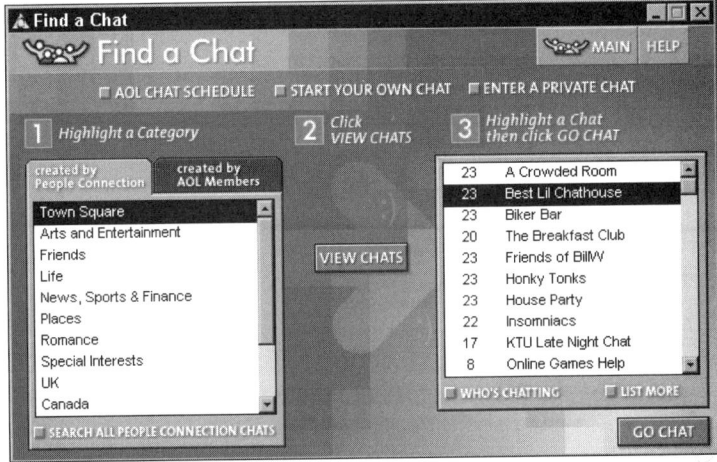

Figure 9-3. The Find a Chat window in People Connection. Select a category on the left and select a chat on the right.

For now, we recommend chat rooms created by People Connection, because they may have hosts who can give you a hand and keep the chat running smoothly. Here's how to access one of these rooms:

1. In the Find a Chat window, highlight the category you want to explore and then click the View Chats button in the middle of the window.

Tip

AOL's chat hosts are people who volunteer to help make the online chat experience rewarding for everyone involved. Like any good host, they welcome you to their chat room, make a few introductions, and explain the ins and outs of that particular room. They also work hard to make their room a pleasant and rewarding place to visit. Hosts receive extensive training before they get a chat room of their own, and they know how to deal with ruffians who like to prey on innocent newcomers. People Connection hosts have screen names that begin with HOST, such as HOSTLeff.

2. Scroll through the list of available chat rooms in the right-hand scroll box and select a room with an appealing title. Over 100 rooms may be listed, and clicking the List More button at the bottom of the scroll box may reveal even more rooms.
3. Click the Go Chat button at the bottom of the window. If the room is already filled to capacity, you may be given the choice to go to another chat like it, because in some cases the AOL service automatically creates additional chat rooms with the same name. So if there's no room for you in Best Lil Chathouse, perhaps there will be room for you in Best Lil Chathouse 2 or Best Lil Chathouse 22.

Tip

To the left of every chat room name is a number. If that number is 23, the chat room has already filled to capacity. You may try to enter that room (because people are coming and going all the time), or you can look through the list for a room that has some space available.

I Need Help!

There's also a dark side to the world of online chat. You can run into people who are rude, offensive, or downright abusive. They may be looking for "cyber" (cyber sex), use language that's far outside your comfort zone, or offer you goodies that turn out to be far from wholesome. Some may be trying to hijack your AOL account, others may want your credit card number, and still others may just want to rattle you. Not every kind of behavior that's offensive to you is a violation of AOL's Terms of Service (TOS), but when it is, AOL makes it very easy to fight back. Just click the handy Notify AOL button in the chat room, and fill in the form.

To learn more about AOL's Terms of Service and how you can better protect yourself, visit AOL Keyword: **I Need Help**. For advice on many aspects of online safety, visit AOL Keyword: **Neighborhood Watch**.

Anatomy of a Chat

After you've found a chat room, you may be wondering what's going on in it. The chat box dominates the chat room window, as shown in Figure 9-4. When you first enter a chat room, you receive an announcement from OnlineHost, identifying the chat room you've entered. Trying to chat with OnlineHost is pointless — she's a computer. Unless the chat room is empty, you begin seeing comments from other people in the room in short order. Each person's comment automatically includes his or her screen name so everyone knows who said what. After the window fills with comments, the text starts scrolling up, like the credits at the end of a movie. Unlike a movie theater, though, you can use the scroll bar on the right-hand side of the chat box to scroll back and review earlier comments.

Figure 9-4. An AOL chat room has a lot in common with an Instant Message.

At the very bottom of the chat window is a text box where you type your comments. The box has room for about one long sentence. This space limitation encourages you to write short comments and send them right to the chat, rather than write the next Great American Novel. Look at your text, make sure it's what you want to say, and click the Send button (or press the Enter key). Now you should see your own screen name and comment up in lights!

Right between the chat and text boxes are a font selection drop-down list and a few styled text buttons. Feel free to dress up your words with a distinctive font and maybe a dash of color.

Only those who have the same font installed on their computers will see the font you've chosen, so try not to use an unusual or exotic font. Use a common font, and make it more distinctive with color, bold, or italics.

Who is in the chat room with you? If other members are *lurking* (just watching), the only way you know it is to scroll through the people list on the right-hand side of the window. If you double-click a name on that list, you can ignore that member (banish his or her chat from your screen), send him or her an instant message, or check his or her member profile.

About the only things left to describe in the chat window are the buttons in the lower-right corner of the window, which may come in handy:

- Find a Chat, Private Chat, and AOL Live are there to make moving from chat to chat a bit easier, and Member Directory helps if you're searching for new (and old) friends.
- Chat preferences enables you to change the way chat is displayed in your chat window and whether you'll be able to hear chat sounds.
- Notify AOL stands at the ready, in case barbarians from the North invade your chat room.

Lurking is not a bad thing in the online world. In fact, it can be downright courteous. It means you've chosen to observe the personalities and customs of the community you're visiting so that when you do start chatting, you'll fit right in.

If someone in the room is behaving badly, you can banish him or her from your sight by using the Ignore feature. Just double-click his or her name in the people list and select the Ignore check box. The neat part is that he or she doesn't know he or she is being ignored. However, if the person leaves the chat room and returns, you have to repeat the steps for ignoring him or her.

What's a Conference Room?

So far, we've been discussing chat rooms, which are the most common group-discussion areas online. The biggest difference between a chat room and conference room is capacity; chat rooms hold 23 visitors, whereas conference rooms hold up to 48. Why don't all chat rooms hold 48 people? The simplest reason is that it's far too confusing to have 48 people chatting at the same time, and the text in the chat window moves by too quickly. Forums use conference rooms when their events need a bit more space, but people won't be chatting much amongst themselves. Events in conference rooms may follow something called "protocol," where folks are asked to speak only when called on. This makes sense when someone is leading a class, or the room is hosting a panel discussion or an interview with an interesting guest.

Chatting

Chatting isn't difficult, but as with any new social situation, you may feel better taking things slow and easy. A chat room can be a busy place, with people coming and going and many conversations happening at once. It pays to sit quietly for a while until you can catch on to the personalities and conversations around you.

Of course, folks may greet you, and it would be rude not to reply, "Hi, Jennifer! I'm new here. I'm just going to lurk a bit."

Whenever you speak, address the person(s) by his or her screen name (or an obvious nickname). With all those conversations going on, it's hard to know who is speaking to whom.

Even the language may be strange. Chatters use all sorts of abbreviations and symbols, such as LTNS, ROFL, {{{{Dave}}}} and :-). To translate, that's "long time no see," "rolling on floor, laughing," enthusiastic hugs for Dave (in this case), and a warm smile (lean your head to the left to see two eyes, a nose and a smiling mouth). The abbreviations are called shorthands, and the symbols are smileys. When you get to know them, you'll be chatting with the best of 'em.

Creating Your Own Chat Room

If you want, you can also create your own chat room. You can make your chat room either a member room, which any visitor to People Connection may find and enter, or a private room, which is open only to those who know (or can guess) the name of the room. The easiest way to create either kind of room is to choose People⇨Start Your Own Chat from the AOL toolbar. You can then select whether you want a member chat or private chat (see Figure 9-5).

You can also exchange Favorite Places in a chat room, but only if your Parental Controls settings have been adjusted to permit it. Because hyperlinks can take you to some dangerous places, AOL has decided to make viewing hyperlinks a conscious decision on your part. If you want to use them, first access Parental Controls from a master screen name, select the screen name you want to modify, and select Chat control in the Custom Controls column. In the Custom Controls Settings Chat window deselect the Block Hyperlinks in Chat check box for those screen names that can be allowed this convenient, if sometimes risky, feature.

The folks at AOL Canada have prepared a delightful introduction to shorthands and smileys, at AOL Keyword: **CDN Smileys**.

Chapter 9 ▲ Chat Rooms and Other Online Forums

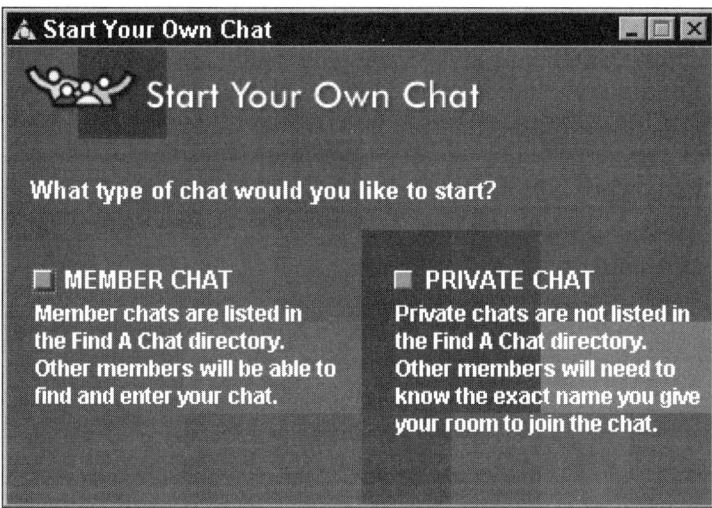

Figure 9-5. Start your own chat — just follow the simple instructions.

If you click the Member Chat button, you can choose the People Connection category in which you want your room to be listed. If you click the Private Chat button, you can create a new private chat, or go to an existing private chat if the name you typed is already in use. As you can see, your room name can be very important. Member chats are listed in People Connection, so it pays to make the name simple and descriptive — "U of M Alumni," for example. To be sure that private chats stay private, private chat names should be a bit more complex.

One important difference between private rooms and all other kinds of chat rooms is that private rooms are really private. Only you and invited guests should be in it, so no Notify AOL button appears in the private room window. In this case, AOL does not get involved in policing violations of the Terms of Service.

A member chat or private chat exists only for as long as the corresponding room is occupied. When the last person exits a room, the room disappears, but you can always create the room again some other day.

Chatters can play special sounds in a chat room. A person in the chat room sends a special phrase to the chat, which looks like this: {S filename. For example, {S welcome plays the "Welcome" you hear when you sign on to the AOL service. The only way the people in the room can hear the chat sound is if the same sound file is on their computer's hard drive. That's why {S welcome, {S goodbye, and {S gotmail are so popular. All three of those sounds are included in your AOL software. If you can't even hear "Welcome" when someone sends {S welcome to the screen, check your chat preferences (click the Chat Preferences button in the chat room window). Be sure that Enable Chat Room Sounds is selected.

You can also create a private chat room by using your Buddy List's Buddy Chat feature, which we describe in Chapter 8.

Tip

If you want to use the same private room on a regular basis, add it to your Favorite Places list. That makes a return trip very simple, and you can use the Favorite Places list to add a hyperlink to e-mailed meeting notices.

Logging a Chat

Sometimes you're just too busy to sit and watch a discussion or meeting in a chat room. With the capability to log a chat, you don't have to. Chat logs save every word displayed in a chat room to a file on your computer's hard drive so you can refer to it later. Just enter the chat room, start your log rolling, and go about your business. As long as you don't close the chat window, the log will keep rolling, and you can read it later when you have more time.

You can start logging a chat at any time by following these steps:

1. Choose File⇨Log Manager from the menu bar. The Logging window that appears (as shown in Figure 9-6) has two sections. We concentrate on the Chat Log section.

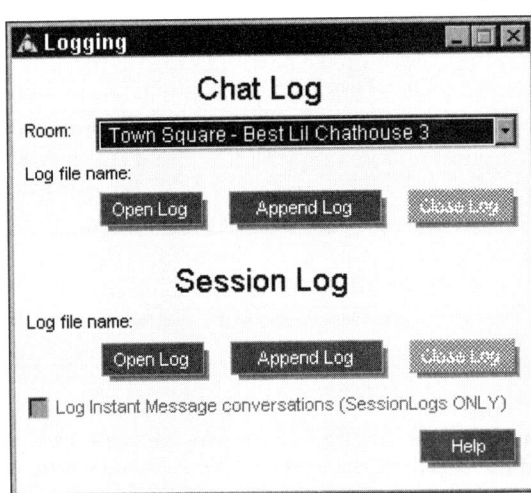

Figure 9-6. The Log Manager. The Chat Log section lists the chat room you're visiting.

2. Click the button that's appropriate for the action you want to take:

   - **Open Log:** Click this button to start a brand new log. The AOL service automatically names the log for the chat room you're visiting, but you can change that if you want.
   - **Append Log:** Click this button to add the latest chat to an existing log file. This is especially useful if your online session is interrupted, and you have to sign back on to resume your chat.

- **Close Log:** Click this button to stop logging cold, which is something you may want to do when your online meeting adjourns and folks hang around to shoot the breeze.

To view your log, choose File➪Open from the menu bar, and use the Open a File dialog box to find and open the file. Log files can become very long, especially when you keep appending chat to the same log file. When log files grow to be over 30K in size, you can no longer open a log file with AOL's software. At that point, you have to use a word processing program to open the log.

Auditoriums

Ladies and gentlemen, step along now, we're about to visit the auditoriums of AOL Live, shown in Figure 9-7. When major celebrities and noteworthy experts come to AOL to chat with the members, AOL Live is usually where you'll find them. Why? The auditoriums at AOL Live can hold thousands of AOL members at one time, not just the 23 that fit into a chat room or the 48 that can squeeze into a conference room. In fact, the current attendance record at an AOL Live event is nearly 400,000 members!

Figure 9-7. AOL Live plays host to some of the biggest names in the entertainment industry.

AOL Live typically hosts several events every day, and because the guests are so popular and the topics so hot, AOL promotes them heavily on the AOL Welcome Screen and when you enter People Connection. If you'd like to pop in to AOL Live, choose People⇨Live Events from the AOL toolbar or use AOL Keyword: **Live**.

An AOL auditorium is like no auditorium you can visit in the physical world. Sure, it has a stage, like any other auditorium. The acoustics in this auditorium are better than most, though. Anything that is said (written) on stage can be heard (read) by everyone in the audience, but no matter how raucous some members of the audience may become, they won't disturb the people on stage or, for that matter, most of the people in the audience.

Each auditorium is made up of rows that can hold from 4 to 16 AOL members. When you enter an auditorium, you're automatically assigned to a row. Each row looks a lot like a regular chat room (see Figure 9-8), but there are a few differences.

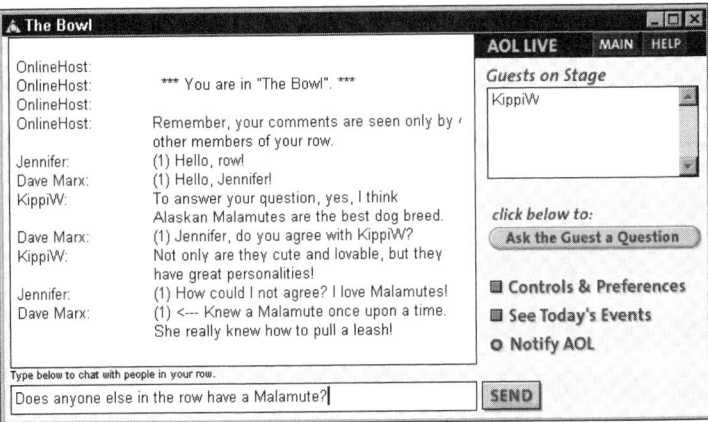

Figure 9-8. A chat row in an AOL auditorium. Every seat in the house is good!

Don't get upset at the people on stage if they seem to be ignoring you. They're not being rude. They can't see you, even though you can see them. Click the Ask the Guest a Question button to send your question or comment to the people on stage.

To chat with other people in your row, type in the box at the bottom of the auditorium window and click the Send button. The large chat box displays chat between people in your own row, plus everything said by the people on stage. Use the scroll bar on the right-hand side of the screen to review earlier comments. You don't see comments by people in other rows, and the people on stage don't see your chat.

The list in the upper-right corner of the window shows the screen names of the people up on stage — the host and his or her guest(s). Clicking the Controls & Preferences button opens a list of those in your chat row, as many as 16 people. Double-click a name to send the person an instant message or to get his or her member profile. Use the Ask the Guest a Question button to send your comments or questions to the folks on stage.

Tip

How do you know whether a comment is being made in your row, or by someone on stage? Everything said by someone in your row will have the row number listed alongside his or her screen name (refer to Figure 9-8), whereas those on stage will only have their screen names listed.

Message Boards

Message boards are a cornerstone of community on the AOL service. You'd be hard-pressed to find an online area that lacks a message board. Message boards turn a one-sided presentation of information into a lively give-and-take among people with common interests.

What precisely is a message board? Imagine a large cork bulletin board. Along the top of the corkboard, you find a row of labels, identifying a variety of topics. Perhaps one of those topics is reserved for official announcements. Beneath each of the other topics people can post written comments, questions, and replies. When folks reply to a particular message, they pin their responses right on top of the original message. When the board gets too cluttered with messages, the oldest messages are removed. Inappropriate messages are removed by the person tending the bulletin board, or moved to a more appropriate place. And when things get out of hand, that same person may remind everyone to tone things down.

Now imagine this bulletin board in an electronic format. Instead of a corkboard and push pins, you have a computer screen and icons. Better yet, you have all the power and convenience you'd normally expect online. This is what we call a message board, shown in Figure 9-9.

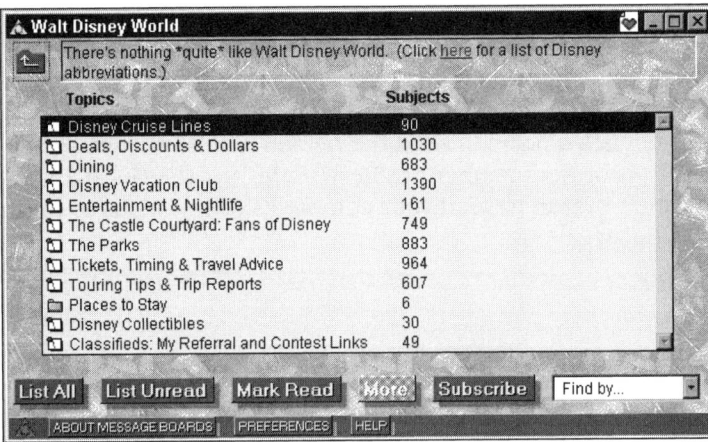

Figure 9-9. A typical message board located at AOL Keyword: **Traveler**. Look at all those topics and subjects!

Unlike a live chat, where you have to be in the right place at the right time to join a conversation, message boards follow a slower, more civilized pace. A person may post a question in the morning, someone else may read it an hour later and post an answer, the original questioner may ask a follow-up question the next day, and other people may chime in on the conversation for weeks to come. Anyone coming late to the discussion can read the whole thing from beginning to end, and if they have a comment, they'll know if someone has already made a similar point.

AOL's message boards follow the bulletin-board model very closely, but thanks to technology, they make it easier to find and participate in this kind of discussion and also keep things neat and tidy. A message board keeps track of which posts and subjects you have read and hides those that you've already seen. The message board also tells you how many topics, subjects, or posts you'll find as you dig down into the contents of the board. You can set your preferences for reading a board, including how you want the messages sorted, whether you want to see posts only on certain topics, or how far back you can look through the messages.

When you open a post, the fun really begins. You can check to see if the author of the post is online. If you reply to the post, you can send your reply via e-mail to the person who made the post and/or post publicly on the board. As with e-mail, you can select text you want to quote in your reply and include a prewritten signature line. And that's not the half of it.

Finding Communities

Finding communities is easy. Finding the right community is a bit harder. Not finding any communities at all is very hard indeed. Pick a forum, any forum! Almost every area in most AOL channels includes some sort of online community. Visit a channel and find an online area with a topic you're interested in or want to learn more about. Are you there yet? (If you're not sure where to go, try AOL Keyword: **Help Community**, shown in Figure 9-10.)

Chapter 9 ▲ Chat Rooms and Other Online Forums

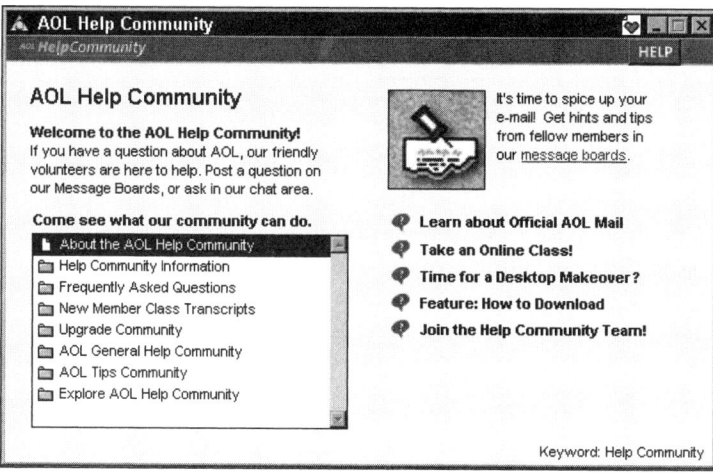

Figure 9-10. The AOL Help Community offers a good message board you can use to get your feet wet.

Take a second or two to look around for a Message Boards or Boards button or link. If you don't see one of those, try a Chat button. Very often, you'll find both message boards and chat rooms when you click a Chat button. Almost any button or link that suggests a discussion of some sort can lead to a message board. If you can't even find that much, perhaps you can find an index of the online area. If you have a choice of areas catering to your topic of interest, try the one with *forum* in its title first, because it's likely to be focused on community interaction.

There's a bit of a difference between finding any community and finding a good community. What is a good community? Consider what you think makes a good community. Do people drop by frequently to see what's happening and contribute their two cents? Are they courteous, friendly to newcomers, patient with beginners, and generous with their expertise? Is the community free of crass commercialism, nastiness, or other inappropriate behavior? Do people take an active interest in maintaining and improving their community? Well, then, we're all in agreement! What's true in your offline community is just as true online.

After you find a promising community, spend a few minutes peeking through the cracks in the fence to see if it's really what you want. As soon as the message board opens onscreen, you begin to get an idea. How many topics do you see? Are there many subjects in each topic? If you open a topic, do

There are several definitions of *forum*. According to the dictionary, it's a place where people meet for free discussion. A forum can also be any online area dedicated to a topic or interest, such as the AOL Families Channel or the Grandstand Soccer Forum (AOL Keyword: **GS Soccer**). To some people, forum means a message board or its equivalent elsewhere in the online world (such as newsgroups).

Many communities exist on AOL, each dedicated to a particular interest. Don't try to make one community serve all your varied interests. Find different communities to serve each of your interests, and keep each community's discussions on topic.

Tip

When you've found a message board you want to call home, add it to your Favorite Places list. Not only can you select an entire message board as a Favorite Place, but you can also make Favorite Places out of individual topics or even messages. See Chapter 14 for more details on adding Favorite Places.

Cross-Reference

You can read more about netiquette in Chapter 4.

you see more subtopics? If you open a topic, do the individual subjects each have two or more posts? If your answer is yes, you've found a thriving community. When it comes to good community, the more messages the merrier!

If you like what you've seen so far, wade in and start reading the messages (we explain just how in the next section). Don't think about adding your own comments, though. If you decide to join the community, you'll have plenty of time for that later. For now, concentrate on getting a feel for how the community operates — see how the conversation ebbs and flows, the kinds of things folks discuss, and the ways they discuss them. Try to become familiar with some of the personalities who make their home there.

Look for the community's message board guidelines and be sure that you understand them. Although AOL's Terms of Service always are in force, many communities post additional guidelines to address issues unique to their community. And, of course, the rules of netiquette are always in force.

Reading Messages

Reading messages is easy, and making your way through a message board is only slightly harder. Message boards are organized by topic, subject, and post. Only forum staff can create a topic (see Figure 9-11), and each topic can be looked upon as a separate message board or set of message boards (depicted by a small folder icon).

Here's a look at the options and buttons of a top-level board (such as the one shown in Figure 9-11):

- ▶ **List All:** Click this button to see every subject within a selected topic, even those you've already read.
- ▶ **List Unread:** This button, as you'd guess, is a bit more selective.
- ▶ **Mark Read:** Click this button to hide every subject in that topic on your next visit, just as if you'd read each one.
- ▶ **More:** This button is active when there are more topics to view than have been displayed on the list. Click this button to add more items to the list.
- ▶ **Subscribe (formerly Read Offline):** Click this button to select that topic so its posts can be saved to your

Chapter 9 ▲ Chat Rooms and Other Online Forums

Personal Filing Cabinet during an Auto AOL session (discussed later in this chapter).

▶ **Find By:** This drop-down menu helps you search for posts containing specific information.

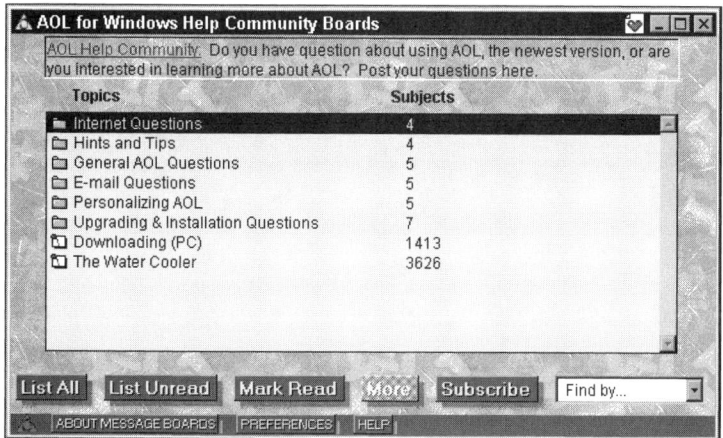

Figure 9-11. The top level of the Members Helping Members message board center at AOL Keyword: **Help Community**. Each topic is a message board in its own right.

To browse a topic, select it and click the List All or List Unread button. Double-clicking a topic is the same as clicking the List Unread button. The topic opens in a new window, displaying a listing of the subtopics or subjects within it, as shown in Figure 9-12.

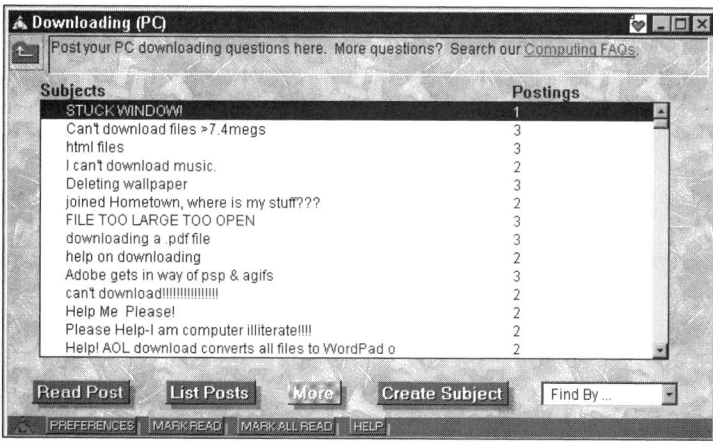

Figure 9-12. A listing of subjects available in the Downloading topic in the AOL Help Community message board.

You can just start double-clicking to read subjects that interest you, or select a topic and click the List Unread button. Alternatively, click the List Posts button to see a list of posts and their authors prior to reading a single post.

Posts look similar to e-mail, as shown in Figure 9-13. They have a subject and date, and identify the person who made the post by screen name.

Note that the screen name is also a hyperlink. If you click the name, AOL checks to see if the person is currently online.

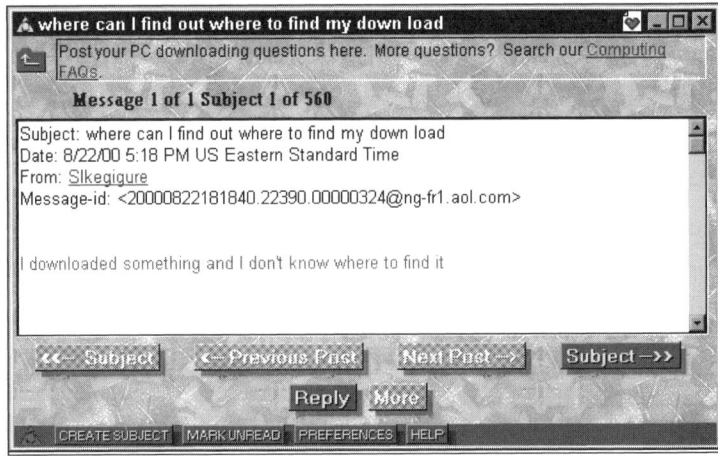

Figure 9-13. A post from the AOL Help Community message board.

Use the buttons at the bottom of the post to move from post to post within a subject, and then move on to the next subject. The More button is available when a post is very long (note that it is "grayed out" and unavailable in Figure 9-13). Click the Mark Unread button if you want to come back to this post later. The Reply and Create Subject buttons belong in our discussion of posting messages, a little later in this chapter.

If you select a topic and click the List All button, you see every subject in that board. Logically, the List Unread button shows you only those subjects you haven't read.

After you've read a post, the message board hides it from your view on the next visit so you don't reread it again, thinking it is a new message. If you want to find the post again, click the Mark Unread button at the bottom of a post's window or click the List All button when you revisit the message board. If, on the other hand, you want to banish posts without reading them at all, select the topic or post and click the Mark Read button at the bottom of the topic window.

Finding Messages

To search message boards, open the Find By drop-down menu in the lower-right corner of a message board and then choose either the topic or subject level (refer to Figure 9-13). You have three main searching options: Custom Search, Word or Phrase, and Date. We recommend that you use the Custom Search option (shown in Figure 9-14), because it provides a more flexible search, although a Word or Phrase search works well for fast-and-simple searches.

Tip

If you want to find all the messages you posted recently, do a search on your own screen name.

Tip

If you prefer to search for posts by date, choose Date from the Find By menu on the message board you want to search. You can search for new posts only (since your last visit), posts in the last *x* number of days (you specify the number of days), or posts between specific dates. Note that the Date search works only for the current message board or topic; it cannot search all AOL message boards.

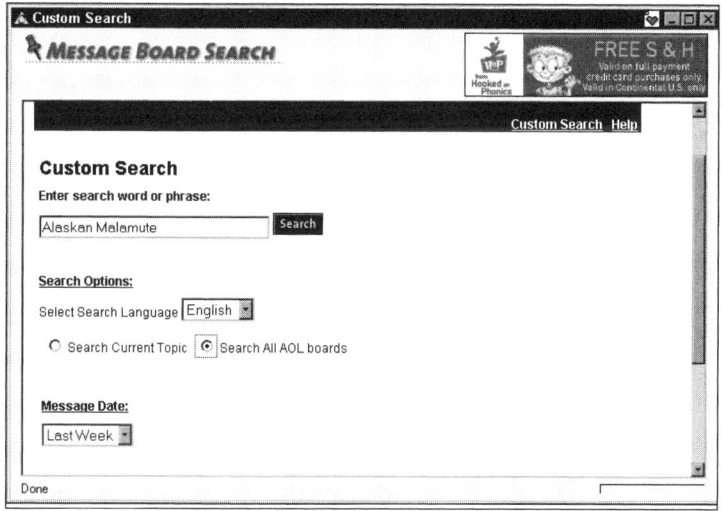

Figure 9-14. The Custom Search window lets you fine-tune your message board search.

Type your search word(s) or phrase in the top field of the search window. For example, we typed **Alaskan Malamute** in the search box in Figure 9-14. For best results, be as specific as possible. Also indicate your searching language (probably English if you're reading this book) and whether you want to search the current topic or all AOL boards. Use the latter option with caution, because it can take some time and return lots of results. If you're performing a custom search, you have some options as to the message date. Choose Last Week (default) or Past Month to find results in either date range.

When you're ready, click the Search button next to the word or phrase field at the top of the window. After a few moments, AOL displays any results found, as shown in Figure 9-15.

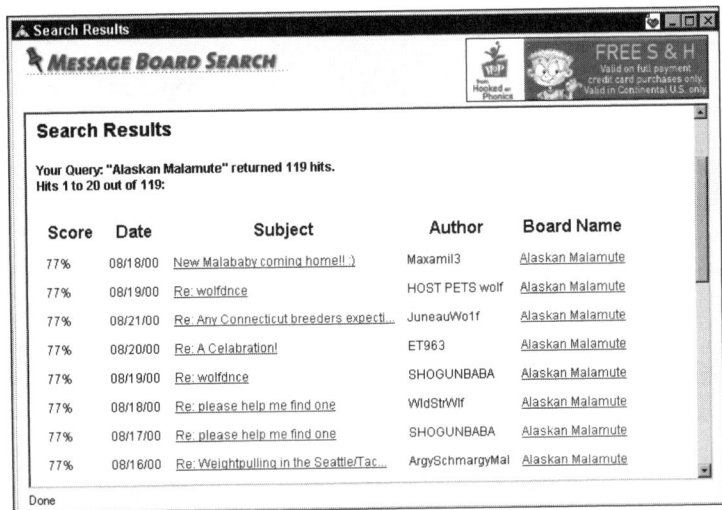

Figure 9-15. The AOL Message Board displays its search results.

AOL lists your results by how closely they match your search word(s) or phrase. Also included is the date of the post, the subject line, the author's screen name, and the message board where the post was found. To read a post, just click the subject line (which is a hyperlink). The message board name is also a hyperlink.

Setting Message Board Preferences

One button that we haven't discussed yet is the Preferences button, found at the bottom of every message board window. Clicking this button opens the Global Message Board Preferences window. Preferences that you select in this window affect every board you visit. The AOL service organizes your message board preferences into three categories: Viewing, Posting, and Filtering (see Figure 9-16).

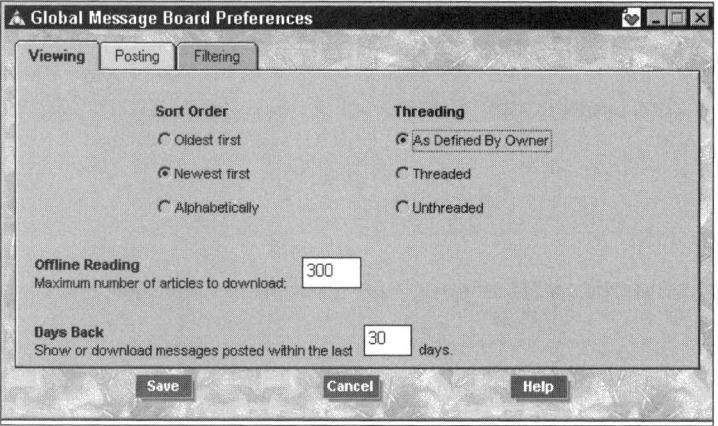

Figure 9-16. The Global Message Boards Preferences window displays your viewing preferences. Click the tabs at the top to view posting and filtering preferences.

Viewing

Click the Viewing tab to open your viewing preferences, which affect the order and accessibility of your message boards. Most people like to see the newest subjects and posts at the top of windows, but you may prefer to choose the Oldest First or Alphabetically option if you're having trouble finding a subject or post.

Threading refers to the way subjects are organized. The As Defined By Owner option accepts the forum staff's recommendation regarding threading. Threaded and Unthreaded give you the choice to overrule the forum staff's judgment and see the message board in your own way. There can be a benefit to selecting Unthreaded and Newest first, which brings all the newest posts right to the top of the board, regardless of which subject they reside in. However, doing so may present too many posts to wade through in a busy board. Feel free to experiment.

Threading connects all the posts for a single subject, like beads on a necklace. This makes it easy to follow the thread of the conversation.

Tip

If you select a board for Offline Reading, go through that board and mark all undesired topics and subjects as read so you don't clutter your Filing Cabinet.

Tip

You can also use viewing preferences to hide or reveal posts based on their age. You can enter a number as high as 9999, which means you'll see all posts available on the board. If a board is very busy, you may prefer to hide posts after seven days or less.

Note

Signatures can contain up to 245 characters of visible text. An additional 217 characters are available to accommodate nonvisible characters, such as formatting (colors, styles, and so on) and hyperlink addresses.

Offline Reading is a setting for Auto AOL. If you've selected one or more message boards for offline reading with Auto AOL, this preference sets limits on how many posts you receive. Limiting the posts prevents the unfortunate accident of downloading thousands of posts from a message board you've yet to read.

Posting

Click the Posting tab at the top of the Global Message Boards Preferences window to access your posting preferences, shown in Figure 9-17. This tab holds your signature (or sig) for your message board posts. You can type whatever you'd like added to the end of your posts in the signature box.

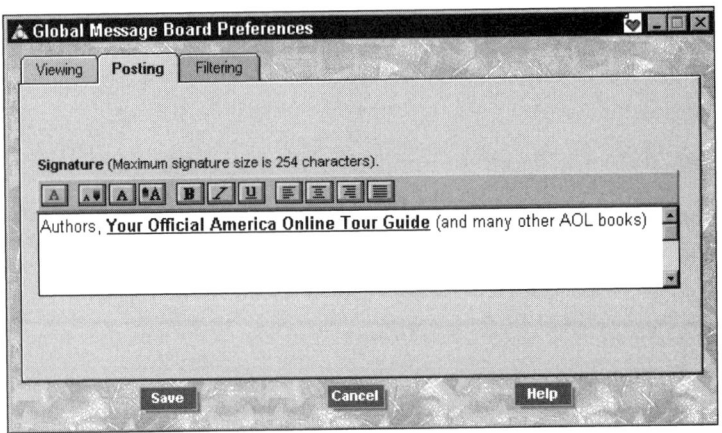

Figure 9-17. The Posting tab reveals our message board signature.

Feel free to use the format toolbar to spiff up your signature. If you want to add a hyperlink, as we did in Figure 9-17, right-click on the signature box and choose Insert a Hyperlink from the drop-down menu that appears.

Filtering

Click the Filtering tab to access your filtering preferences, which let you hide posts you don't want to see and/or read. You can filter out posts with subjects containing certain words or phrases, or posts written by individuals you find objectionable (see Figure 9-18).

Chapter 9 ▲ Chat Rooms and Other Online Forums

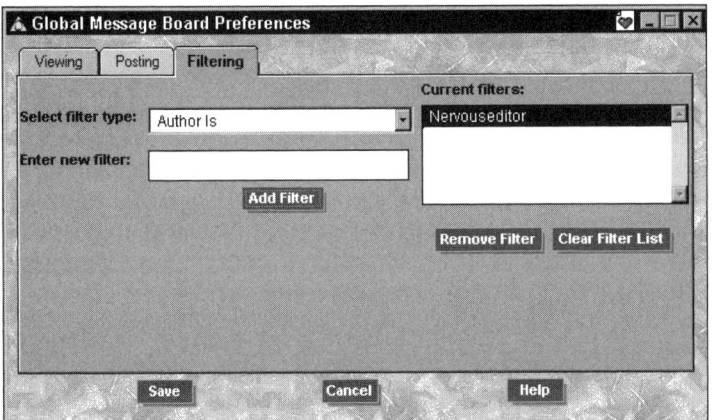

Figure 9-18. Filtering preferences displayed in the Global Message Board Preferences window.

To create a filter, follow these steps:

1. Choose a filter type from the Select Filter Type drop-down menu (Subject Contains, Subject Matches, or Author Is).
2. Type in the word(s) or screen name you want to filter in the Enter New Filter text box.
3. When you're finished, click the Add Filter button. AOL adds your filter to the Current Filters list on the right. You can add up to 25 filters.

To remove a filter, select it from the Current Filters list and click the Remove Filter button. Or click the Clear Filter List button to remove all filters.

When you're finished setting your preferences, click the Save button to preserve your settings. Any change that you make to your message board preferences goes into effect the next time you open a message board. To see how the changes affect the current board, you have to close that board and then open it again. Feel free to try out new settings and see how they affect a board. You can always change them back afterward.

Posting Messages

Message boards, like e-mail, give you two basic choices. You can reply to the post you're currently reading or create the

Your message board signature is different than the one(s) you may have created for your e-mail. If you want a message board signature, you have to create one in the Global Message Board Preferences window. If you already have an e-mail signature that you like, consider copying it to your Global Message Board Preferences. To do so, open a Write Mail window, click the Insert Signature File button, and then select the signature of your choice. After that, you can drag and drop (or copy and paste) the signature from the e-mail window into the Global Message Board Preferences window.

See our signature suggestions in Chapter 6, which apply to message board signatures as well as e-mail signatures.

first post of a new subject. The steps and options for creating a new subject are simple, so we start with them.

For this example, go back to the AOL Help Community message boards (AOL Keyword: **Help Community**); we're sure you must have some sort of question about AOL. Just find the topic that corresponds with your question, open that topic, and click the Create Subject button in the lower-right corner of the window. A Post New Message window appears, as shown in Figure 9-19.

You can learn about creating new e-mail and replying to e-mail messages in Chapter 5.

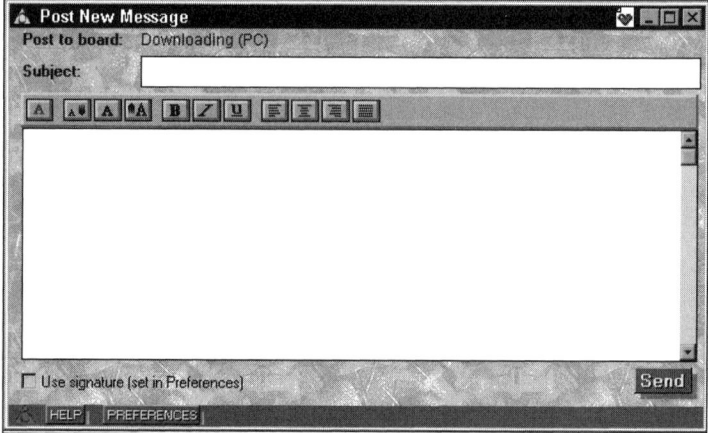

Figure 9-19. The Post New Message window looks a lot like a Write Mail window, doesn't it?

If you have set a signature in your message board preferences, the Use Signature (Set in Preferences) check box will always be selected by default. Thus, if you don't want to use your signature, be sure to deselect it.

Each Post New Message window lists the name of the message board in which the subject will be posted and has text boxes for a subject and a message. You also find a format bar with styled text buttons of the same sort found in the Write Mail window. Instead of the Insert Signature File button that you find in an e-mail window, you find the Use Signature (Set in Preferences) check box in the lower-left corner of the window. If you included a signature in your message board preferences (discussed earlier in the chapter) and you don't want to use your signature in your post, be sure that the check box is deselected.

Every post must have a subject. Be sure that folks reading the subject will understand your question or comment without having to read the post itself. After you double-check and spell-check your post, click the Send button in the lower-right

Chapter 9 ▲ Chat Rooms and Other Online Forums

corner of the window. AOL confirms that your message has been sent to the message board by displaying a message box. Click OK (or press Enter) to dismiss it.

To see the post you've just made, close the message board and reopen it. Your new subject should be there for all to see!

Replying to Messages

Now that you know how to create your own subject, replying to someone else's post should be even easier, right? Well, replying is definitely easy, but you're faced with a few new options in the Reply window, shown in Figure 9-20. To open this window, click the Reply button.

When you've finished writing your post, reread it. You cannot unsend a message board post, so be sure you've said what you mean and that it's in line with AOL netiquette, AOL's Terms of Service, and the guidelines for that board. We also recommend that you check the spelling by choosing Edit⇨ Spell Check from the menu bar (or just press Ctrl+=).

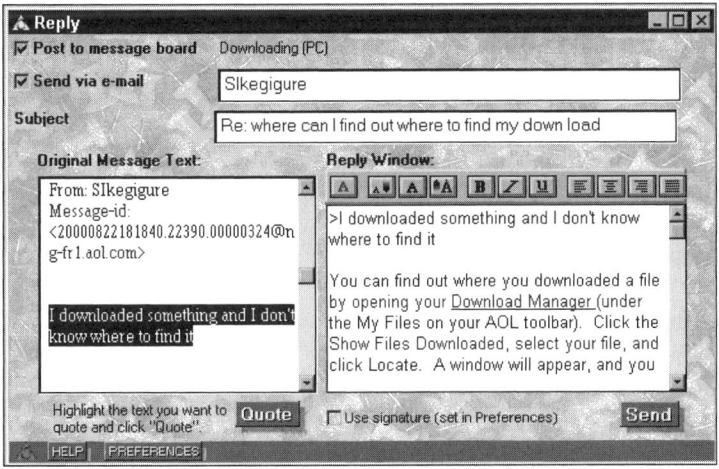

Figure 9-20. The Message Board Reply window offers all kinds of options.

Replies can be posted on the message board and/or sent via e-mail to the person who wrote the post; just use the options in the upper-left corner of the Reply window. After all, some responses should be shared with everyone, and some things are best said privately. Just select one or both of the check boxes to turn those options on or off.

It's always helpful to include quotations from the post(s) you're replying to, and AOL makes quoting very easy. The original message is displayed in a field on the left-hand side of the

If you select the Send Via E-Mail option, your post is sent to the screen name in the adjacent field. You can, however, edit the screen name if you prefer to send the e-mail to another member or even to yourself for your records.

Reply window. Just highlight the text you want to quote and click the Quote button. AOL adds the selected text to the text box on the right. You can even continue typing below the quotation and add an additional quote later on.

Finally, to round out your reply, you can choose whether or not to use the signature you created. Remember, if you created a signature, it will be used automatically, and you must deselect the Use Signature check box if you want to eliminate it.

When you're finished typing your reply, double-check and spell-check it, and then click the Send button just as you do when creating new subjects. That's all there is to it!

Newsgroups

If you enjoy message boards but hunger for discussions with a wider range of participants, you're ready to step up to newsgroups. Thanks to the fact that newsgroups originated years ago on the Internet, more people (and a more diverse group of people at that) frequent newsgroups in general. Newsgroups also offer more control over posting your own messages and reading others' posts. On the downside, Internet newsgroups are usually not monitored, meaning you're more likely to find objectionable material and advertising on them. Even so, if you can navigate the obstacles, you're likely to find strong communities and fascinating conversations.

Finding Communities

Speaking of finding things, how do you find newsgroups? Unlike message boards, which are more often than not scattered throughout the AOL service, newsgroups are mostly clustered in one area on AOL.

Follow these steps to find a newsgroup:

1. Use AOL Keyword: **Newsgroups** to open the Newsgroups window, shown in Figure 9-21.

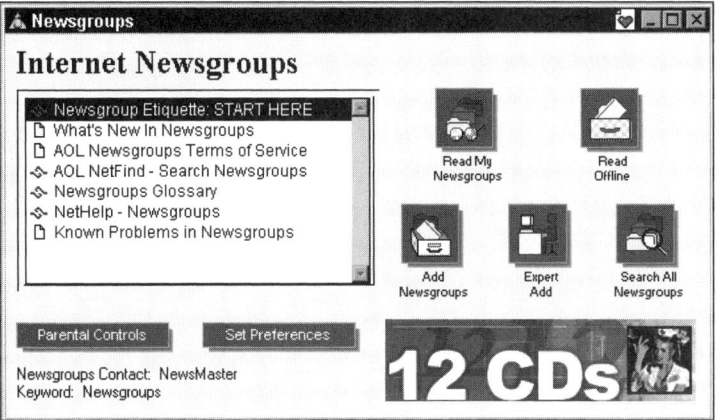

Figure 9-21. AOL offers a convenient and friendly gateway to Internet newsgroups.

2. If you get a message from America Online about selecting the Preferences button, just click OK. We get to the preferences later in this chapter.
3. Click the Search All Newsgroups button on the right side of the window. The Search All Newsgroups window appears.
4. Type your search word(s) in the resulting window and click the List Articles button to see a list of newsgroups that match your interest.
5. Double-click any listed newsgroup to see a description of the newsgroup and hyperlinks that you can use to preview the newsgroup's contents or subscribe to the newsgroup.
6. If you don't get any valid results, modify your search word(s) and search again.

Another good place to look for newsgroups is at AOL Search. Follow these steps to find a newsgroup with AOL Search:

1. Use AOL Keyword: **Newsgroup Scoop** to open the Search Newsgroups page.
2. Select the Descriptions radio button, type in your search word(s), and click the Find button. AOL Search lists the results, if any, by how closely it "thinks" it matches what you were seeking (see Figure 9-22).

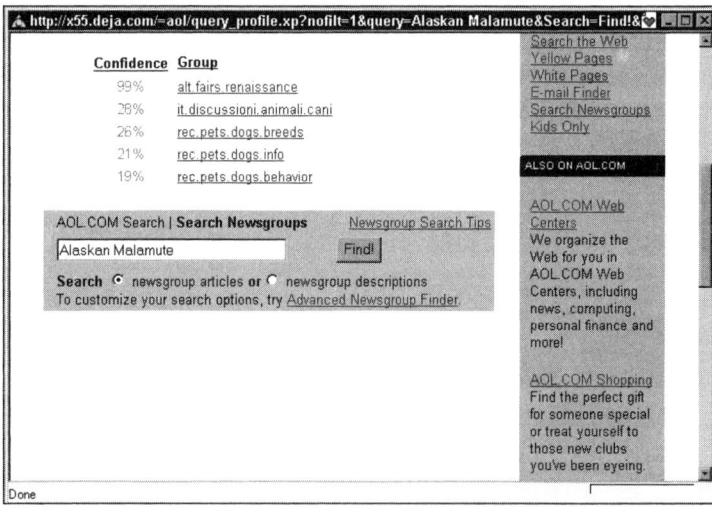

Figure 9-22. AOL Search returns newsgroups that match your search criteria.

After you find a newsgroup, the next step is to take a closer look. The best way to do this is to open the newsgroup and read a few messages, just as you would on a message board. You can find out more about reading newsgroup posts later in this section.

Subscribing to Newsgroups

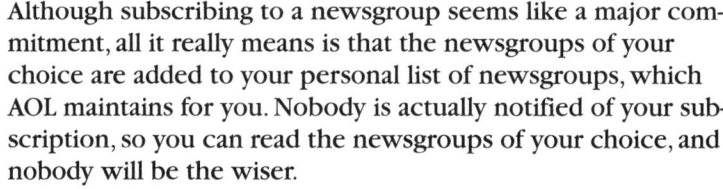

If you're having trouble finding or subscribing to newsgroups, you may want to check your Parental Controls settings (AOL Keyword: **Parental Controls**). Some types of newsgroups are blocked by default. Then again, maybe Mom and Dad have your best interests at heart.

Although subscribing to a newsgroup seems like a major commitment, all it really means is that the newsgroups of your choice are added to your personal list of newsgroups, which AOL maintains for you. Nobody is actually notified of your subscription, so you can read the newsgroups of your choice, and nobody will be the wiser.

AOL automatically subscribes you to a handful of useful newsgroups, through which you can learn more about newsgroups and practice your newsgroup skills. Just go to the AOL newsgroups area (AOL Keyword: **Newsgroups**) and click the Read My Newsgroups button to view the list.

You can add newsgroups to a list three ways:

▶ **Search All Newsgroups:** Click this button to find a newsgroup by topic. Open the newsgroup's description, and click the Subscribe to Newsgroup link.

- **Expert Add:** Click this button when you already know the name of the group you want to join. If you found a newsgroup's name by using AOL Search, this is where you type in that name, such as `rec.collecting.sport.baseball`, which is a haven for baseball card collectors.
- **Add Newsgroups:** Click this button to open a list of newsgroup categories. Each category hosts newsgroups of a particular type or sponsored by a particular organization. When you find the newsgroup you want, click the handy Subscribe button.

Reading Newsgroup Messages

Reading newsgroups is very similar to reading message boards, which we describe earlier in this chapter. Begin by opening the Newsgroups window (at AOL Keyword: **Newsgroups**) and then click the Read My Newsgroups button. Your list of subscribed newsgroups appears in alphabetical order in the Read My Newsgroups window, shown in Figure 9-23.

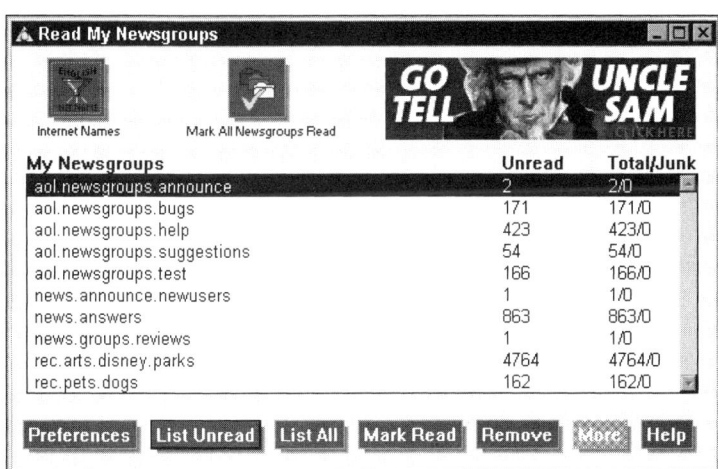

Figure 9-23. Our list of subscribed newsgroups. We have a lot of messages to catch up on!

The newsgroup address is listed in the far-left column, followed by the number of unread posts, the total number of posts, and the number of posts that AOL believes to be junk (such as advertisements). The buttons along the bottom of the window work just as they do in a message board. The Remove button allows you to unsubscribe a newsgroup. At the top of the window, you find two more unfamiliar buttons: Internet Names and Mark All Newsgroups Read. Internet Names displays descriptions of your newsgroups. Use Mark All Newsgroups Read to hide all existing posts. This option "cleans house" so the next time you visit your newsgroups, you'll see only newly posted messages.

To open a newsgroup, simply select the newsgroup and click the List Unread or List All button. Double-clicking the newsgroup also works (which is the same as clicking List Unread). A newsgroup's list of subjects is pretty straightforward — subjects appear on the left and the number of posts in the thread appears on the right, as shown in Figure 9-24.

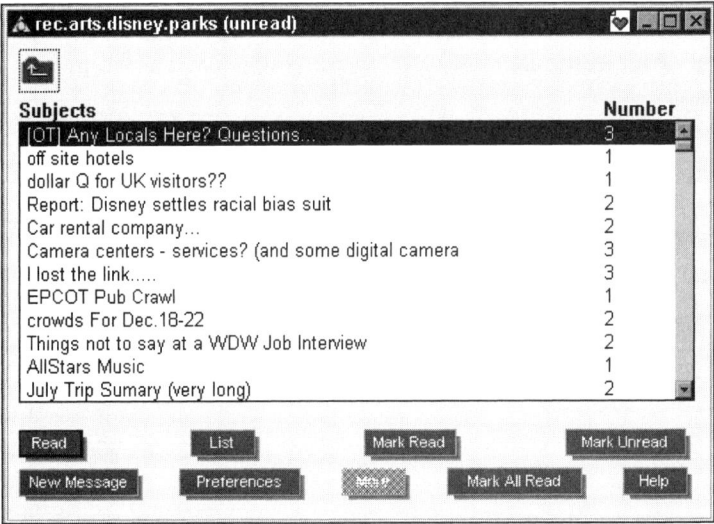

Figure 9-24. The rec.arts.disney.parks newsgroup for Walt Disney World and Disneyland enthusiasts.

You may need to click the More button to see all the subjects in a newsgroup, particularly those that are very active (such as rec.arts.disney.parks).

Reading newsgroups works the same as reading messages on a message board. Double-click a subject to read the first post in the thread, or click the List button to see a list of all the posts in a given thread. Use the Mark Read and Mark Unread buttons as needed.

Setting Newsgroup Preferences

Unlike message boards, you can choose to apply newsgroup preferences globally (that is, your settings affect all newsgroups) or only to a specific newsgroup or set of newsgroups. Your global newsgroup preferences are accessible by clicking the Set Preferences button in the Newsgroups window (AOL Keyword: **Newsgroups**). Global newsgroup preferences look very similar to global message board preferences, with Viewing, Posting, and Filtering tabs, as shown in Figure 9-25.

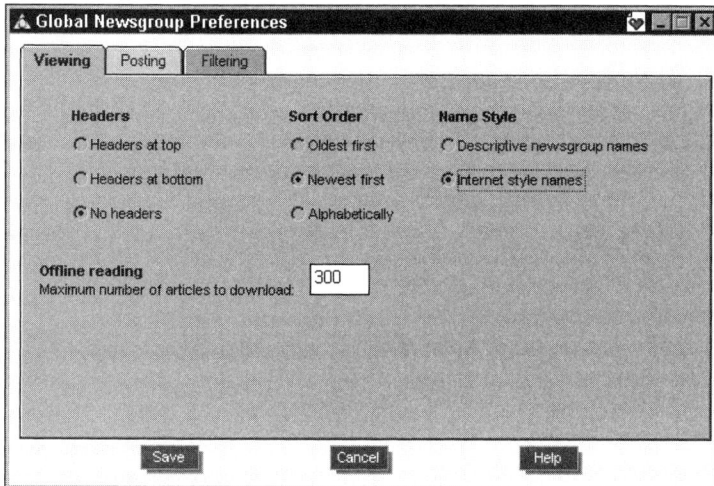

Figure 9-25. Set your global newsgroup preferences. Don't overlook the Posting and Filtering tabs at the top, which lead to more preferences.

Rather than go through each setting, we just detail those preferences that differ from your global message board preferences. Here's how the viewing preferences differ:

▶ **Headers:** A newsgroup header comprises a set of technical information about how the newsgroup was posted. You can choose to view newsgroup headers at the top of a post, at the bottom, or not at all (default).

▶ **Name Style:** Choose between descriptive newsgroup names (simple English) or the Internet-style names (technically correct but often obtuse).

The posting preferences differ in these ways:

- **Real Name:** Use this option to display your real name in posts, if you want others to know it. Anything you type in the Real Name field appears in parentheses after your screen name in all your posts (considered polite in newsgroups). For example, when we make newsgroup posts, readers see jenniferanddave@aol.com (Jennifer Watson and Dave Marx).
- **Junk Block:** Specify a phrase that will appear after your screen name to thwart junk mailers from harvesting your name in newsgroups. For example, if we type **nojunk** in the field, our name appears as jenniferanddave@aol.comnojunk. The automated programs that junk mailers use to harvest names end up with an undeliverable address. Human beings are smart enough to remove "nojunk" and send e-mail to your proper address.
- **Signature:** This option allows you to include a signature with your post. You set a newsgroup signature as you would a message board signature, except that you cannot format the signature or include hyperlinks.

Filtering preferences differ in the following ways:

- **Excessively Cross-Posted or Repeated Messages:** Select this check box to hide posts that meet this description, which are also known as *spam*.
- **"Make Money Fast" and Similar Messages:** Select this check box to hide posts that meet this description.
- **Messages Longer Than x Characters:** Select this check box to hide long posts.
- **Forged Messages:** Select this check box to hide posts that AOL determines to be falsified.
- **Binaries Posted to Nonbinary Newsgroups:** Select this check box to hide posts with binary information (usually graphics or programs).

Newsgroup-specific preferences are accessible via the Preferences button at the bottom of any newsgroup window. Use these newsgroup preferences (shown in Figure 9-26) to fine-tune your settings. New options include the following:

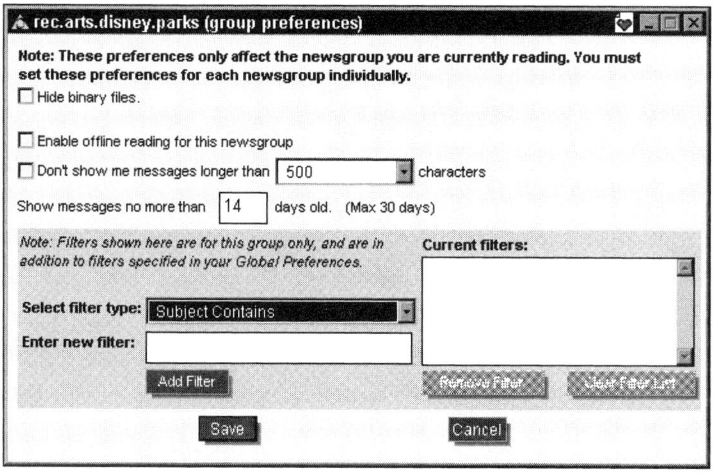

Figure 9-26. Get down to the nitty-gritty with your newsgroup preferences.

- **Enable Offline Reading for This Newsgroup:** Select this check box if you want to use Auto AOL to download posts.
- **Show Messages No More Than *x* Days Old:** Decrease this number if you want to see only the most recent posts.

Additionally, you can add filters that affect only that specific newsgroup.

Finding Newsgroup Messages

Although newsgroup windows don't contain a nifty Find button or menu, you can still search newsgroups. Here are two ways:

- To search just the subject lines in a newsgroup, begin by opening the newsgroup that you want to search and make sure all the subjects appear in the list box (you may need to click the More button a few times). Then choose Edit⇨Find in Top Window from the menu bar to search for words or phrases in the subjects.
- To search the contents of newsgroup messages, use AOL Keyword: **Newsgroup Scoop**. Enter your search word(s) or phrase, select the Newsgroup Articles radio button, and click the Find button.

Find It Online

Another place to search for newsgroups is at Deja.com (www.deja.com/usenet). This community-oriented service offers lots of searching and reading options, including ways to find all posts made by individuals. You can also access Deja's newsgroup search from its home page (www.deja.com). Look for the Search Discussions link in the search section at the top of the page.

Posting Messages

Posting to a newsgroup is similar to posting to a message board. The biggest differences aren't technical, but cultural. Each newsgroup has its own culture, social rules, and quirks; we strongly recommend that you get to know a newsgroup by reading it first before you post in it. Read the Newsgroup Etiquette article at the top of the Newsgroups window (AOL Keyword: **Newsgroups**) for a general set of guidelines to follow when posting to newsgroups.

When you're ready to contribute something of your own, you can start a new thread by clicking the New Message button at the bottom of a newsgroup window. This button works almost exactly the same as the Create Subject button does in a message board, which is described in the "Posting Messages" section, earlier in this chapter. To see your post, close the newsgroup and reopen it — you may need to give it a few minutes to show up.

You can also reply to posts. Just click the Reply button in a post that you want to respond to and type your message. The newsgroup Reply window is identical to the message board Reply window (but without the format toolbar).

If the person posting the message used a junk block in his or her address (it's usually obvious) and you want to send him or her e-mail, you need to remove the junk block in the screen name field before you click the Send button. If you're not sure what is and isn't a junk block, check the original post – the message often specifies what words and/or letters to remove from the address in order to send the e-mail.

Downloading Messages

Do you love to read messages but just can't keep up with everything? Or do you wish you could keep records of your messages to read later at your leisure? Both desires are possible with AOL's Offline Reading feature. You can download posts on message boards and newsgroups, organize them in your Filing Cabinet, and read them whenever you like (online or offline). This also means you can search the post easily with the Find feature in your Filing Cabinet.

To mark a message board for offline reading, follow these steps:

1. Open the message board, select the topic you want to download, and click the Subscribe button at the bottom of the window. We recommend that you try only one message board your first time out.

2. Click the Preferences button to open the Global Message Board Preferences window.

If clicking the Reply button results in a note that reads `Follow-up to newsgroups is allowed via posting only`, this simply means that the poster cannot receive e-mail. You can reply to his or her post in the newsgroup as normal, however.

3. Indicate the maximum number of articles to download. You may want to decrease this number to something reasonable if the message board you marked for offline reading is particularly active.
4. Click Save to keep your changes.

To mark a newsgroup for offline reading, follow these steps:

1. Open the Read My Newsgroups window, open one of your newsgroups, and click the Preferences button at the bottom of the window.
2. In the window that appears, select the Enable Offline Reading for This Newsgroup check box and set the number of days for which you want to see messages. Again, you may want to decrease this number if the newsgroup has a lot of posts. Click the Save button when you're done.

To actually download the messages in the boards or newsgroups you've marked for offline reading, you use Auto AOL. We explain how Auto AOL works in Chapter 10.

The Subscribe feature is very useful, even if you never use Auto AOL. You can access every message board that you subscribe to by using AOL Keyword: **My Boards**. It's like having a Favorite Places list just for message boards, except that you can even access them if you sign on to AOL as a guest.

Putting Your Knowledge to Work

One of the most amazing things about AOL is its people. You may be sitting alone at your computer, but when you're on AOL, people surround you. And unlike being alone in a crowd of people in a mall or at a stadium, you can reach out and connect with people online. The term *global village* was never truer than with AOL.

Now that you know where to find people and how to connect with them, we heartily recommend that you take advantage of your power. Invite your friends to a virtual party or your family to an online reunion. If your friends and family aren't on AOL, invite them over with AOL Keyword: **Friend** or AOL Keyword: **Instant Messenger**.

All this talk of community leads us right into to our next topic: downloading files. AOL members share special files with one another, which you can download and enjoy on your computer.

CHAPTER

10

DOWNLOADING FILES

Quick Look

▶ Downloading Files   page 210

AOL has thousands and thousands of files available online. You can download these files (save them to your computer) by using your AOL software to transfer them. Visit AOL Keyword: **Download Center** for libraries of files you can download.

▶ Avoiding Viruses   page 218

If you download files, you're susceptible to getting computer viruses or Trojan horses that can harm the data on your computer. To guard against this, visit AOL Keyword: **Virus**, where you'll find information, tools, and resources for virus prevention.

▶ Download Manager   page 220

Your AOL software comes with a tool to organize and control the files you want to download (or have already downloaded). This tool is called the Download Manager, and you can access it under the File menu.

Chapter 10
Downloading Files

IN THIS CHAPTER

Learning how to download and upload files

Protecting yourself from viruses

Using the Download Manager

Managing your files with Automatic AOL

AOL is truly a goldmine of free and low-cost treasure. The newly acquainted often overlook it, or worse yet, don't realize it even exists. We have the treasure map to the goodies, and we'll show you the way in this chapter.

Downloading Files

Did you hear about the prisoner whose mother baked a file into a chocolate cake? If you have, forget about it; the files we're talking about have nothing to do with escaping from jail. When we refer to *files,* we are talking about information stored in a computer or transported between computers.

A word processing document and a picture viewed on a computer screen are both files. Computer programs such as America Online 6.0 are made up of many files, each of which fulfills a certain purpose. Some of those files contain program instructions so that you can view Web pages, visit chat rooms, and receive e-mail. Other files contain information, such as the contents of your Filing Cabinet, a photo of your sister Sara, or the voice of the "You've Got Mail!" guy. Some files store special program settings so you can customize AOL to your own tastes. Of course, some files are games, utilities, and business applications.

Definition

Downloading is the act of transferring something from someone else's computer (such as AOL's) to your own computer. You can download files, and then the files you've downloaded are then referred to as downloads.

Many types of files are associated with AOL, but those of most interest in this chapter are those you can download. If you don't yet know how to download files, AOL offers a useful area filled with help and tips with this process, as described in the next section.

How to Download

The folks at the Computer Center are downloading maniacs. Well, actually, they'll download just about anything, not just maniacs — computer programs, sound files, videos, graphics, the works. The Computer Center has devoted an entire area to teaching you how to download called, appropriately enough, How to Download (see Figure 10-1). You can find it quickly at AOL Keyword: **How to Download**.

To get started, click the Watch the How to Download Movie link near the top of the How to Download window. If you need more hands-on help, click the Take a Class link on the right side of the How to Download window; this opens the AOL 101 – Downloading Files window, shown in Figure 10-2.

Figure 10-1. How to Download teaches you the art and science of downloading.

AOL 101 – Downloading is a free online course designed to help you learn about downloading files from live instructors. A link to the classroom, transcript, and a new user computer guide are available here also.

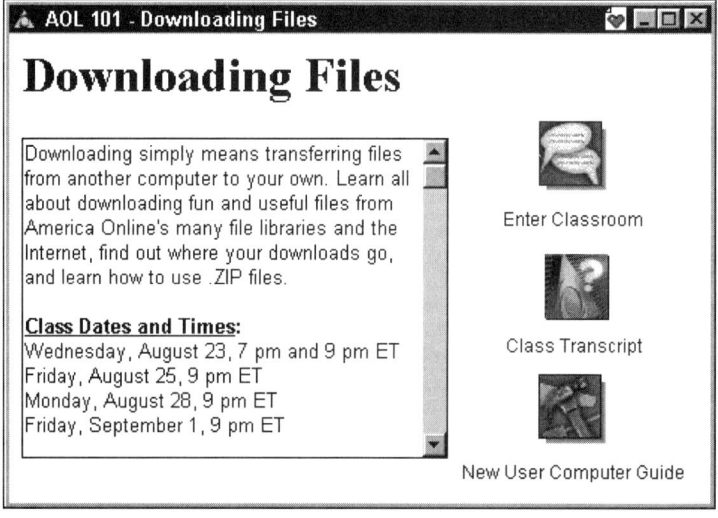

Figure 10-2. Get help downloading at the AOL 101 – Downloading Files class.

If you're in a hurry to learn how to download, follow these easy steps:

1. Locate a file that you want to download. We offer tips on finding files later in this chapter, but if you need a file to download now, use AOL Keyword: **Daily Download** and click the Download It Now button on the left side of the resulting window.
2. In the resulting window, choose a location on your hard drive for your new file. Make a note of the filename and the location so you can find your file later. AOL 6.0 now assists the users by asking if they want to access the folder immediately after download.
3. Click the Save button and then wait as AOL transfers the file from its computers to your hard drive, displaying a progress meter as it goes. If you need to cancel the download process, click the Cancel button. Click the Finish Later button if you want to complete the download later (see "Download Manager," later in this chapter, for details). If your file was compressed, AOL also decompresses it for you.
4. When the download (and decompression) is complete, AOL notifies you and offers to locate your file for you now. We recommend that you click Yes if you're new to downloading.

Unless you changed the default location, your file is probably located in the Download folder within your America Online folder on your hard drive. You can now open or run your file if you want. If the filename ends in .zip, this means the file was compressed, and AOL probably already decompressed it — look for a folder with the same name as the file instead. AOL automatically decompresses your files (unless you disable this setting in the Download Preferences dialog box).

After you understand how the download process works, you're likely to be eager to download a file or two (or three or 30). Where do you actually find files? You will encounter them throughout your AOL travels: attached to e-mail, under icons and hyperlinks, in lists, and on the Web. The greatest concentration of files is found in file libraries, of which there are hundreds (if not thousands) on AOL.

Before you download any file, read the "Viruses and Trojan Horses" section, later in this chapter.

AOL automatically creates a folder on your hard drive to receive downloaded files, and uses that folder as the default destination for all downloads originating from AOL. You can change that default in your download preferences (see Chapter 12). The download folder is located within your AOL software folder, for example: C:/America Online 6.0/download.

Don't confuse the name of the file saving window (which is called Download Manager) with the Download Manager feature found under the My Files icon on the toolbar, which we describe in detail later in this chapter.

File Libraries

You can use the Find Files feature to locate recently downloaded files on your hard drive. Choose File⇨Download Manager⇨Show Files Downloaded⇨Locate from the menu bar.

File compression is common with files found on AOL and the Internet. Files are compressed so they are smaller and thus faster to download. A compressed file may also be called a zipped file due to the `.zip` extension at the end of its filename.

If you want to bypass the file description and download the file immediately, click the Download Now button in the file library window. You may instead decide to click the Download Later button to add it to a list of files to be retrieved later (see "Download Manager" later in this chapter).

If the term *file library* conjures up thoughts of hushed tones and towering stacks of floppy disks, you're in for a treat. AOL's file libraries are not so inconvenient. File libraries are collections of related files, which you can browse, sort, and/or search. Virtually every forum online has a file library (usually several), though the greatest concentration of file libraries are in the Computer Center. File libraries are usually identified by name, but you may also recognize them by their distinctive appearance (see Figure 10-3).

Figure 10-3. A typical file library, listing filenames and relevant information.

Upon opening a file library, AOL lists the files in the order they were uploaded to the library. To change this order, click the Sort Order drop-down menu at the bottom of the window and choose a new order; you can sort the list by subject (alphabetically), download count, or download date. Download count is an indicator of a file's popularity. A file's download count is listed beside the file's subject, along with the date it was last downloaded (on the far right) and the date is was uploaded (on the far left).

Use the buttons arrayed along the bottom of a file library to gain more information. First select a file in the list (highlight it) and then click the Read Description button for a file description containing detailed information (see Figure 10-4). The Upload button lets you send your own file to the library. The List More Files button shows the next 20 files in the library; if you're looking for something but can't find it, click this button to see more files.

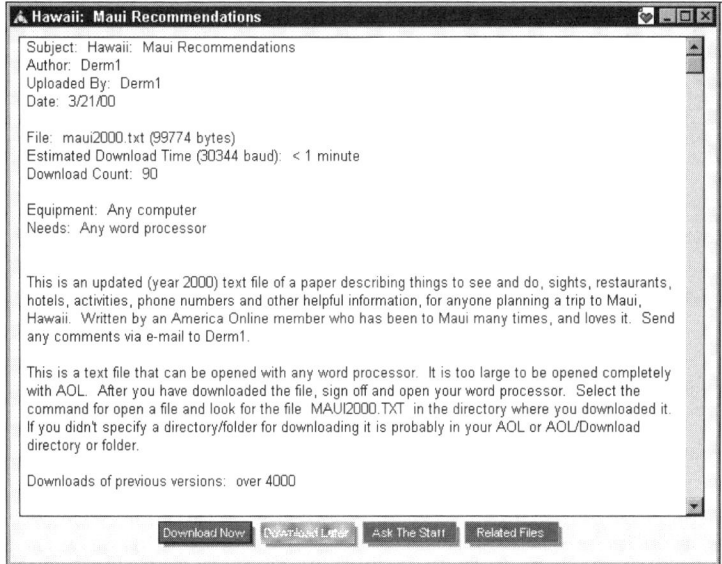

Figure 10-4. Every file in a library has a description similar to this one.

We recommend that you read file descriptions carefully before downloading a file. Descriptions list the subject, author, screen name of the person who uploaded the file, date uploaded, filename, estimated download time, and download count. More importantly, descriptions tell you what you need to have to use the file and how the file itself works. You may want to save this file description to your hard drive so you can refer to it at a later time (just press Ctrl+S when the description window is open).

We've discussed browsing and sorting libraries, but how about searching them? You need to visit the Download Center for a more comprehensive search, which just happens to be next on our tour!

Tip

Click the Ask The Staff button at the bottom of any File Description window if you have a question about that file or click the Related Files button to return to the library.

Download Center

Now that you're a pro at downloading, where can you find more files to download? The Download Center (shown in Figure 10-5) offers tens of thousands of files, including graphics, sounds, and programs. Just type AOL Keyword: **Download Center** to find this area.

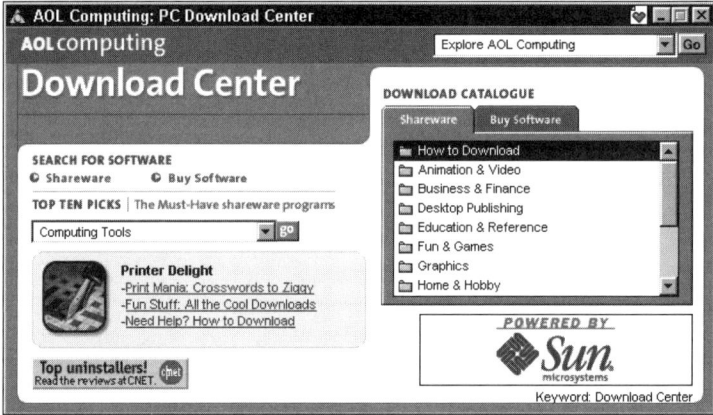

Figure 10-5. Dive into the downloads at the Download Center.

The Download Center search encompasses almost all Computer Center libraries, but very few libraries in other channels on AOL.

You can find files two different ways at the Download Center: by searching or by browsing. We recommend searching for a file if you know what you're seeking. Browsing, on the other hand, works best when you know what kind of file you want, such as a game or utility, but not the specifics of it. We take a closer look at both searching and browsing through the Download Center in the next two sections.

Searching for Files

If you're seeking shareware files, follow these steps:

1. Go to AOL Keyword: **Download Center**.
2. Click the Shareware button in the Search for Software area of the Download Center window. This brings up the Software Search window (shown in Figure 10-6), in which you can choose your search parameters.

Chapter 10 ▲ Downloading Files 217

Figure 10-6. Use the Software Search window to find shareware files.

3. Choose a time frame if you're looking for a recent file; otherwise, you can leave it set to All Dates.
4. Select a category to narrow down your search.
5. Type your search word(s) in the text box at the bottom of the window. You can use Boolean operators such as AND, OR, and NOT to fine-tune your search.
6. When you're ready, click the Search button (or just press Enter) to start your search.

AOL displays the first 20 results in the window, as shown in Figure 10-7. If there are more than 20 results, you can click the List More Files button at the bottom of the window to display the next 20 matches. You can get a closer look at your search results by double-clicking a file in the Search Results window. You then see a description of the file, which we explain in more detail in the "File Libraries" section, earlier in this chapter.

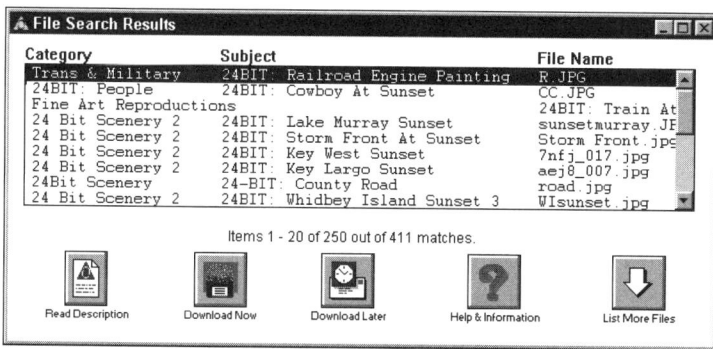

Figure 10-7. AOL displays your search results in a new window.

Tip

If you're in the market for commercial software, click the Buy Software button in the Download Center. This leads you to SoftwareBuys.com, which you can access directly with AOL Keyword: **SoftwareBuys**. SoftwareBuys.com offers a large selection of commercial software. Begin a search for commercial software by typing your search word(s) into the Search field and clicking Go. Read more about online shopping and shopping carts in Chapters 15 and 19.

Browsing Files

If you're the type who likes to just stroll through the aisles, make a beeline for the Download Catalogue on the right side of the Download Center window. Here you'll find collections of libraries organized by topic, category, and subcategory. First, find a topic from the list in the Download Center and double-click the selection. This opens a topic window, shown in Figure 10-8.

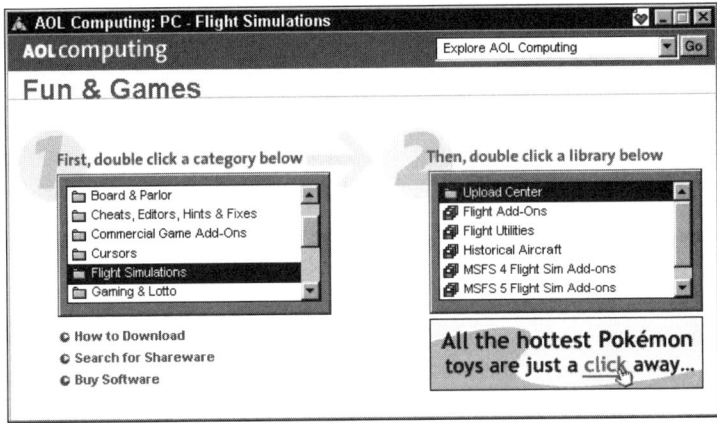

Figure 10-8. A download category window containing collections of libraries.

Note

The Buy Software tab above the list box in the Download Center window leads to SoftwareBuys.com, which we describe earlier in this chapter.

Double-click a category in the left-hand list box to see a list of libraries, which appears in the right-hand list box. Double-click a library to open it and begin browsing. Be sure to use the scroll bar to see all categories and libraries available.

Those of you who love to browse but don't know where to start may enjoy the Top Ten Picks, available in the Download Center window. Just choose one of the topics from the Top Ten Picks drop-down menu and click the Go button to see a list of recommended files.

Cross-Reference

You may also find files in your e-mail! To learn more about downloading files from e-mail, see Chapter 5.

Viruses and Trojan Horses

Along with the benefits of downloading files, you must also accept the risks — namely, contracting viruses or encountering Trojan horses. Thankfully, most files available in file libraries have been carefully scanned for viruses and Trojan horses before they were released to the public. However, due to the proliferation of viruses, not to mention their tenacity, AOL cannot guarantee that all files available are safe. Even so, it isn't difficult to avoid viruses and Trojan horses with some prevention and a lot of common sense.

Your first line of defense against viruses and Trojan horses is knowledge. For this, we direct you to the Anti-Virus Center at AOL Keyword: **Virus**. Here, you can find plenty of information about what constitutes a virus, a Trojan horse, or just a hoax. You can also download demo versions of antivirus programs or purchase commercial software.

Keep your antivirus program up-to-date by checking for virus definition updates on a regular basis. Depending on which antivirus program you go with, you can find these updates in AOL's file libraries or on the program's Web site.

In addition to an antivirus program, it helps to use common sense before you click that Download button. Download files from people and sources you feel you can trust, and avoid strangers and disreputable Web sites. If something sounds too good to be true (such as a free, full-featured word processing program or adult software), it probably is a Trojan horse; resist the temptation to check.

If you must download a file and you aren't sure of its contents, first make sure that your antivirus program is up-to-date and functioning. You can then download the file to a floppy disk and scan the file on the disk. If the file is infected, you can safely delete it without worrying that any harm was done to your computer; the simple act of downloading a file is not dangerous in itself. In order to do damage, a virus or Trojan horse must be executed (run) or loaded into software that can run it. It is always a wise precaution to keep a full backup of your data in the event that your computer is ever infected with a virus.

If you think your computer is infected with a virus or has encountered a Trojan horse, stay calm. Immediately stop what you're doing, exit your programs, and turn off your computer. Restart your computer, open your antivirus program, and scan your computer. If you don't find anything, visit your antivirus program's Web site, download the latest file descriptions, and scan again. You may also want to scan your computer with

Definition

Viruses are specific kinds of files designed by their programmers to cause damage. Viruses generally damage the files on your computer's hard drive. *Trojan horses*, on the other hand, are dangerous files disguised as useful or desirable programs. Trojan horses generally contain objectionable or inappropriate images, conceal viruses, or even compromise your AOL account or credit card information.

Definition

An *antivirus program*, properly installed and updated, can scan your computer and all the files you download for possible viruses. We strongly recommend that you use an antivirus program if you download files from AOL and/or the Internet, or even simply receive files from friends or coworkers.

Visit www.drsolomon.com for information and updates on Dr. Solomon's antivirus programs. Visit www.mcafee.com for McAfee's antivirus programs. Or visit www.symantec.com for Symantec's antivirus programs.

Just because your computer acts funny or strange doesn't mean it contracted a virus. You may have a hardware problem instead (in which case you may want to visit AOL Keyword: **Hardware**).

For more information on viruses and what to do if you think you've been infected with one, visit the Computer Protection Center at AOL Keyword: **Virus Info**.

another antivirus program. If your antivirus program finds a virus, it can usually eliminate the virus. Do not upload any files, attach any files to e-mail, or exchange floppies with anyone until you're sure you've eradicated the virus; otherwise, you'll spread the virus to others.

Download Manager

The Download Manager keeps track of the files you've downloaded and those you chose to download later, and it knows where those files have been stored on your hard drive. If you've selected several files to be downloaded later, clicking the Download Manager's Download button collects the entire list of files. You can also use the Download Manager to decompress zipped files, access your download preference settings, and decide where files will be stored on your hard drive.

You can reach the Download Manager, shown in Figure 10-9, by choosing File⇨Download Manager from the main menu or by using AOL Keyword: **Download Manager**.

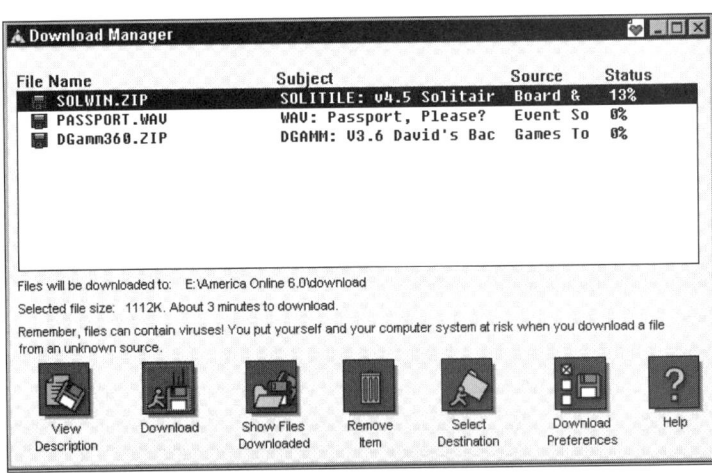

Figure 10-9. The Download Manager displays files waiting to be downloaded.

Buttons along the bottom of the Download Manager window give you access to your downloads. Here's what those buttons do:

- **View Description:** Shows the file description for the highlighted file
- **Download:** Retrieves the selected file right then and there
- **Show Files Downloaded:** Shows a list of files you've already downloaded
- **Remove Item:** Deletes the highlighted file from the download list (but doesn't actually delete the download if you've already downloaded it)
- **Select Destination:** Changes the default download folder
- **Download Preferences:** Makes changes to your download-related settings
- **Help:** Gives you additional assistance

When you're trying to figure out what you've downloaded and where you put it, click the Show Files Downloaded button in the main Download Manager window. By default, the Files You've Downloaded window (shown in Figure 10-10) lists the past 100 files you've downloaded (click the Download Preferences button to adjust the number of files listed).

If you can't remember what the downloaded file is, click the View Description button. The Locate button finds the folder on your hard drive that contains the downloaded file, and the Decompress button unzips zipped files on command. Altogether, the Download Manager is a handy manager to have around.

You can also view downloaded files (or those ready to be downloaded) in your Personal Filing Cabinet — choose File⇨Filing Cabinet from menu bar, and click the Downloads tab near the top of the window.

The Download Manager only lists files that have been attached and downloaded from e-mail or from AOL file libraries. If you download files from a Web site, they won't be listed here.

If an interruption occurs during a download from an e-mail or an AOL file library, you can visit the Download Manager to resume that download. AOL displays the filename in the Download Manager, along with the percentage of the file that has already been downloaded. Click the Download button at the bottom of the File Manger window to resume the selected download.

Figure 10-10. Files You've Downloaded is your downloading lost and found.

Automatic AOL

If you've always wanted your very own robot, Automatic AOL may be the robot for you! Automatic AOL can run down to your AOL e-mail box to send and collect your e-mail, download your files, and collect and send message board and newsgroup postings. All this fetching, sending, and saving can be done automatically — while you sleep or even while you're on vacation. When you return home, just open your Personal Filing Cabinet, and everything is there waiting for you.

Automatic AOL is easy to set up. Just choose Mail⇨Automatic AOL from the toolbar. The setup process asks you to answer a series of simple questions, and after you're finished, your little robot is ready to go! You can change your settings at any time by returning to the Automatic AOL preferences window, shown in Figure 10-11.

Tip

Many people depend on AOL's software to automatically decompress files when they sign off AOL. If you downloaded a zip file and would rather not sign off before using it, the Decompress button in the Files You've Downloaded window is a very handy thing to have around.

Note

Your computer must be turned on and your AOL software must be running in order for Automatic AOL to work.

Tip

You can set up Automatic AOL another way, too: Choose Settings⇨Preferences, click the Auto AOL link, and click the Walk Me Through button.

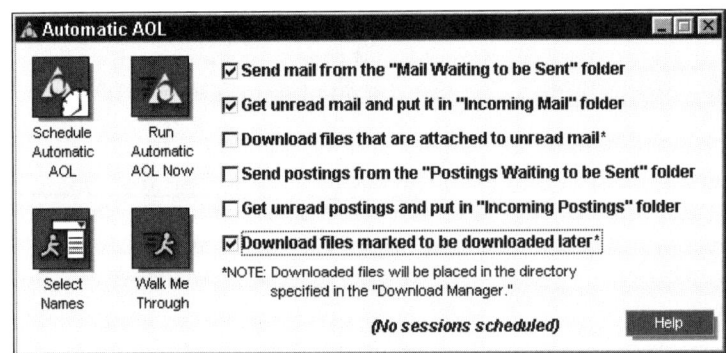

Figure 10-11. Select your Automatic AOL options in the Automatic AOL preferences window.

Automatic AOL sessions can be set to take place as often as every half hour, seven days a week, regardless of whether you're around. Just click the Schedule Automatic AOL button in the Automatic AOL preferences window to see scheduling options in the Schedule Automatic AOL window, shown in Figure 10-12. You can also use Automatic AOL to "make the rounds" whenever you like, even if you never schedule an unattended session. Just choose Mail⇨Run Automatic AOL Now, and head to the kitchen for a snack.

Chapter 10 ▲ Downloading Files

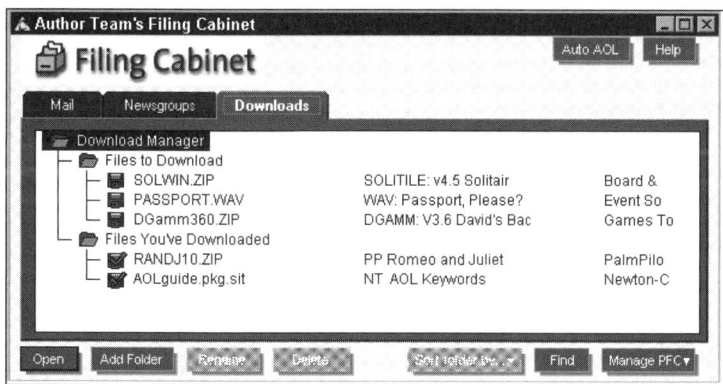

Figure 10-12. The Schedule Automatic AOL window, the autopilot for your online world.

After an Automatic AOL session, visit your Filing Cabinet and find any e-mail, posts, and/or files it collected. Note the three tabs at the top of the Filing Cabinet: Mail, Newsgroups, and Downloads, which help you find the items you seek (see Figure 10-13).

Figure 10-13. The Personal Filing Cabinet stores and organizes the results of your Automatic AOL sessions.

Tip

If you're a fan of message boards and newsgroups, you can download posts from any boards or newsgroups to which you've subscribed (subscribing is discussed earlier in this chapter). Make sure that the Get Unread Postings and Put in "Incoming Posts" Folder check box is selected in the Automatic AOL window. After your next Automatic AOL session, choose File⇨Offline Newsgroups from the menu bar to read your new posts. Just as with e-mail, you can compose your replies and new subjects offline and have them posted automatically during the following Automatic AOL session.

Putting Your Knowledge to Work

An entire world of software awaits you on America Online. At one point — many, many years ago — we had a good handle on the scope of files you could expect to find online. No longer. The availability of files for downloading has grown in such scope and magnitude that it is almost overwhelming. Suffice it to say if you're looking for something, you can probably find it somewhere online.

If you're reading between the lines, you may wonder if we're hinting that commercial software is available for free online. The answer is yes, though only in the back alleys and black markets of the Internet. You download any such software at your own risk, and we do mean risk — viruses, Trojan horses, and other dangers run rampant in such places. You get what you pay for, after all. Enough said.

So where do you go to find quality software on your own? Beyond your favorite forum's libraries and the Download Center, we recommend www.shareware.com for a large collection of valuable downloads. CNET's www.download.com is also an excellent source.

All this talk of downloading leads us right into our next topic: "You've Got Pictures." With "You've Got Pictures," you can get your snapshots online, share them with family and friends, and download them to your computer.

CHAPTER

11

"YOU'VE GOT PICTURES"

Quick Look

▶ **Get Your Photos Online**   page 227
Visit AOL Keyword: **Photo Developer** to find a place to drop off your film for "You've Got Pictures" developing.

▶ **See Your Photos Online**   page 227
After your film is processed and available online, you can click the "You've Got Pictures" button on the Welcome Screen to view your photos.

▶ **Create an Online Album**   page 233
Once your pictures are available at "You've Got Pictures," it's easy to create online photo albums that you can share with your friends and family.

▶ **Download a Photo to Your Computer**   page 235
When you see a photo you want to save to your computer, select the check box beside the picture and then click the Download Pictures button.

Chapter 11

"You've Got Pictures"

IN THIS CHAPTER

Getting your film developed and viewing your pictures online

Saving your pictures and creating online photo albums

Downloading your online pictures to your hard drive

Sharing your pictures with friends and family

AOL's "You've Got Pictures" is more than just a cute icon on the Welcome Screen. With "You've Got Pictures," you don't have to buy a digital camera or scanner to put your pictures online. All you need is a regular 35mm or Advantix camera, or even one of those inexpensive disposable cameras. When you drop off your film to be developed, ask for "You've Got Pictures!" Not only will you get your prints as usual, but your pictures will be online in a matter of days.

Of course, if you have a digital camera or scanner, "You've Got Pictures" provides an easy way to order prints and store and share your digital pictures, too.

Dropping Off Your Pictures

The next time you drop off your film to be developed, look for signs offering, "You've Got Pictures." Thirty-eight-thousand developers offer the "You've Got Pictures" service. These locations include most Kodak processing centers, one hour photo labs, like Wolf Camera, and leading mail order photofinishers. You can find one in your area at AOL Keyword: **Photo Developer**.

When you drop off your film at a participating photo developer, keep these two important points in mind to get your pictures online with "You've Got Pictures":

- You must ask for the "You've Got Pictures" service. You should find a check box right on the film processing envelope.
- When you fill out the film processing envelope, be sure to supply your AOL screen name. Otherwise, the photo processor won't know where to send your digital pictures when they're finished.

Your AOL account can have up to seven screen names, and you can send your pictures to nearly any screen name you choose. The exception? Screen names with Parental Controls set to Kids Only or Young Teens cannot access "You've Got Pictures." You can learn more about Parental Controls in Chapter 4.

Viewing Your Pictures Online

When your pictures are ready, you hear "You've Got Pictures!" when you sign on and/or you receive an e-mail from screen name AOLYouveGotPics (see Figure 11-1), letting you know that your pictures are ready. Just click the "You've Got Pictures" icon on your Welcome Screen to go to your pictures. You can also access your pictures through AOL Keyword: **Pictures**.

After you drop off your film, your pictures are uploaded and online within 48 hours. If you drop off the roll at a participating one-hour photo finishing lab, your pictures could be online in a matter of hours.

Note

You must be signed on to AOL using the screen name you gave to the photo lab to hear "You've Got Pictures!" and/or receive an e-mail.

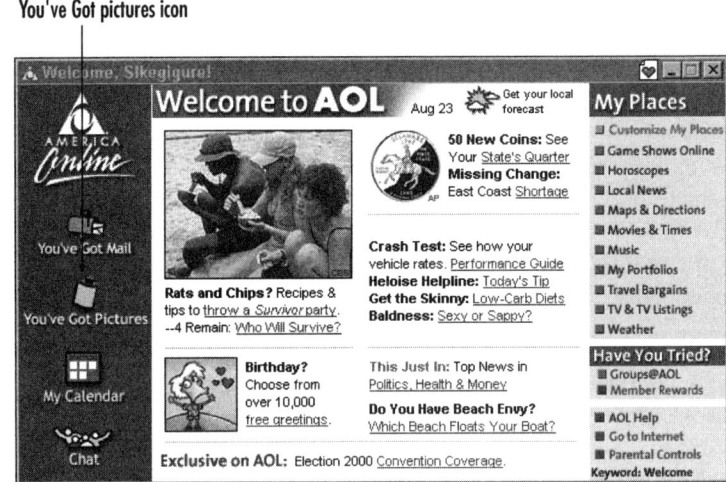

Figure 11-1. The "You've Got Pictures" icon on the AOL Welcome Screen, indicating that we have pictures waiting!

The main page of "You've Got Pictures" (shown in Figure 11-2) is an excellent introduction to "You've Got Pictures," offering step-by-step instructions, tips, photo galleries, and helpful information. Feel free to spend some time exploring this area. We particularly recommend the tutorial on getting your pictures online, which you can access by clicking the Learn How link.

Tip

When you receive pictures for the first time, click the "You've Got Pictures" icon to go to the main page. After that first time, you can click the icon to go directly to your pictures!

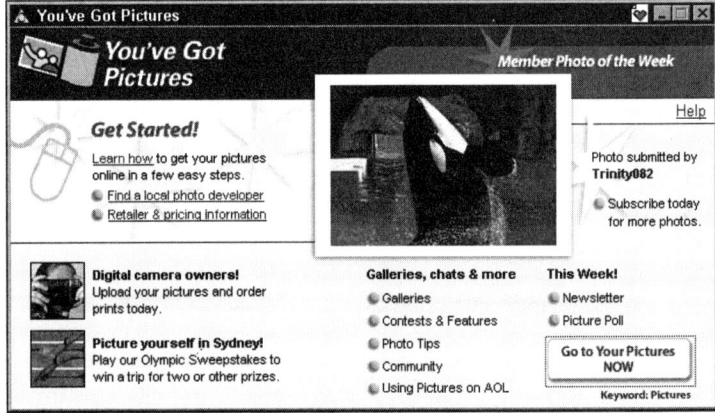

Figure 11-2. The "You've Got Pictures" main page.

Viewing a Roll

When you're ready to see your pictures, follow these steps:

1. If you are using "You've Got Pictures" for the first time, click the Go to Your Pictures Now button in the lower-right corner of the "You've Got Pictures" window. This opens the My Pictures page, shown in Figure 11-3.

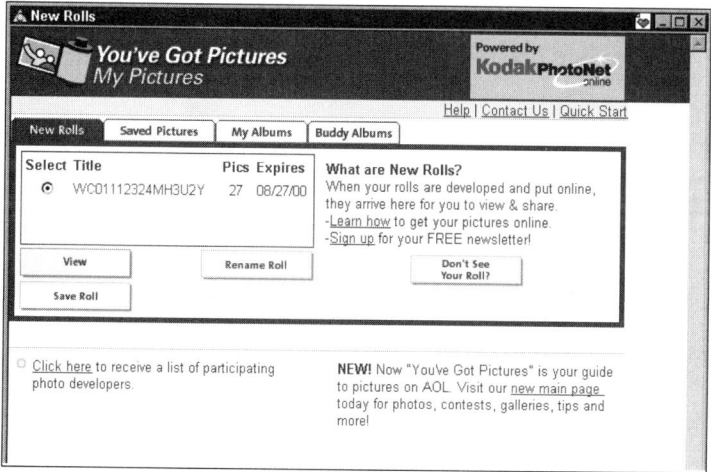

Figure 11-3. The My Pictures page, where you can find your photos.

Note

Your new roll remains in the New Rolls area of My Pictures for 30 days from the day it is delivered to your AOL account. As expiration nears, you will receive two e-mail reminders from screen name AOLYouveGotPics, letting you know that your roll is about to expire. After your pictures expire, they are deleted from the system, so be sure to save the pictures you want to keep as soon as possible.

2. Near the top of the "You've Got Pictures" window, you find four tabs — New Rolls, Saved Pictures, My Albums, and Buddy Albums. If the New Rolls tab isn't already selected, click it to display the New Rolls area. If you have a roll (or rolls) waiting for you, the New Rolls area is displayed automatically.

Every new roll you receive is stored here for 30 days, and listed next to each roll is its title, the number of exposures, and the expiration date of that roll. Any images that are not saved by the end of that 30 day period are deleted, just like the way old e-mail is deleted from your online mailbox (see the "Savings Pictures and Rolls" section, later in this chapter).

Note

What happens if that happy voice doesn't say, "You've got pictures!" (or you don't get e-mail from AOL)? When you receive your regular prints, a claim card is enclosed in the envelope containing a unique Roll ID and Owner's Key number for "You've Got Pictures." You can use this information to retrieve your digital pictures from "You've Got Pictures" (see the "Viewing a Roll" section).

3. Click the Select radio button alongside the roll you want to view and click the View button. Within moments the Roll Viewer page appears, displaying every image on that roll, as shown in Figure 11-4.

Figure 11-4. The Roll Viewer page displays every photo on your roll.

Those images are pretty small (otherwise they wouldn't all fit on one page), but if you click one of the images, a new page appears, showing a larger version of that same picture, as shown in Figure 11-5. As an alternative, you can select the check box alongside a picture, and click the View Full Picture button at the bottom of the Roll Viewer page.

Ah, that's better! Now you can really see what's going on. The Next Picture and Previous Picture buttons appear below the larger picture, along with thumbnail (small-sized) previews of other pictures. Just click either button to move through your roll, displaying a larger-sized image of each photo as you go.

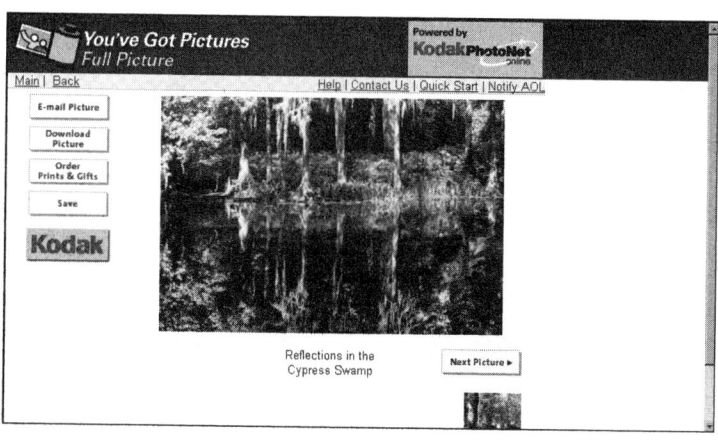

Figure 11-5. You see a larger image by clicking the thumbnail.

Renaming a Roll

After you've had a good look at a roll of pictures, you may just want to change the roll's title from WC01112324MH3U2Y (or whatever name the photo developer gave you) to something a little bit more descriptive. If you're not already there, return to the New Rolls area, click a radio button to select the roll you want to rename, and click the Rename Roll button at the bottom of the New Rolls page.

Finding a Missing Roll

What if you can't find one or more of your new rolls? To look for your missing pictures, follow these steps:

1. Click the New Rolls tab on the My Pictures page.
2. In the New Rolls page, click the Don't See Your Roll button. This opens the Don't See Your Roll page, shown in Figure 11-6.
3. Type the Roll ID and Owner's Key into the appropriate text boxes and then click the OK button at the bottom of the page. Every roll of film scanned by "You've Got Pictures" gets a unique Roll ID and an Owner's Key, which are printed on a card that comes inside the envelope containing your prints. As long as the initial 30-day period hasn't expired, the roll will appear as a New Roll. If the 30-day period has expired, you'll receive a message explaining that the pictures are no longer available.

If you'd rather not step through the roll one shot at a time like a slide show, click the Back link at the top left of the Full Picture window. You skip right back to the Roll Viewer page, where you can select a different picture to view up close.

The roll name you create can contain 20 characters, including letters, numbers, spaces, and common punctuation marks. The name change is only for your convenience. The original Roll ID and Owner's Key don't change. If you just got 11 rolls back following your vacation, Rename is a very handy feature.

Tip

If you're sure you should have pictures, go to the Don't See Your Roll page, and look for the tip that says `If a claim card was not included with your prints, or if you need further assistance, click here for Customer Service`. The Customer Service Roll Assistance window will help you find your missing pictures.

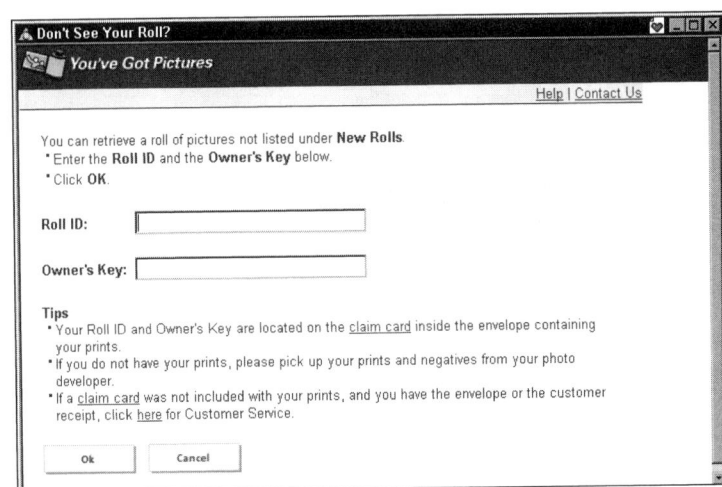

Figure 11-6. Retrieve missing rolls on the Don't See Your Roll page.

Saving Pictures and Rolls

Your digital pictures are stored online at "You've Got Pictures." Every screen name gets free, unlimited storage on "You've Got Pictures" as long as you are an AOL member and you access "You've Got Pictures" once every six months. You can save individual pictures or entire rolls online, and if you prefer, you can download pictures to your hard drive (which we discuss a little later in this chapter). If you don't go to the "You've Got Pictures" area at least once in a six-month period, your saved pictures will be deleted.

You can save an entire roll with a few clicks of your mouse. Just follow these steps to save your roll:

1. Click the New Rolls tab on the My Pictures page.
2. Select the Select radio button adjacent to the roll you want to save.
3. Click the Save Roll button toward the bottom of that page.
4. A new window appears, asking whether you're sure you want to save the roll. Click OK, or Cancel, depending on your needs.

After your roll has been saved, you'll find all the pictures under the Saved Pictures tab.

Creating an Album

Albums are a fun, easy way to organize your favorite photos and share them with others. Online albums can consist of up to 100 photos, which can be gathered from "You've Got Pictures" and/or uploaded from your own computer. After you've chosen the photos for your album, you can personalize the presentation with background colors, titles, and captions. When your album is ready, you can share it with friends and family anywhere, regardless of whether they have AOL.

 **Note**

Albums can only be viewed online, and can only be created from pictures stored online at "You've Got Pictures."

The easiest way to create a new album is to follow these steps:

1. Visit AOL Keyword: **Pictures** and view a roll. You can also begin in Saved Pictures or Buddy Albums, if you prefer.
2. With the Roll Viewer open and displaying photos, select the photos you want to display in the album. To select a photo, just select the check box to the left of a photo — a check mark appears in the box to indicate it is selected, as shown in Figure 11-7.
3. Now click the Create New Album button. "You've Got Pictures" displays the photos you selected for your new album, along with a default title (your screen name and the current date).
4. At this point, you have three choices: customize your album, save your album, or cancel. For now, click the Save button — you can return to customize it later.
5. You're prompted to agree to the "You've Got Pictures" terms. After you accept, your new album is created, as shown in Figure 11-8.

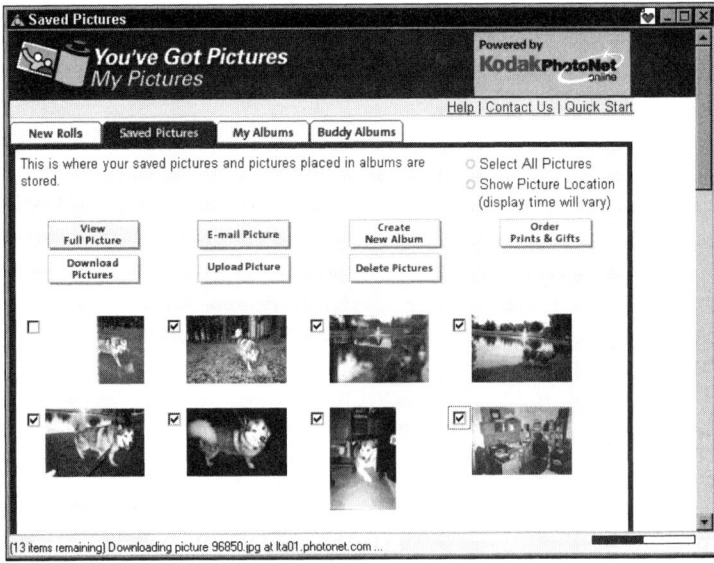

Figure 11-7. Select the photos for your new album.

Once you have a snazzy album filled with your favorite photos, you can access it anytime you want by clicking the My Albums tab at the top of the My Pictures page.

Take a look at your new album by clicking the View button. Your default title is displayed at the top, followed by your photos, and then an array of options along the bottom. Here are some of those options:

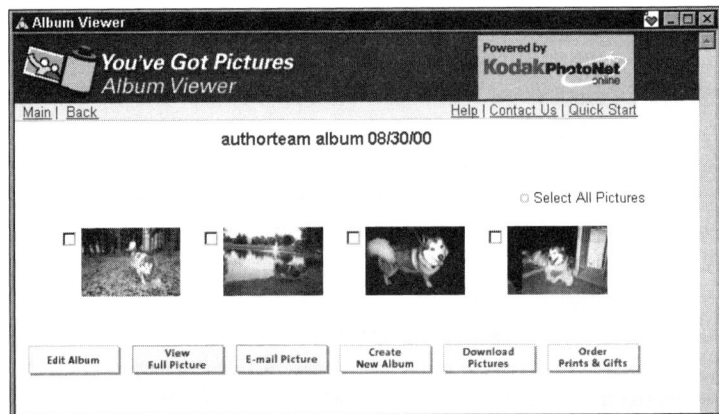

Figure 11-8. A new album, fresh from the computer.

- **Edit Album:** Click this button to customize the look of your album with layouts, backgrounds, and captions.
- **View Full Picture:** Click this button to see a selected photo up close.

- ▶ **E-Mail Picture:** Click this button to send a picture to a friend.
- ▶ **Create New Album:** Click this button if you want to create another album.
- ▶ **Download Pictures:** Click this button to download a picture to your computer (discussed in the next section).
- ▶ **Order Prints & Gifts:** Click this button to purchase photo prints and gifts (discussed later in this chapter).

You can also share your album with family and friends by sending it as a Buddy Album.

Downloading Pictures to Your Computer

"You've Got Pictures" makes it easy to download digital pictures to your computer. When you select a picture to download, you're looking at a small version of your image. In fact, your picture is available in several different resolutions.

Here's how to download one or more digital pictures to your computer:

1. Go to AOL Keyword: **Pictures**.
2. Find the picture(s) you want to download. If you previously saved the picture(s), click the Saved Pictures tab. If the picture(s) is part of a New Roll, click the New Roll tab, select the roll you want to view, and click the View button.
3. Select the check box next to each picture that you want to download. You can download more than one picture at a time by selecting more than one check box.
4. Click the Download Pictures button.
5. When your digital pictures are delivered online, they're available in several different qualities (resolutions). Select one of these three resolutions:
    - **E-Mail & Web Page Quality:** This quality looks very good on your computer screen and downloads quickly. This makes it perfect for sharing as an

attached file or image imbedded in e-mail, or for display on your home page. It will look grainy if printed or enlarged on screen. Resolution: 384 x 256. Download time at 56 Kbps: 8 seconds. Cost: Free

- **Print Quality:** This quality is suitable for snapshot-sized prints on a color ink jet printer, or when you need to edit or crop a picture before using it online. Resolution: 768 x 512. Download time at 56 Kbps: 45 seconds. Cost: Free
- **Premium Offer:** The premium service from "You've Got Pictures" enables you to download a high-resolution version of your digital pictures. This quality is useful for projects where maximum resolution is critical, such as professionally printed brochures. Resolution: 1,024 x 1,536. Download time at 56 Kbps: 2 minutes. Cost: $1 per image, $3 minimum per order

The higher the resolution, the larger the picture, the longer the download, and the better the print quality. Lower resolutions are more appropriate for online use like e-mail and the Web. If you'll be editing your pictures, the middle or high resolutions offer more digital information to play with.

If you click the E-Mail & Web Page Quality or Print Quality button an additional page comes up with instructions for actually getting and saving the selected pictures; continue with Step 6.

If you clicked the Premium Offer button, a new window records what you have selected to download, how many pictures you are downloading, and the unit and total costs. Each row corresponds to a single item in your "You've Got Pictures" shopping cart; an item can consist of more than one digital picture. In this window, you can complete your order, change or cancel it, or continue shopping in the "You've Got Pictures" store. After you've completed your order the downloading procedure begins, in a manner similar to Step 6.

6. Click the Download Pictures button when you're ready to go. The File Download window comes up; make sure that the Save This Program to Disk check box is selected. Then click OK.

7. In the Save As dialog box, indicate where you want the picture(s) to be saved, and then click the Save button.

Note

When you download pictures, the default destination for the files is the AOL Download folder. It's usually fine to accept that choice in the Save As dialog box. However, "You've Got Pictures" attempts to save *all* downloaded pictures with the filename `photos.exe`. Because every picture you download to the AOL6.0/Download directory will have the same name (`photos.exe`), the second picture file you download will *overwrite* (replace) the previous picture file, the third will replace the second, and so on. If you don't want to lose all those files rename each `photos.exe` file in the Save As dialog box as you download them. Don't download digital picture(s) until you've opened and renamed the previous pictures you've downloaded!

As the picture(s) downloads (is copied from "You've Got Pictures" to your computer), the Windows Download dialog box tracks its progress.

8. When the Download is complete, you see the Download Complete message in the Windows Download dialog box. Click the Done button and continue your online activities.

Sharing Your Pictures

Taking pictures is one thing, and developing pictures is another, but why bother at all unless you can share those pictures with friends and families? "You've Got Pictures" makes it easy to share photos through e-mail, Buddy Albums, and Prints and Photo Merchandise.

E-Mail a Picture

Sharing pictures via e-mail couldn't be easier with "You've Got Pictures" — you don't have to know anything about inserting pictures in e-mail, downloading, or file attachments. Just select the picture you want to share from any "You've Got Pictures" page (only one picture per e-mail), click the E-Mail Picture button, and fill in the onscreen form. Supply the recipients e-mail addresses, add an appropriate message, and click the Send button.

AOL members will receive e-mail from screen name `AOLBuddyPics` containing an embedded image (see Chapter 6). Recipients who are not on AOL receive e-mail from your AOL screen name. containing an attached JPG file of the picture. All e-mailed pictures also include your message and a hyperlink so your friend can view the picture online and order prints or other photo merchandise if they so desire. The e-mail also contains an invitation to try "You've Got Pictures," and may also include special offers from "You've Got Pictures." Altogether, it's a fast, simple, and safe way to share your pictures with your friends and family.

If your recipient is an AOL member, you do not need to type @aol.com after that person's screen name; all other e-mail addresses do require the @ symbol and the domain, however.

"You've Got Pictures" maintains a list of up to 10 e-mail addresses you've previously sent "You've Got Pictures" e-mail. The next time you want to send one of them a picture, select a name from the Recent Recipients drop-down list on the E-Mail Pictures page.

Buddy Albums

You can share the albums you create with anyone who has an e-mail address. People you share with receive your album as a Buddy Album. To send a Buddy Album, follow these steps:

1. Click the My Albums tab, select the album you want to share, and click the Share button. A new page appears, where you can indicate who should receive your album.
2. To add a name to the list of folks who can access your album, type each individual's exact e-mail address in the top field and click the Add Name button.
3. When your list is complete, click the OK button to save your list and share your album.

"You've Got Pictures" sends e-mail to all the recipients on your list, announcing the availability of the new album, and adds your album to their individual lists of Buddy Albums. This process may take a few minutes. When complete, a confirmation page appears, displaying the address of each person who successfully received access to the album.

Prints and Photo Merchandise

The uses for digital photos are endless. Gift-giving is perhaps one of the more popular uses, and certainly one of the easier uses, thanks to the power of digital photos. In fact, you can order photo gifts online directly through "You've Got Pictures." You, or anyone to whom you send a Buddy Album, can order prints in three sizes. Would you like your child's sunny face on a coffee mug, or your favorite landscape on a jigsaw puzzle? They can do that, too. And proud grandparents can order T-shirts and sweatshirts emblazoned with their favorite group photos. Just look for the Order Prints and Gifts button when you view Saved Pictures or Albums, and start clicking options in the "You've Got Pictures" Picture Store, shown in Figure 11-9.

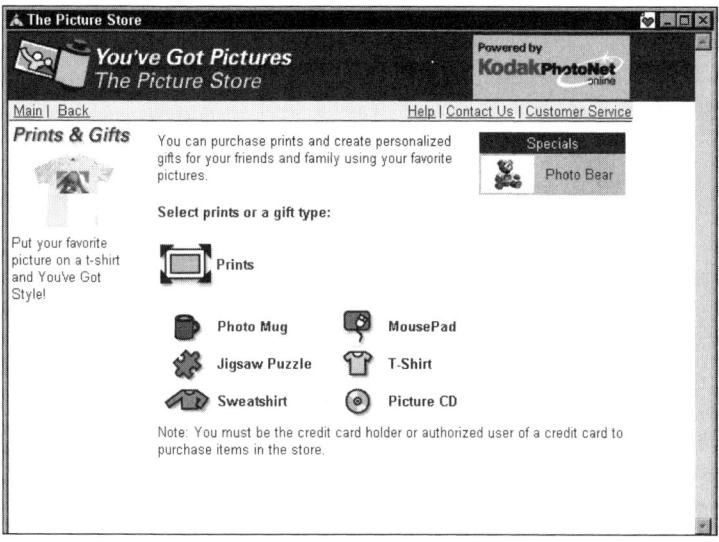

Figure 11-9. The "You've Got Pictures" Picture Store offers prints, mugs, puzzles, sweatshirts, mousepads, T-shirts, and Photo CDs.

Safety Considerations

America Online has a well-deserved reputation for providing a safe and secure online environment, and as you may expect, "You've Got Pictures" reflects AOL's values. Whether you're concerned about objectionable or unsolicited images, your children's safety, your personal privacy, or secure online commerce, you'll find your concerns have been addressed. "You've Got Pictures" provides a thorough discussion of online safety and security issues in its Help area, which you can reach by clicking the Help link in any "You've Got Pictures" window or by using AOL Keyword: **YGP Help**. We don't have room in this book to duplicate all that information, so be sure to visit this area very soon.

Parental Concerns

"You've Got Pictures" is also integrated with AOL's Parental Controls, so you can protect your children from unsolicited, inappropriate images and prevent them from ordering services without your permission. If you set Parental Controls for

Caution

"You've Got Pictures" is covered by AOL's Terms of Service (TOS), which governs member's conduct on AOL. "You've Got Pictures" has its own set of rules to govern the special conditions that can arise at "You've Got Pictures." In addition to the usual prohibitions of sexually explicit, obscene, and/or defamatory material, there are rules regarding issues such as solicitation of business and copyright infringement.

your children's screen names to Kids Only or Young Teens, they cannot receive Buddy Albums. Access to "You've Got Pictures" is determined in the Custom Web Controls area at AOL Keyword: **Parental Controls**. Set Custom Web Controls to Access Only Kid Approved Sites or Access Only Teen Approved Sites to block access to Buddy Albums for any screen name.

Secure Commerce

AOL also makes online commerce safe, easy, and reliable. "You've Got Pictures" is part of AOL's Certified Merchants program, which guarantees the safety of your credit card information and sets stringent standards for customer support and accountability to consumers.

Putting Your Knowledge to Work

We've only scratched the surface of what you can do with "You've Got Pictures." If this feature intrigues you, we recommend that you get a roll of pictures processed and experiment with all the things you can do in "You've Got Pictures!"

- ▶ Visit the "You've Got Pictures" main page to find picture galleries or contests where you can enter your own pictures.
- ▶ Add your pictures to your AOL Hometown home page and share them with your group at Groups@AOL.
- ▶ Order photo-quality prints from your digital camera: Just upload the pictures to "You've Got Pictures" and place your print order.

PART III

CUSTOMIZING YOUR AOL

Chapter 12
AOL Anywhere and Preference Settings

Chapter 13
My Calendar

Chapter 14
Favorite Places

Chapter 15
Shopping Preferences

Chapter 16
AOL Hometown

CHAPTER

12

AOL ANYWHERE AND PREFERENCE SETTINGS

Quick Look

▶ Screen Names   page 244
You can create up to seven screen names on one AOL account. Screen names can be up to 16 characters long. Use AOL Keyword: **Screen Names** to create, delete, and restore screen names.

▶ Passwords   page 247
Passwords are the key to your AOL account, and they should be created and used carefully. The more difficult your password is, the harder it is for another person to guess. You can change passwords any time you're online at AOL Keyword: **Password**.

▶ AOL Anywhere   page 251
The "AOL Anywhere"℠ service is a next-generation customizable news and information resource offering up-to-the-minute headline news, stock quotes, sports scores, weather, and more, based on preferences selected by members. It's a quick and easy way for members to get round-the-clock updates on the topics that matter most to them — from one convenient Web page.

▶ Preferences   page 253
Your AOL software comes with a built-in control panel for setting your preferences. You can use your AOL preferences to change the look and feel of your AOL interface. To access your preferences, choose Settings⇨Preferences from the AOL toolbar.

Chapter 12
AOL Anywhere and Preference Settings

IN THIS CHAPTER

Creating a distinctive new screen name

Discovering how to create a secure password

Customizing your AOL experience with AOL Anywhere

Setting your AOL preferences to your taste

Preferences are your ticket to a customized AOL experience. You can personalize screen names and customize your e-mail, chat rooms, downloads, Filing Cabinet, the AOL toolbar, and your Buddy List. The privacy-minded can protect themselves and their families with features such as Parental Controls and privacy preferences. And, of course, there's the ever popular "much, much more!"

Screen Names and Passwords

Your AOL account can hold up to seven different screen names for yourself and/or other members of your family. Every screen name on an account comes with its own rights and privileges. Each screen name has its own Buddy List, Filing Cabinet, online mailbox, member profile, News Profile,

Interest Profile, Stock Portfolios, e-mail signatures, Web home page, FTP storage, and My Calendar (we discuss many of these features later in this chapter).

Why so many screen names? In the online world, having the option to create multiple screen names affords you some real benefits. Different screen names allow you to separate business activities from pleasure. You can also have one screen name for family and friends to use and one for the personality you present in a favorite chat room. If you join an e-mail discussion group (or two), a different name helps you separate all the discussion group e-mails from the rest of your correspondence.

The most important benefit of those seven names, though, is that each member of your family can have his or her own name (unless your family is the size of the Brady Bunch). Multiple screen names is more than just convenience, because your family can save the expense of having to purchase additional AOL accounts for various family members. Additionally, AOL's Parental Controls allows you to tailor your family's access to AOL's many features on a name-by-name basis. Thanks to Parental Controls, AOL knows exactly what your children are allowed to do and see online.

For all these reasons (and especially the last), it's important that every family member with access to AOL has his or her own screen name, and parents should be sure that junior members of the family have access only to their own screen names. Each screen name requires a separate password, each password should be unique, and those passwords should all be carefully safeguarded.

Caution

If someone other than you has your password, that person can pose as you, and you will be held responsible for his or her actions. This is an especially important point for parents, because your kids could assume your identity and change the Parental Controls on their own screen names. Children should also know to carefully safeguard their own passwords. If one of their "friends" uses that password to borrow your child's identity and violates AOL's rules, AOL can cancel your AOL membership, and the whole family is out of luck.

Choosing Screen Names

Think about this for a second: AOL may have 24 million members by now, and each of those members can have seven screen names. That's 168 million possible screen names on AOL! Consider that every one of those screen names has to be unique, and the task of coming up with a new and unique screen name becomes absolutely mind-boggling. After all, there are probably tens of thousands of John Smiths in the United States, but there can be only one John Smith on AOL.

Note

If you're hoping for a screen name with only your first name, don't get your hopes up. Can you imagine the odds against becoming the only *Jennifer* on AOL? Suffice it to say, for common names like that, you can be sure someone else got there first!

Caution

You may be tempted to try a few tricks if your first screen name choice isn't possible, but we don't recommend them. For example, you can use a zero in place of the letter *O*, or a one in place of the letter *l*. The problem with this idea is people will misread your name and send e-mail to the wrong person. Somewhat safer are intentional misspellings, like *Dayve* instead of *Dave*. Still, people will forget the misspelled version and send their e-mail to Dave anyway.

Devising an absolutely unique screen name can be quite a creative challenge. And finding out that someone else has already used the wonderfully imaginative name you cooked up can be the height of frustration. It always pays to have one or two names in reserve, just in case your first choice has been taken.

Here are some important facts to keep in mind when choosing a screen name:

- All screen names can contain up to 16 characters (including spaces).
- All screen names must begin with a letter, rather than a number. (AOL automatically capitalizes the first letter in the name.)
- Screen names can be any combination of numbers and letters, but you can't use punctuation marks and symbols such as the ampersand (&).
- Screen names can contain any combination of upper- and lowercase letters, and AOL will always display your name the way you first typed it. However, screen names are not case sensitive or space sensitive. There's only one John Doe, so whether your friends address their e-mail to `John Doe` or `johndoe`, it will still arrive at your doorstep.
- Screen names are the property of AOL and are only yours to use as long as you continue to be a member.
- Some screen names cannot be created. Certain terms such as `HOST` are reserved for AOL staff. Vulgar terms and terms that could be used in a fraudulent manner may also be recognized and rejected if you use them when you try to create the name.
- You cannot pose as someone else. This goes for AOL staff identities, celebrity names, government officials, private individuals, and company names and trademarks that do not belong to you.
- Screen names cannot contain sexually explicit, vulgar, suggestive, or racially or ethnically offensive language. They also can't include telephone numbers, include or promote a Web site, include individually identifiable information about a minor (such as a full name, home address, Social Security number, telephone number, or name of the child's school), or advertise products or services.

Choosing Passwords

Passwords are the key to your account, so make sure that your key is difficult to copy or guess. Longer passwords are more difficult to guess than shorter ones. Passwords should not contain easy-to-guess information about you or your family members (don't use the name of the family dog, for instance). Totally random passwords containing a combination of letters and numbers are much more secure, but much harder to remember.

You'll probably want to write down your password in case you forget it. If you do, be sure it's in a secure place. People have a way of losing their daily planners, and if you write the password on a sticky note and put it on your computer monitor or hide it under your keyboard, you may as well not use a password at all.

Creating, Deleting, and Restoring Screen Names

To create an additional screen name on your account, follow these directions:

1. Sign on to AOL using a master screen name (such as the original name created when you joined AOL).
2. Choose Settings⇨Screen Names from the AOL toolbar. (Alternatively, you can use AOL Keyword: **Screen Names**.) The AOL Screen Names window, shown in Figure 12-1, displays all the screen names on your account.

Consider choosing the initials of an easy-to-remember phrase for your password, such as "Four score and seven years ago . . ." (FSASYA) and intersperse it with numbers, such as F4SAS7YA. We don't recommend this particular example, though, because the phrase is much too well known, and the numbers are direct substitutes for the words in the phrase. (Besides, you should never use passwords you've seen in examples.) Choose a line from a favorite poem or song, and make sure the numbers are unrelated to the phrase.

If you do forget a password, call AOL Member Services at 888-265-8004. After you properly identify yourself as the account holder (have your contact and billing information handy), AOL gives you a new temporary password. Be sure to change the temporary password as soon as you sign back on to AOL.

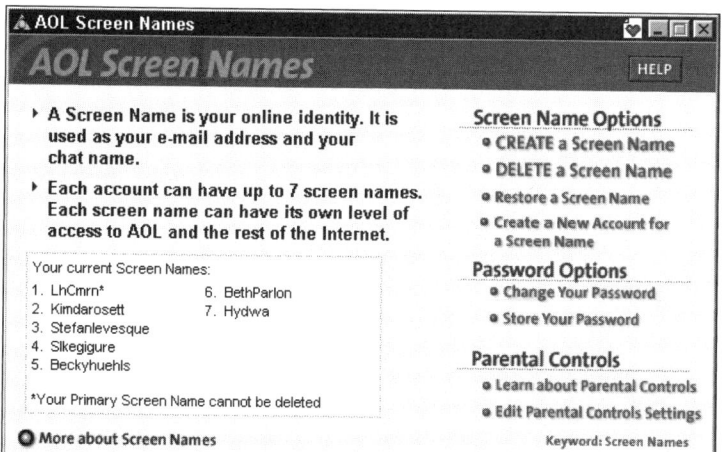

Figure 12-1. The AOL Screen Names window is screen name central.

The AOL Screen Names window lets you create, delete, or restore a deleted screen name, change and store passwords, and access Parental Controls. It pays to review all the information provided in this window.

3. Click the Create a Screen Name link. A small window appears, asking if you are creating this screen name for a child — respond appropriately.

4. Review the instructions presented and then click the Create Screen Name button. The Choose a Screen Name window appears, as shown in Figure 12-2.

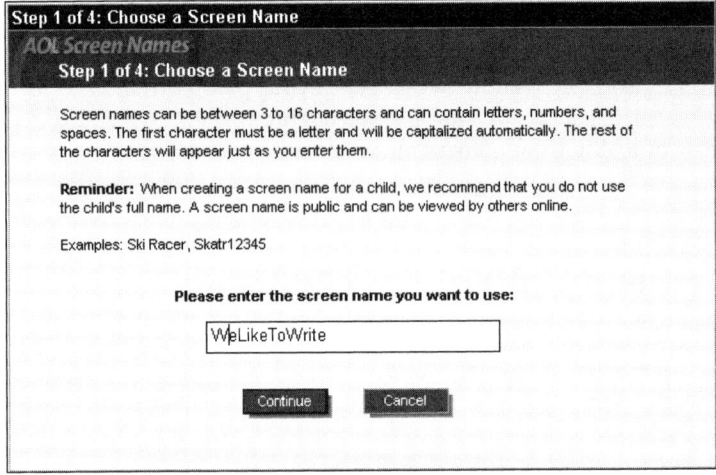

Figure 12-2. Type in your first choice for a screen name.

If your screen name choice is already active or has been used sometime in the recent past, you're advised to try a different name. If the next name you try has also been used, AOL recommends a name that will work (although it probably won't be very appealing to you). You can keep trying until you succeed, though.

5. Type in the screen name you want to use in the screen name field and click the Continue button. AOL then checks its records, and if the name you want is available, the Choose a Password window appears, as shown in Figure 12-3.

6. After you have an acceptable screen name, enter a password in the first password field and then verify the password by reentering it in the second password field. After you type in your password and click Continue, the Select a Parental Controls Setting window appears, as shown in Figure 12-4.

7. Choose a parental control setting for the new screen name. You have four choices: General Access (18+), Mature Teen (16-17), Young Teen (13-15), or Kids Only (12 and under). After making your selection, click the Continue button.

8. You now have the option to customize the Parental Controls settings. For now, you'll probably want to pass on this option.

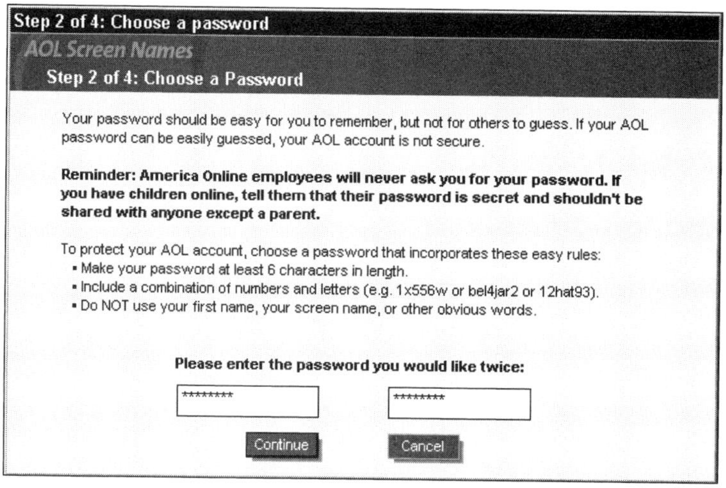

Chapter 12 ▲ AOL Anywhere and Preference Settings

Figure 12-3. Type your sufficiently complicated and hard-to-guess password twice.

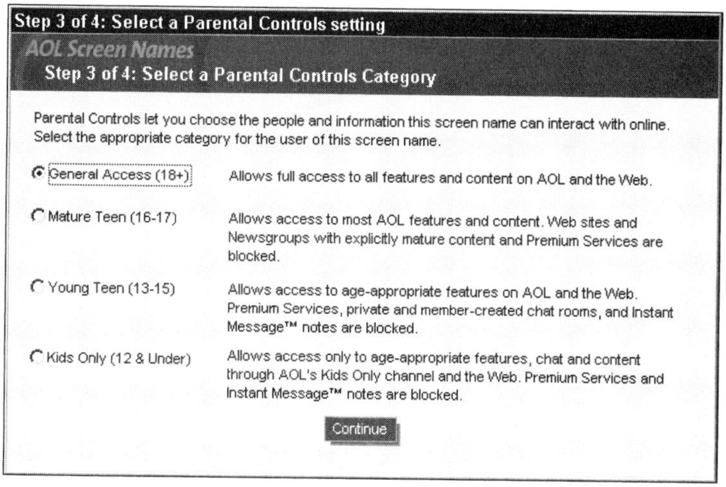

> **Tip**
>
> If you assigned Parental Controls to the screen name, sign off AOL and exit the AOL software to be sure that the Parental Controls are properly established. The next time you sign on to AOL, click the arrow button to the right of the Select Screen Name box, and you'll see the new name in the drop-down list.

Figure 12-4. Choose the appropriate access level for your new screen name.

9. Click the Accept Settings button. The new screen name is ready to use. AOL displays it in the AOL Screen Names window (refer to Figure 12-1).

What happens when you tire of a screen name, or you've used all seven available names and want to create a new one? You can delete any screen name on your account with the exception of the name created when you established your account. Just sign on with a master screen name, choose Settings⇨ Screen Names from the AOL toolbar, and click the Delete a Screen Name link in the AOL Screen Names window.

If you delete a screen name by accident (or on purpose), you have a six-month grace period during which you can restore the old name (provided your account has room for another screen name). All you have to do is return to the Screen Names area and click the Restore a Screen Name link.

Changing Passwords

To change a password — and we recommend you do change yours periodically — follow these directions:

1. Sign on to AOL.
2. Choose Settings➪Passwords from the AOL toolbar. (Alternatively, you can use AOL Keyword: **Password**.)
3. Read AOL's brief advice about choosing passwords and click the Change Password button.
4. In the Change Your Password window, shown in Figure 12-5, type your current password, press the Tab key, type your new password, press the Tab key again, and type your new password again.
5. Click the Change Password button, and your new password goes into effect immediately.

Each character you type appears as an asterisk on-screen to protect your password from anyone who may be looking over your shoulder.

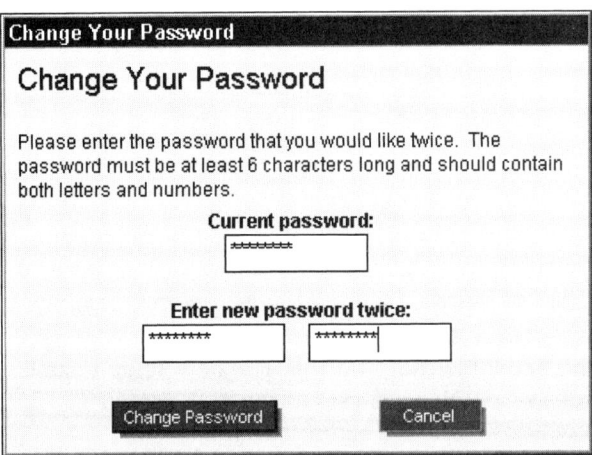

Figure 12-5. Changing a password requires knowing the old password.

AOL Anywhere

Ever wish you had your own personal staff of news writers and editors working around the clock to put out a newspaper designed especially for you? With the new AOL Anywhere service provided as part of AOL 6.0, such a dream can finally become reality. A simple click on the AOL Anywhere button on the main toolbar displays the fully customizable AOL Anywhere Web page, shown in Figure 12-6.

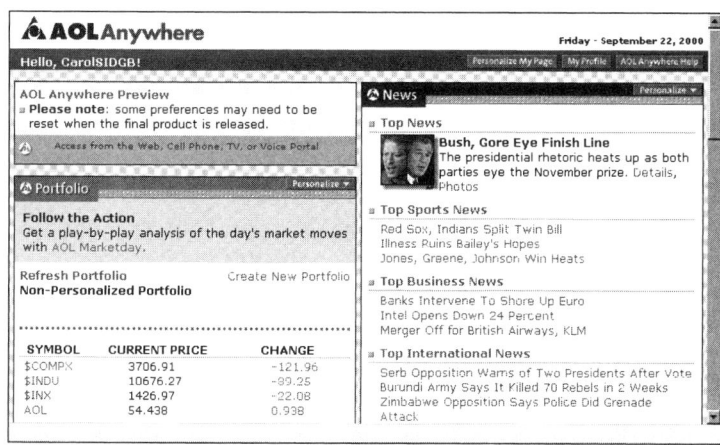

Figure 12-6. The AOL Anywhere Web page gives you a daily dose of the news that's important to you.

For the most part, the major content areas of the AOL Anywhere service mirror the kinds of information you would see in a big city newspaper. The following list gives the details on the kinds of features that appear when you first open the AOL Anywhere Web page:

- ▶ **Headline news from top news services:** Get the scoop on up-to-the-minute business, entertainment, sporting, and world news — all based on what interests *you*. You can choose from many categories to create your own online newspaper with stories from the Associated Press, Reuters, and Bloomberg Business News.

- ▶ **Weather forecasts from more cities than any other source:** Whether you're looking for an extended local forecast or want to know what the weather is like in another city, AOL Anywhere has you covered. With the

Tip

Use the My Profile button in the top right of the AOL Anywhere page to provide information (such as birth date and Zip code) to have your local weather forecast, horoscope, and movie schedule automatically generated for you.

Web's most extensive weather database, AOL Anywhere offers forecasts for over 34,000 cities around the world.

▶ **Calendar:** Proving that the AOL service can offer features that even the most prestigious big city papers can't, AOL Anywhere automatically displays any of the day-to-day appointments you may have set using up using AOL's My Calendar. AOL Members can check their day's schedule at a glance or even add new events to the My Calendar feature directly from their personalized AOL Anywhere page. (For more on the regular My Calendar feature, see Chapter 13).

▶ **Horoscopes:** AOL Anywhere greatly enhances the customization capabilities of this popular feature. Members can now see their personalized daily horoscopes every time they open AOL Anywhere.

▶ **Stocks:** The My Portfolio feature offered by the Personal Finance Channel is now accessible from AOL Anywhere. Members can view constantly updated information on the stocks in their portfolio by visiting their personalized AOL Anywhere page.

▶ **Sports:** Customized sports scoreboards are continually updated throughout the day and displayed on the AOL Anywhere home page.

▶ **The Lighter Side:** What would a newspaper be without a daily crossword puzzle, advice from Ann Landers, or the most popular comic strips? AOL Anywhere not only offers these features, but also throws in links to the Game Parlor, Game Shows, and Xtreme Games areas of the Games Channel.

The features offered on your start-up AOL Anywhere Web page are certainly impressive, but that's no reason to stay with the original lineup. You can customize your page by adding, deleting, or rearranging sections at any time. Here are some tips for customizing your page:

If you add AOL Search to your AOL Anywhere page, you can conduct AOL searches anytime, anyplace.

▶ To add to your page, scroll to the bottom to find the Add Content to the Left Side and Add Content to the Right Side pull-down menus. Select a content area from the Left Side and/or Right Side menu(s) and click the Add button to place the new content area on your page. You have the choice to add TV listings, local traffic reports, AOL Search, a recipe finder, product reviews from the Computing Channel, and much more.

- To delete a content area from your page, click the Personalize My Page button at the top right of the AOL Anywhere page. In the dialog box that appears, deselect the check boxes next to areas you want to delete and then click the Save button. *Note:* You can use the Personalize My Page dialog box to add sections to your page, but any sections you add using the Personalize My Page button are automatically placed on the left side of your page.

- To move a content section from one place to another, click the long gray box just below the section's Personalize button and drag the section to another location on the page. When you see the words "Reposition Here" on your screen, you can drop the window by releasing the mouse button.

- To customize the information *within* a particular section, click the section's Personalize button. If content can be personalized, select Customize and follow the on-screen directions.

With all the customized information available on your AOL Anywhere page, it would be a shame if you could only access such information from your home computer with your AOL software. Luckily for you, the "Anywhere" in the title of AOL Anywhere is meant to be taken literally. If you are on the road and don't have access to your home computer, you can access your AOL Anywhere page with the help of a Web browser from any available Internet connection. Just point your browser to my.aol.com.

Chapter 24 shows you how to use your wireless phone service to access the many features of AOL Anywhere.

AOL Preferences

You can access most AOL software preferences by choosing Settings⇨Preferences from the AOL toolbar. Doing so opens the Preferences window, shown in Figure 12-7. The following sections detail the kinds of preferences you can set.

Whenever suitable, we note the *default* settings, which are the settings that are standard when AOL comes "out of the box" for a new account. If you have upgraded to AOL 6.0 from an earlier version of AOL software, your previous preference settings have been copied, for your convenience.

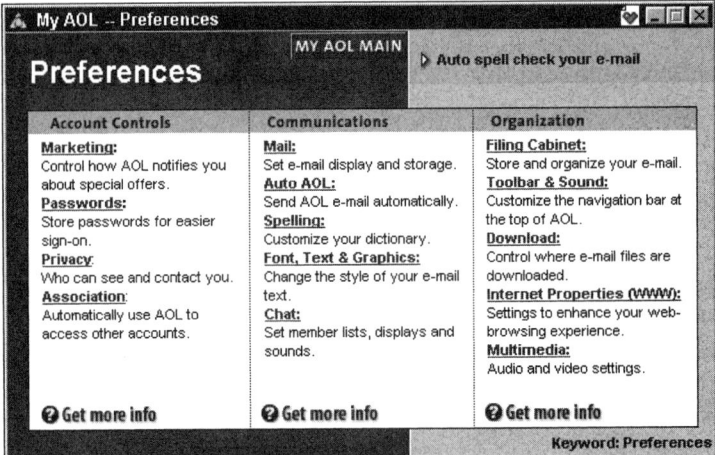

Figure 12-7. Your preferences are always within reach in the Settings menu on the AOL toolbar.

Marketing

AOL is the world's largest online shopping destination and uses many different methods to reach its membership with product and service offers. AOL doesn't want to alienate you with undesired offers or make you feel like your privacy has been breached, so it offers marketing preferences to give you a choice in these matters. To open the Marketing Preferences window, shown in Figure 12-8, click the Marketing link in the Preferences window. You must be signed on to AOL to set your marketing preferences.

Here's a listing of the different marketing preferences:

- **U.S. Mail from Other Organizations:** AOL sells its mailing list (but not your screen name) to other companies. Here's your chance to get off the mailing list. (Default: Yes)
- **U.S. Mail from AOL:** AOL also sells products and services to its members via U.S. Mail. You can opt out of this mailing list, too. (Default: Yes)
- **Telephone:** AOL offers products and services to its members via the telephone, too. This option does not affect calls that AOL may make that are related to the status of your AOL account. (Default: Yes)

- ▶ **E-Mail:** AOL sends a confirmation e-mail when someone has made a purchase and includes additional product offers in that e-mail. Use this option to let AOL know whether you want this e-mail. (Default: Yes)
- ▶ **Pop-Up:** These product-offer windows may appear when you first sign on to AOL or at other times during your online session. AOL promotes special offers on products and services that will help members get the most out of their computing experience. These offers are not made to Kids Only, Young Teen, or Mature Teen screen names. (Default: Yes)
- ▶ **Additional Information:** AOL also provides information on how to get off other companies' mailing lists and provides a link to Interest Profiles, which give you the option to receive e-mail about areas and activities on AOL that match your personal choices.

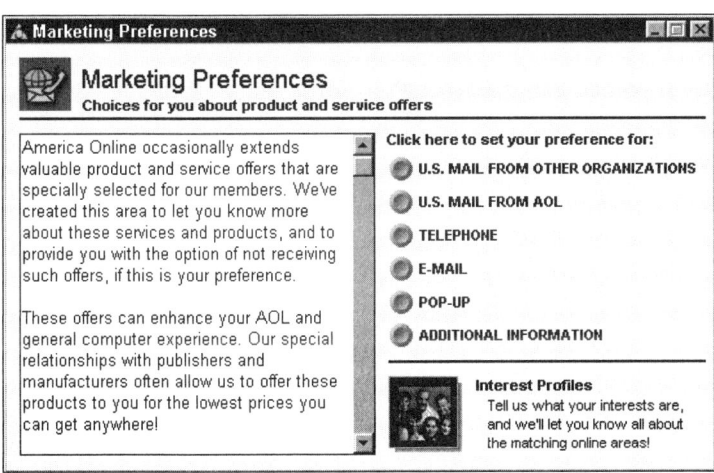

Figure 12-8. Protect your personal information with these marketing preference settings.

Passwords

The Password settings let you store your password. This means you can, in effect, bypass your password when you sign on to AOL. This preference also lets you add a password to your Filing Cabinet so that it's more secure. It's unlikely that you'll use both of these options at the same time, because one reduces security and the other enhances it. You can change these settings only when you're signed on to AOL, and they're available only for the screen name you're currently using, which is listed in the lower-left corner of the Store Passwords window, shown in Figure 12-9.

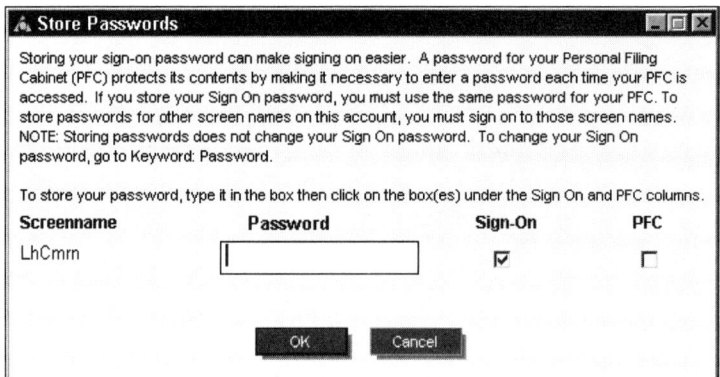

Figure 12-9. Use password preferences to store your passwords for sign-on and your Filing Cabinet with caution.

When you access the Store Passwords window, this is what you see:

- ▶ **Password field:** If you plan to use the Sign-On option, enter the password you use to sign on to AOL in this field. If you plan to use only the PFC option, you can use any password you please. (Default: blank)
- ▶ **Sign-On check box:** Selecting this check box stores your password on your computer and thus eliminates the need for you to enter your password before you sign on to AOL. This reduces the security of your account, because anyone with access to your computer can use your account and screen name. (Default: Off)
- ▶ **PFC check box:** Selecting this check box adds password protection to your Filing Cabinet (PFC). If this option is deselected, anyone with access to your computer and AOL software can access the contents of your Filing Cabinet. When this option is selected, your Filing Cabinet cannot be accessed without entering the password, regardless of whether you're signed on. (Default: Off)

Privacy

Privacy preferences relate to Buddy Lists and instant messages. You can access privacy preferences in either the Buddy List

Setup window or the Buddy List Preferences window, shown in Figure 12-10. For privacy preferences, you first have to choose the kind of preferences you want and then apply those features either to just your Buddy List or to both the Buddy List and instant messages. The following lists explain the options for choosing and applying preferences.

> **Cross-Reference**
>
> See Chapter 7 for a discussion of instant message–related privacy preferences, and Chapter 8 for discussion of Buddy List–related privacy preferences.

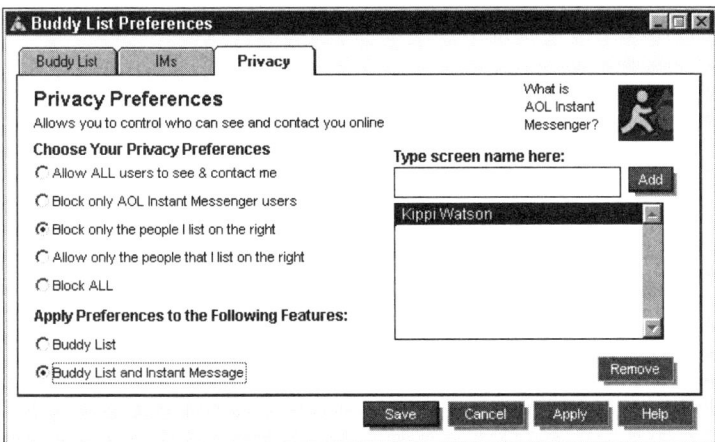

Figure 12-10. Privacy preferences let you designate who can and cannot see you in Buddy Lists and instant messages.

When choosing privacy preferences, select one of the following options:

- **Allow All Users to See & Contact Me:** Anyone on AOL (or using AOL Instant Messenger via the Internet) can view you on his or her Buddy List and send you an instant message. (This is the default.)
- **Block Only AOL Instant Messenger Users:** AOL members have full Buddy List and/or instant message access, but instant messenger users (Internet users) do not.
- **Block Only the People I List on the Right:** Create a list of the people you never want to hear from, and/or banish yourself from their Buddy Lists. Anyone else can still access you.
- **Allow Only the People That I List on the Right:** This option provides a high level of personal privacy, because only those screen names you place on your list can send you instant messages and/or see you on their Buddy Lists.

- **Block All:** This is the maximum privacy setting. Nobody can see you on his or her Buddy List, and/or nobody can send you an instant message.

After choosing a privacy preferences option, select one of these options to apply it:

- **Buddy List:** People you've blocked can't see you on their Buddy Lists, but they can still send you instant messages.
- **Buddy List and Instant Message:** You won't be seen on Buddy Lists or receive instant messages from those names you've blocked.

If you choose to block or allow only certain people, you need to add those people's screen names or Internet addresses to the list on the right side of the window. To add a name, type it into the box in the top-right corner of the window and then click Add — the name appears in the list below once added. If you select the Block Only Those People option, any addresses in your list are blocked. If you select the Allow Only Those People option, all addresses except those in your list are blocked.

Association

The Windows desktop can have icons for browsing the Web, sending e-mail, and reading newsgroups. When you click one of the icons, the application *associated* with that icon immediately opens. Because Windows is a Microsoft product, the default applications associated with these icons are also Microsoft products (Internet Explorer, for example). The association settings in AOL allow you to designate AOL as the application you want to use when you click those icons on the Windows desktop, or when you click an e-mail link or Web link in programs that take advantage of this feature.

Mail

Mail preferences provide greater control over mail you read, send, and save in your Filing Cabinet. In the Mail Preferences window, shown in Figure 12-11, the preferences are divided into three categories: Reading Mail, Sending Mail, and Writing Mail.

You can also access some association settings from the Windows Control Panel: Choose Start➪Settings➪Control Panel from the Windows Start menu. After the Control Panel window opens, double-click the Internet Options icon and click the Programs tab. Select the default E-Mail and Newsgroups applications by using the drop-down lists for each of those two functions. If you connect to AOL via an Internet service provider or local area network, you may prefer to retain other programs as your defaults, such as the Netscape Navigator browser or the Microsoft Outlook e-mail reader, and open AOL only when you need it.

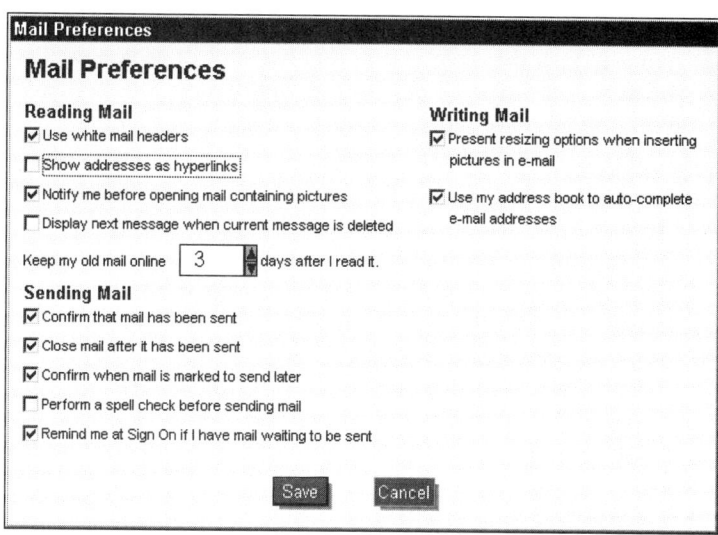

Figure 12-11. Get control of your e-mail by setting your mail preferences.

Here are the Reading Mail options:

- **Use White Mail Headers:** If you change the page background color (see the "Fonts, Text, and Graphics" section, later in this chapter), this option makes sure that the address information on the e-mail you send is still legible, because you can't change the color of e-mail headers to contrast with the background color. If the page background color contrasts well with black text, the e-mail may look better with this option turned off. (Default: On)

- **Show Addresses As Hyperlinks:** E-mail addresses in the e-mail header (not the body of the message) are displayed as hyperlinks. Click a hyperlink to open a preaddressed Write Mail window with the same subject as the original message. (Default: Off)

- **Notify Me Before Opening Mail Containing Pictures:** Embedded photos and images in e-mail are convenient, but they can be offensive if sent by the wrong person. AOL notifies you before you view such images in the event you want to decline doing so. (Default: On)

- **Display Next Message When Current Message Is Deleted:** When this option is selected, you save some steps (and time), because the next e-mail in your online mailbox or Filing Cabinet opens automatically when you delete a message. If you receive a lot of junk e-mail, however, you may prefer to deselect this option so that you don't accidentally add more junk to your Filing Cabinet. (Default: Off)

▶ **Keep My Old Mail Online <*number*> Days After I Read It:** AOL automatically deletes your e-mail three to seven days after you first read it. If you receive a lot of e-mail, you may want to set this preference for fewer than seven days, but most people prefer the full seven days. To change the number of days, type a number between three and seven in the box or use the up and down arrows to increase or decrease the number. You must be online to adjust this setting. (Default: 3 days)

The Sending Mail options are as follows:

▶ **Confirm That Mail Has Been Sent:** The confirmation message is a reassuring reminder that your e-mail was sent successfully. On the other hand, the OK button, which pops up to tell you that your e-mail was sent, is one more button to click when you're in a hurry; deselect this option if you find it annoying. (Default: On)

▶ **Close Mail After It Has Been Sent:** This feature reduces screen clutter and helps confirm that your e-mail has been sent successfully. Some people may prefer to keep the e-mail window open so they can modify the text, change the address, and send e-mail to other people. (Default: On)

▶ **Confirm When Mail Is Marked to Send Later:** This is another reassuring reminder, especially if you accidentally click the Send Later button, rather than the Send Now button. If you use Send Later frequently, this reminder may not be necessary. (Default: On)

▶ **Perform a Spell Check before Sending Mail:** Spell-checking your e-mail can prevent embarrassment. If you select this option, clicking the Send button in an e-mail window automatically initiates a spell check. When you're in a rush (or if you're an excellent speller), this feature may be annoying, because you can't send the e-mail until the spell check has been completed. Keep in mind that the Write Mail window contains a spell check button for when you need it. (Default: Off)

▶ **Remind Me at Sign On If I Have Mail Waiting to Be Sent:** AOL prompts you when you sign on to send your waiting mail, if you want. This feature can be helpful, depending on how often you queue mail for later transmittal. (Default: On)

Here are the Writing Mail options:

▶ **Present Resizing Options When Inserting Pictures in E-Mail:** When you insert a large graphic into your e-mail, AOL offers to resize (shrink) it to fit the e-mail. This is generally a good idea, because it reduces the time needed to send and receive the e-mail, but it can also degrade the image quality. Deselect this feature to bypass the option window and always insert graphics at full size. (Default: On)

▶ **Use My Address Book to Auto-Complete E-Mail Addresses:** A new feature in AOL 6.0 is auto-completion, which means AOL recognizes e-mail addresses from your Address Book when typing e-mail. This feature is usually quite helpful, but it can be annoying if you use similar e-mail addresses. (Default: On)

Automatic AOL

Automatic AOL can send and retrieve your e-mail, file downloads, and message board postings while you're asleep or even out of the country. The Automatic AOL window, shown in Figure 12-12, contains the following options:

To learn more about Auto AOL, see Chapter 10.

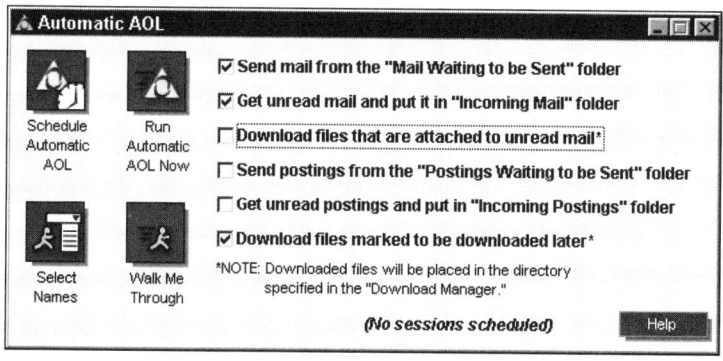

Figure 12-12. Choose the items you want Automatic AOL to perform when it is enabled.

See Chapter 5 to learn more about downloading files from e-mail.

See Chapter 9 for more details on message boards and Internet newsgroups.

See Chapter 10 for more details on downloading files.

- **Send Mail from the Mail Waiting to Be Sent Folder:** Sends e-mail you wrote offline or specified to be sent later when you were online. (Default: Off)
- **Get Unread Mail and Put It in Incoming Mail Folder:** Retrieves unread e-mail from your online mailbox and saves it in your Filing Cabinet (Default: Off)
- **Download Files That Are Attached to Unread Mail:** Automatically downloads files attached to e-mail. The Get Unread Mail preference must be selected for this option to be available. This is a security risk, because you may receive attached files from strangers that contain viruses or Trojan horses. If you prefer, deselect this option and download only the files you want by accessing the Old Mail folder in your online mailbox. (Default: Off)
- **Send Postings from the Postings Waiting to Be Sent Folder:** For those message boards and Internet newsgroups that you designated to be read offline, you can also reply to and/or compose new postings offline, via your Filing Cabinet, and send them later, using Automatic AOL. (Default: Off)
- **Get Unread Postings and Put in Incoming Postings Folder:** Retrieves unread message board and Internet newsgroup postings for those boards and newsgroups you designated to be read offline. Postings are stored in your Filing Cabinet. (Default: Off)
- **Download Files Marked to Be Downloaded Later:** Downloads all files (whether attached to e-mail or in AOL file libraries) that have been designated to be downloaded later. (You can find a list of these files in your Download Manager.) (Default: Off)

Additional buttons along the left side of the window offer these options:

- **Schedule Automatic AOL:** Select the day(s) of the week, the starting time, and how often an Automatic AOL session will take place. The Enable Scheduler option must be selected in order for the scheduled session(s) to take place. (Default: Off)
- **Run Automatic AOL Now:** Click this button to run a session for the current screen name, regardless of whether you're currently signed on.

- **Select Names:** Select the screen name(s) to be included in the Automatic AOL session and enter the passwords for each of those screen names. When the session is run (either by using Schedule Automatic AOL or Run Automatic AOL Now), AOL performs all activities that have been set in preferences for each selected screen name. (Default: Off, no passwords)
- **Walk Me Through:** This feature explains the Automatic AOL preferences and options and sets them based on your responses.

Spelling

The AOL spell checker can fix common grammar, punctuation, and typing errors. Spelling preference settings give you control over which rules will and will not be enforced and gives you access to a personal spelling dictionary. The Spelling Preferences dialog box, shown in Figure 12-13, lists the following options:

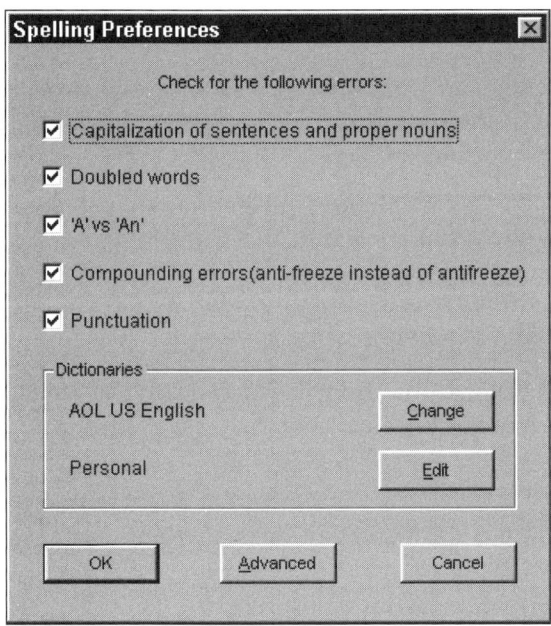

Figure 12-13. Fine-tune your spell checker in the Spelling Preferences dialog box.

- **Check for the Following Errors:** Specify whether you want the spell checker to check the capitalization of sentences and proper nouns, doubled words, *a* versus *an,* compounding errors (for example, anti-freeze instead of antifreeze), and punctuation. (Default: All On)

▶ **Dictionaries (AOL US English and Personal):** The Change button permits a switch to a different language dictionary, which must be supplied by AOL. The software supplied to AOL International services, such as AOL Canada, may come equipped with multiple dictionaries. The Edit button allows you to add to or modify the personal dictionary that is created when you click the Learn button during a spell check.

▶ **Advanced:** Click this button to bring up the Advanced Spelling Preferences window, which offers a list of over a dozen kinds of grammatical and formatting errors corrected by the spell checker. Click a rule in the list to view a full description of that rule. You can disable a rule by selecting the Current Status On radio button while that rule is highlighted. (Default: All On)

Font, Text, and Graphics

You can make all your e-mail, chat, and instant messages distinctive by changing your font preference settings. AOL provides sample text in the Font, Text, and Graphics window so you can see how new font and style settings will look.

In the Font, Text & Graphic Preferences window, shown in Figure 12-14, the formatting toolbar includes the following menus and buttons (from left to right). (If you allow your mouse pointer to hover over a button, a *bubble help* window containing the button's function name appears.)

▶ **Font name:** Select a font from the drop-down font list. (Default: Arial)

▶ **Text size:** Select a text size from the drop-down list. (Default: 10)

▶ **Text color:** Click this button and select a color from the palette. (Default: black)

▶ **Text background color:** Click this button and select a color. (Default: clear)

▶ **Page background color:** Click this button and select a color for the entire page. (Default: white)

▶ **Text attributes:** Select any combination of **bold,** *italic,* and underline. (Default: none)

Note

The font, text, and graphics settings apply to every e-mail, chat, and instant message used on your account, regardless of screen name, so there's room for family disagreements. Also note that the fonts you use must also be installed on the computers of those who receive your e-mail and chats; otherwise, the recipients will see a common, generic font, rather than the fancy one you selected.

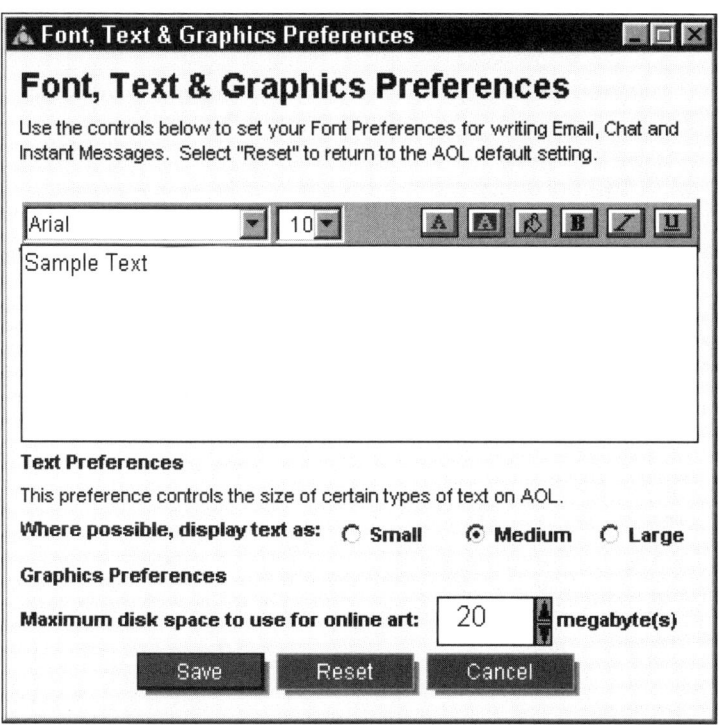

Figure 12-14. Spice up your e-mail, chats, and instant messages by setting your font preference settings.

The options at the bottom of the window control the text size and the amount of hard drive space allotted to online art:

- **Where Possible, Display Text As: Small, Medium, Large:** This setting does not affect all text in all AOL windows. *Large* may be easier to read but can cause the text for some labels and captions to be cut off or overflow the space. (Default: Medium)

- **Maximum Disk Space to Use for Online Art: <*number*> Megabyte(s):** AOL stores some of its artwork used on the service to your hard drive so you don't have to download it each time you visit an area. As you visit more and more areas on AOL, you accumulate more and more artwork on your hard drive. This setting limits the amount of space AOL can use so that it doesn't totally fill your hard drive. When you reach this limit, AOL stops storing new art, which can slow down your online experience. This setting allows your computer to reach a balance between speed and available hard drive space. (Default: 20MB)

Chat Preferences

Chat preferences affect features in AOL chat rooms, private rooms, conference rooms, and auditoriums. You can access these preferences by clicking the Preferences button in a chat room or by choosing Settings⇨Preferences and clicking the Chat link. The Chat Preferences window, shown in Figure 12-15, has the following options:

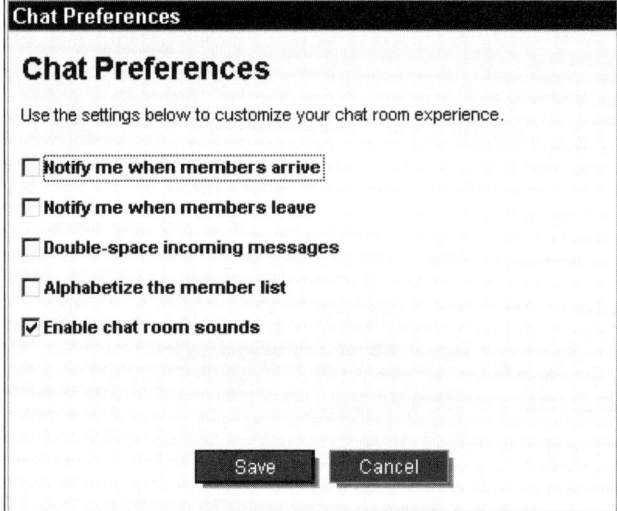

Figure 12-15. Enhance your chats with these chat preference settings.

- ▶ **Notify Me When Members Arrive:** The Online Host announces that a member has entered the chat room. (Default: Off)
- ▶ **Notify Me When Members Leave:** The Online Host announces that a member has left the chat room. (Default: Off)
- ▶ **Double-Space Incoming Messages:** This formatting may make it easier to read conversations in chat rooms. It also makes the chat conversation scroll twice as fast, so it may be difficult to follow conversations in a busy chat room. (Default: Off)
- ▶ **Alphabetize the Member List:** Normally, the member list in a chat room displays names in the order in which members entered the chat room. Alphabetizing this list makes it easier to find a specific member's name so that you can access information about that member or send him or her an Instant Message. (Default: Off)

▶ **Enable Chat Room Sounds:** People in chat rooms can play sounds so that others who have the same sound files installed on their hard drives can hear the sounds. Some people love this feature, but others are distracted or annoyed by it. (Default: On)

Filing Cabinet

Your Filing Cabinet (PFC) can take up a lot of hard drive space, so AOL provides settings in the Personal Filing Cabinet Preferences window that limit and manage the hard drive space occupied by your Filing Cabinet files. You'll also find a couple of settings in the same window that affect file deletions in your Filing Cabinet, Favorite Places, and online mailbox. The Personal Filing Cabinet Preferences window, shown in Figure 12-16, has the following options:

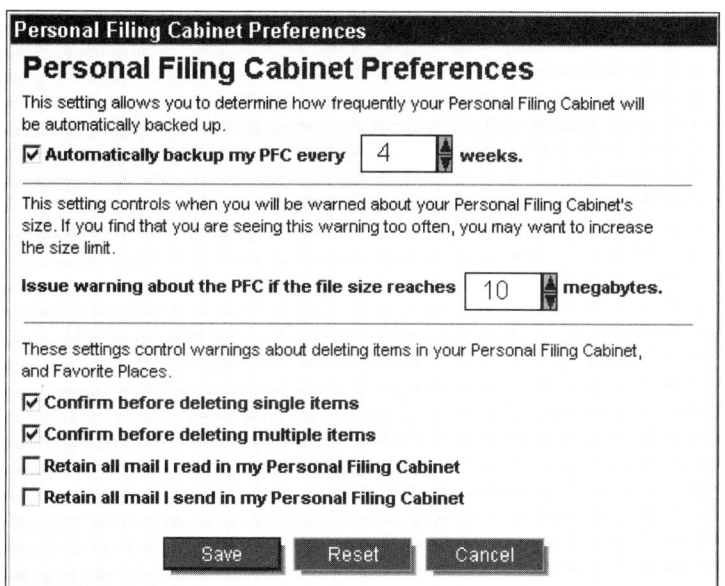

Figure 12-16. Configure your saved mail and postings in your Personal Filing Cabinet preferences.

▶ **Automatically Back Up My PFC Every <*number*> Weeks:** This setting provides a built-in safeguard for your important data in the Filing Cabinet. If you use the PFC, we recommend you keep this setting at four weeks or even more frequently. It can be a lifesaver if you find a crash has damaged your Filing Cabinet. (Default: Four weeks)

- ▶ **Issue Warning About the PFC If File Size Reaches <*number*> Megabytes:** This option helps limit the hard drive space occupied by your Filing Cabinet. When you reach the preset file size, you're advised to either delete items from your Filing Cabinet or increase the setting. (Default: 10MB)
- ▶ **Confirm Before Deleting Single Items:** To prevent accidents, you receive a warning before deleting an item from your Filing Cabinet, Favorite Places list, or online mailbox. Expert users may prefer to forgo the warning. (Default: On)
- ▶ **Confirm Before Deleting Multiple Items:** To prevent accidents, you receive a warning before deleting multiple items from your Filing Cabinet, Favorite Places list, or online mailbox. Expert users may prefer to forgo the warning. (Default: On)
- ▶ **Retain All Mail I Send in My Personal Filing Cabinet:** This option saves a copy of all sent e-mail on your hard drive, where you can refer to it long after it disappears from your Online Mailbox. We recommend selecting this option unless you have a shortage of hard drive space or a need for privacy. (Default: Off)
- ▶ **Retain All Mail I Read in My Personal Filing Cabinet:** This option saves a copy of all e-mail you read on your hard drive, where you can refer to it long after it disappears from your Online Mailbox. We recommend selecting this option unless you have a shortage of hard drive space or a need for privacy. (Default: Off)

Toolbar & Sound

You can customize the AOL toolbar to your needs with the help of the Toolbar Preferences window, shown in Figure 12-17. The options are as follows:

- ▶ **Toolbar Appearance:** The Icons and Text option is the normal appearance. The Text Only option removes the icon graphics to supply more space in the main AOL window. (Default: Icons and Text)
- ▶ **Location:** The Move to Top option places the AOL toolbar at the top of the window. The Move to Bottom option places the toolbar at the bottom of the screen,

the same place that most people have their Windows taskbar. (Default: Move to Top)

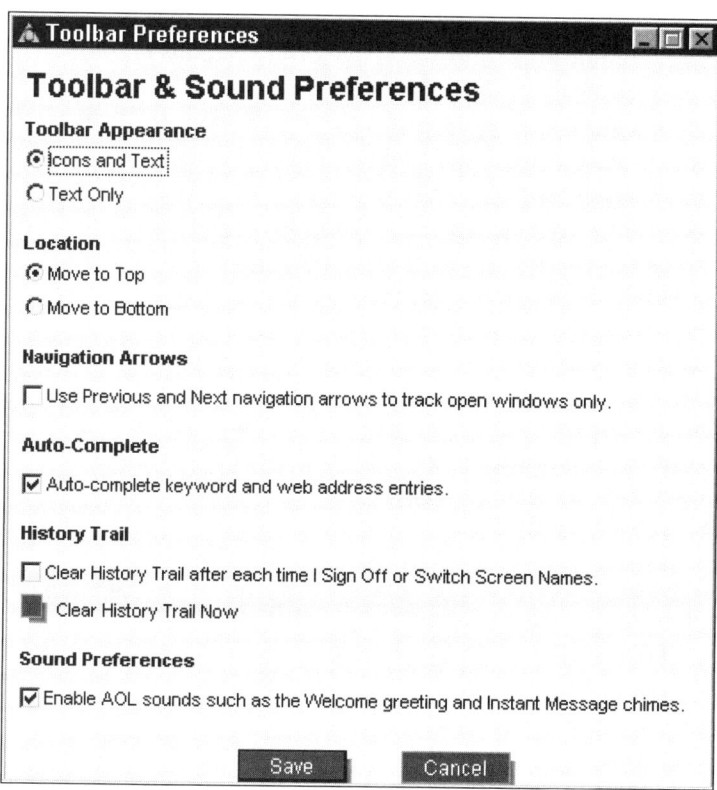

Figure 12-17. Change the appearance and functionality of your AOL toolbar with the toolbar preference settings.

- **Navigation Arrows (Use Previous and Next Navigation Arrows to Track Open Windows Only):** When you deselect this option, you can use the navigation arrows on the toolbar to reopen windows you've recently closed. When this preference is deselected, you can only step through windows that are still on-screen. (Default: Off)
- **History Trail:** The history trail normally remembers the online areas and Web pages you've visited so you can return again, even if you signed off in the interim. In this area, you have two options:

Tip

If you share your computer with other members of the family, you may prefer to have AOL erase the history trail every time someone signs off. On the other hand, because the history trail can record your children's online activities, some parents may prefer to leave the history trail on. You can have the best of both worlds (privacy for the parents and a history trail for the children). Leave the history trail on, but click the Clear History Now button whenever you want to erase your trail.

Cross-Reference

See Chapter 10 for more details on downloading files.

- **Clear History Trail After Each Time I Sign Off or Switch Screen Names:** With this option selected, the history trail is cleared each time you sign off or switch screen names, and the record of the online areas and Web pages you visited is erased. (Default: Off)
- **Clear History Trail Now:** This option manually clears the history trail whenever you feel it is appropriate. (Default: Off)
- **Enable AOL Sounds Such As the Welcome Greeting and Instant Message Chimes:** This setting sets the play of online event sounds. (Default: On)

Download

Download preferences affect files you download from AOL's file libraries and forums, and attached e-mail files. The Download Preferences window, shown in Figure 12-18, offers the following options:

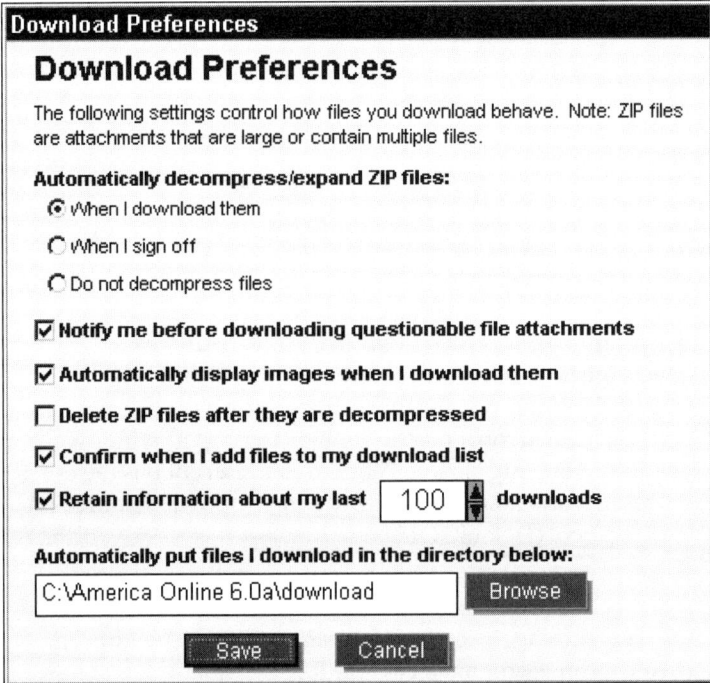

Figure 12-18. Control your file downloads with the download preference settings.

- **Automatically Decompress/Expand ZIP files:** Files compressed in ZIP format can be automatically decompressed when you download them, when you sign off from AOL, or not at all. Automatic decompression can save you a lot of time and trouble, but some folks prefer to decompress the files at a different time or with different software. (Default: When I Sign Off)

- **Notify Me Before Downloading Questionable File Attachments:** AOL takes your security seriously and will notify you before you download any file, because it may contain a virus or Trojan horse. If you don't need this warning, go ahead and deselect this option; otherwise, we recommend that you keep it on. (Default: On)

- **Automatically Display Images When I Download Them:** If you download a graphic in GIF, JPG, BMP, or ART format, AOL can start to display the image while it is downloading. The image won't be complete until the download is finished, but you can watch it emerge. If you prefer to view the image at a later time, deselect this preference. (Default: On)

- **Delete ZIP files after Decompression:** After a file has been decompressed, you have the original ZIP format and a new file (or files) in its original, uncompressed format. You may find it handy to keep the original ZIP file, either to share with friends or to use as a backup in case you have trouble with the uncompressed file(s). However, you can also waste a lot of hard drive space with old, unneeded ZIP files. If you prefer, have AOL delete the ZIP file as soon as it has finished automatically decompressing it. (Default: Off)

- **Confirm Additions to My Download List:** When you click the Download Later button, you get a message that confirms you've added the file to your Download Manager's download list. If you do a lot of downloading this way, you may prefer to save some time and bypass the message by deselecting this option. (Default: On)

- **Retain Information about My Last <*number*> Downloads:** This option controls whether your Download Manager keeps track of the files you've downloaded, and if so, how many of those downloads will be stored in your Download Manager. People interested in the privacy of their download information may prefer to deselect this feature. Active downloaders may

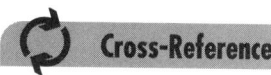

Cross-Reference

Learn more about the Download Manager in Chapter 10.

prefer to increase the number of downloads retained on their lists. (Default: On, 100 downloads)

▶ **Automatically Put Files I Download in the Directory Below:** By default, AOL places all downloaded files in a Download folder within the America Online software folder. If you prefer to download to another folder, such as the My Documents folder, click the Browse button to select the folder of your choice. (Default: `C:\America Online 6.0\download`)

Internet Options (Web Preferences)

Web preferences are a complex set of tools, just as your Web browser is a complex bit of software. These preferences affect your built-in AOL browser (Microsoft Internet Explorer). If you're using a separate browser (such as Netscape Navigator), you have to open your browser to find its preference settings.

Web preferences are divided into four sections: General, Security, Content, Web Graphics, and Shopping Assistant. Click the tabs at the top of the screen to switch among these sections.

General Web Preferences

Your General Web preferences is the first set of options you see when you access your Web preferences. Options include settings for your home page, temporary Internet files, history trail, colors, fonts, languages, and accessibility. The General tab of the AOL Internet Options dialog box, shown in Figure 12-19, includes the following options:

▶ **Home Page:** Determines which page opens when you open Microsoft Internet Explorer or when you click the home page icon in Microsoft Internet Explorer (this setting does not affect AOL 6.0). Type the URL of the page you find most useful. The Use Default button restores AOL.COM as your home page. (Default: www.aol.com, AOL's home page on the Web)

▶ **Temporary Internet Files:** Your browser automatically saves Web pages and other Web files on your hard drive. This means you can access these files again, offline, and it also speeds access of those pages if you revisit them online. This can use a lot of disk space and may hurt your computer's performance.

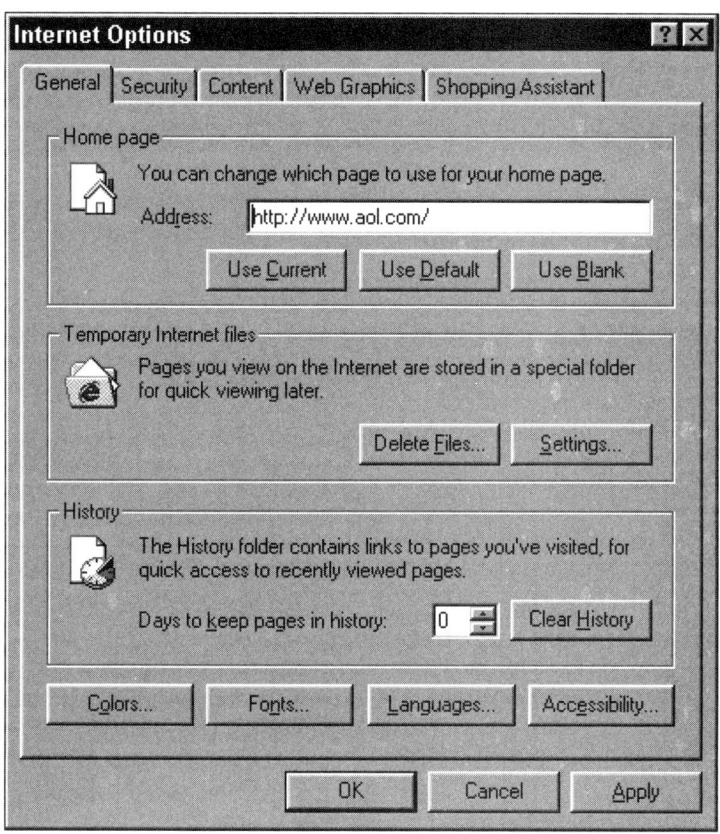

Figure 12-19. Web preference settings provide a wide range of control over your Web browser. Note the tabs at the top of the dialog box, which lead to entirely different sets of controls.

- **History:** Keeps track of your recent travels on the Web. This history trail is a separate function of the Microsoft Internet Explorer browser, unrelated to the history trail we mention in the "Toolbar & Sound" section. This History feature has no effect when you browse the Web from within AOL, but it is valid if you open Internet Explorer as a separate application, outside of AOL. The AOL history trail is permanently set to 25 items. You can set the number of days (0 to 99) you want to keep the pages. You can also click Clear History to clear your history trail at anytime.
- **Colors:** Affects the text and background color of your browser window and the color of hyperlinks displayed in the browser.

- **Fonts:** Enables you to select the fonts and alphabet you see if a Web page's designer doesn't specify a particular font. (Defaults: Language script — Latin based; Web page font — Times New Roman; Plain text font — Courier New)
- **Languages:** Some Web pages are available in more than one language. This preference determines your choices, if available, in order of priority. (Default: English–United States)
- **Accessibility:** If you have trouble reading a computer screen (for example, you have a visual impairment), you may want to override the Web page designer's font and color choices and create a standard style sheet of your own.

Security

The security preferences built into Microsoft Internet Explorer are independent of the Parental Controls that AOL provides. They can be used to restrict access not only to particular Web sites, but also to various features of Web pages that may be hazardous when used by less-than-scrupulous Web site operators who may be out to steal your password or credit card number. The Security tab of the AOL Internet Options dialog box, shown in Figure 12-20, includes the following options:

Many Web security settings fall beyond the scope of this book. *Your Official America Online Internet Guide* by David Peal discusses all the ins and outs of these options.

You can define security settings for each of four zones: Internet (all sites that have not been specified as either Restricted or Trusted), Local Intranet (most home users won't be connected to an intranet, which is a private computer network that functions like the Web), Restricted Sites, and Trusted Sites. Click the icon for a zone to access the settings for that zone.

- **Sites:** Click this button to create lists of sites that are either Trusted (less-restrictive security settings) or Restricted (highest security settings). This button is grayed-out for the Internet zone, because its settings apply to all sites not otherwise listed as Trusted or Restricted.
- **Security level for this zone:** Move the slider control to adjust the general level of security for Trusted Sites and Restricted Sites. We recommend the maximum settings for all zones until you feel more comfortable using the Web.

▶ **Custom level:** Access all the various security settings for the zone you're currently adjusting.

▶ **Default level:** Restore the factory settings if changes to settings have been made.

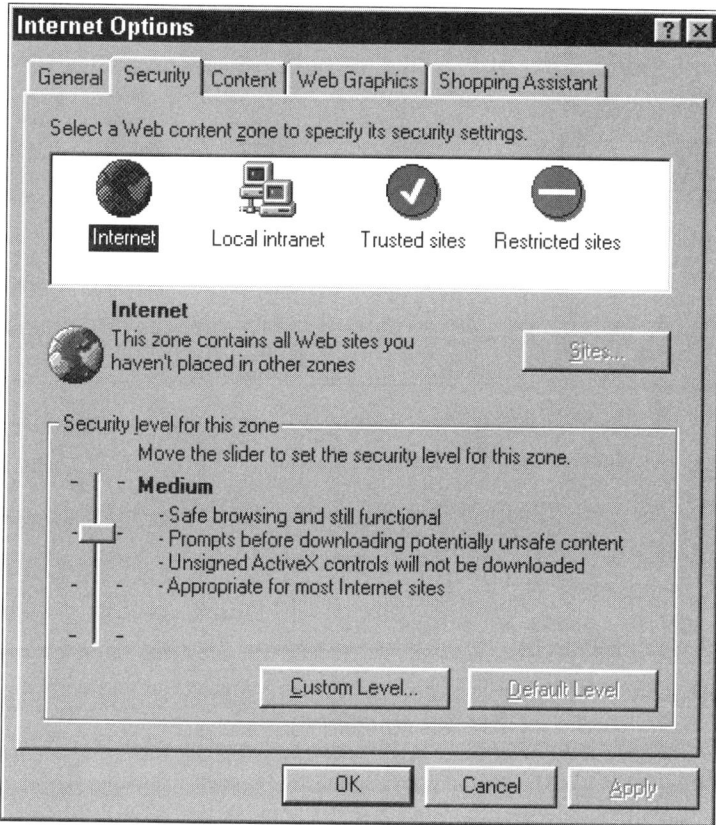

Figure 12-20. Your Web security preferences let you safeguard yourself, your family, and your computer.

Content

The name of this group of settings is a bit misleading, because AOL disabled the Content Advisor feature of Microsoft Internet Explorer in favor of its own Parental Controls. The remaining settings in this area relate more to security than the content of Web sites you can visit. The Content tab of the AOL Internet Options dialog box, shown in Figure 12-21, has the following options:

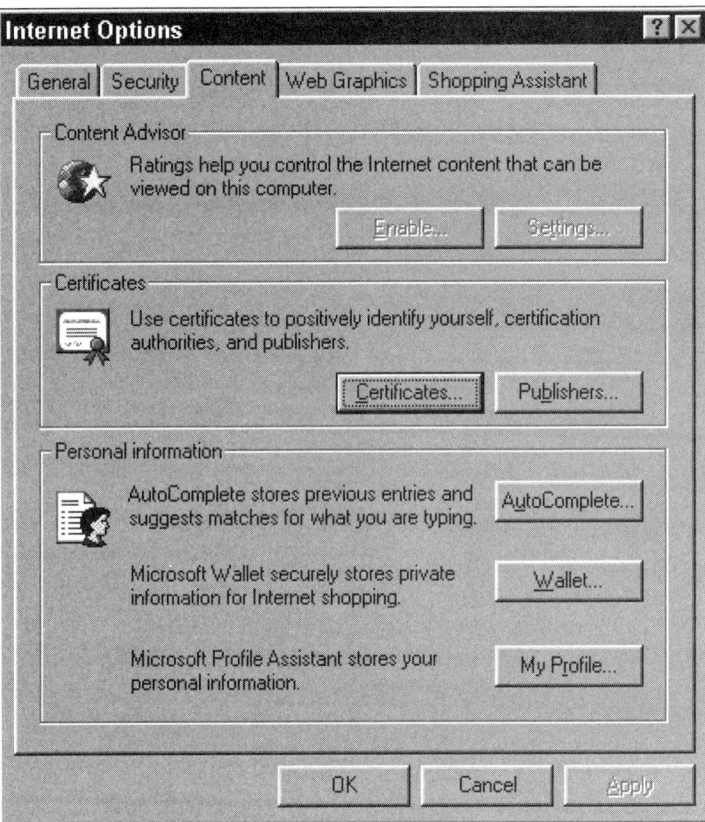

Figure 12-21. Web content preference settings give you greater control over the information coming to and going from your computer.

If you have to manually import, export, or remove certificates, click the Certificates button to reach the Certificate Manager window. Certificates relate to access you've been granted to specific sites, whereas Publishers refers to a list of software publishers whose products you have accepted as safe to download and automatically install on your computer without further notice to you. Click the Publishers button to manually remove publishers from your list.

- **Content Advisor:** This feature is disabled. See Parental Controls in Chapter 4.
- **Certificates:** *Certificates* are special small files that are exchanged with Web sites. They can either identify you as a trusted visitor or identify software as coming from a trusted source. Under most circumstances, certificates are automatically installed when you're granted access to sites that require certificates.
- **Personal Information:** The AutoComplete feature remembers passwords and other entries you have made at Web sites. When you revisit a site, it "suggests" your previous entries, such as automatically entering your username and password. The Microsoft Wallet feature stores private information that is used for Internet

shopping. You must download additional software from Microsoft to use this feature, and it only works at Web sites that incorporate this technology. The Microsoft Profile Assistant feature stores personal information that can be exchanged with Web sites. Again, you must download additional software from Microsoft to use the feature, and it only works at Web sites that incorporate this technology.

Web Graphics

Graphics files can be large and time consuming to transfer over the telephone lines that most people use to access AOL. To speed up the process, AOL can *compress* those files as they travel from AOL to your computer. Although the results of this compression technology are generally quite good, the process can seriously degrade the appearance of some images. You can choose whether to have AOL compress graphics through the Use Compressed Graphics option on the Web Graphics tab of the AOL Internet Options dialog box. (Default: On)

Shopping Assistant

The Shopping Assistant Bar assists you with online shopping, making recommendations, offering Internet searches, and providing additional information. (We discuss this feature in more depth in Chapter 15). If you want to deselect this feature, the Shopping Assistant tab of the AOL Internet Options dialog box is the place to do it. (Default: On)

Multimedia

The final set of preference settings included in the Preferences window is entitled Multimedia. Your multimedia preferences are simple: You can enable or disable AOL's automatic attempt to play all multimedia content with the internal player. We recommend that you leave this setting enabled. You may want to disable it if you want to designate other media-playing software on your computer to open by default (as defined in your Windows Settings). (Default: On)

Tip

If the images you're viewing seem unclear, or the colors are muddy or mottled, deselect the Use Compressed Graphics option on the Web Graphics tab of the AOL Internet Options dialog box. You may also have to reload the Web page to receive a new, uncompressed graphic.

Connection and Setup Preferences

You can access setup options in the Setup and Sign On screens when you're offline. You selected connection and setup preferences when you first set up your AOL account. However, you may want to change these settings if you install new computer hardware, add a new connection method (such as a cable modem), or have performance problems with your AOL connection.

You may have to change your AOL access number(s) and/or add a new location if you move or if AOL adds a new access number in your area. To change your connection and setup preferences, click the Setup button in the lower-left corner of the Sign On screen. The AOL Setup window appears, as shown in Figure 12-22.

- ▶ **Add Number:** Click this button to add a new access number to your setup.
- ▶ **Edit Numbers:** Click this button to change an existing access number.
- ▶ **Add Location:** Click this button to create a new group of access numbers.
- ▶ **Add Modem:** Click this button to add or change your modem, LAN/ISP, or other connection.

Figure 12-22. AOL Setup lets you change your access and connection methods.

Putting Your Knowledge to Work

As you can see from the length of this chapter, AOL offers a wide array of customization options. You don't need to customize AOL, of course, and you may find that the default settings work just fine for you. But if you want to tweak and fiddle with your settings, go ahead. We recommend you make small changes at first, live with them for a few days or a week, and then decide whether you want to keep them or change back to your previous settings. If you or someone else with access to your computer makes a bunch of changes and you want to reset them, just use this chapter to determine the default settings.

The next chapter discusses My Calendar, another highly customizable feature in AOL. Turn the page and learn how you can use My Calendar to organize your life.

CHAPTER 13

MY CALENDAR

Quick Look

▶ Get Started With the "My Calendar"℠ service   page 283
Take a few minutes to set up and explore My Calendar, AOL's interactive electronic personal date book. You'll be asked to supply some basic information so your calendar can best suit your needs. You'll also find out how to make your way around the calendar.

▶ New Appointments   page 286
Adding a new appointment to your calendar is very easy. Click the Add button, type a description, and select a date, time, and duration, and you're on your way. Add recurring appointments and notes, too, to be sure nothing is forgotten.

▶ Event Directory   page 289
Plan your business and personal life with the help of nearly a dozen directories. Add dates from financial calendars to your personal calendar. Schedule your television viewing. Plot out your favorite team's season and order tickets to all the home games. It's all possible with the Event Directory.

Chapter 13
My Calendar

IN THIS CHAPTER

Making your way around My Calendar's Month and Day views

Typing new appointments right into the monthly calendar display

Picking up quick tips for the day from the Idea List

Adding events from the Event Directory

So much to do, so little time! Now that you've added AOL to your social life, how can you keep track of all the online chats, meetings, TV shows, play dates, ball games, and cultural events that fill your days (and nights)? Turn to AOL's My Calendar to get your life in order.

My Calendar is a good bit more than an old-fashioned appointment calendar. You can access My Calendar anywhere you have access to AOL or the Internet. Jump from date to date with a few clicks of your mouse, add listings of recurring events with a few more clicks, and store far more information than you could ever fit on a regular calendar. My Calendar also includes an Idea List and Event Calendar that list online chats, TV programs, movies, sports, and cultural events that you can add to your calendar with just a click or two of your mouse. Customize your calendar by selecting a one-day calendar view, and add local weather forecasts, your daily horoscope, and your choice of national and religious holidays. After you get started with My Calendar, you'll be amazed by just how much you can do with it.

Getting Started

You can get started with My Calendar several ways:

- ▶ Click the My Calendar icon on the AOL Welcome Screen or the Calendar icon on the AOL toolbar.
- ▶ Choose AOL Services⇨Calendar from the AOL toolbar.
- ▶ Use AOL Keyword: **Calendar**.

As a first-time visitor, you're asked to supply your time zone and zip code so My Calendar can suggest events happening in your area. If you want, select a location so AOL can add weather forecasts, and choose a Zodiac sign if you want a daily horoscope. You can always change any of these settings by clicking the Settings button (the small wrench) at the top right of the main Calendar window, shown in Figure 13-1.

Note

You have offline access to My Calendar from your primary computer (and any other computer that has AOL 6.0 software installed). Just select your screen name in the Sign On screen and click the Calendar icon on the toolbar.

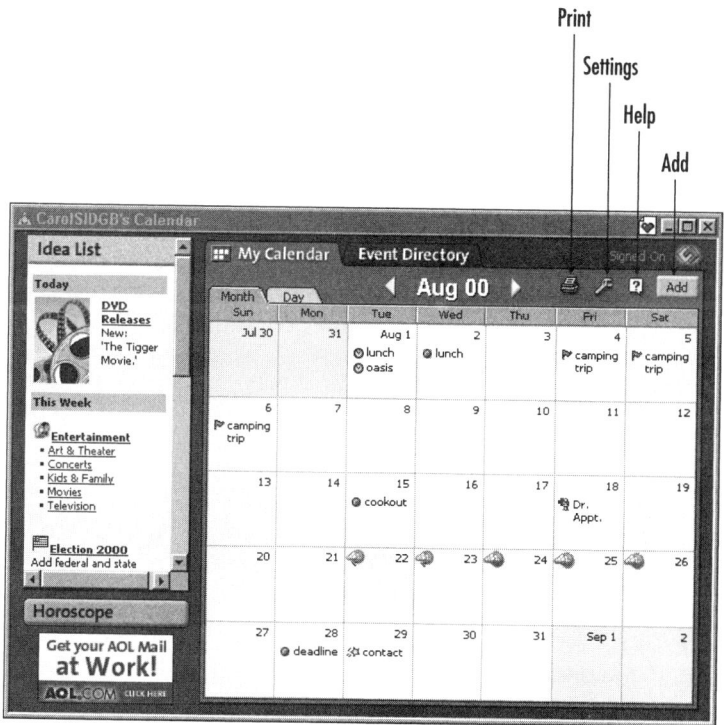

Figure 13-1. My Calendar opens with a monthly overview of your schedule.

The first time you visit My Calendar, you see the Month view, which has the familiar appearance of a wall calendar. Click the Day tab to see the kind of detailed daily listing you'd see in an appointment book, as shown in Figure 13-2.

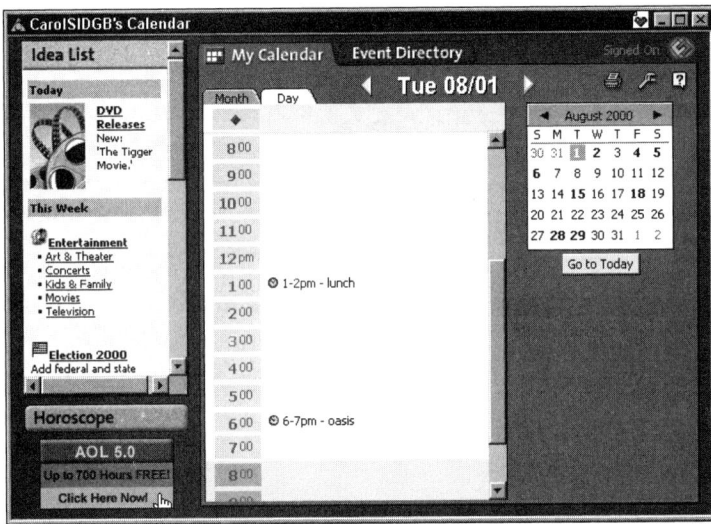

Figure 13-2. My Calendar's Day view.

Each item you add to your calendar has a brief description right on the calendar, and if you click that listing, you can view or edit all the details and reschedule or delete the listing. If you choose the weather forecast option, the calendar displays icons representing the day's weather conditions.

Flipping the pages of your calendar is very simple. Here's how:

My Calendar remembers whether you last used Month or Day view and returns to that view the next time you open your calendar.

▶ **Month View:** To move from month to month in the Month view, just click the left or right arrows that flank the date at the top of the calendar (refer to Figure 13-1). To jump to another month or year, click the date at the top of the calendar and select the year and month from the drop-down list.

▶ **Day View:** You can move from day to day by clicking the arrows that flank the date at the top of the calendar. To the right is a small, monthly calendar (refer to Figure 13-2). To jump around within a month, just click the desired day, or switch months by clicking the arrows at the top of the small calendar. Click the Go to Today button to get back to your starting point.

My Calendar Settings

My Calendar offers a few easy-to-change settings so that you can customize your calendar to your needs. Click the Settings button located near the top right of the Calendar window (it's the button with the small wrench on it). The Settings button opens the Options window, in which you can adjust your settings (see Figure 13-3).

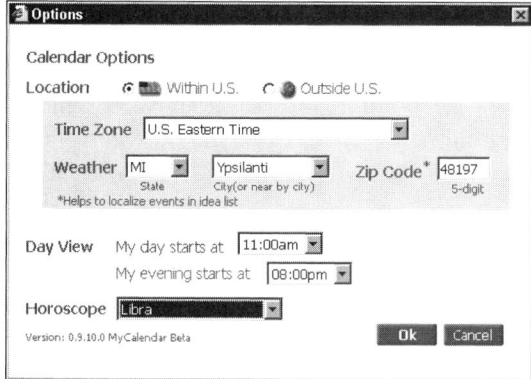

Figure 13-3. Set your calendar display options.

Here's a summary of your calendar settings:

▶ **Location:** Indicate whether you're within or outside the United States. This information affects your time zone and weather forecast options.

▶ **Time Zone:** Select your local time zone.

▶ **Weather:** If you live in the United States, choose a state and nearby city. If you live outside the United States, select a region, country, and nearby city from a series of drop-down lists. Once you've set your location, the weather forecast appears as small icons on the days of your calendar. Click a weather icon to get more detailed weather information. You can select a blank location to banish the weather forecast.

▶ **Zip Code:** Entering your U.S. zip code tailors the Idea List.

- **Day View:** Specifying when your day begins and ends enables the Day view to focus on your active hours.
- **Horoscope:** Select your Zodiac sign or the Don't Show Horoscope option from the drop-down list.

My Calendar View

Click the My Calendar tab to view and add appointments to your personal calendar. As we mention earlier, you can select either a Month view, which displays a traditional calendar with briefly noted appointment listings, or a Day view, which resembles a daily appointment book. To toggle between Month and Day view, click the appropriate tab below the My Calendar tab.

Once you have appointments in your calendar (which we show you how to do soon), you just click an appointment listing in the Month view to open its Appointment Details listing. You can also click any date in your calendar to reveal a larger version of the day's schedule.

The Day view is organized in one-hour increments, and a monthly calendar appears on the right side of the window. Not only does the monthly calendar give you the traditional overview of the month, but you can click it to move to another date.

Adding New Appointments to My Calendar

You can add a new appointment to your calendar several ways. The most obvious way is to click the Add button at the top of the calendar. My Calendar automatically opens the Add New Appointment window (shown in Figure 13-4), which is set to whichever date was most recently selected on the calendar.

Chapter 13 ▲ My Calendar

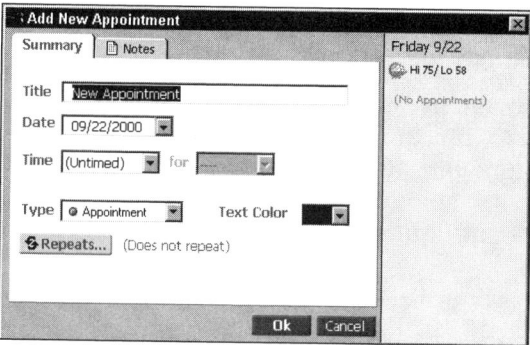

To open the Add New Appointment window preset for the desired date and time, switch to the Day view to select a date and then click the desired time for the appointment.

Figure 13-4. The Add New Appointment window. Note the Repeats button.

The Add New Appointment window offers you a wide range of options for your appointment. Click the Summary tab to record the basics of your appointment and click the Notes tab to record the details. And to the right of the window, you can find a list of existing appointments for that day. Here's a rundown of the available features on the Summary tab:

- ▶ **Title:** Type a brief description of the appointment.
- ▶ **Date:** Select a new date from the drop-down calendar.
- ▶ **Time:** Choose a time (or the Untimed option) from the drop-down list.
- ▶ **For:** Enter the expected length of the appointment (from 15 minutes to 23 hours).
- ▶ **Type:** Label your appointment with a category and mini-icon.
- ▶ **Text Color:** Color code the appointment for importance or visibility.
- ▶ **Repeats:** Click this button to set the repeat cycle for recurring events from every day to every fourth year, and set an end date as needed.

In the Month view, you have several other appointment-adding options. Click individual appointments to add details to those listings. When the mouse pointer becomes a small box containing a plus (+) symbol, just click and type a new appointment description right into the calendar. Later you can click the appointment to add additional details. Alternatively, move the mouse pointer to the top of a specific day's grid to reveal a rectangular button. Click this button to open a box showing a larger-sized version of the day's appointment list along with

To add an appointment to your calendar quickly, use AOL Keyword: **Add2Cal**. This keyword produces a small window in which you can type the title of your appointment, the date, and the time. Clicking Add to My Calendar adds the new appointment with or without having your calendar open on-screen.

an Add Appt button and your expanded weather information (if available).

To add an appointment in the Day view, just click an hour to open the New Appointment window, preset to the desired time. Setting the appointment details in Day view works the same way as it does in Month view. Of course, you can click any existing appointment to make changes.

Idea List

You can do far more than create your own appointments. My Calendar's *Idea List* and *Event Directory* open the door to thousands of events that you can add to your calendar with just a few clicks of your mouse.

The Idea List, shown in Figure 13-5 is always visible on your calendar, suggesting things you can do today and delivering shortcuts to lists of this week's popular entertainment and sporting events in the Event Directory. You'll also find a collection of useful online Tools & Tips.

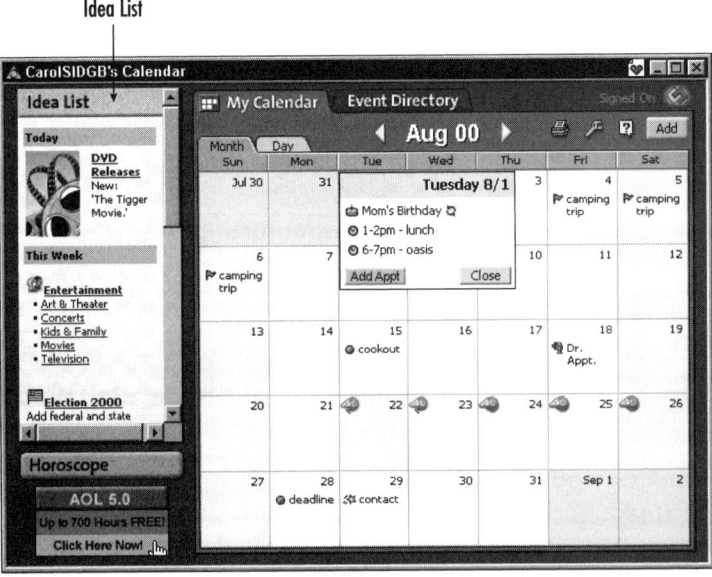

Figure 13-5. My Calendar's Idea List.

Event Directory

For a far greater selection of things to do than is listed in the Idea List, check out the Event Directory. Click the Event Directory tab at the top of the Calendar window to see this list of activities. You can do far more than create your own appointments. My Calendar's Event Directory, shown in Figure 13-6, offers easy links to thousands of TV shows, plays, concerts, sporting events, and family activities that you may wish to add to your calendar.

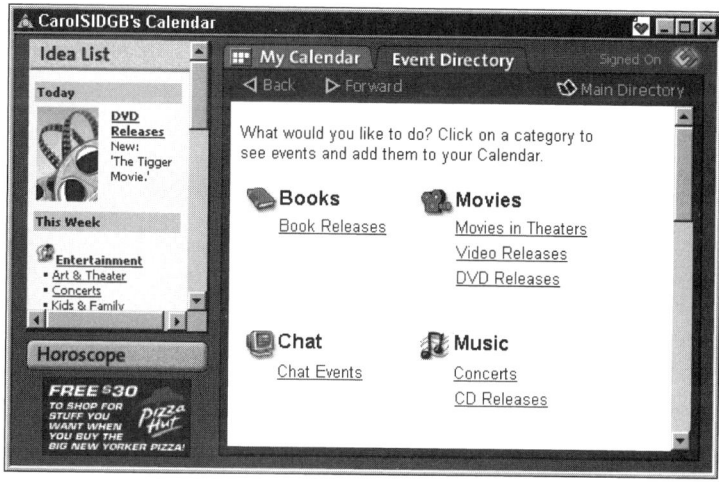

Figure 13-6. The Event Directory's Main Directory.

The Event Directory offers listings of everything from book and movie releases to cultural events, family events, and trade shows to financial calendars listing dividend dates, Initial Public Offerings, stock splits, and earnings announcements. These listings are prepared by such well-known names as Digital City, TV Guide, CultureFinder, and Moviefone. If you're interested in any listed event, click its hyperlink to view more details and click the Add to Your Calendar button to include it in your calendar. You may even be able to purchase tickets or tell a friend.

Putting Your Knowledge to Work

You should also keep your eyes open for the My Calendar icon wherever you travel on AOL and the World Wide Web. If you see it, click it to add that item to your calendar.

Travelers and business people can access My Calendar from any computer with Internet access, even if AOL software hasn't been installed. Just visit the My Calendar home page (calendar.aol.com) or follow the links to My Calendar when you visit AOL.COM.

CHAPTER 14

FAVORITE PLACES

Quick Look

▶ Favorite Places List   page 293
You can add frequently visited AOL Internet destinations to a drop-down menu on the AOL toolbar with a quick move of your mouse. Just find the heart icon in any window and then drag that heart to the My Favorites button on the toolbar.

▶ Organize Your Favorites   page 296
Open the Favorite Places window to bring order to your Favorite Places list. Add folders and subfolders to the list and drop your Favorite Places into appropriate folders — they'll appear as submenus the next time you open your Favorite Places list.

▶ Copy Your Favorites to Another Screen Name   page 298
Click the Save/Replace button in the Favorite Places window to save your Favorite Places list as a file. That file can then be copied to another screen name on the same computer by using the same Save/Replace button.

▶ Customize My Places   page 299
Take control of your Welcome Screen. The My Places area, on the right side of the Welcome Screen, consists of ten buttons that you can customize to your needs. Click the Customize My Places button on the Welcome Screen and take your pick from many of AOL's most popular destinations.

Chapter 14
Favorite Places

IN THIS CHAPTER

Collecting your favorite AOL and Internet destinations

Reorganizing your Favorite Places list by adding folders

Sharing your Favorite Places with friends and family

Adding up to ten of your favorite destinations to the Welcome Screen

AOL and the Internet offer so much to see and experience, but the journey from link to link to link can be long and tiring. Wouldn't it be wonderful to store all your favorite destinations so you can return to them in one or two clicks? You can!

Favorite Places make getting to where you want to go fast and easy. Each one of your screen names has its own Favorite Places list, which appears when you click the My Favorites button on the AOL toolbar. After you add a Favorite Place to your list, all you have to do is click the Favorites menu, choose the Favorite Place from the drop-down menu (shown in Figure 14-1), and you're on your way.

Chapter 14 ▲ Favorite Places

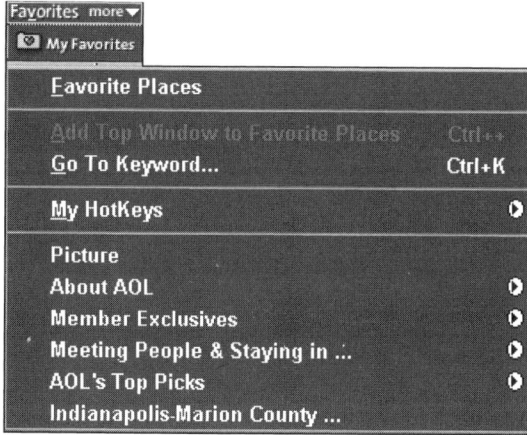

Figure 14-1. Open the Favorites menu on the AOL toolbar to see your Favorite Places list.

Finding and Adding Favorite Places

AOL lets you create a Favorite Place for nearly any window you can open on AOL, including any place on the Web. Navigate to the area you want to add to the list, and look for the little red-and-white heart icon on the right-hand side of the window's title bar, as shown in Figure 14-2. If it has one, you're in luck.

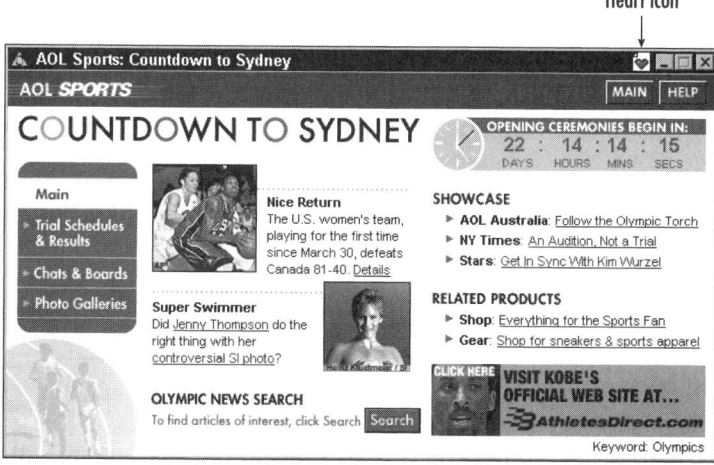

Figure 14-2. The heart icon is the key to saving and sharing your favorites.

To add a Favorite Place, follow these steps:

1. Click the small heart icon once. The small window that appears (shown in Figure 14-3) contains these buttons: Add to Favorites, Insert in Instant Message, or Insert in Mail.
2. For now, just click the Add to Favorites button.

After making your selection, the window disappears, and the location is added to your Favorites menu. If you check the Favorites menu again, you see the new addition, as shown in Figure 14-4.

Figure 14-3. You have several options when you click a Favorite Place icon.

You just added the location to your Favorite Places list. There are other ways of adding Favorite Places, as well as methods of adding Favorite Places to e-mail and instant messages to share your favorites with your friends. You can also drag that heart icon to make saving and sharing Favorite Places even easier. Here are all the details:

- To add an area to your Favorite Places list, drag the heart icon to the My Favorites button on the AOL toolbar.
- Another way to add an area to your Favorite Places list is to choose Favorites➪Add Top Window to Favorites from the AOL toolbar.
- To manually add an area to your Favorite Places list, first open your Favorite Places window (click the My Favorites button on the AOL toolbar). Now click the New button in the Favorite Places window to open the Add New Folder/Favorite Place window. Type or paste

the Internet address and a description in the appropriate text boxes.

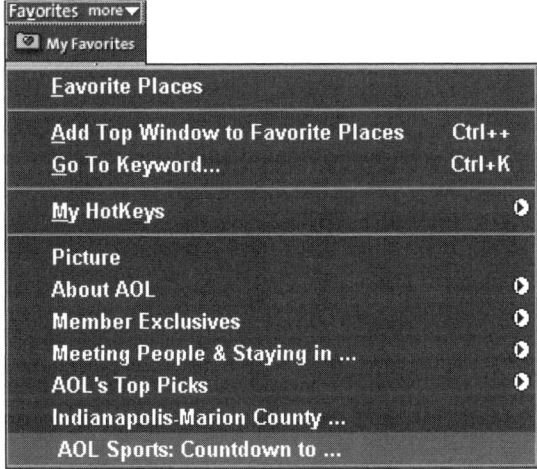

Figure 14-4. Your Favorites menu automatically updates.

- To add an area to the AOL toolbar, drag the heart icon anywhere on the toolbar. In the resulting window, select an icon and assign a label to that icon. Your new area appears in the purple section of the AOL toolbar with the icon you selected. If you want to later remove an item from the purple section of the AOL toolbar, right-click on the item and choose Remove from Toolbar.
- To add a hyperlink to an e-mail, an instant message, or Chat, drag a heart icon to a text box.

See Chapter 2 if you're unfamiliar with *dragging* something.

Use your Favorite Places list when you're offline to start the sign-on process and go directly to your desired destination.

Favorite Places Window

The Favorite Places window gives you the power to edit and reorganize your Favorite Places list, to share your favorites with your friends, to make a backup copy of your Favorite Places list, and even install your favorites on a different computer or under a different screen name.

Editing and Organizing Your Favorite Places List

Your Favorite Places list can become long and unruly. If it becomes too long, a *More Favorites* menu option appears at the bottom of your Favorite Places list. But don't worry! You can bring order to the chaos by adding new Favorite Places folders, rearranging the places in your list, deleting unwanted items, and otherwise organizing your Favorite Places.

Follow these steps to reorganize items in your Favorite Places list:

1. Click the My Favorites button, or choose Favorites⇨ Favorite Places from the AOL toolbar to open the Favorite Places window, an editable version of your Favorite Places list (see Figure 14-5).

2. Click the New button to create a new item. The Add New Folder/Favorite Place window appears.

3. Select the New Folder radio button to create a subfolder and then type a descriptive name for the new folder (see Figure 14-6). Click OK when you're finished. The new folder should now appear in your Favorite Places list.

4. Drag the heart icons from existing items in your list to place them into your new folder (see Figure 14-7).

Chapter 14 ▲ Favorite Places

Figure 14-5. The editable Favorite Places list.

Figure 14-6. Creating and naming a new folder for the Favorite Places list.

You can select multiple Favorite Places by holding down the Shift key while you click each one. Hold down the Ctrl key instead as you click if you want to select items that aren't adjacent to each other.

Figure 14-7. Organizing favorites into a new folder.

The Save/Replace button gives you the power to preserve your Favorite Places list in case of disaster by installing a copy of that list on another screen name or by installing it on another computer running AOL. To install a copy of a list on one screen name to another, just save the list on the first name, change to the second name, and replace the list.

5. Use the Edit, Delete, and New buttons at the bottom of the window to edit the titles (or URLs) of existing Favorite Places or folders (see Figure 14-8), delete unwanted items, and even create new Favorite Places if you happen to know the URLs of the Web pages.

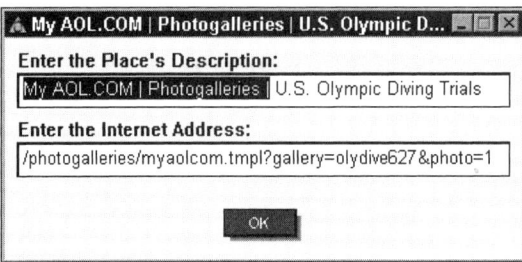

Figure 14-8. Editing the name of a favorite.

Sharing Favorite Places

Half the fun of having favorites is sharing them with your family and friends. Earlier in the chapter, we describe how you can drag heart icons from an AOL area or Web page into e-mail, instant messages, and chat rooms. Here we describe how you can also drag heart icons from your Favorite Places window. Drag a bunch of hearts into a single e-mail to build a complete mini-favorites list!

The Save/Replace button in your Favorite Places window lets you save your entire Favorite Places list for installation on another computer (see Figure 14-9). Follow these directions to save a copy of your Favorite Places list:

You can also use Save/Replace to copy your Favorite Places list to another screen name on the same computer.

1. Click the My Favorites button on the AOL toolbar.
2. Click the Save/Replace button.
3. Verify that the Save the Favorite Places for Your Current Screen Name option is selected and then click OK.
4. Choose a location for your saved list and click Save.
5. Click the Write button on the AOL toolbar.
6. Click Attachments and then click Attach to locate the file you just saved and attach it to your e-mail.
7. Address your e-mail, add a message about your list, and send it.

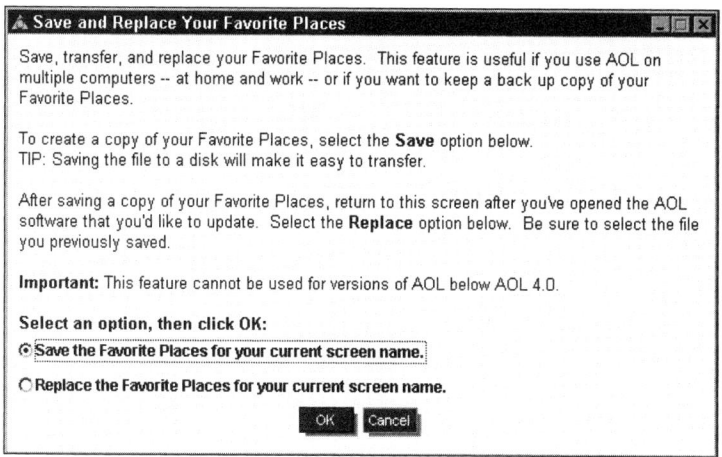

Figure 14-9. Saving a list of Favorite Places.

My Places

Customize your AOL Welcome Screen with My Places! You can put ten of your favorite AOL destinations right there on the Welcome Screen and change them whenever you want. To get you started, AOL has already selected some of its most popular sites, but you can change any or all of them with a few quick clicks.

Here's how to do it:

1. Open the AOL Welcome Screen (choose the item that begins with "Welcome" from the Window menu).
2. Click the Customize My Places button to open the Change My Places window, shown in Figure 14-10 (or use AOL Keyword: **Set My Places**).

Figure 14-10. The Customize My Places window.

3. Click any one of the Choose New Place buttons to open a drop-down list and then select a place from the list. Note that the list only includes the top sites AOL members have deemed worthy.
4. When you're done, click the Save My Changes button. Your Welcome Screen updates with your changes.

Putting Your Knowledge to Work

Now that you know how to add to and organize your Favorite Places list, why not go on a grand scavenger hunt for all your regular online haunts and destinations? Don't stop with favorite Web sites and informational resources. You can save your favorite public and private chat rooms, message board topics, and newsgroups, too!

CHAPTER

15

SHOPPING PREFERENCES

Quick Look

▶ **Quick Checkout** **page 302**
Zip through the online "express lane" with Quick Checkout. Quick Checkout allows shoppers to store billing and shipping information securely on AOL and shop without having to repeatedly enter this information at each store they visit. Shopping online is smooth, fast, and secure with Quick Checkout. Learn more and sign up at AOL Keyword: **Quick Checkout**.

▶ **Gift Reminder Service** **page 305**
Remember important holidays, birthdays, and anniversaries with AOL's free reminder service. It can be set up to remember important dates, and AOL will even send a reminder e-mail message ahead of time. Get started at AOL Keyword: **Reminder**.

▶ **AOL Shopping Guarantee** **page 308**
Worried about shopping online? Thanks to the AOL 100% Shopping Guarantee, you can relax while shopping through AOL Certified Merchants, all of whom meet or exceed AOL's stringent standards of customer service. Learn more at AOL Keyword: **Guarantee**.

Chapter 15
Shopping Preferences

IN THIS CHAPTER

Learning how to shop online

Shopping quickly and easily with Quick Checkout

Staying safe with the AOL Shopping Guarantee

If you enjoy mail-order catalogs, you'll enjoy the convenience of shopping online. You're free to browse at any time of the day or night, with no salespeople to pressure or intimidate you. AOL offers shopping services to make your experience safe and easy, including Quick Checkout, the Gift Reminder Service, and the AOL Shopping Guarantee.

Ringing Up the Sale with Quick Checkout

Welcome to the Express Checkout lane! With a little help from Quick Checkout, you can fly through the online stores in record time. Sign up for Quick Checkout (it's free!) by visiting AOL Keyword: **Quick Checkout** (see Figure 15-1), or click the Quick Checkout button at any of the Shop@AOL merchants that accept Quick Checkout.

Figure 15-1. At Quick Checkout, the express lane is always open!

After you've experienced the ease of online shopping, and it becomes a regular part of your shopping routine, you may want to take advantage of ways to make the experience even easier. Online shopping often requires you to reenter your credit card information each time you make a purchase, but Quick Checkout can save you some of that time and trouble, and help you avoid typing errors. Quick Checkout conveniently and securely stores information for up to 10 of your credit/debit cards and 50 shipping addresses of your friends and relatives, so you can quickly finish paying for things and get back to the fun of shopping.

When you reach the checkout at a participating AOL merchant, Quick Checkout provides your preferred credit card and shipping information to the merchant to complete the transaction. If you want to use a different credit card or ship the goods to someone else listed in your Quick Checkout address book, just select the desired changes.

Quick Checkout is the place to go if you want to add, delete, or modify credit card and address information, or get in-depth information on how Quick Checkout works. You can use a special Quick Checkout Customer Service number (877-385-2330) if you have problems or questions regarding your Quick Checkout account.

Note

Provide your credit card information only to established and trusted retailers, such as AOL's Certified Merchants. Beware of any individuals asking for your information, or anything suspicious during transactions. No AOL employee will ever ask you for your credit card information online (though you may be required to provide it if you call AOL regarding a billing issue).

Cross-Reference

See Chapters 4 and 11 for more information on security and creating good passwords, and refer to the section titled "Surfing Safety" later in this chapter.

Definition

SSL encryption is the industry standard for secure Web transactions.

Shoppers should make certain that their credit card information is safe and secured when it is entered online. Shop@AOL considers the safety of its consumers to be the top priority, and has taken steps to ensure that shoppers will be safe online:

▶ Your Quick Checkout account is protected by a separate shopping password. The first time you use Quick Checkout during an online session, you'll be asked for that password.

▶ If you forget your shopping password, Quick Checkout asks you a security question, the answer for which you provided when you first set up your Quick Checkout account. When you answer the question correctly, Quick Checkout e-mails you a temporary password.

▶ Your information is protected from prying eyes. After it has been entered into the system, your credit card numbers will not be displayed on-screen. Only the last four digits of your card number will be shown so you can recognize the card.

▶ Your information is stored at AOL on computers that are not accessible via the Internet.

▶ The highest level of SSL encryption available with your browser protects credit card information as it flows between your computer and AOL (128 bit with Internet Explorer 5.5, which is the browser supplied with AOL 6.0).

▶ Only screen names with Parental Controls set to 18+ or Mature Teen may create Quick Checkout accounts.

▶ You are free to delete information on your account at any time, and AOL erases that information immediately.

Of course, computer security becomes even more important after you set up a Quick Checkout account. Be sure that your passwords are unique, hard to guess, and hard for others to find (if you write them down). AOL will not let you use the same password for your AOL account and Quick Checkout.

Using the Reminder Service

Has all this talk of shopping reminded you of anything? Like an upcoming birthday or holiday, perhaps? If you're still drawing a blank, you may need a reminder. The Reminder Service (see Figure 15-2) is a free tool that lets you save dates of birthdays, holidays, and so on, and then reminds you beforehand so you don't miss them. See AOL Keyword: **Reminder**.

Figure 15-2. Never forget a date with AOL's Reminder Service.

Reminders are sent via e-mail messages two weeks before the date; users have the option of being sent a second reminder four days beforehand, too. It's a simple, but effective tool for remembering important holidays and events that you may need to make a purchase for. Click the Create Your Reminder button in the Reminder Service window to begin the registration process (see Figure 15-3).

In the registration window, you can choose whether you'd like the 4-day reminder in addition to the 14-day reminder. You can also choose to be automatically reminded of up to seven major holidays; just click the boxes to the left of the name to select them. When finished, simply click the Continue button. You are now registered and will see your reminder list, as shown in Figure 15-4.

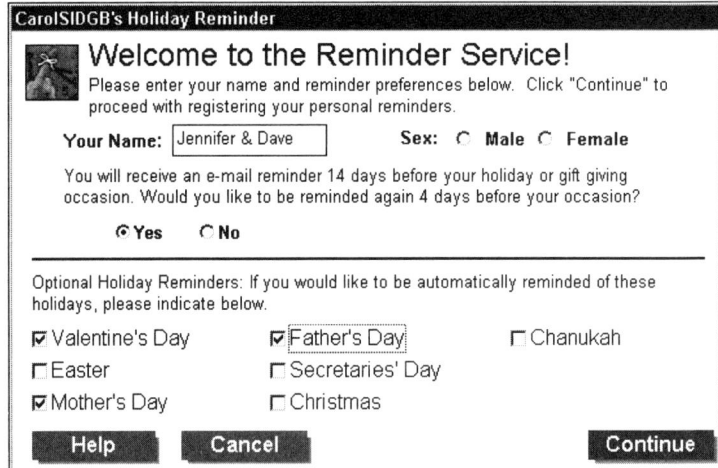

Figure 15-3. Registration for the Reminder Service is free and easy.

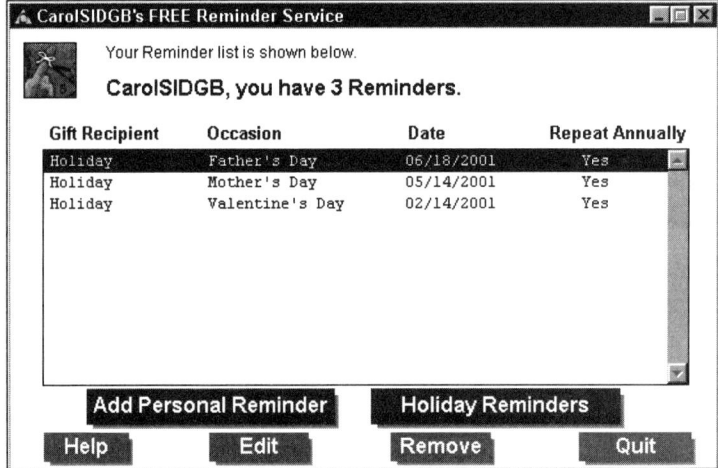

Figure 15-4. Our new reminder list.

Any holidays you chose when you registered appear on the reminder list, organized alphabetically by occasion. Note the columns indicating recipient, occasion, date, and repeat rate. To create a new reminder, click the Add Personal Reminder button near the bottom. Fill out the reminder form as requested. Note that only the gift recipient's name and the date are required. When you're finished, click the Save button to create your reminder. The new reminder now appears in your reminder list.

Reminders are easy to edit. Just select a reminder in your reminder list, click the Edit button, make your changes, and click Save again. If you'd rather just delete a reminder, simply select it in the reminder list and click Remove. Use the Holiday Reminders button to add or remove the automatic holiday reminders in your list. The reminders are easy to use, and a great way to stay on schedule successfully!

The Gift Reminder area also offers easy access to Shop@AOL's Gifts & Specialty Shops, which consist of a Great Gift Ideas area, offering gift suggestions for all holidays and occasions, and Specialty Shops that focus on events, interests, or lifestyles.

Along with helping you remember birthdays and holidays, the Reminder Service can remind you to pay your bills when they are due, get to meetings on time, and more! Simply type the occasion (meeting, bill payment due) in the field marked "Other" when creating a reminder.

Getting Good Customer Service

AOL's hallmark is its customer service. AOL's goal is to ensure that shoppers have a successful experience while visiting Shop@AOL.

Shop@AOL expects its merchant partners to adhere to AOL's strict customer service policies. Its Certified Merchants Program has been established to ensure that merchants place a high priority on the safety and satisfaction of AOL's customers.

If you do have a problem with a merchant, your first stop should be that store's customer service department. AOL's Certified Merchants Program requires merchants to provide a high level of customer service, including clearly-stated return policies and information on how to reach them by phone or e-mail. AOL works only with merchants who are dedicated to providing the consumer with a successful shopping experience.

Specially-trained customer service experts are on hand at Shop@AOL to answer online shoppers' questions and provide personal assistance. AOL's customer service representatives are on duty from 8 a.m. to 2 a.m. eastern standard time to help answer any of your shopping questions. You can chat with them online, speak with them on the phone, send them e-mail, or post your question on a message board. Shop@AOL Customer Service is easy to find; just click the Customer Service button on the Shop@AOL main screen, or use AOL Keyword: **Shopping Customer Service** (see Figure 15-5).

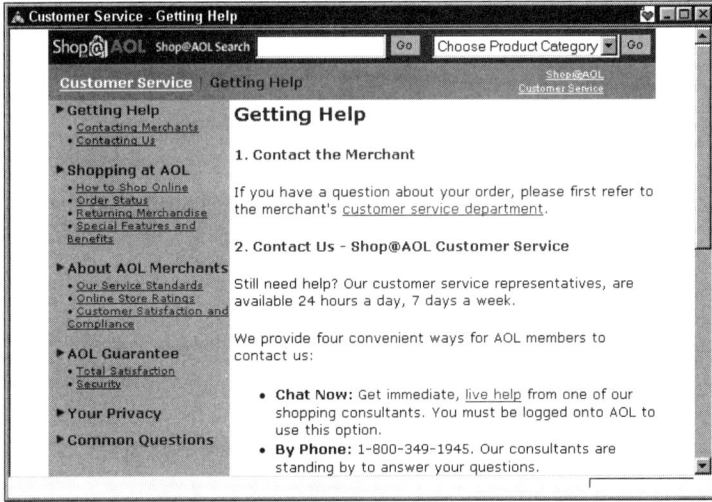

Figure 15-5. Find answers to your shopping questions at Shop@AOL Customer Service.

Note

Contact Shop@AOL Customer Service by sending e-mail to screen name `ShopHelp`. You can also phone 800-349-1945 any time between 8 a.m. and 2 a.m. eastern standard time.

If you do have a problem with a shopping transaction that wasn't satisfied by the merchant, please have as much information available for the AOL customer service representative as possible, including the name of the merchant, the date of purchase, the price you paid, and a description of steps you've taken to resolve the problem and how the merchant responded.

Shopping with Confidence with the AOL Shopping Guarantee

Shop@AOL's cutting-edge shopping experience brings together more than 300 brand-name retailers. AOL's Certified

Merchants Program, introduced in 1995, was created to ensure the best possible online experience and the highest level of customer satisfaction. AOL requires that each of its Certified Merchants meets its high standards for customer service, security, and privacy protection, and supports AOL's 100% money-back guarantee of satisfaction and security. This comprehensive guarantee applies to all goods and services purchased on Shop@AOL (see Figure 15-6).

Shop@AOL Customer Service provides more than help with problems. The service representatives will help you with just about any online shopping-related question, including where to find the most unusual kinds of merchandise.

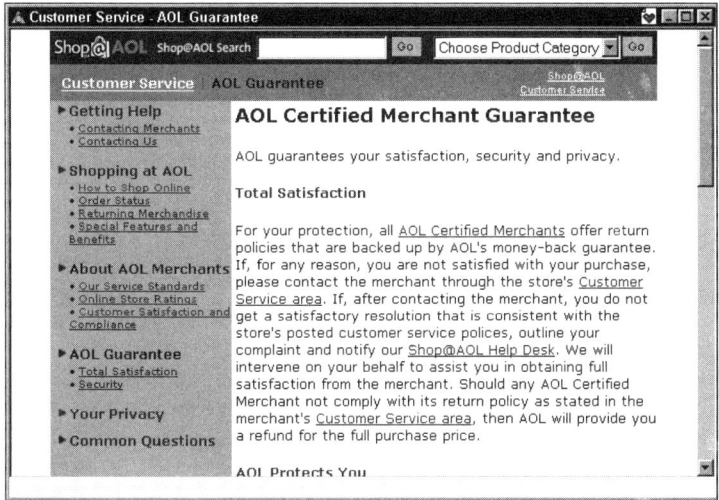

Figure 15-6. AOL's 100% Shopping Guarantee.

Getting Help from the AOL Shopping Assistant

New for AOL 6.0 is the AOL Shopping Assistant, a shopping feature that offers easy access to services that enhance the online shopping experience. The AOL Shopping Assistant appears as a bar at the top of your browser window when visiting qualifying Web sites, such as bn.com (see Figure 15-7).

310   Part III ▲ Customizing Your AOL

Figure 15-7. The AOL Shopping Assistant Bar pops up at the top of your browser window.

 **Note**

You must have the AOL Shopping Assistant preference enabled to see it while shopping. To check, choose Settings⇨Preferences, click the Internet Properties link, click the Shopping Assistant tab, and verify that a check appears to the left of View the Shopping Assistant. Of course, if you find you do not need the Shopping Assistant, this is also the place to disable it.

The AOL Shopping Assistant Bar appears after you begin browsing the store. The bar provides several helpful features:

▶ **Shop@AOL Search:** Just type in a product or brand name, click Search, and Shop@AOL returns matching results in your browser window. Shop@AOL Search is discussed more in Chapter 19.

▶ **Explore Shop@AOL:** This drop-down menu in the upper-right corner of the AOL Shopping Assistant Bar gives you access to the many departments available in Shop@AOL.

▶ **This Store:** Click the small white arrow (when available) to learn more about the store you are currently visiting, including its online store rating, whether it is an AOL Certified Merchant, and whether the merchant accepts Quick Checkout (see Figure 15-8). Click the white arrow again to hide the information.

Figure 15-8. The AOL Shopping Assistant provides handy information about this store.

- **Other Stores:** When looking at a particular product (for example, the latest Harry Potter book at Barnes & Noble), click the Other Stores arrow to display information about other Shop@AOL partners who carry the product. You can also compare the other stores' ratings as well as check availability and prices of the product, all without having to leave the current site. Click the white arrow to hide the information again.
- **Help (?):** Click the small white arrow beside the question mark on the right side of the bar to learn more about the AOL Shopping Assistant and select the services that the AOL Shopping Assistant provides.

If you need more room in your browser window and just want to hide the AOL Shopping Assistant temporarily, click the white arrow on the left side of the bar to minimize it.

No, big brother isn't watching. The AOL Shopping Assistant does not track or store any information about your shopping habits.

Surfing Safety

Did you know that shopping on AOL is safer than shopping at your local mall? Besides avoiding the obvious safety considerations such as potential accidents while driving to and from the mall, purse and wallet snatchers, your credit cards are also more secure on AOL than in a mall. How does AOL do it? Shop@AOL provides a secure environment for credit card transactions by encrypting all data sent and received during the purchase. This means that even if someone intercepted the transmission, that person wouldn't be able to make heads or tails of the information.

AOL guarantees this secure environment only with its Certified Merchants. Be careful not to give your credit card information or any other personal information to an unauthorized party. If you receive what you believe is a fraudulent credit card request, notify AOL immediately at AOL Keyword: **TOS**. You can also send e-mail to screen name `MarketMail`.

More consumer tips on shopping online are available on the Web from the Federal Trade Commission. Visit www.ftc.gov/bcp/menu-internet.htm for more details.

Putting Your Knowledge to Work

Shop@AOL makes shopping online easy, convenient, and fun! You can use AOL services from start to finish: AOL's Reminder Service can send you a reminder of your Dad's birthday in two weeks, the AOL Shopping Assistant can help you compare prices for that book you want to buy for him, AOL's 100% Guarantee of Satisfaction and Security will put your mind at ease about making the purchase, and AOL Quick Checkout can get you in and out in a flash. Shop@AOL can even make recommendations and point you to stores, which you discover in Chapter 19.

You may have noticed that most of the destinations in this chapter are Web sites. If you're wondering about Web sites, perhaps even thinking about creating your own, the next chapter is for you. We show you how to create your own Web site on AOL — at no additional cost!

CHAPTER 16

AOL HOMETOWN

Quick Look

▶ **1-2-3 Publish**   **page 316**
Create your first Web page with this incredibly easy-to-use feature. Select a topic or theme for your page, click a few buttons, fill in a simple form, and you've got your own, free home page at AOL Hometown.

▶ **Easy Designer**   **page 320**
When you're ready to be more creative with your Web page designs, Easy Designer is ready to help. Drag and drop text and images anywhere you like on the page — add one of the 5,000 free pictures — add hyperlinks to text and pictures, and customize text colors and backgrounds. You don't even have to install any software. Easy Designer is another one of the free services available at AOL Hometown.

▶ **Groups@AOL**   **page 325**
Bring your friends, relatives, or coworkers together in a private online area. Maintain an event calendar; communicate with a group mailing list, instant messages, buddy chat, and a message board; and share photos, profiles, and personal favorites.

Chapter 16
AOL Hometown

IN THIS CHAPTER

Creating Web pages and finding a community that interests you at AOL Hometown

Converting your first, 1-2-3 Publish Web page into a masterpiece with Easy Designer

Finding recipes for better home pages at AOL Hometown's Build Better Web Pages

Keeping in touch with friends and family with Groups@AOL

Inviting your friends to a holiday feast with AOL Invitations

Part of the magic of the Web is that everyone can have his or her own place on the Web. For AOL members, that place is *AOL Hometown,* a busy community where *home page* means more than just a lonely Web site drifting in cyberspace. You'll find neighborhoods of people with similar interests with whom you can share and interact. What's more, it costs nothing but your time and creativity to get started. AOL provides all the tools you need to create a simple home page and more advanced tools for building more sophisticated pages — all without installing a single byte of software or learning a single word of the HTML language used to build Web pages. It's as easy as 1-2-3!

The Hometown Community

The Web is huge and intimidating, whether you are brand new to the online world or have been trotting the virtual globe for many years. Wouldn't it be nice to have a community of supportive friends to help you build your own home on the Web? That's just what the AOL Hometown community offers. You can find people who share both your personal interests and your interest in creating Web pages. Even before you create your own Web page, you may want to explore the communities of AOL Hometown, view members' pages, and decide how you and your page might best fit in. Use AOL Keyword: **Hometown** to go to this area, shown in Figure 16-1.

You and your friends can access AOL Hometown directly on the Web, at `hometown.aol.com`.

Click the Get a Quickstart link on the AOL Hometown main page for a complete introduction to AOL Hometown.

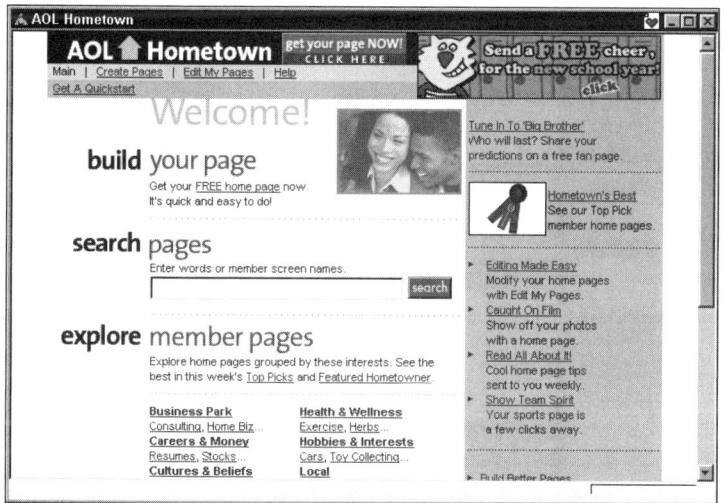

Figure 16-1. AOL Hometown's main page — creativity and community.

AOL Hometown is open to AOL members only.

AOL Hometown gives you 12MB of free Web storage space for every screen name on your AOL account — that's 84MB per account on AOL 5.0 and above.

The AOL Hometown main page is packed with all sorts of useful links. Search and explore AOL Hometown's many communities, take a look at Hometown's Best, build your own page, and learn how to build even better pages. It's all here, and much more.

Located at the top of every page, the AOL Hometown navigation bar (shown in Figure 16-2) is a handy resource wherever you travel in AOL Hometown. You're never more than a click away from all the tools you need to publish your own pages and manage the pages you've already created.

Figure 16-2. The AOL Hometown navigation bar — tools at your fingertips.

The Create Pages link is a particularly useful resource. Here's what it has to offer:

- **Create:** Make a home page with 1-2-3 Publish.
- **Move:** List your pages at a different Hometown community.
- **Describe:** Edit the descriptions of your existing pages.
- **Add All:** Make all your AOL Hometown pages searchable in AOL Hometown.
- **Add:** Transfer your pages from Members.AOL.com to AOL Hometown.
- **Upload:** Upload existing pages at AOL Keyword: **My FTP Space**.
- **Edit:** Modify pages you created with 1-2-3 Publish or Easy Designer.

Of course, you can't do most of these things until you have a home page of your own. Do you want to get started with the least fuss and bother? Try AOL's 1-2-3 Publish.

1-2-3 Publish

How easy is it to create your first home page? Three minutes may be all you need with 1-2-3 Publish, AOL Hometown's introductory-level Web-page creation tool. 1-2-3 Publish is a breeze for anyone who knows how to get around AOL. All you have to do is click some links and buttons, fill in a simple form, and you're ready to preview your first Web creation.

For your very first page, AOL Hometown suggests one of five basic themes. After that, you can add more pages with the help of the 60 templates 1-2-3 Publish makes available to you. Templates range from personal and business profiles to pages about your interests, thoughts, favorites, family, hobbies, sports, and cities. Each template has the same basic features, but offers a different look and suggestions for the kind of content you can add to your page. Figure 16-3 shows the My Loveable Pet Page template.

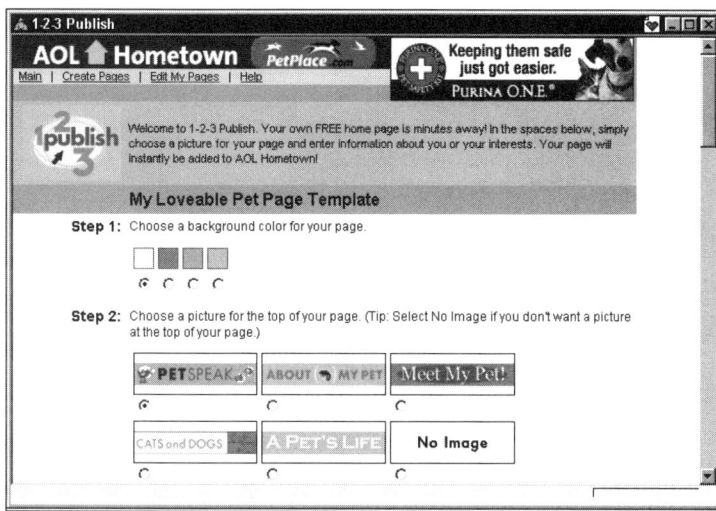

Figure 16-3. Meet My Pet Page template.

1-2-3 Publish makes it easy for you to design your own Web page by presenting the Web page creation process in a series of steps. Here's a listing of the steps you need to follow:

1. Go to AOL Keyword: **123 Publish**. The 1-2-3 Publish page appears, as shown in Figure 16-4.

Figure 16-4. Choose a template to get started with 1-2-3 Publish.

Tip

Don't be afraid to browse through the templates until you find one you like. With a little creativity, you can make almost any template serve your purpose.

Tip

Spend some time thinking and writing offline. Type your thoughts into a new AOL document (choose File⇨New) and then copy and paste the text into the template after your text has been nicely polished. Don't bother formatting your text, though, 1-2-3 Publish ignores existing formatting.

Tip

You can also click E-Mail This Page on the confirmation screen or above the page to share your creation with others.

2. Click the appropriate link to select a template from the offerings listed. The page for the particular template you have chosen appears.

3. Choose a background color by selecting a radio button beneath one of the four color-coordinated background options.

4. Select a banner to run across the top of your Web page from the available options. Banners allow you to set the theme for your page with a ready-made graphic.

5. Enter a title for your page in the Title text field. Think up your own title, or your page will have the same title as many others.

6. If you want, click the Browse button to find a picture on your computer's hard drive to add to your Web site. 1-2-3 Publish will automatically upload that image so it can be used on your Web site.

7. Choose a divider style for your Web page by selecting a radio button beneath one of the available options. Dividers allow you to separate each section of your page with an attractive divider image.

8. Add text to your Web page by filling in the text fields. 1-2-3 Publish gives you three sections to work with. Each section has a suggested title (such as *My Pet's Favorite Activities* and *Funny Pet Stories*), but you can easily substitute a more appropriate heading. Write as little or as much as you'd like in each of these sections.

9. You can enter the URLs (Internet addresses) of up to three Web sites you recommend — including, perhaps, other pages you've created — into the online links text fields. 1-2-3 Publish formats them as hyperlinks on your Web page so that visitors can check out your favorite Web sites with a simple click of the mouse.

10. To include a banner for AOL that lets you earn up to $50 for every member you recruit who stays with AOL for at least 90 days, select the Make Money with Your Home Page check box.

11. To add an AOL Instant Messenger Remote to your page so that visitors can meet you online, select the AOL Instant Messenger Remote check box.

Chapter 16 ▲ AOL Hometown

12. Click the Preview My Page button to take a look at your creation before you place it on the Web.
13. Click the Modify button if you want to make any changes. After making these changes, click the Preview My Page button again.
14. Click Save to save your finished page to AOL Hometown. When you save your page, it is automatically categorized in AOL Hometown, based on the template you selected.

Congratulations, you have your own home page! In fact, on the next page that appears, that's just what AOL tells you when you're done (see Figure 16-5). On this page, AOL tells you where to find your new page; offers you a chance to send e-mail to friends and family announcing your page; tells you how to edit, view, and move that page to another AOL Hometown community; and offers a subscription to a free, weekly Home Page Tips e-mail newsletter.

Note

What's the address of your new page? Whenever you create a new page at AOL Hometown, you receive an e-mail from HMTWN@aol.com that includes the new page's address plus many tips for getting the most out of AOL Hometown.

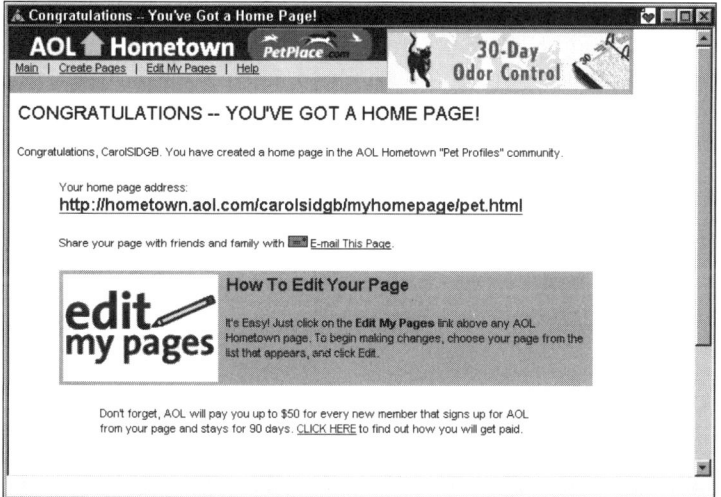

Figure 16-5. Congratulations! Now that your page is done, AOL tells you what's up next.

From now on, whenever you enter AOL Hometown, you can click the Edit My Pages link on the AOL Hometown navigation bar. This link takes you to the Edit My Pages window, shown in Figure 16-6, in which you can view, edit, or delete any page you created with 1-2-3 Publish.

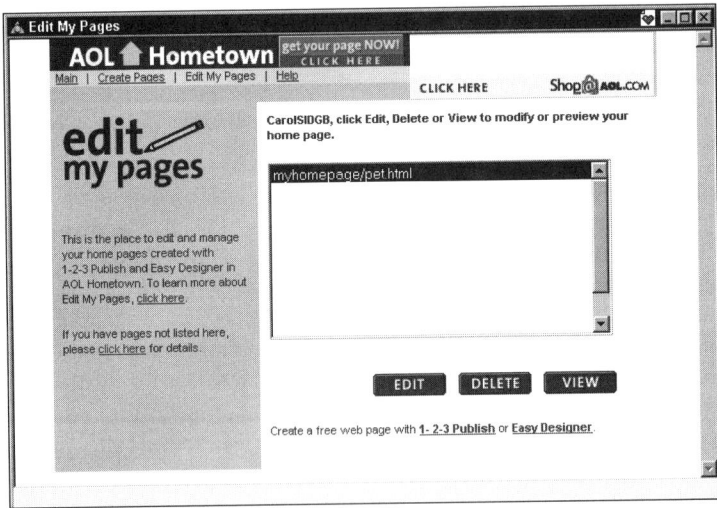

Figure 16-6. Edit, delete, or view any page you created with 1-2-3 Publish.

Clicking the Edit button in the Edit My Pages window opens the same, familiar 1-2-3 Publish window you used to create your page. Simply change whatever you want and save it when you're done. Take care if you decide to delete your page — your page will disappear without a trace, and there's no chance of recovery.

Now that you've made your first small steps into the world of Web publishing, you may be ready to create something a bit more imaginative. AOL's Easy Designer may be just the ticket!

Easy Designer

Note

Easy Designer is automatically sent to your computer every time you open it. It even provides a little game to play while you wait for the program to load.

If you've exhausted the creative possibilities of 1-2-3 Publish and yearn to do more, Easy Designer gives you room to grow. Easy Designer gives you the freedom to drag text, hyperlinks, and graphics anywhere on the page until you're satisfied with the results. You can add as many hyperlinks, photos, and graphics as you'd like, and advanced users can insert their own HTML code to extend their page's capabilities. You can even enhance the pages that you created with 1-2-3 Publish. Despite all this publishing power, Easy Designer is incredibly easy to master. You'll be designing great Web pages before you can say, well, Easy Designer!

Chapter 16 ▲ AOL Hometown

To create a Web page in Easy Designer, follow these steps:

1. Go to AOL Keyword: **Easy Designer** or follow one of the links you find on the Create Pages page and other locations around AOL Hometown. The main Easy Designer page, appears, as shown in Figure 16-7.

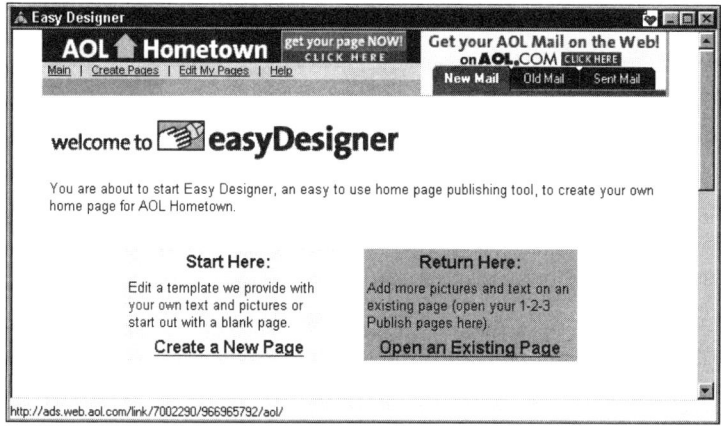

Figure 16-7. Welcome to Easy Designer.

2. Click the Create a New Page link.
3. Click the Get Started button.
4. In the Select a Template dialog box, select a template for your page. You can choose from over two dozen templates or start with a blank page. First select a category from the list on the left and then a topic from the list on the left. When you're finished, click the Next button.
5. In the Select Your Layout dialog box, select a page layout and then click the Next button.
6. In the Select a Color Style dialog box, choose from dozens of different ready-made *color styles.* Color styles consist of a text color, hyperlink color, visited-hyperlink color, and background. Backgrounds can be solid colors or tiled graphics. If you don't like the ready-made color styles, click the Customize button to customize them with your own choice of colors and background images, and even upload your own background image for tiling. Click the OK button when you're done. Easy Designer then displays a short list of Quick Tips.

 **Definition**

A *tile* is a small graphic image used for the background of a Web page. The image is repeated, much like floor tile, so it covers the entire page.

Advanced users: Insert an object that contains your own HTML code. Choose Advanced HTML from the Insert menu to open the HTML Source Code Editor window.

Meta tags are a hidden part of a Web page that make it easy for Search Engines to find and categorize your page. To boost your visibility, access your meta tag from the Edit menu and add lots of search words that accurately reflect your Web page's content. For example, if your page is dedicated to your favorite pet, include the pet's breed, type, name, color, and any other descriptive words that might help other pet lovers find your page.

7. Now that you've created the foundation for your Web page, click the Let's Go button to see the Easy Designer window, shown in Figure 16-8.

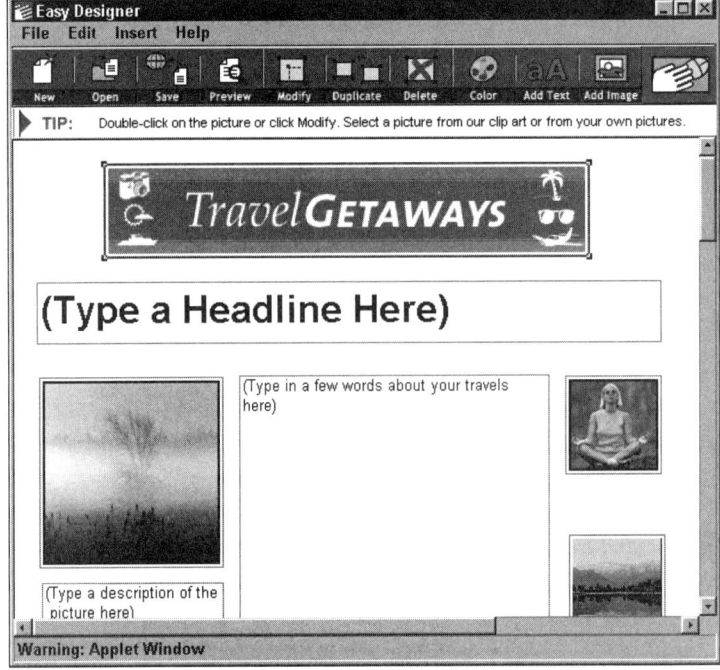

Figure 16-8. The Easy Designer workspace is loaded with tools and creative power.

8. Customize your Web page in the Easy Designer window. Here's a quick look at the main buttons on the Easy Designer toolbar:
   - **New:** Displays the Select a Template window (Step 4) so you can create a new page.
   - **Open:** Work on any of your existing AOL Hometown pages.
   - **Save:** Displays a window so that you can title your page, enter a filename, and publish your page.
   - **Preview:** See your page as it will appear online.
   - **Modify:** Edit the selected text or image object (if you have an object selected in the page), or select new images from Easy Designer's Picture Gallery (or upload your own).

Chapter 16 ▲ AOL Hometown

- **Duplicate:** Copy the selected text or image object (especially useful for preserving existing layout and formatting).
- **Delete:** Delete the selected text or image object on the page.
- **Color:** Modify the default text color, hyperlink color, and background for your page.
- **Add Text:** Open the Text Editor window and create a new text object. You can also create hyperlinks in the Text Editor. Double-click the text you want to become a hyperlink; select the specific word(s); click Link This Text. Then in the Easy Designer – Link To dialog box (see Figure 16-9), enter a Web address, AOL Hometown Page, or E-Mail Address; click OK; and click OK again.

You cannot overlap objects (either text or images). Simply reorganize and resize the boxes on-screen so that they don't overlap by clicking the object and dragging it with your mouse.

You can upgrade any 1-2-3 Publish page in Easy Designer. Just choose File⇨Open and then find your page in the list that appears. 1-2-3 Publish pages begin with My Homepage in the list.

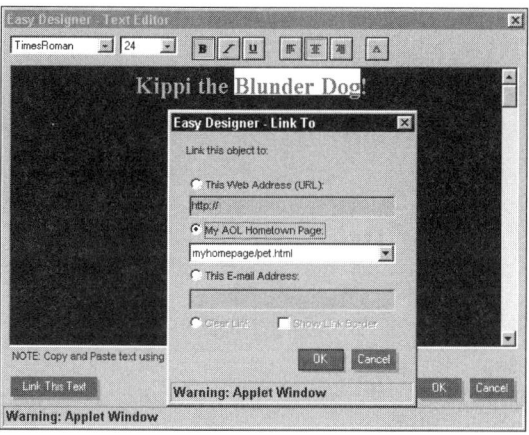

Figure 16-9. The Easy Designer Text Editor makes it easy to add a hyperlink.

- **Add Image:** Open the Easy Designer Picture Gallery to select a new image object. Select from thousands of images in the Picture Gallery, your online Web storage area, or upload your own picture (see Figure 16-10).

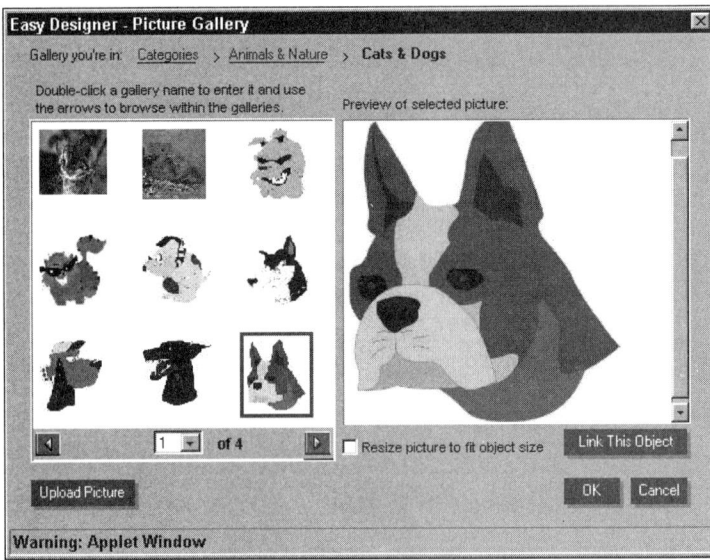

Figure 16-10. The Easy Designer Picture Gallery browses Easy Designer's own collection and the images in your AOL Hometown storage area.

Advanced Authoring

After you've mastered the basics of Easy Designer, where do you turn? For a start, turn to Build Better Pages at AOL Hometown. Just look for the link of the same name on the bottom right-hand side of the main AOL Hometown window. Here's a quick rundown of what you'll find:

- ▶ **Home Page Recipes:** Find suggestions on how to build online resumes, fan clubs, family albums, newsletters, and home pages for your small business.
- ▶ **Adding Extras to Your Page:** Learn how to earn money from Digital City by linking to local content; create animated images; add links, sounds and downloadable files; and create image maps.
- ▶ **Advanced Features:** Discover counters, forms, guest books, tables, frames, passwords, drop-down menus, and tips on creating complex home pages. Be sure to click the Advanced Tools link for information about

other tools, useful tips, free trial versions of advanced HTML editing software, plus a wide range of tutorials and classes.

As you probably know, building advanced Web pages and complete sites is far too big a topic to cover here. One place to turn is AOL Keyword: **Web Page**, part of AOL's Computing Channel (see Figure 16-11). Click the Advanced Web Publishing tab and select a topic you're interested in learning more about.

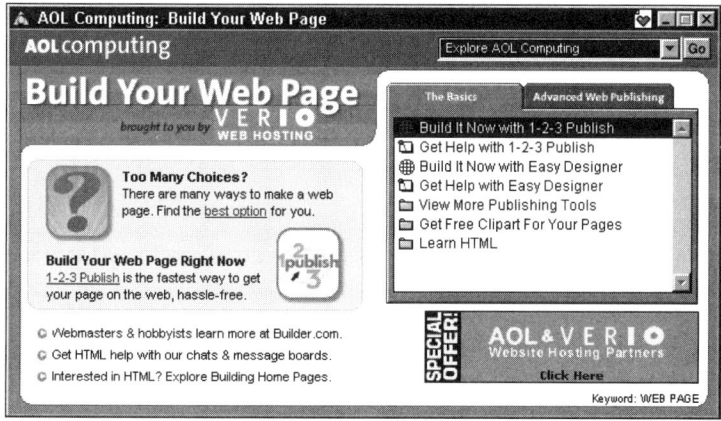

Figure 16-11. AOL Computing's Build Your Web Page, with help for advanced Web designers.

Another useful resource is the *America Online Guide to Creating Web Pages,* 2nd Edition, by Ed Willett, available from AOL Press. You can buy it online at AOL Keyword: **AOL Book Shop**.

Groups@AOL

Web pages are a fun way to share information with the whole world, but how would you like a private space in which to plan a family gathering, hang out with your old school buddies, or manage the local little league? Maybe it's time to take a look at Groups@AOL, shown in Figure 16-12.

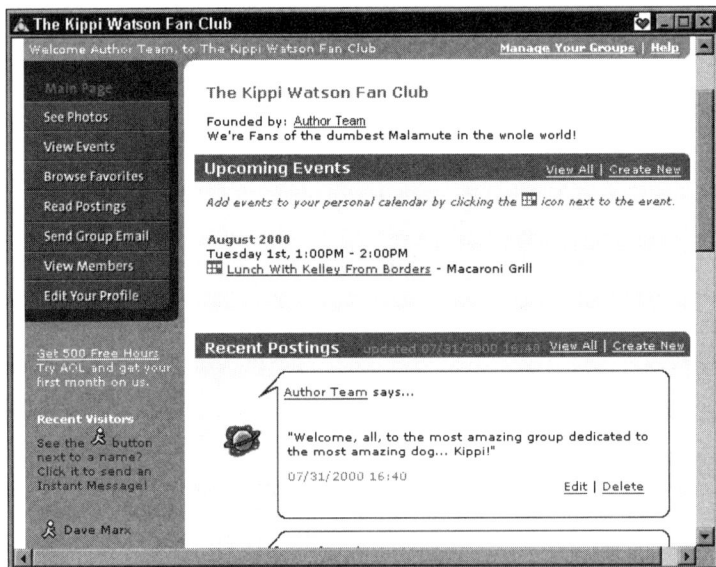

Figure 16-12. Groups@AOL offers a private spot to share information and keep in contact with family and friends.

Groups are private, invitation-only online areas. Prospective members are invited by e-mail and receive the URL (Internet address) to the group's area. To set up a group, go to AOL Keyword: **Groups@AOL**.

What can you do in a group?

- ▶ **Exchange messages:** Post and reply to messages, and (optionally) distribute those messages by e-mail.
- ▶ **Create a photo collection:** Caption the photos and use message postings to exchange comments.
- ▶ **Maintain a group calendar:** Post deadlines, schedules, and important information. Distribute the same notice via e-mail to the group. Group members can add these events to My Calendar, their personal online calendar.
- ▶ **One e-mail address for the group:** Use the built-in e-mail form or use regular AOL e-mail.
- ▶ **Exchange instant messages and chat:** See which group members are online.

- **Create lists of favorite things:** Each group member can suggest favorite Web sites, books, TV shows, and much more.
- **Create personal profiles:** Share information about yourself with the group.

Only AOL members can create groups, but anyone with Internet access can be invited to join (and access the group) so long as they get a free AOL screen name. The person who created the group has the power (and responsibility) to manage the group as its *founder;* that person can invite and remove members, send administrative e-mail as the owner, delete and edit other members' content, and give similar *owner* rights to other members of the group.

Because groups are private places that can't be monitored, AOL takes special pains to be sure parents can control their children's membership in groups. The parents of children with Kids Only or Young Teen accounts will receive an invitation to join every group their children are invited to join. Parents should monitor the group before allowing their kids to visit (and on an ongoing basis), and if the parents quit as members, their children are automatically removed from the group.

AOL Invitations

AOL Invitations are similar to Groups@AOL, but they're designed with a different purpose in mind. They are meant to be used for a single event — a birthday party, meeting, holiday celebration, hike, or maybe a dinner date.

AOL Invitations combine e-mail and a private Web page to send out simple e-mail invitations that contain hyperlinks to the Invitation page. When the guests arrive, they can RSVP, view the guest list, post messages for or send e-mail to the other guests, add the event to their personal AOL Calendar, and view a map with driving directions.

To send an invitation, go to AOL Keyword: **Invitations**, or choose People➪Invitations from the AOL toolbar. Follow the on-screen directions to choose your event type, images, dates, places, and addresses for those who should receive an invitation. When you're finished, you'll be able to preview your invitation (see Figure 16-13).

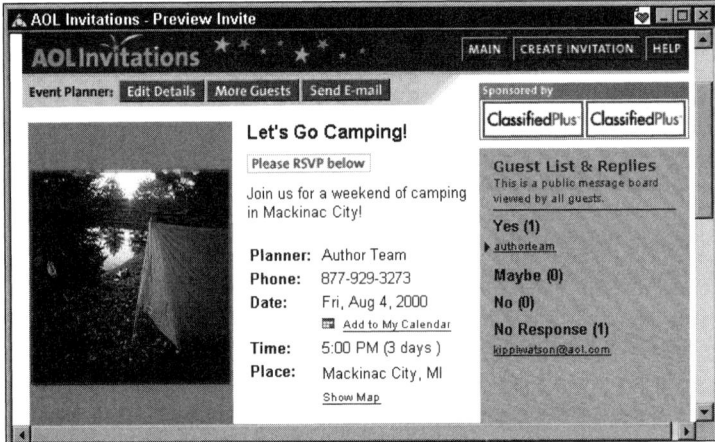

Figure 16-13. Invite your friends, relatives or colleagues to your next party.

Putting Your Knowledge to Work

After learning how easy it is to build Web pages, organize your group, or put together a party using AOL, how can you not be tempted to play around just a little? Build a Web page celebrating your favorite interest or hobby, and find new friends with this common interest at AOL Hometown.

PART IV

SEARCHING ON AOL & THE INTERNET

Chapter 17
AOL Search Tools

Chapter 18
People Search

Chapter 19
Internet Shopping

Chapter 20
Business and Information Channels

Chapter 21
Personal Enrichment and Information Channels

CHAPTER

17

AOL SEARCH TOOLS

Quick Look

▶ AOL Search   page 332
Looking for something but don't know where to start looking? Use AOL Search, which can quickly search both the AOL service and the Web at the same time. You can even narrow your search to news articles, message board posts, and so on. Just click the Search button while the text box is empty to reach AOL Search and jumpstart your search.

▶ Channel and Local Searches   page 338
Go straight to the source to find something specific by using content channel and local searches. You can initiate channel-level searches at AOL Keyword: **Channels**; you can do local searches on the area or forum level.

▶ AOL Keyword Search   page 340
AOL Keywords can also be search words. If you don't know the keyword to an area, enter a search word that seems close in the Address box on the navigation bar or in the Keyword window (press Ctrl+K to open this window). If the word you enter doesn't lead to an area, AOL Search will search on your word automatically and deliver the most relevant results from across the AOL service and the Internet!

Chapter 17
AOL Search Tools

IN THIS CHAPTER

Exploring with AOL Search

Honing in with content channel searches

Going to the source with local searches

Mining with AOL keyword searches

In the hunt for great information, picture the AOL service as a whopping, big-city main branch library. The librarians maintain numerous indexes and catalogs and many methods of searching those catalogs for just the information you need. When you know how to use all these search methods, the information you seek will be delivered to your computer screen.

AOL Search

AOL Search does something that no other search tool can do. It searches both the AOL service and the Web in one easy step. You can reach the AOL Search page in three ways:

▶ Type your search word(s) into the Search box at the far right end of the navigation toolbar and then click the Search button. (See Figure 17-1).

Search box

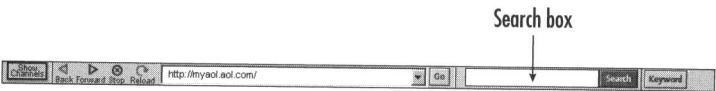

Figure 17-1. The Search box in the navigation bar.

▶ Click the Search button beside the Search field when the field itself is empty.
▶ Use the AOL Keyword: **Search**.

AOL Search is fast and easy to use. Just type a word or phrase that best describes what you are seeking into the Search box on the navigation bar or at the top of the AOL Search page (shown in Figure 17-2) and then click the Search button. After you click Search, AOL Search immediately begins looking for areas that match your word or phrase and then displays the results, as shown in Figure 17-3.

Figure 17-2. AOL Search stands ready to search for you.

If a box pops up and informs you that you are about to send information to the Internet zone, go ahead and click Yes. (You can learn more about this setting in Chapter 12.)

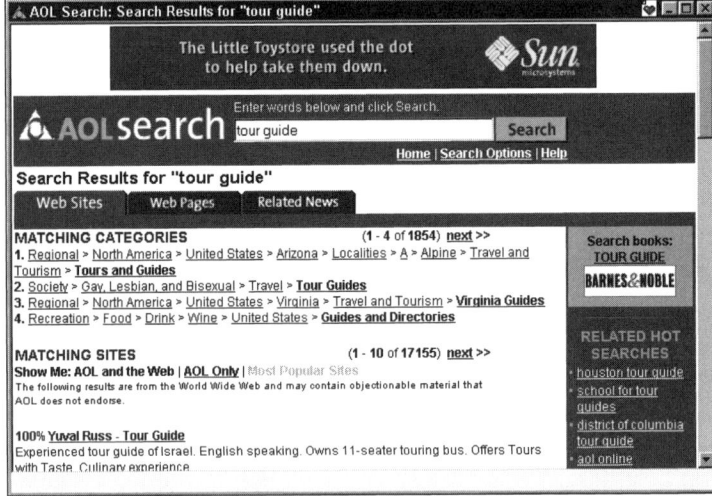

Figure 17-3. AOL Search displays the top matching categories and sites.

You can find out more about hyperlinks in Chapter 2.

A *path* on the Web is the set of links that lead you (or led you) to a particular destination. When a path is shown in a Web page, you can often jump back or forward along the path by clicking one of the hyperlinks in the path.

Take a closer look at the AOL Search results page. Near the top of the page is a search field, in which you can enter another search term when you're ready. Below this are the Home link (which leads back to the main AOL Search page), the Search Options link (which leads to more options for searching), and the Help link. In the main section of the page are the main matching categories, followed by the matching sites.

Take a look at the matching categories first. If AOL Search finds entire categories that match your search word or phrase, it displays the results near the top of the page. Click one of these words or phrases to see a list of sites within a given category, which may or may not offer what you need. Note that AOL Search displays the entire path of the matching categories — this means you must click the last item in the path (the word at the end of the line) to go to the matching category. If you click anywhere else in the matching category's line, you may go to another section within AOL Search's hierarchy.

Matching sites link you directly to areas or forums that usually contain information and/or articles with information matching your word or phrase. Note that the matching sites are displayed in order of relevancy. If AOL Search finds more results than it is capable of displaying on the initial page, the Next link is active on the right side of the page — click it to see more matches.

Arrayed beneath the Search box on the main AOL Search page is a group of very handy tabs to other results for your search. Web Sites is the default tab, but you can also view matches on the Web Pages, Related News, and Related Music tabs. Along the right side of the page are related searches — created by other members — that you may find useful, too.

You can also browse at AOL Search. Browsing means to follow links from one page to another in succession, stopping when you see something of note and then continuing to click links that interest you. You can use the links in the main portion of the AOL Search page to browse categories, subjects, and topics. You'll also notice more links at the bottom of the page for things such as the White Pages and Yellow Pages — we discuss these topics in the Chapter 18.

Still no luck with your search? Click the Search Options link to narrow your search and hone in on exactly what you seek. The Search Options page lets you define your search in more detail by defining where you want AOL Search to look for matches and how exact those matches should be. You can also enter additional words to further narrow your search.

Another way to narrow your search is to start with good search words and phrases — read the sidebar "Searching for Information" to learn how to craft good searches.

Special Searches

At the top of the AOL Search page, you can find links to specialized search engines that enable you to search different areas of AOL (refer to Figure 17-2). Here are a few examples of these specialized search engines:

- **Shopping Search:** Click this link to go to the Shopping Search, where you can search for any product that you're interested in buying. Just enter the product name or product category in the search field, and the Shopping Search will provide a list of online merchants from which you can buy the product. (See Chapter 19 for more on shopping on AOL.)

- **Message Board Search:** Click this link to go the Message Board Search, where you can search the message boards for a specific word or phrase. This feature enables you to limit the messages on a particular subject. For example, you can limit the subject *photography* by entering the search term **wildlife photography** in the message board search box. (See Chapter 9 for more on message boards.)

- **Job Search:** Click this link to go to the Job Search, powered by Monster.com. This handy search engine enables you to search online for a job. Enter the city and state you're interested in, select the job title, and, if you want, enter any terms that may further define the job you're seeking. Then click the Search button to see your results. (See Chapter 20 for more on searching for jobs.)

- **Yellow Pages:** Click this link to go to the Yellow Pages, where you can search for businesses. To conduct a simple search, enter the name of the business, the business category (click the List link to see a list of categories to choose from), and the city and state, and then click the Search button. (You can find more information on the Yellow Pages in Chapter 18.)

In addition to the searches highlighted in the preceding list, you can also search these areas: White Pages, Downloads, Shopping, Home Pages, Maps, Stock Quotes, Classifieds, Government Guide, News, Kids Only, and Encyclopedia.

Searching for Information

If you're looking for news articles, use AOL Keyword: **News Search**.

Learning to use search methods is easy. But like volunteering and voting, searching is also a matter of "getting out of it what you put into it." If you really want to hone in on what you're looking for through a search, you need to choose your search words and phrases carefully. Here are our best tips and techniques to help you craft good search words and phrases:

- **Be specific.** If you're looking for information about your new dog, type the dog's breed such as **Alaskan Malamute** rather than simply **dog**. Alternatively, try phrases like *dog groom* or *dog train*. If you're looking for an exact phrase (such as *dog bark*), put quotes around it, or you may end up with articles about the bark of the dogwood tree.

- **Use Boolean operators.** This is just a fancy way to say, "Use AND, OR, and NOT in your searches." Including these words limits your search and generally produces better results. For example, type **malamute or husky** to find all articles matching either breed of sled dog (and an occasional article about burly football players), but not both. You can also type an asterisk (*) as a wildcard, which is useful when you want to find everything that contains a word or set of characters. For example, searching on **dog*** finds doghouse, dogma, dogwood, and so on. If you're not sure how to spell a word, type it as best you can and then add the tilde (~) character — this finds results with similar spellings.

- **Don't worry about case.** Capitalization rarely matters. We recommend that you just type in all lowercase — it's faster.

- **Don't worry about suffixes either.** Most search engines treat the words *bark, barks, barked,* and *barking* as the same word.

The computer-run search engines have the benefit of impartiality, but they can be too literal-minded. Their careful methods miss countless gems that human intelligence can unearth, and they present lists with millions of selections that are barely relevant to your needs. All too often, the best resource on the Internet for your needs is item number 1,574 on a list of 11,933.

> **You Can't Search AOL from There**
>
> It is important to note that if you're seeking information specifically on the AOL service, you need to use an AOL search tool. An Internet-only search tool such as Yahoo! or Excite cannot search the AOL service, because AOL's on-line areas are available exclusively to AOL members through AOL software. The only exception is the information that AOL posts at its own Web site, AOL.COM.

Channel Searches

Another way to search for content on the AOL service is to go straight to the source. In this case, that means searching on the channel level. Channel-level searching is most useful when you have a general idea where to find something. For example, because you know that gymnastics is somewhere in the Sports Channel, a channel search would likely be fruitful.

To do a channel search, follow these steps:

1. Go directly to the channel that most likely contains the information you're seeking. The quickest way to get to a channel is via an AOL keyword (and all channel names are also keywords).

    If you're not sure which channel you need, use the Channel window on the left side of your screen (click Show Channels if you don't see it) or go to AOL Keyword: **Channels** to select one.

2. After the channel of choice is open on your screen, look for an option called Search & Explore or simply Search — it is usually near the bottom of the channel window. Alternatively, use AOL Keyword: **Channel Guide**, choose a channel, and look for the Search option. Regardless of how you find it, click the channel's Search option to open it.

    A channel's search and explore window appears (as shown in Figure 17-4), which generally offers an A–Z guide of all forums in the channel, as well as links to popular or helpful features.

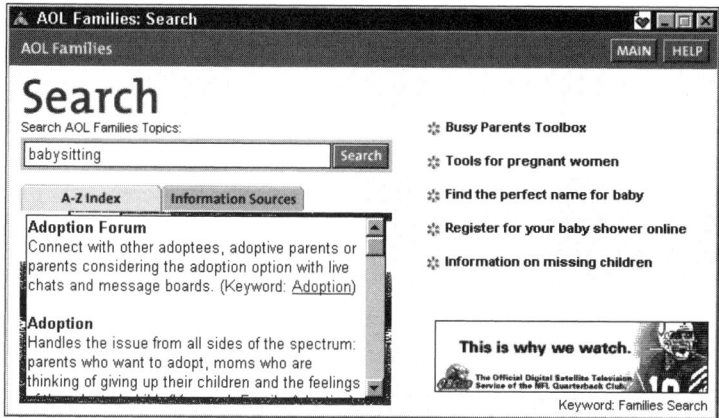

Figure 17-4. Exploring the AOL Families Channel.

3. If you don't find what you're looking for in the text, type your search word(s) in the Search box and click the Search button to scan for more content. Searches initiated from channels usually use the same AOL Search functionality, which means you search all of the AOL service and the Web.

Local Searches

Sometimes there's just no substitute for being there. In the same way you'd head to your local library to search through the local papers, it often pays to head directly to a forum to search through its content. You often get more detailed, specific results with a local search on the forum level. The downside is that you're only searching one forum's content and thus won't find anything that isn't available in the forum.

To perform a local search, go directly to the forum in question by using its keyword. Alternatively, use AOL Keyword: **Channel Guide** to open the Channel Guide window (shown in Figure 17-5). Then browse the forums available in each channel and choose one.

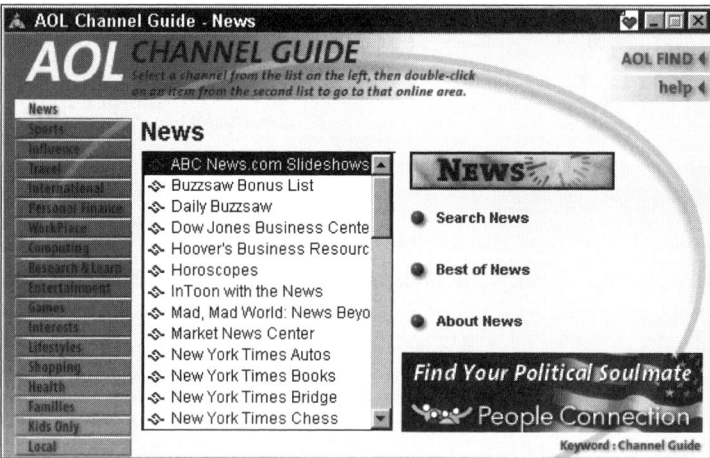

Figure 17-5. The Channel Guide can be your navigator.

Finding a search option in a forum is more hit or miss than in a channel — not every forum can be searched. If you see a Search or a Find link, click it. Otherwise, your best bet is to look for a Help or Site Map link. Search pages differ from forum to forum, but all should offer a text box for your search word or phrase and a Search or Find button to initiate the search. If you get lost, look for a Help button — they're often treasure troves of information.

Keyword Searches

If you're searching for the latest additions to the AOL service, pay a visit to AOL Keyword: **New**. Although What's New on AOL doesn't include a search engine, you may find things listed here that haven't been added to the official search engines yet.

AOL keywords are another useful tool for finding information on the AOL service. Although you may generally use keywords to reach areas you're already familiar with, you can also use them to explore new areas. One way you can do this is to simply guess a keyword. Type in a keyword in the Address box on the navigation bar or in the Keyword window (which you can reach by pressing Ctrl+K). Chances are your search word is a keyword and may lead to the exact information you seek. This technique works best when you use general search words rather than specific ones. If your search word isn't a keyword, the AOL service automatically initiates an AOL Search on your search word.

Another technique for locating information with keywords is via the keyword list. Search the keyword list online at AOL Keyword: **Keyword**. You can browse keywords in order of popularity (the top ten), alphabetically, and by channel. Alas, the online keyword list has no built-in search option.

Putting Your Knowledge to Work

Probably the most fruitful exploration you can pursue following this chapter is the search for an eloquent search phrase. As you've probably already noted, a search engine can produce radically different results based on a very small change in a search phrase. Why not focus your energy on creating the best possible search phrase for one particular search, on one particular search engine? Don't make the topic too broad, or you may never get the results down to a manageable size. Be sure to find that search engine's search tips or help area, and learn more about how to get the most out of that search engine.

Putting a bit of time and effort into mastering search engines will result in major time-savings in the years to come.

CHAPTER

18

PEOPLE SEARCH

Quick Look

▶ People Directory   page 344
Search for fellow AOL members in the People Directory. All members with profiles can be searched by name, location, sex, hobbies, and so on. Go to AOL Keyword: **Members** to do a Quick Search (or click the Advanced Search tab for a more in-depth search).

▶ Yellow Pages   page 348
Look up the phone number of virtually any business in the Yellow Pages. Just use AOL Keyword: **Yellow Pages**, enter a business category or business name, a city and state, and click the Find button.

▶ White Pages   page 350
You can find phone numbers and addresses of individuals online, too! Use AOL Keyword: **White Pages** to search for a long-lost family member or even your neighbor. Use links in the Search Results window to search for an e-mail address, to save the address, to send a greeting, and to find services in an individual's neighborhood.

▶ E-Mail Finder   page 351
If you're looking for the e-mail address of an individual who isn't an AOL member, make AOL Keyword: **Email Finder** your first stop. Enter the person's last name, first name, city, state, and country, if known. Results won't show the actual e-mail address found, but you will be able to send an e-mail to that address.

Chapter 18
People Search

IN THIS CHAPTER

Searching the People Directory for AOL members

Browsing the Yellow and White Pages for addresses and phone numbers

Using the E-Mail Finder to find e-mail addresses outside of AOL

AOL and the Internet are great places to find information. And what better information can you find than the e-mail address of a long-lost friend or relative? Your search can start right in AOL's own People Directory and spread outward from there. Searching for friends and relatives isn't quite as straightforward as browsing through a telephone book. For a variety of good reasons, finding individuals online can be difficult, unless they want to be found. Still, searches like these can be far more fruitful than flipping through a telephone book or dialing directory assistance, because you don't need to know the city or state.

People Directory

Are you looking for a fellow AOL member? Head for the AOL People Directory. Every AOL member with a member profile is listed in the People Directory, which is completely searchable. You can find someone by name, location, or just about any criteria. The catch is that the information must be in a profile, or you won't find it. If a member lists only a first name in his or her profile and you search on a first and last name, you won't find that person. This is the exception, however — we've found many long-lost friends and elusive colleagues by searching the People Directory.

To do a Quick Search of the People Directory, follow these steps:

1. Open the People Directory by choosing People⇨ People Directory from the AOL toolbar or by using AOL Keyword: **Members**. The Member Directory window then appears, as shown in Figure 18-1.

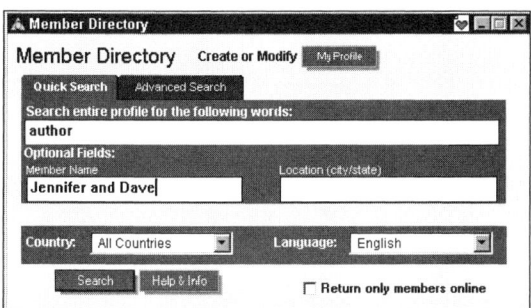

Figure 18-1. Performing a quick search of the directory.

2. In the resulting window, type in a search word or phrase in the first field, which is a catchall field for something that might appear anywhere in a member profile. Alternatively, you can type a name (first, last, or both) in the Member Name field and/or a location (city, state, country, and so on) in the Location field to refine your search. You do not need to have information in every field, but you do need to enter something in at least one field.

3. Click the Search button (or press Enter) to begin your search. AOL displays the search results in the Member Directory Search Results window, shown in Figure 18-2.

If a member is online at the time of the search, a red arrow appears next to his or her listing in the Search Results window.

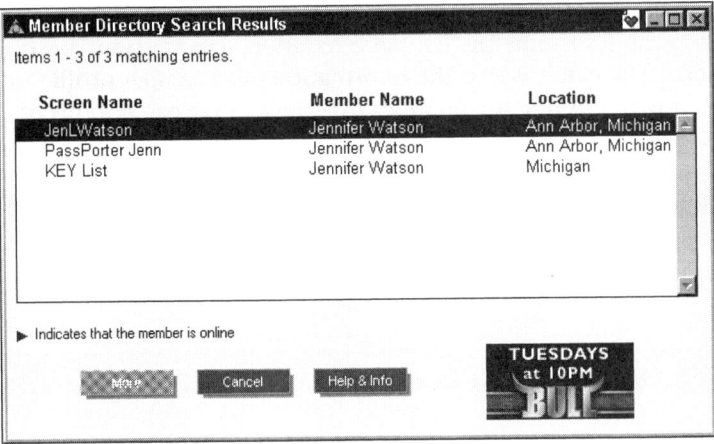

Figure 18-2. The search results.

The Search Results window lists the first 20 profiles that match your search word or phrase. You can scan the screen names (and corresponding member names and locations) of each matching profile. If more than 20 matches are found, the More button at the bottom of the window becomes active — just click it to view the next 20 matches. The results aren't listed in any logical order, so you may need to browse through them to find what you're seeking. Double-click a screen name to view the Member Profile window, shown in Figure 18-3.

Six buttons are arrayed along the bottom of the Member Profile window:

- **Locate:** Click this button to find out if the member is online right now.
- **E-Mail:** Click this button to open a new e-mail window, addressed to the member.
- **Create a Home Page:** Click this button to go to 1-2-3 Publish (discussed in Chapter 16).
- **Online Greetings:** Click this button to send a free electronic greeting to the member.
- **Notify AOL:** Click this button to report inappropriate information (refer to AOL's Terms of Service, which is described in Chapter 4).
- **Help & Info:** Click this button for more searching tips and assistance.

Note

In addition to the screen name, a profile lists all information volunteered by a member. This may include member name, location, birth date, gender, marital status, hobbies, computers, occupation, and a personal quote. If all this information isn't listed in a profile, it simply means that the member left the associated field blank when filling out the profile form.

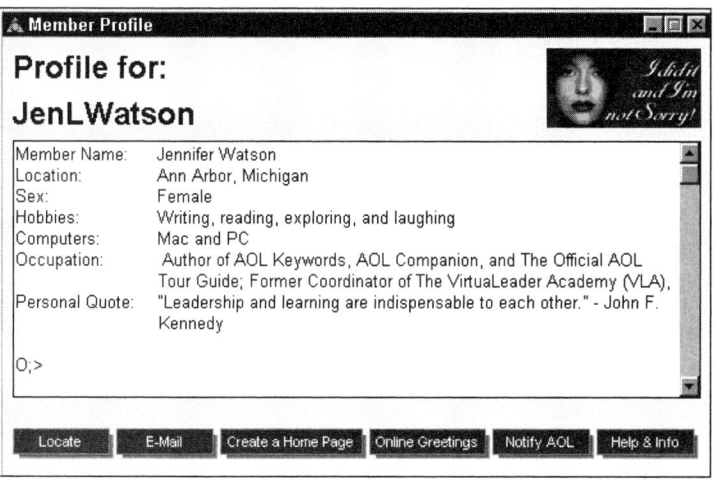

Figure 18-3. Author Team's AOL member profile.

If your search returns many results, you will discover that your search is limited to 100 matches. This can be a real problem if your friend turns out to be number 101. Besides, although you could browse 100 member profiles, who wants to? Instead, get fewer (and better) results with an advanced search. Click the Advanced Search tab in the Member Directory window (refer to Figure 18-1) to get more search fields, as shown in Figure 18-4. Now you can further define a search by gender, marital status, hobbies, occupation, computers, and quote.

Select the Return Only Members Online check box in the Member Directory window to return profiles of members who are currently online and no others.

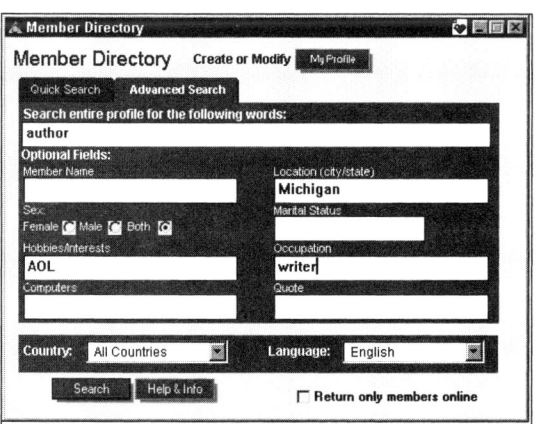

Figure 18-4. Digging deeper with the Advanced Search feature.

Yellow Pages

When you need to find a business, its address, and its phone number, where better to turn than the Yellow Pages? To go the old-fashioned yellow pages one (or two) better, an AOL Yellow Pages listing includes a map, driving instructions, and (sometimes) fax numbers and e-mail addresses! AOL's Yellow Pages are part of AOL Search (which is described in Chapter 17). You can reach the Yellow Pages by using AOL Keyword: **Yellow Pages** or by choosing People⇨Yellow Pages from the AOL toolbar.

On the Yellow Pages search page, shown in Figure 18-5, you can search for businesses by either business category or business name, and you must narrow the search by selecting which state to search. If you know which city to search, so much the better!

Category searches are most accurate if you select a category from the Yellow Pages' Category list. Click the Category List hyperlink on the search page and select the appropriate category (see Figure 18-6). Once a category is selected, you are taken back to the Yellow Pages search page with the selected category filled in.

Business searches work best when you know the exact name of the company you seek, as well as its location. Just type the company's name in the Business Name field and then fill in the City and State fields, as shown in Figure 18-5.

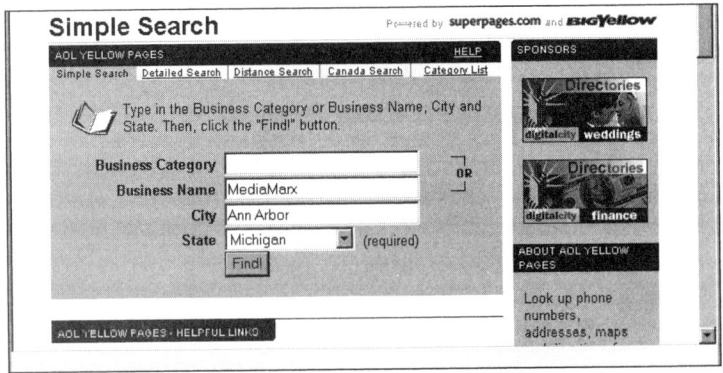

Figure 18-5. Searching for a business name in the AOL Yellow Pages.

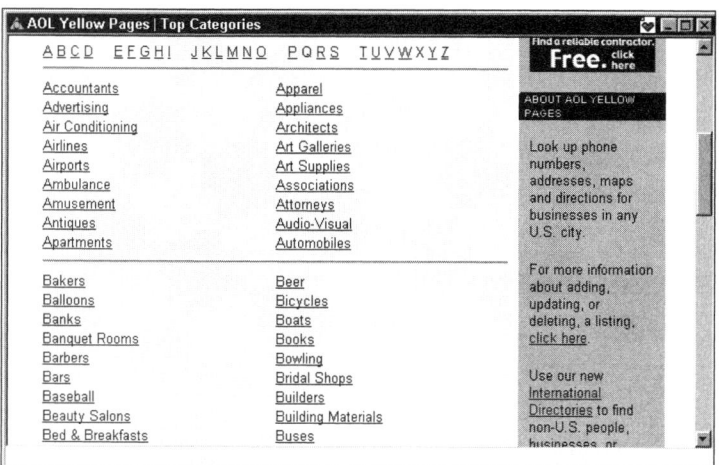

Figure 18-6. Choosing categories in the AOL Yellow Pages.

You can perform additional types of searches by clicking these links:

- ▶ **Distance Search:** This option helps you find businesses within five miles of home.
- ▶ **Detailed Search:** This option lets you search by useful keywords, such as free delivery. You can also use the detailed search to get a business's address, map, and driving instructions, as shown in Figure 18-7.

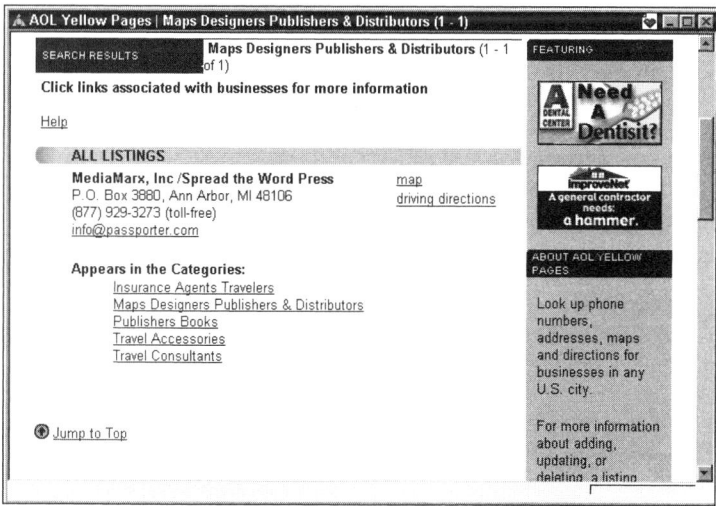

Figure 18-7. Search results in the AOL Yellow Pages.

Like any telephone directory, the AOL Yellow Pages listings can be a bit out of date, but unlike the paper-and-ink version, a business can create or update its own listing by clicking the handy link right on the search page. One thing's for sure: You'll always know where to find your copy of AOL's Yellow Pages.

White Pages

Not everyone has an e-mail address. AOL recognizes this and makes an international, fully searchable White Pages available. The White Pages can virtually eliminate the need to call directory assistance! Best of all, the White Pages contains more information than your run-of-the-mill directory assistance offers. In addition to phone numbers, it offers e-mail addresses, street mailing addresses, neighborhood maps, driving directions, lists of nearby businesses, and more. You can reach the AOL White Pages by using AOL Keyword: **White Pages**. Alternatively, choose People⇨White Pages from the AOL toolbar.

The White Pages search window, shown in Figure 18-8, asks for much the same information as the E-Mail Finder (described in the next section). The biggest difference is the addition of the Metro Search check box. If you select this check box, the search encompasses an entire metropolitan area, rather than just the city proper.

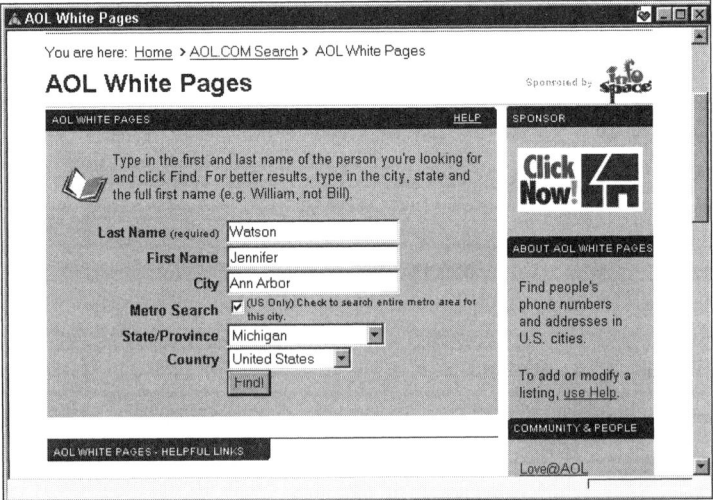

Figure 18-8. The AOL White Pages makes it easy to find someone.

Updating Your Listing

When you're checking out the White Pages, do a search on yourself. Did you find a listing (or two)? Chances are you will, but the information may be too specific or inaccurate. If you want to change the information displayed by the White Pages, click the update link to the right of your listing. You need to provide your e-mail address and your updated information. Note that even if your information is correct, you can use the Update feature to add more information. Alternatively, you can click the Delete link to remove your listing entirely.

E-Mail Finder

The AOL Member Directory is a powerful tool for finding people on AOL, but what about people who aren't on AOL? The AOL E-Mail Finder can help you locate virtually anyone with an e-mail address, whether they're AOL members or not. Use AOL Keyword: **Email Finder** to go directly to the Web-based search page, shown in Figure 18-9.

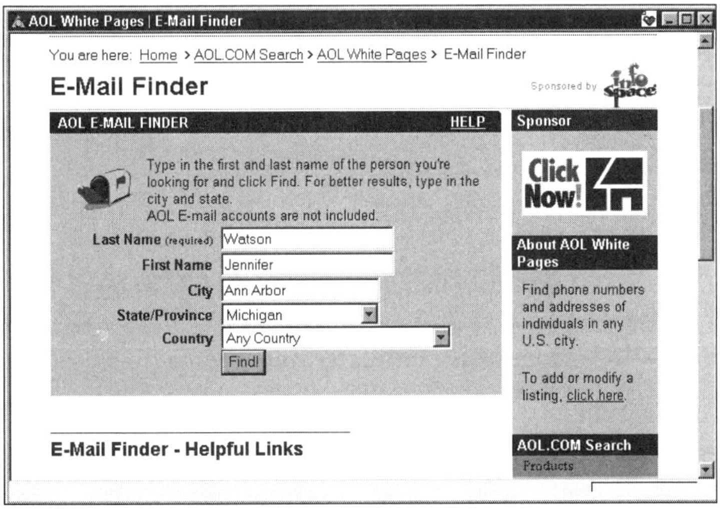

Figure 18-9. The AOL E-Mail Finder searches a vast database of e-mail addresses.

Because of the sheer number of people and e-mail addresses, the E-Mail Finder works best when you provide as much information as possible. Type in a last name (required), followed by a first name (or initial), city, state, and country. Check that your spelling is as accurate as possible and then click the Find button. AOL displays the results in the same window, as shown in Figure 18-10.

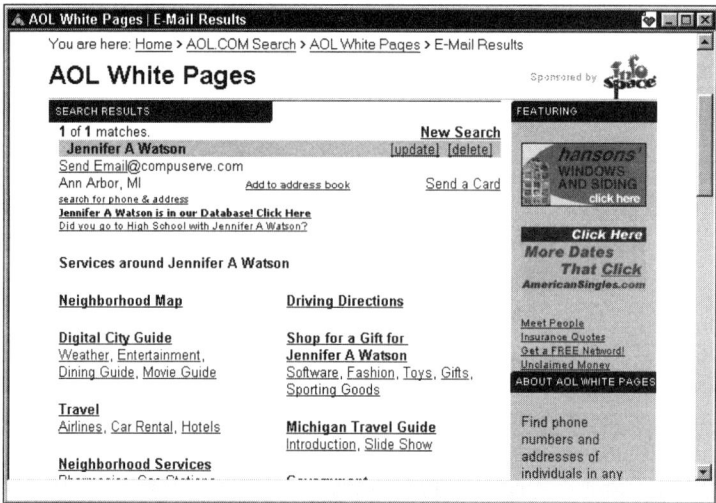

Figure 18-10. The E-Mail Finder's search results.

A search is limited to 250 results. If you reach this limit, refine your search for fewer results.

The E-Mail Finder only finds e-mail addresses outside of AOL.

The E-Mail Finder lists results in alphabetical order by name. The page displays only five records at a time, so you need to click the Next link to view the next five matches.

Each record includes other available information, such as an address, a city, a state, or a country. What isn't included is the e-mail address itself — only the words *Send Email* and the domain name are given (for example, `Send Email@compuserve.com` or `Send Email@netscape.net`). To actually send an e-mail, click the blue Send E-Mail link and fill out the e-mail message form, shown in Figure 18-11.

It may seem odd that the E-Mail Finder doesn't list the individual's e-mail address, but AOL is protecting each individual's privacy by not revealing his or her actual e-mail address. You can obtain the actual e-mail address when your recipient replies to your message — just be sure you type your own e-mail address correctly in the Web e-mail message window.

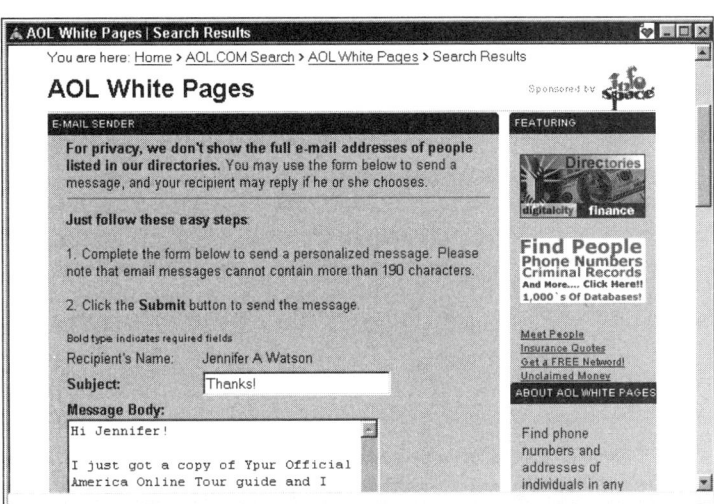

Another way to find people is through the Personals (choose People➪Personals from the AOL toolbar). You can search and browse the personals, learning all sorts of juicy details about people. Of course, you can create your own personal and let others find you, too!

Figure 18-11. Sending e-mail from E-Mail Finder.

Putting Your Knowledge to Work

Now that you know how to find people online, why not search for a long-lost friend? You may be surprised to learn just how easy it is to find someone! Chances are, of course, that as soon as you find that long-lost friend, you'll realize you just missed his or her birthday. Need a gift quick? Shopping is fast and simple on AOL, which offers a vast array of products. The next chapter takes a closer look at the benefits of shopping online.

CHAPTER 19

INTERNET SHOPPING

Quick Look

▶ Shop@AOL   page 356

AOL offers an entire channel devoted to shopping online: Shop@AOL. The channel offers online retailers, organized by category, as well as a way to search for brands and products. You can reach the Shopping Channel with AOL Keyword: **Shopping**.

▶ Chic Simple   page 360

Need a little help finding that perfect dress for the party? Pay a visit to Chic Simple for fashion advice from Kim and Jeff. It's a fast, easy way to shop with style. See AOL Keyword: **Chic Simple**.

▶ AOL Shop Direct   page 361

Whether you want to upgrade your computer or just want to show your AOL pride with a T-shirt, AOL Shop Direct comes through. You can find hardware, software, books, AOL logo merchandise, and deals for AOL members at AOL Keyword: **Shop Direct**.

Chapter 19

Internet Shopping

IN THIS CHAPTER

Finding the stores and shops that have what you want

Searching the stores quickly and easily

Finding advice on stylish shopping

Getting shopping deals for AOL members

Shopping on America Online is even better than shopping on Rodeo Drive or in the streets of Paris. You can find a wide variety of items within every price range on AOL, and you can shop from the comfort of your desk — no sore feet, no overflowing bags, and no parking problems. So grab your shopping lists, and come with us as we explore the shops and stores of America Online.

Browsing the Categories

Although you'll find shopping opportunities in many of AOL's channels and forums, AOL's Shopping Channel (also known as Shop@AOL; see Figure 19-1) is the best place to start. Click the Shopping button in your Channel list (on the left side of your screen), or use AOL Keyword: **Shopping**.

Figure 19-1. Shop@AOL is an electronic bazaar of goods and services.

The Shopping Channel offers more than 200 retailers displaying their wares in more than 15 categories, from some of America's oldest household names to the hottest "dot.coms." You can find all the great brands you know and trust, and browse or shop in a safe and secure environment at Shop@AOL (see Figure 19-2).

Figure 19-2. The Kids, Toys & Babies department at Shop@AOL.

Tip

Click the A–Z Store Listing of Stores link in the Shop@AOL window to get a list of all stores at Shop@AOL.

When you think about AOL's Shopping Channel, think *shopping mall*. Think really, really *big* shopping mall. Many of the retailers in the Shopping Channel's categories are familiar shopping mall names, from big department stores such as J.C. Penney and Macy's to specialty shops such as Godiva Chocolates, Gap, Victoria's Secret, and Eddie Bauer. Mail-order favorites L.L. Bean, Lands' End, Spiegel, Lillian Vernon, and Chef's Catalog, among others, have also set up shop online. Door-to-door specialist Avon comes calling, and you can "call" 1-800-Flowers. Just about the only thing you can't get at this shopping mall is a burger and a haircut (although you *can* buy a frozen steak from Omaha Steaks).

Although the procedures vary a bit from store to store, making purchases is very straightforward. As you browse through a store and find something you like, you "toss" it in your *shopping cart* — choose the item you're interested in and click the Order, Purchase, Add, or OK button with your mouse. You may be asked questions about size, color, and other options. See Figure 19-3 for an example.

Figure 19-3. Click the Add to Shopping Cart button when you see something you like, such as this way cool watch from DisneyStore.com.

The stores maintain an electronic shopping cart that holds all the items you select until you're ready to check out. You're free to check the contents of your shopping cart, add items to or remove items from your cart, or quit shopping altogether without spending a cent or divulging your personal information. Many stores are able to retain the contents of your shopping cart, even if you leave the store, though this isn't true of all stores. When you're finished in a store, click the Begin Checkout button (see Figure 19-4). During the checkout process, you are asked for payment and shipping information, and then you're done!

If you find yourself shopping online often, consider signing up for AOL Quick Checkout (described in Chapter 15). It can save you plenty of time when shopping from qualifying merchants.

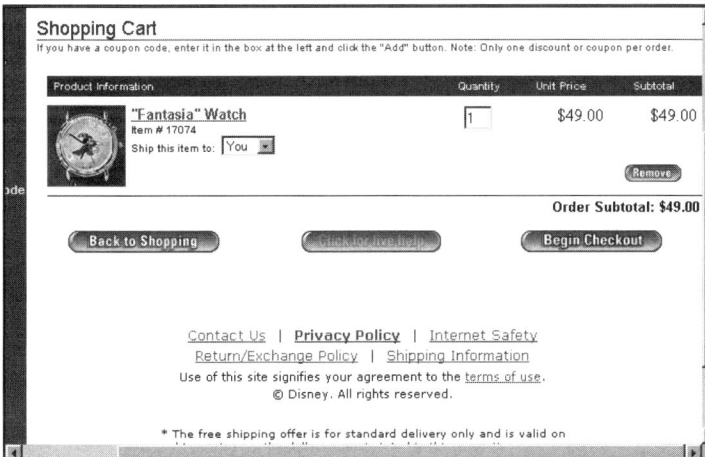

Figure 19-4. Click the Begin Checkout button when you're ready to purchase your items.

Shopping Search

Can't find what you want? Use the Shopping Search. Just type a product or brand name in the Shopping Search field in the main Shop@AOL window, and then click Search. AOL returns all the matching products (see Figure 19-5).

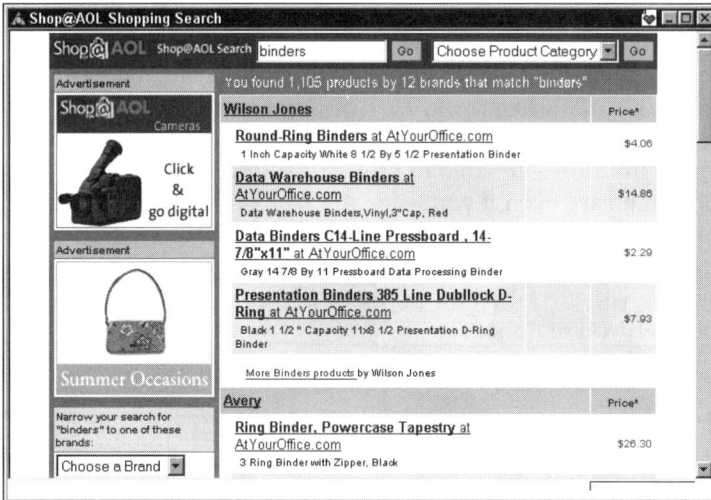

Figure 19-5. Shop@AOL search results are easy to browse.

You can also use the Shopping Search box at the top of each category window to zero in on the product you're seeking.

Results are ranked by relevancy and include short descriptions, prices, and hyperlinks to go directly to the stores that carry the matching products. If your search returns too many results, narrow your search by using brand names or descriptive words, such as "ring binder" or "binder accessory."

Chic Simple

Do you ever go shopping with a friend whose taste, shopping savvy, and sense of style is "to die for"? AOL figures everyone can use the kind of advice that leaves you looking outrageous for far less than you thought you'd pay, so Kim Johnson and Jeff Stone of Chic Simple are now fixtures at Shop@AOL. Chic Simple puts together seasonal wardrobes with items selected from merchants throughout Shop@AOL. Everything from tops and bottoms to undies and accessories are selected with an eye for comfort, value, and style. If you're really stumped, you can even ask Kim for a bit of help. You can find links to Chic Simple right on the Shopping Channel's front page and in many other departments around the Shopping Channel, or use AOL Keyword: **Chic Simple**.

Shopping AOL Shop Direct

AOL Shop Direct (AOL Keyword: **Shop Direct**) is America Online's very own store, offering just the kind of merchandise you need for a great online (and offline) experience (see Figure 19-6).

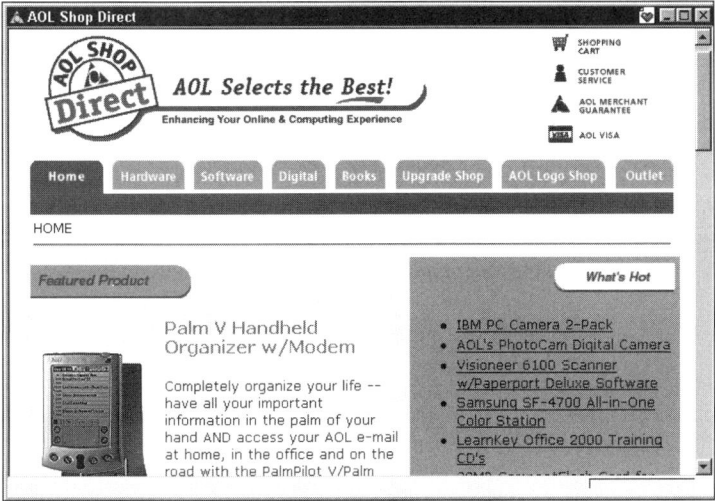

Figure 19-6. AOL Shop Direct offers great deals to AOL members.

Everything from computers, modems, and digital cameras to software, books, and logo merchandise has been selected and pre-tested for value, ease of use, and suitability to an AOL member's needs. Shop Direct turns up some great bargains and its Outlet center is a fun place to look for close-out merchandise, so it pays to visit AOL Shop Direct.

Putting Your Knowledge to Work

Our brief tour of AOL's shopping district barely skims the surface of what awaits you at AOL Shopping, in other areas on AOL, and out on the wider Internet. If you're half the shopper we think you are, you'll have to come back some other time to shop in earnest. When you do, keep some of these tips in mind:

- Be the same careful consumer you'd be anywhere else. Visit the shops' customer service areas, read the fine print, and be sure that you understand all the ins and outs before you commit real cash.
- If you're a serious wheeler-dealer and bargain hunter, you may want to check out an online auction. You'll find several examples of this hot new way to buy and sell merchandise at the AOL Shopping Channel — just click the Auctions & Collectibles button.
- Some apparel shops let you build an electronic mannequin so you can see how their clothes look on someone who looks like you. Mix, match, and see how an ensemble will look on you. Pretty neat!

Now that you know how to spend your money on AOL, we're going to show you where you can earn more of it. At the next stop on our tour, you get a chance to explore the business-related channels and forums on AOL.

CHAPTER

20

BUSINESS AND
INFORMATION
CHANNELS

Quick Look

▶ **Channel Bar**   **page 365**

Your AOL remote control — the Channel bar — is always accessible with the Show/Hide Channels button on the left end of the navigation bar. Use your Channel bar to surf the channels quickly and easily.

▶ **Weather**   **page 368**

AOL offers up-to-the-hour weather conditions and forecasts for your hometown or travel destination. Just go to AOL Keyword: **Weather**, type your zip code, city, or country, click Search, and choose your community. You are rewarded with stats, maps, and forecasts.

▶ **Job Search**   **page 376**

You can search more than 350,000 job listings online to find that perfect job. Go to AOL Keyword: **Job Search**, click Job Search, enter your information, and click Search for your results.

▶ **Ask-a-Teacher**   **page 382**

When you (or your kids) need help with a homework assignment, just ask a teacher ... on AOL! At AOL Keyword: **Ask a Teacher**, you can look up answers to previously asked questions, post your question on a message board, get live help from a teacher, or e-mail your question to a teacher. This free service is available for students in elementary school, middle school, high school, college, and beyond.

Chapter 20

Business and Information Channels

IN THIS CHAPTER

Surfing the AOL channels

Staying informed at the News Channel

Going around the world at the International Channel

Making money at the Personal Finance and Careers & Work Channels

Learning more at the Computer Center and Research & Learn Channels

Visiting the neighbors at the Local Guide Channel

AOL's business and information channels offer all the resources and tools you need to stay on top and stay up-to-date. You'll find business forums, financial tools, research libraries, extensive news coverage, career aids, and computing resources.

The Channels

We start this tour with a quick visit back to the Channel bar, which we describe in Chapter 1. The Channel bar is fully

Chapter 20 ▲ Business and Information Channels

integrated into the navigation bar — anytime you want to visit a channel, just click one on the Channel bar on the left side of your screen. If you don't see the Channel bar, click Show Channels on the Navigation Bar (see Figure 20-1).

Figure 20-1. The Channel bar is the perfect jumping-off spot.

Flipping the channels at AOL is nearly as simple as changing channels on your television. Think of the Channel bar as a remote control. Click once, and the screen is instantly converted to the desired channel.

If you don't flip for that method, AOL offers a couple more:

- ▶ **Try keywords.** Every channel name is also a keyword. Just type the channel name in the navigation bar's text box, and click Go (or press Enter).
- ▶ **Use AOL Keyword:** Channels. The Channels window has a large, colorful button for every channel.

You can use some other advanced methods (like Favorite Places), but this should be enough to get you started. The next time someone loses the remote control, you can still switch channels.

News Channel

It's huge! If you had to carry it in from the front stoop, you'd need a forklift, but fortunately, all you need is your mouse and all the time in the world. This is AOL News, your route to what's happening now throughout the world at AOL Keyword: **News** (see Figure 20-2).

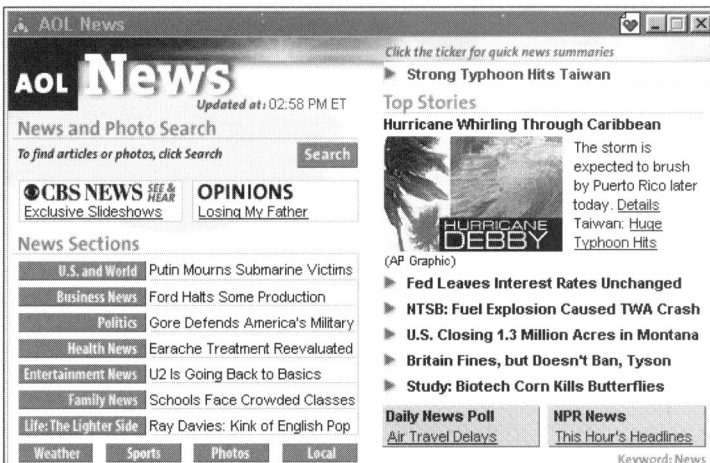

Figure 20-2. AOL's News Channel — all the news that fits, and then some!

The News Channel gathers news from many of the top sources online, in print, and on the air. Among AOL's news gathering partners are CBS News, National Public Radio, TIME magazine, The New York Times, the Associated Press, Reuters, and Bloomberg.

The AOL News Channel screen is packed tightly with news headlines and features. If you click any one selection, you'll be swept deeper and deeper into the news. If the headline leads to a news story, the story probably will be accompanied by a photograph and/or collection of additional stories on the same topic. Other buttons lead to entire news departments, such as Business News or U.S. & World News, and still others lead to news-gathering organizations such as CBS News. The News Search feature can find hundreds of articles on a given topic, and surveys or quizzes are always available for those who want to lend their voice or test their knowledge.

You can expect to find the following things on the front screen of AOL News:

- **News and Photo Search:** Type your search phrase, and be prepared to dive into an ocean of search results. You'll find more here than ever makes it to the front page. Use AOL Keyword: **News Search**.
- **CBS News:** See slide shows of CBS news reports, prepared especially for AOL. Hear the reports, and see an ever-changing series of still photos. You'll also find links to CBS News top stories and On Air, featuring transcripts and reports from CBS News magazines such as 48 Hours, 60 Minutes, and the CBS Evening News. Use Keyword: **CBS News**.
- **Opinions:** AOL News collects editorials and commentaries from its diverse partners, including The New York Times and National Public Radio. You can also make yourself heard at the many chats, message boards, and surveys offered at the bottom of the Speak Out window. Use AOL Keyword: **Speak Out**.
- **U.S. and World:** Here's all the news you'd expect to find, and a good bit more. Search around a bit (by clicking the More Stories button, for example) for collections of world news organized by region and by nation, and news from Washington, D.C. Use AOL Keyword: **US World**.
- **Business News:** Track the course of commerce and finance at AOL Business News. The AOL Business News Center is shared by AOL's News, Personal Finance, and WorkPlace Channels, and features stories from Bloomberg News, AP, and Reuters. A stock ticker highlights top financial averages and provides links to AOL Personal Finance's Market News Center (MNC). Top Stories, Business News Search, Overseas Markets, News Summary, Technology, Economy, International, Industry,

Tip

How fresh are the headlines at the News Channel? A quick glance at the top of the News Channel screen, where AOL posts the time of the last update, tells you. If the headlines don't seem quite fresh enough, close and reopen the window. If there's been another update, you receive it! No matter what happens, the headlines on the news ticker (discussed later) in the upper-right of the screen are constantly changing.

Tip

For even more international news, visit the AOL International Channel's News department at AOL Keyword: **Intl News**. Among its fascinating resources are links to hundreds of online newspapers throughout the world, many in their native languages. We discuss this channel later in the chapter.

and Consumer Briefs all have a home here. Use AOL Keyword: **Business News**.

▶ **Politics:** Learn more than you wanted to know about politicians, lawmakers, and elections from the major news organizations. Of course, what's politics without a link to NewsTalk, where the soapbox is king (or president)? Use AOL Keyword: **Politics**.

▶ **Health News:** Today in Health offers news and articles of interest from AOL's Health Channel. Use AOL Keyword: **Today in Health**.

▶ **Entertainment News:** Showbiz news from AOL's Entertainment Channel. Read the hot news, and find links to the entertainment news sections of PEOPLE Online, E! Online, Entertainment Weekly, and SonicNet. Use AOL Keyword: **Ent News**.

▶ **Family News:** This is the human-interest side of news with late-breaking stories, today's Features, and in-depth coverage of news that matters to families. Use AOL Keyword: **Family News**.

▶ **Life: The Lighter Side:** Gossip, gossip, and more gossip. Check this section out when you need the dirt. Use AOL Keyword: **Life News**.

▶ **Weather:** Visit AOL Weather Central for the national weather map, local weather conditions, and torrents of useful news at AOL Keyword: **Weather**. Just enter an area code, zip code, city, or state into the Search box to get a detailed forecast for your hometown or anyplace else in the United States (see Figure 20-3).

Add an icon for your local weather forecast to your AOL toolbar for one-click access to current weather information. Call up your local forecast at the AOL Weather Center, drag its Favorite Places heart to the AOL toolbar, select an icon (the sun-and-clouds icon works well), and add a caption (see Chapter 14 for more details on Favorite Places). You'll never have to look out your windows again!

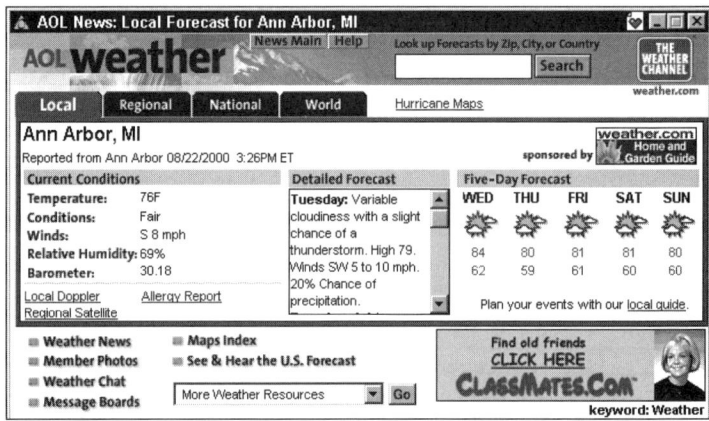

Figure 20-3. Get the local conditions in Ann Arbor, Michigan, from AOL Weather Central.

- **Sports:** This is actually a link to the Sports Channel, where you'll find the latest scores and top sports stories. For more on the Sports Channel, see Chapter 22.
- **Photos:** Really "see" the news with photo galleries related to top stories. Use the arrows to flip the photos one by one, or click the thumbnail to jump to the photo you want. Use AOL Keyword: **Photo News**.
- **Local:** AOL News and Digital City have teamed up with local news organizations across the country to bring a local slant to the AOL experience. Get local news, sports, and weather from your old hometown, from just around the block, or for the city you'll be visiting tomorrow. Use AOL Keyword: **Local News**. See the section on the Local Guide Channel, described later in this chapter.
- **News Ticker:** Up-to-the-moment headlines flash across the top of the News Channel window, just the way they do in New York City's Times Square. The similarity ends there, though. Just one click on the headline brings you the stories behind the headlines from the U.S. and World News Summary.

International Channel

When you got this book, did you think you'd be traveling the world? Thanks to AOL's International Channel (see Figure 20-4), the entire world is only seconds away. The folks at AOL International have prepared a warm welcome for travelers from every modem on the globe (at AOL Keyword: **Intl**).

Despite its name, America Online is a worldwide phenomenon. AOL has services in Canada, Brazil, Mexico, the United Kingdom, France, Germany, Sweden, Austria, Switzerland, Japan, Hong Kong, and Australia — all in the native languages. Services for Argentina and other countries are also in development. AOL International gives you a chance to sample some of those services and to interact with fellow AOL members around the globe.

Tip

The headline that's visible when you click the News Ticker is the first story that is displayed when the summary appears. Wait for the ticker to come back around to the story you want to see, click, and that item will be right at the top of your summary. Or just click the News Ticker, and scroll down to that story. Pretty slick, huh?

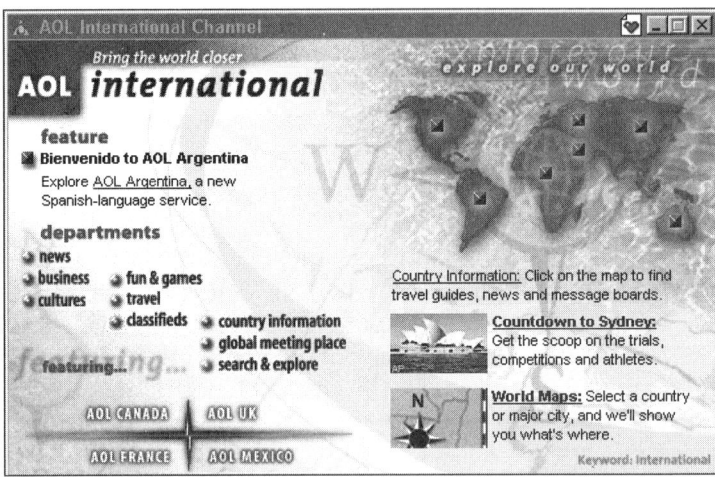

Figure 20-4. AOL's International Channel — an entire globe to explore!

Tip

What does AOL U.K. have that AOL U.S. does not? How about BBC News Online? For a taste of Great Britain's legendary news source, head for AOL International News, select AOL's Foreign News Sources from the list, and then select AOL UK News. The "Beeb" should be right there on the AOL UK News front screen.

AOL International ranges far beyond the boundaries of those 12 national services. World travelers, students of foreign cultures, and just plain folks will find information on more than 210 countries and political subdivisions. The folks at AOL International have knit together in-depth guides to each of these places, combining travel, economic, cultural, and political information in an easy-to-use format that is consistently applied from country to country.

The International Channel hides a wealth of information and community activities behind its uncluttered main screen, as the following list makes clear:

▶ **News:** What more can the AOL International Channel News offer? How about the entire AOL Canada, AOL Mexico, AOL U.K., AOL Australia, AOL France, and AOL Germany news departments? How about world news organized by country, overseas weather forecasts, links to hundreds of newspapers around the world, and TIME magazine's Asia edition? Does that sound like a good reason to visit AOL Keyword: **Intl News**? We certainly hope so!

▶ **Business:** The global economy is never at rest, but the resources of AOL International Business, at AOL

Keyword: **Intl Business**, can help you rest a bit easier. Research world market conditions with the Financial Times. Dig deeply into global economic conditions with the Economist Intelligence Unit. AOL International Business also delivers Business Week International, information for those working abroad, exchange rates, and a currency conversion calculator.

▶ **Cultures:** Whether you're headed for Korea or the kitchen, International Cultures has the recipe for greater understanding of people, their languages, and cultures at AOL Keyword: **Intl Cultures**. Planning a dinner at home or boning up on what you can expect to eat while abroad? Visit The Global Gourmet (AOL Keyword: **GG**). They serve up a huge menu of authentic recipes and delightful, food-oriented destination guides for 40 countries and regions (see Figure 20-5).

One of the less-heralded gems of International Channel is its collection of language dictionaries and resources (AOL Keyword: **Foreign Dictionary**). From Afrikaans to Zulu, dictionaries and language aids are available by the dozen.

Figure 20-5. The Global Gourmet's pantry is stocked with international cuisine.

▶ **Fun & Games:** AOL International's Fun and Games forum crosses oceans and continents to gather games, quizzes, contests, and entertainment news that help you learn a bit more about the world and the people in it.

▶ **Travel:** When you've finished your virtual world tour on America Online, AOL International Travel stands ready to help you travel the globe at AOL Keyword:

Intl Travel. Preparing for vacation and business travel has never been easier, thanks to the many resources gathered here.

▶ **Country Information:** AOL International maintains profiles on more than 210 countries around the globe (see Figure 20-6) at AOL Keyword: **Countries**. Whether you're planning a visit, researching a school project, or looking for new friends from your old homeland, you'll find everything you need in rich detail.

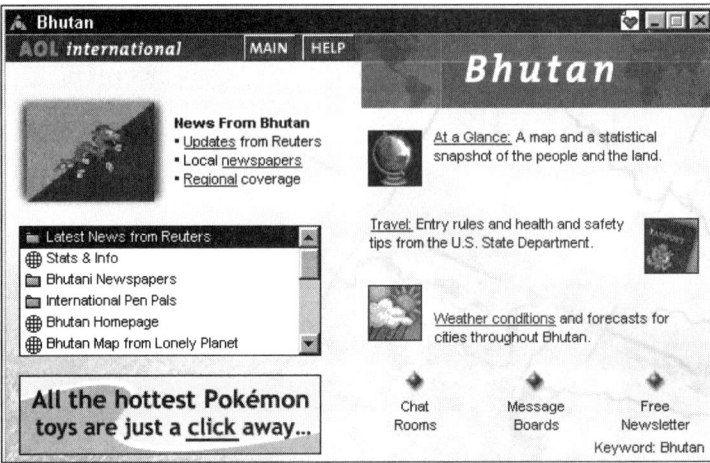

Figure 20-6. You can find Bhutan, sandwiched between China and India, and located at AOL Keyword: **Bhutan**.

▶ **Global Meeting Place:** If you'd like to teach the world to sing in perfect harmony, you'll find few better places to start than AOL International Channel's Global Meeting Place (AOL Keyword: **Global Meeting**). You can visit chat rooms in the U.K., Germany, Canada, and Australia, search for a pen pal (although perhaps "keyboard pal" would be the better term), and find romance in Passport to Love. Perhaps AOL is the true international language! Be sure to stop in The Bistro, which offers live chat in more than 30 different languages at AOL Keyword: **Bistro**.

Personal Finance Channel

AOL has managed to pack every financial service from Wall Street to Main Street into one little channel: AOL Personal Finance. This channel is for the homeowner, the stockholder, and the just-plain-everyday person who strives to put his or her life and finances in order, and for all of us who want to make the most of our economic resources. Although the main screen looks like something created for stock market fanatics, far more lurks beneath the surface. See what it has to offer at AOL Keyword: **PF** (see Figure 20-7).

> **Tip**
>
> You can track nearly 210 stock indices and other measures of market and investment performance in My Portfolio. For a complete listing of the indices and their symbols, click the Help button on either the My Portfolios screen or one of your personal Portfolio windows, select Index Quotes, and click the hypertext link for the "complete and printable list of Indices." For more information on portfolios, see Chapter 12.

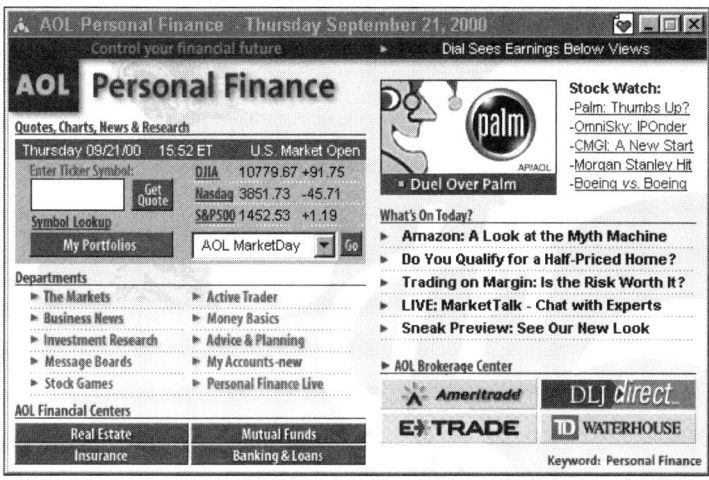

Figure 20-7. AOL Personal Finance is a rich resource.

Quotes, Charts, News & Research

AOL packs just about everything an investor needs to track the stock market, individual stocks, and personal portfolios in one small, unassuming box at AOL Keyword: **Quotes**. In the stock ticker, type the symbol for nearly any stock, mutual fund, or stock index on U.S. and major international exchanges, and you'll receive a snapshot with all the key trading statistics, pertinent news articles, and charts of historic performance for that stock, fund, or index. Access your online portfolios (you can have up to 21 portfolios per screen name), keep an eye on the major market averages, and pull up news reports on a wide variety of key indicators.

Departments

Whether you're a buy-and-hold investor, a day trader, or someone who's just beginning to explore your financial options, the departments of Personal Finance stand ready to serve your needs. The Markets and Money Basics are two of the more popular departments:

▶ **The Markets:** Clicking The Markets link leads to the Market News Center (AOL Keyword: **MNC**), a one-stop shop for current events in the major financial markets, with charts, news headlines, and detailed reports of every description (see Figure 20-8). With a few clicks, the Market News Center can go from a general overview of the major markets to specialized views of stocks and mutual funds, bonds, currencies, the U.S. economy, international markets, and futures trading.

Figure 20-8. Track the markets with a few quick clicks at the Market News Center.

Cross-Reference

The extensive news resources of AOL Business News (AOL Keyword: **Business News**) are discussed earlier in this chapter, in the News Channel section.

▶ **Money Basics:** This area of AOL is ready to school you in all the ins and outs of investing. (Access it at AOL Keyword: **Money Basics.**) Take an eight-step course in how to become an investor. You can sample Investing Basic's full portfolio of forums and tutorials. Or visit The Motley Fool (AOL Keyword: **Fools**) to learn the Fool's not-so-foolish approach to investing. The wisdom you can learn here is priceless.

Financial and Brokerage Centers

The AOL Financial Centers — Real Estate, Insurance, Mutual Funds, and Banking & Loans — are a gold mine of information, advice, and services. These four areas are accessible through the four buttons in the lower-left corner of the Personal Finance window. With a little help from AOL's partners and experts, you can calculate the what-ifs of almost any real estate transaction and search for a new home (see Figure 20-9) at AOL Keyword: **Real Estate**.

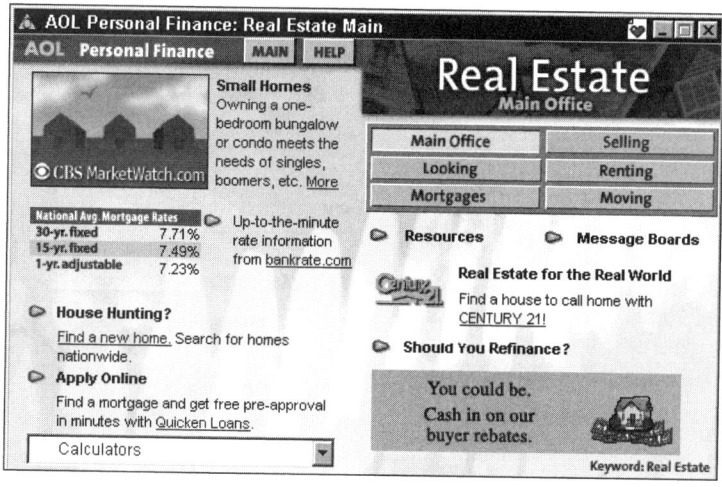

Figure 20-9. Real Estate helps you get a piece of the American Dream. Open the drop-down list in the lower left to access more than 21 financial planning calculators.

You can also comparison-shop for all sorts of insurance coverage, research mutual funds, and discover the joys of online banking. The Brokerage Center is a gateway into the world of online investing, where you can learn about investing through discount brokers and engage the services of some of the best-known online brokers in the business.

Whew! Who'd have thought that so much economic potential lurked within those seemingly simple surroundings? Invest a bit of your time here sometime soon, and you may reap rich rewards later on.

Careers & Work Channel

The Careers & Work Channel is a great place to turn for information on finding a job, starting a business, and improving your career. The first rung on the ladder begins at AOL Keyword: **Careers & Work** (see Figure 20-10).

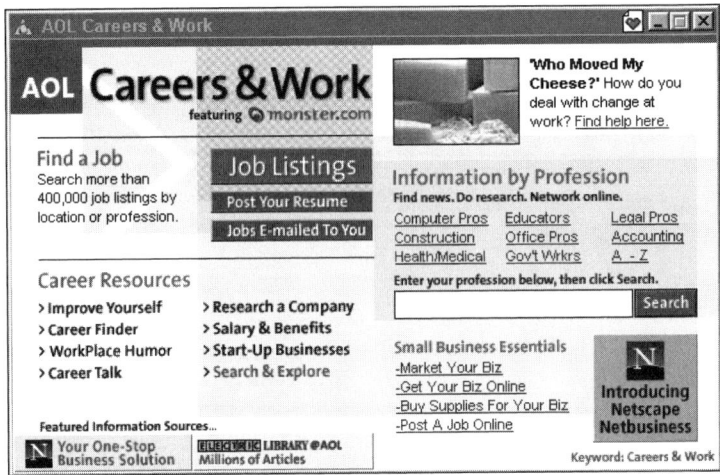

Figure 20-10. Get ahead with AOL's Careers & Work Channel.

Job Search

Today's job market isn't just about finding a job — it's about finding the best job for you. Job Search is sponsored by Monster.com, the granddaddy of job search sites. Just click Job Search; enter your location, profession, and keywords; and click Search. Your matches appear (see Figure 20-11).

Monster.com searches more than 350,000 job listings. And if that's not good enough, you can post your own resume at AOL Careers & Work for free. You can even control who sees your contact information.

If you want a new job, but you're too busy to search, let the jobs come to you! You can get available job postings sent to you via e-mail as soon as they become available through the Careers & Work Channel.

Chapter 20 ▲ Business and Information Channels

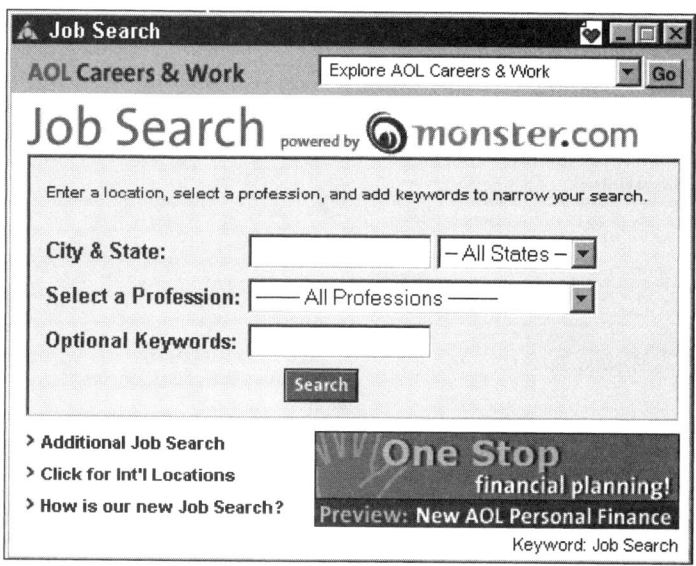

Figure 20-11. Job Search lets you hone in on the job you want.

Career Resources

For those on the corporate career path, Career Resources is the route to the next rung on the corporate ladder. You can improve your career potential, find the right line of work for you, enjoy a knowing laugh with a daily dose of Dilbert, and network with colleagues. Additional resources let you research a potential employer, compare the cost of living in two cities, and get helpful advice on start-up businesses. And if your career is already firmly established, the Careers & Work Channel stands ready to help you update your skills, network with your peers, and get the latest information on what matters in your job.

Computer Center

No channel lineup on AOL would be complete without a channel dedicated to computing. The Computer Center Channel (shown in Figure 20-12) offers virtually everything you need to know to make your computer hum at AOL Keyword: **Computer Center**.

Figure 20-12. Learn to make the most of your computer at the Computer Center Channel.

AOL's Computer Center Channel is founded on a very basic truth: If you're using AOL, you're using a computer, and the more you know about your computer, the more you'll get out of your AOL experience.

CNET

CNET is known for its computer-oriented television programming and extensive Web sites dedicated to (you'll never guess in a million years, will you?) ... computers! CNET's Consumer Guide (available by clicking the CNET icon in the opening screen of the Computer Center Channel, shown in Figure 20-12) supplies computer hardware and software reviews, an interactive guide to buying the right computer, and a search engine to reach deep into CNET's archives. CNET contributes its articles and expertise throughout the Computer Center Channel, including the Get Help Now department. If you want to visit CNET's home page, AOL Keyword: **CNET** will take you right there.

Download Center

The Computer Center Channel is also home to the Download Center, where you can find computer software of nearly every description. When you use AOL Keyword: **File Search** (discussed in Chapter 10), you are searching the contents of the

Download Center. Whether you're looking for freeware, shareware, or shrink-wrapped applications, this is the first place to turn.

Help and Education

Whether you just bought your first PC or have already worn out your fifth computer, the Computer Center Channel's help desk (AOL Keyword: **Get Help Now**) and online classrooms have a lot to offer.

Use AOL Keyword: **Get Help Now** (see Figure 20-13) to get help with computer software and hardware problems and access links to AOL's Member Help area for problems relating to AOL's own software and service. You can find answers to frequently asked questions about using your computer and how-to guides to computing and AOL. Among the how-to guides is Help Illustrated, a visual guide to using dozens of AOL's features. And from 9 p.m. to 11 p.m. eastern standard time every night, Computer Center Channel volunteers are on hand live to answer your questions about PC and Mac computing.

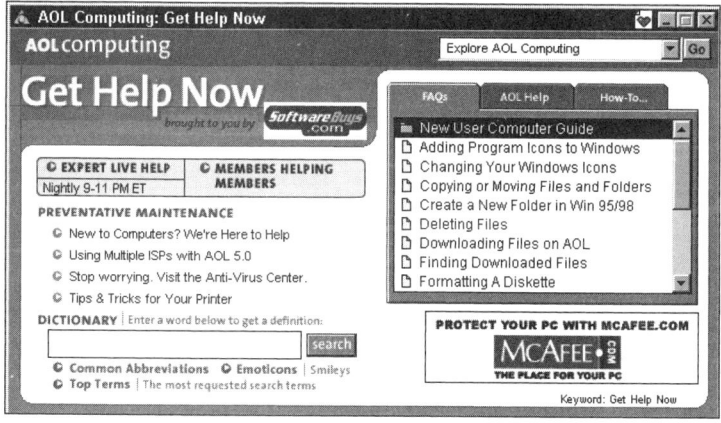

Figure 20-13. Get Help Now at the Computing Help Desk — open 24 hours a day.

AOL Keyword: **Online Learning** offers tutorials and courses in everything from AOL basics to Microsoft advanced networking system certification. Many courses are free, taught by volunteer community leaders, whereas others are provided for a fee by organizations such as `tutorials.com`. You can study desktop computing, computer graphics, and computer programming, or become a Webmaster. You can also reach the Online Learning center from the link in the main Computer Center Channel window.

Communities

Tucked quietly away behind the main screen of the AOL Computer Center Channel are dozens of vibrant areas dedicated to all aspects of computers and computer use. These are home to the AOL Computer Center's Anti-Virus Center (AOL Keyword: **Virus**), the Desktop Publishing Community, PDAs & Palmtops, the Windows Community, and many more groups with a passion for their topic. You'll find answers, wisdom, and lots of good people at AOL Keyword: **Computing Communities** (see Figure 20-14).

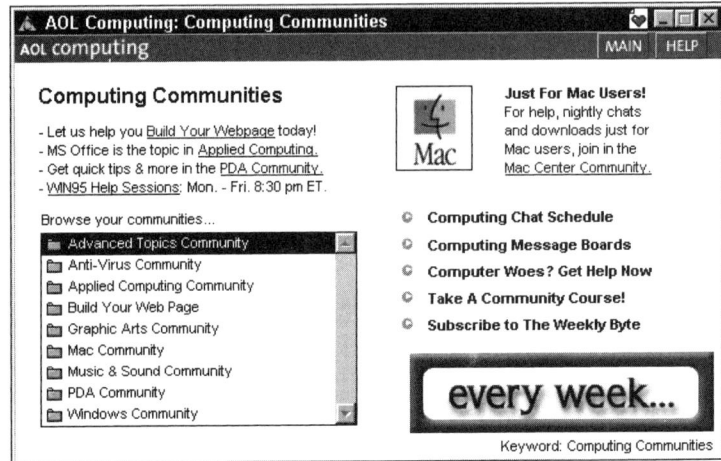

Figure 20-14. AOL Computing Communities is all about people sharing their passion for computing.

Research & Learn Channel

Whether you need general reference resources or help with schoolwork, college admissions, enhancing your child's education, or furthering your own professional education, the AOL Research & Learn Channel is a great place to turn (see Figure 20-15).

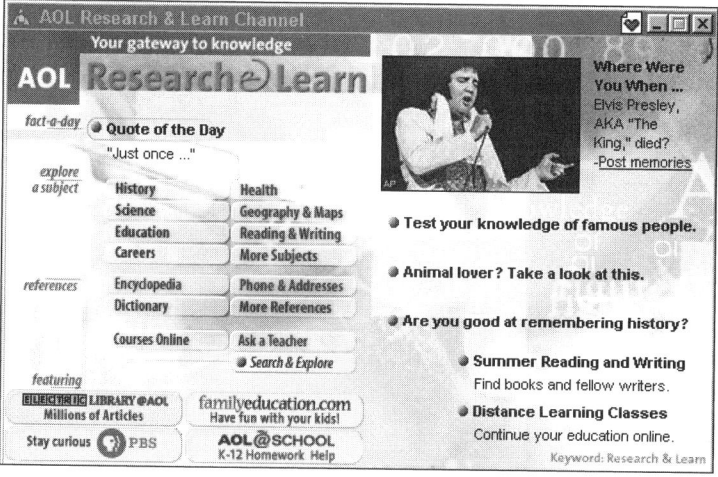

Figure 20-15. Learn something new at the Research & Learn Channel.

Explore a Subject

When general references manage to skim only the surface, try one of the Research & Learn specialized topic areas. The list looks like a school curriculum: History, Science, Education, Careers, Health, Geography & Maps, and Reading & Writing. The More Subjects section covers the Arts, Business Research, Consumer & Money Matters, and Law & Government, among other topics. Each of these subjects is available through buttons in the main Research & Learn Channel window.

References

Research & Learn offers a handy collection of desktop references. Take your pick of two general-purpose online encyclopedias: Compton's Encyclopedia Online and The Concise Columbia Electronic Encyclopedia, plus a handful of specialized encyclopedias on topics such as baseball, chemistry, and mythology. Business-minded folks will appreciate the collection of telephone and address listings, including the Chamber of Commerce Directory. Electronic Library@AOL is a commercial reference service that offers access to articles on a wide range of topics. You can try the Electronic Library for a free trial period and, if you like, subscribe to the service on a monthly basis. Research & Learn is also home base to AOL Keyword: **Dictionary**, the Merriam-Webster Collegiate

The online dictionary is surprisingly powerful. If you don't know the spelling of a word, you can replace the letter(s) you're unsure of with an asterisk. For example, n*bor will fetch neighbor. If you're looking for synonyms or alternate spellings, you can search the full text of the dictionary's definitions, too.

Dictionary online (see Figure 20-16). This is the kind of resource worth adding to your AOL toolbar. The same dictionary is available from the Edit menu, too.

Figure 20-16. The online dictionary places thousands of words at your fingertips.

Look for the Other Dictionaries button at the bottom of the Dictionary window, which opens the pages of another dozen specialized dictionaries.

Ask-a-Teacher

Although we've all been told to look it up, Research & Learn is also home to Ask-a-Teacher, the AOL Academic Assistance Center at AOL Keyword: **AAC** (see Figure 20-17). The thousands of volunteer teachers of the AAC provide targeted assistance for every age group from elementary school through college. Okay, so one of the first things you see at Ask-a-Teacher is a link to the Look Up Answers area — which features thousands of answers prepared by the AAC staff to commonly asked questions. If you don't find your answer there, you can post a question on one of hundreds of topic-specific message boards. Or if your need is more urgent, send e-mail to a teacher or get live help from teachers during the evening (check the daily schedule for times and subject matter).

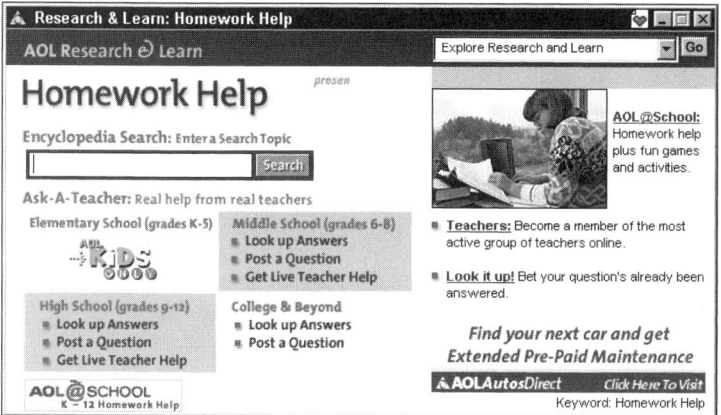

Figure 20-17. Ask-a-Teacher offers personal help with schoolwork for students of all ages.

Education and Courses

The Education Resources department covers every education-related topic, from Study Skills and Resources for Parents K-12 through College Prep, Financial Aid, and Resources for Educators. Featured in this area is the Family Education Network, a must-visit for any parent. To reach this area, click the Courses Online button in the main Research & Learn Channel window.

If you're interested in furthering your own education, check the offerings in Courses Online. The Online Campus (AOL Keyword: **Courses**) offers hundreds of enrichment courses in a wide range of topics for fees typically in the $25–50 range. The University of California Extension Online at AOL Keyword: **UCAOL** (get it?) offers college-level instruction, and grants course credits that are accepted at the University of California and other degree-granting institutions. Peterson's `LifeLongLearning.com` (AOL Keyword: **Petersons**) is a database that lists distance-learning offerings from colleges and universities throughout the U.S., including Regents College, a degree-granting virtual university.

Local Guide Channel (Digital City)

The last channel in this chapter covers the quaint, ethnic neighborhoods of America Online. Well, in this case, quaint and ethnic really refer to the cities of Digital City, from Milwaukee to Miami, Seattle to San Diego, and many places in between (see Figure 20-18) at AOL Keyword: **Local Guide**.

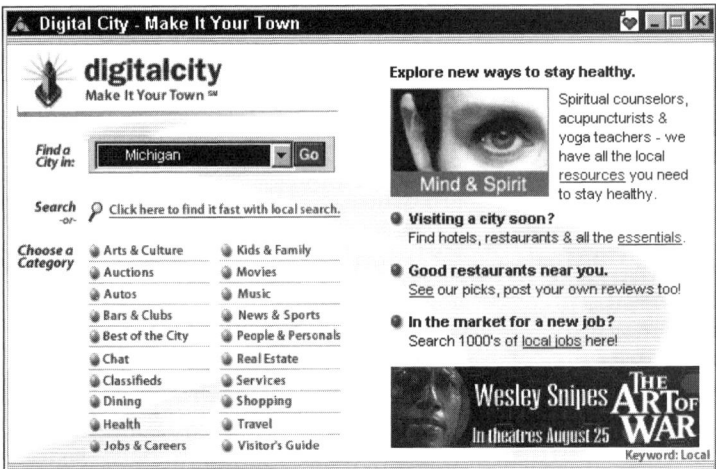

Figure 20-18. Choose a state from the drop-down menu to find a nearby city.

Digital City operates local city guides, delivering everything from local news, traffic, movie listings, and dining out guides to personal ads, job listings, and a real estate section (see Figure 20-19). If this sounds like your local newspaper, you're right. Many Digital City guides are produced in cooperation with local newspapers, magazines, or TV stations — organizations that know their towns very well.

Figure 20-19. Read the "front page" for Detroit, Michigan.

You can go directly to the Digital City for your city — the city's name is also its keyword — or you can use AOL Keyword: **Digital City** to get started. Choose a state from the drop-down menu, and then choose a nearby city from the resulting page. The main page also displays a list of the categories for Digital City, which you can also use as a jumping-off point for your travels.

Digital City is currently the largest service of its type in the U.S. (although competition is fierce). If the city you want isn't listed yet, it may be coming soon.

 Tip

You can use a keyword to jump to Digital City departments for many cities. Just use this pattern: **CITY + DEPARTMENT**. For example, AOL Keyword: **Detroit Movies** takes you to the Movies department of Digital City Detroit. Although it doesn't work for every department in every Digital City, it's sure convenient when it works.

Putting Your Knowledge to Work

As you can see, AOL's Business and Information channels are extensive. We covered a lot in this chapter, but it's really only a fraction of what AOL's business channels have to offer.

Although this chapter's tour hasn't all been business, there haven't been many opportunities for fun and frolic either — but tomorrow, as Scarlet O'Hara said, is another day. Turn the page to learn more about the personal enrichment and entertainment sites of AOL.

CHAPTER

21

PERSONAL ENRICHMENT
AND INFORMATION
CHANNELS

Quick Look

▶ Travel Reservations   page 391
You can research and book flights, hotels, and rental cars without ever leaving your computer or picking up a phone. Use AOL Keyword: **Preview Travel** to access AOL's virtual travel agency and sign up for your free membership.

▶ Interactive Games   page 397
Computer game enthusiasts will love the interactive games available online in the Games Channel at AOL Keyword: **Games**. Play against a friend or find a new opponent in one of the many games available. Gameplay is free or fee-based, depending on the complexity and nature of the game.

▶ Communities   page 399
AOL plays host to many thriving communities online. Virtually every interest, lifestyle, and hobby has a community.

▶ Kids Only   page 407
Kids can have their own version of AOL, complete with a kid-style Welcome Screen and kid-appropriate content. Visit AOL Keyword: **Kids Only** for a look through kids' eyes and learn more about configuring AOL for your child.

Chapter 21

Personal Enrichment and Information Channels

IN THIS CHAPTER

Getting involved with Sports and Travel

Having fun with Entertainment and Games

Exploring new and familiar interests

Enriching your life with Shopping and Health

Getting in touch with Families and Kids Only

As they say, "All work and no play makes for a dull day." Now that you've visited the business and information channels of America Online, let's paint the town red! Pleasure-seekers will find much to do on America Online, whether their interest is in travel, entertainment, or shopping.

Sports Channel

If you're into sports, you'll want to get into the Sports Channel. Virtually everything related to sports, for both spectators and participants, is available here. It's like a huge sports complex, complete with stadium, arena, track, field, and, of course, a pro shop (see Figure 21-1). Just type AOL Keyword: **Sports** into your AOL Toolbar and click the Go button.

Figure 21-1. The Sports Channel provides 'round-the-clock sports coverage for fans of all games.

Scoreboard

Have you ever tried following scores of several games at once on the TV or radio? You end up doing lots of channel flipping just to keep up with two or three games. If this sounds familiar, you're going to flip for the Scoreboard at AOL Sports (use AOL Keyword: **Scoreboard** to go there directly). Virtually every major and minor league game score is available, up to date, and accurate. Better yet, the scores don't disappear after the post-game wrap-up — results are kept online for you to check at your own convenience. Just choose a league (click its name), and the scores are displayed (see Figure 21-2).

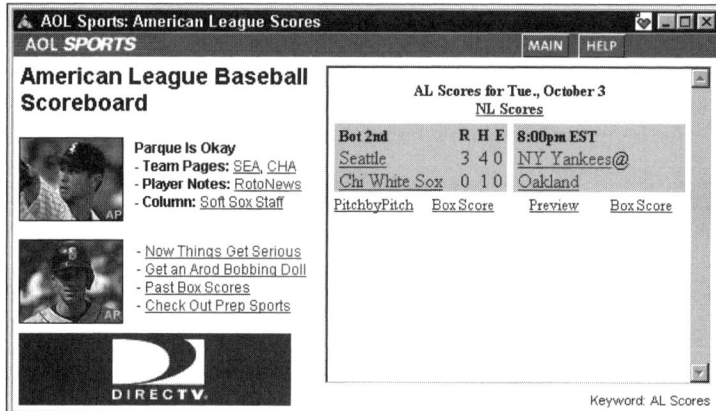

Figure 21-2. Scoreboard for the American League shows game recaps and box scores.

Grandstand

If you love to talk sports, we have to talk ... about the Grandstand. This forum's main events are the message board and chat rooms, in which discussions between sports fans take the field. The Grandstand has a community for almost every sport, from baseball to women's sports. The Grandstand even hosts fantasy leagues to put you in the middle of the action. You can get to the Grandstand directly using AOL Keyword: **GS** (see Figure 21-3).

Figure 21-3. The Grandstand's focus is on community among fans, players, and experts.

We think a visit to AOL Sports is the ultimate spectator sporting event. It's like having a virtual VIP box seat to monitor your favorite teams and games. But you don't have to put up with lines, bad seats, sunburns, or rain-outs. Of course, if you get a hankering to watch the real game "up close and personal," AOL can help you plan a trip to any stadium or arena in the world.

Travel Channel

If our travels throughout America Online have piqued your wanderlust, you're going to love the Travel Channel. It's a destination designed for travelers, whether their trips are for pleasure or business. Even armchair travelers (or should we say "desktop travelers"?) can find a home here. Everything you need to daydream and plan the perfect trip is gathered in the Travel Channel, from information on vacation resorts and exotic ports to traveler reports and news of all sorts. To reach the Travel Channel, choose Travel from the Channels list or simply use AOL Keyword: **Travel** (see Figure 21-4).

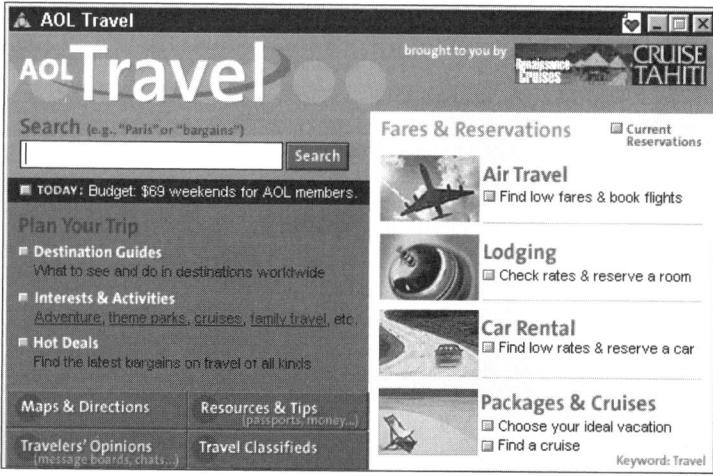

Figure 21-4. The Travel Channel is a complete travel service, offering information, resources, traveler exchanges, and a full-service travel agency.

Tip

Visit AOL Keyword: **Member Opinions** for a collection of message boards, chats, polls, and newsletters devoted to travel destinations (you may also find this area by returning to the main Travel Channel window and clicking the Travelers' Opinions button).

From the Travel Channel window, you can explore destinations, find bargains, make reservations (including air, car, hotel, and cruise reservations), get the latest travel news, and much more. It's a bit like standing at a crossroads with signs going off in all directions: "Amazing Travel Bargains — Next Stop on the Left" and "World Famous Travel News Served 24 Hours a Day — Turn Right Here!" What's your dream destination? If you're not sure, click the Destination Guides link (or use AOL Keyword: **Destinations**) to orient yourself and home in on just what you need (see Figure 21-5).

Figure 21-5. Destination Guides from the Travel Channel let you discover and explore destinations within the U.S. and around the world.

After you've narrowed your list to a handful of potential destinations, we recommend that you gather opinions from other travelers before you make a final decision. This is where America Online and the Internet really shine for travel planners. Nowhere else will you find such easy access to thousands of first-hand experiences, and opinions from folks who've really been there.

Fares & Reservations

After you've decided on your destination, make your reservations at Travelocity (an AOL partner). This online travel agency lets you search and book flights, rental cars, hotel rooms, and packages — right from your computer. To begin, click one of the buttons below Fares & Reservations on the Travel Channel window, such as the Air Travel button. The Travelocity window for air travel appears, as shown in Figure 21-6.

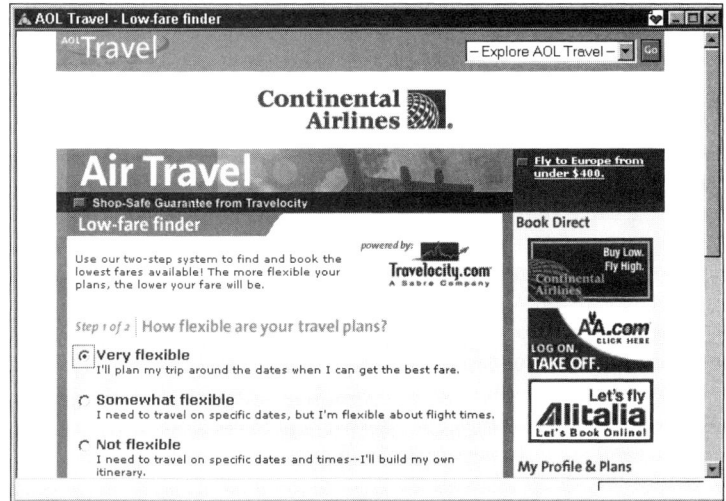

Figure 21-6. Find the lowest airfares at Travelocity.

You can begin browsing available airfares, hotels, car rentals, and packages immediately — no need to sign in. If you find something you like and you want to book it, just click the Book Now button. If you aren't already a member of AOL Travel/Travelocity, you'll be prompted to join first. AOL Travel walks you through the free sign-up process. Be sure to save your user ID and password in a safe place for future visits.

The Travelocity system gives you many of the same tools that travel agents use to make reservations. You can search by destination, travel dates, and a whole slew of other preferences. Help is always at hand (look for the Help hyperlink), and the process is quite simple.

The Independent Traveler

Imagine a club of travelers who congregate to swap stories of their journeys, exchange tips and tricks, and plan their next adventures. You might call it an adventurer's club, though on America Online this traveler community goes by the name of

Tip

Within The Independent Traveler, one resource in particular stands out: the Travel Boards. Whether your interest is in cross-country road trips or around-the-world journeys, you'll find a message board that suits you. Every state and country is represented, as well as places like Walt Disney World. Also of interest is a Travel Issues message board, covering topics from aerophobia (fear of flying) and airfare secrets to volunteer vacations and youth hostels. We estimate that you'll find more than 300 message boards with hundreds of thousands of posts just in The Independent Traveler. See Chapter 7 for more details on using and searching the message boards.

The Independent Traveler (at AOL Keyword: **Traveler**). It's one of the few forums that has been around since the early days of AOL, meaning its collection of articles, photos, tips, reports, and discussions is truly phenomenal! The Independent Traveler offers very active message boards, regular chats, trip reports, article and photo libraries, travel book reviews — the list goes on and on (see Figure 21-7).

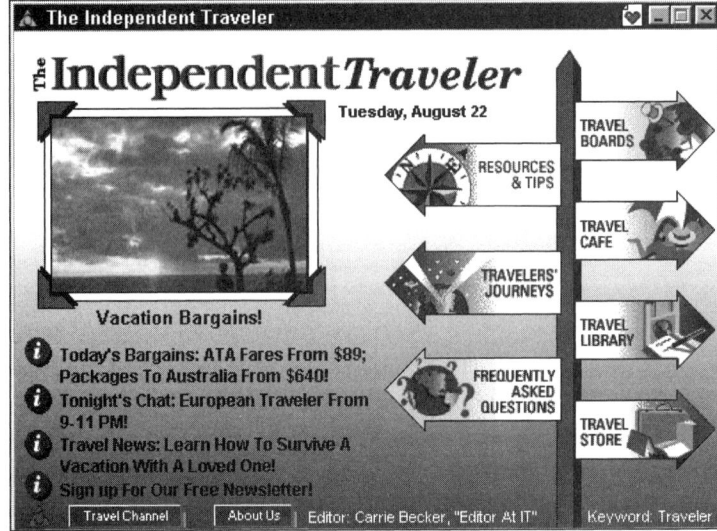

Figure 21-7. The Independent Traveler is the best place for travelers' tales, tips, and tricks.

Entertainment Channel

The Entertainment Channel really speaks for itself. And sings, and dances, and performs up a storm! Show times, movie reviews, concert dates, or celebrity news — you name it, the Entertainment Channel has it. Use the AOL Keyword: **Entertainment** to reach the Entertainment Channel (see Figure 21-8).

Figure 21-8. Entertainment Channel, the Hollywood-and-Vine of America Online.

Movies, music, and TV are in the spotlight at the Entertainment Channel. Click Movies (or use AOL Keyword: **Movies**) for a list of what's playing in theaters, show times (more on this later), movie reviews, moviegoer opinions, behind-the-scenes glimpses, and movie news. Click a movie name for fact sheets, related reviews, trailers, photos, interviews, and discussion boards. This is also the place to find out what movies are coming out on video.

The Music section covers the stage from rock to jazz to classical. Click a category for reviews and clips of the latest releases. Use the Music Index drop-down menu to get concert tour dates, online events with artists, information on record labels, and the latest charts. Rolling Stone Online is also here, along with MTV.

When was the last time you wondered what was playing at the movie theaters? If your town is anything like ours, it has only a few good theaters, and you have to phone each one to listen to their barely audible recorded listings. Or you may buy the local paper just to get the list of movies and times. If this seems familiar, you're going to love Moviefone. To use it, just go to Moviefone (AOL Keyword: **Moviefone**), click the What's Playing in a Particular Theater button, type your zip code and any other search criteria, and click Go (see Figure 21-9).

Sounding Great with Spinner and Winamp

Not only does AOL offer music information and news, but it provides the means to actually hear music through AOL as well! Two musical plug-ins come as standard equipment with AOL 6.0: Spinner and Winamp. So what's the big deal? With Spinner and Winamp onboard, you can now download music through AOL and hear it immediately — no muss, no fuss. To see what we mean, try a few of the hyperlinks at AOL Keyword: **Music** — look for the Listen to Online Radio and Download Digital Music links. You may need to sign up with one of the online music sites before you can hear your tunes. Also note that you need a sound card and speakers installed in your computer before you can hear glorious music.

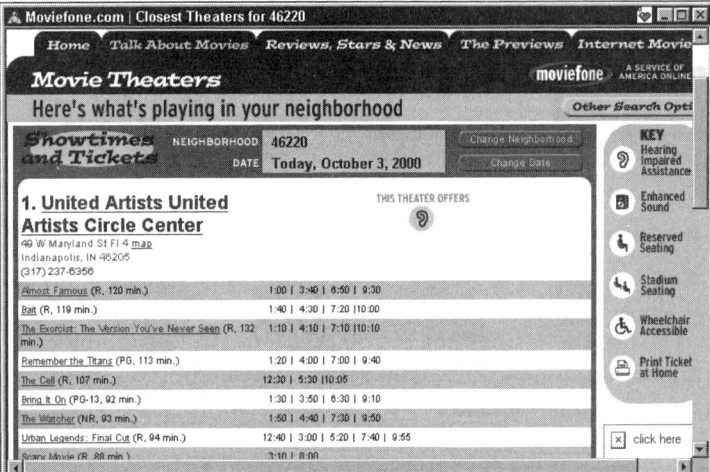

Figure 21-9. You can find listings for local theaters, movies, and show times at Moviefone.

Your local movies and show times pop up on the screen, based on your search criteria (by theater, by movie, by actor/actress, by time, and so on). One of the nifty features is that Moviefone is smart enough to indicate which show times are sold out. And if you click the movie name's hyperlink, you can get more information about the movie — synopsis, cast list, and so on. It's wonderfully convenient, fast, and easy. You may never have to call the theater again! But should you want to, Moviefone also displays the theater's phone number.

If you're a frequent movie-goer, look up your theater express code from the list so you can zip right to your local theater. Also, create a Favorite Place for Moviefone (see Chapter 14 for details on creating Favorite Places).

Games Channel

Warning! This channel contains highly addictive, interactive games that can cause a sudden drop in boredom levels. Members should be free of finger injuries, mouse problems, and time constraints. You must be as least as tall as your computer to enter the Games Channel. Keep your arms inside the room at all times.

Well, that last rule bends a bit if you're using a laptop on the beach, but that's part of the fun and excitement of the Games Channel. It's total fun and games, 24 hours a day, 7 days a week, 365 days a year — and it goes anywhere your computer goes. If you think you can handle it, use AOL Keyword: **Games** to enter the Games Channel (see Figure 21-10).

Figure 21-10. The Games Channel offers 100 percent pure recreation.

The Game Parlor

Note

To play a game, you must first download the software. Begin by choosing a game from the list, and click the Play button in the resulting window. If you agree to the game charges, click Agree and then download the game (which requires its own software). Downloads can take a while, so you may want to use this opportunity to take a break. Oh, and don't worry — you won't rack up game charges during the download.

Tired of playing solitaire? Step up to classic parlor games that you can play online, such as backgammon, bridge, cribbage, hearts, and poker. What makes these games any better than solitaire? Simple. You can play these games head-to-head with other players! All this fun comes at a price, however — games at The Game Parlor are 99 cents per hour (at the time of this writing). To see the list of available games and get more information on pricing, visit AOL Keyword: **Parlor** (see Figure 21-11).

Figure 21-11. Sit in on a game in The Game Parlor.

Xtreme Games

Note

If you get a message stating that your screen name is blocked from playing games, your Parental Controls are set to prevent premium game play (and associated charges). AOL blocks premium services on secondary screen names by default. The master account holder can change this setting at AOL Keyword: **Parental Controls**. Refer to Chapter 4 for more information on setting Parental Controls.

If you prefer action and adventure games, make Xtreme Games your Holy Grail. They offer such games as Air Warrior III (aerial shoot 'em up game), Dragon's Gate (text-based adventure game), and Warcraft II (graphic-based strategy game). Like The Game Parlor, Xtreme Games are a premium service, though these are a bit more expensive at $1.99 per hour. Again, these are addictive games — be sure that you've got plenty of time and money before you get hooked! But what fun they are! The action begins at AOL Keyword: **Xtreme**, which you may also reach by clicking the Xtreme Games link at either the bottom of The Game Parlor window or on the main Games Channel window.

Game Shows Online

If you love games, but don't have the money for the premium games, head for Game Shows Online. Here you'll find a collection of no-charge games, such as BUZZTIME Trivia (formerly NTN trivia), Puzzle Zone (word puzzles), and Slingo (a cross between bingo and a word game). Don't be fooled by their low, low price tag — these games are first-rate and fun! Like The Game Parlor, many of the games on Game Shows Online require that you download software before you can play, but the download times are generally much shorter. BUZZTIME Trivia (see Figure 21-12) is the notable exception — it has nothing to download! Come on down to Game Shows Online with AOL Keyword: **Game Shows** or click Game Shows either at the bottom of the Xtreme Game window or on the main Games Channel window.

Figure 21-12. Play trivia to your heart's content with BUZZTIME Trivia.

Autos Channel

The Autos Channel reminds us of those new, gleaming auto malls you see these days. No matter whether you're looking for a new or used car, a Nissan or a Cadillac, a coupe or a convertible — you can find it here. If you can buy a car online, what's next? Traffic citations for speeding along the information superhighway? And if you're an auto enthusiast, you'll find articles, message boards, libraries, and guides on how to jumpstart a car, change a flat, and even accomplish parallel parking. Use AOL Keyword: **Autos** and observe posted limits (see Figure 21-13).

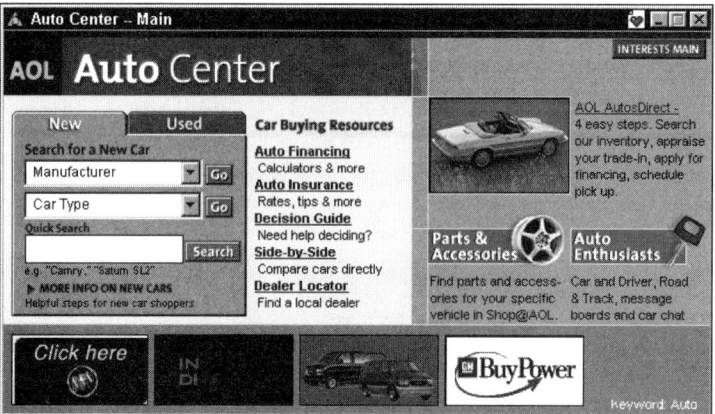

Figure 21-13. Auto Center puts you in the driver's seat.

House & Home Channel

The House & Home Channel offers tips, advice, and information on gardening, home improvement, and decorating. This channel can help you add style and comfort to any home, however modest or grand. The key to a comfortable, relaxing home is under the doormat at AOL Keyword: **House & Home** (see Figure 21-14).

Figure 21-14. Everything for the homefront is available at the House & Home Channel.

Women Channel

Back when America Online started, women made up only a small percentage of the AOL population. Women now make up 51 percent of AOL's members. Accordingly, AOL offers a new channel called Women, with a range of helpful resources and unique forums to help women manage their increasingly busy lives. AOL Keyword: **Women** opens the door (see Figure 21-15).

Figure 21-15. Women have their own space in cyberspace on AOL.

Notable within Women is Oxygen, an umbrella forum for several familiar faces including Thrive Online, Moms Online, Electra, and more. The goal is to incorporate humor, honesty, and heart into the relationship between women and the media. You can visit the site directly at AOL Keyword: **Oxygen**.

Shopping Channel

We discuss shopping in much more depth in Chapters 15 and 20.

Shopping opportunities are available practically everywhere at AOL. Tour almost any channel, and you'll find virtual shops and stores sprinkled throughout. If you're a serious shopper, you may prefer to go directly to the stores rather than hunt for them during your travels. AOL won't disappoint you. The Shop@AOL Channel is AOL's equivalent of a major marketplace, complete with large department stores, specialty shops, outlet stores, and even grocery stores. Best of all, they are available from your desktop, 24 hours a day, 7 days a week. To reach the Shop@AOL Channel, use AOL Keyword: **Shopping**.

Health Channel

The virtual road to wellness begins at the Health Channel. This channel offers healthy coverage of conditions and their treatments, as well as nutrition, fitness, health care, and alternative medicine. This is a haven for all, healthy and hope-to-be-healthy alike, offering support groups and experts in the many topics that are covered here. If you're ready to take your health seriously, use AOL Keyword: **Health** to enter the Health Channel (see Figure 21-16).

allHealth.com

Information and community are the cornerstones of allHealth.com. Beyond the articles, resources, and "Experts" features are heart-warming and handholding chats, message boards, and support groups. Click the Resources drop-down menu for a listing of major centers within the forum, covering topics such as Alternative Health, Cancer Center, Emotional Health, Living with HIV, and Senior Health. Use AOL Keyword: **AH** to get to allHealth.com (see Figure 21-17) or find it by clicking the allHealth.com icon below the Other Useful Sites section on the main Health Channel window.

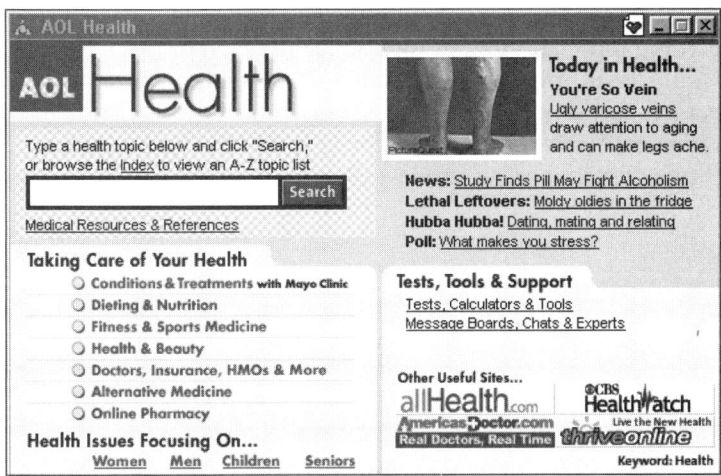

Figure 21-16. Stay healthy and happy with the Health Channel.

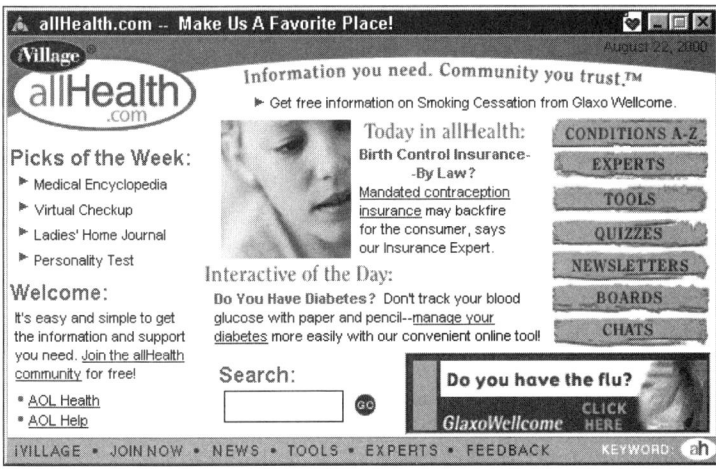

Figure 21-17. allHealth.com offers information and community.

Thrive Online

Thrive Online is a hip, straight-to-the-point wellness forum offering resources on physical, emotional, and sexual health. If that last item got your attention, you won't be disappointed by Thrive Online's Sexuality area — it's honest and, best of all, comprehensive. It offers tips on staying healthy and happy, having fun in bed (or staying out of it, as the case may be), and learning more about your own sexuality. Each of the Thrive Online areas offers a similar scope, along with community features like chats and message boards. Start thriving at AOL Keyword: **Thrive**, which you can also find by clicking the Thrive Online icon on the main Health Channel window.

Parenting Channel

If family ties are tying you down, the Parenting Channel may have the solution. This channel provides resources, support, and access to experts on the topic of family, all from the comfort of your family nest. AOL Keyword: **Parenting** takes you to the Parenting Channel (see Figure 21-18).

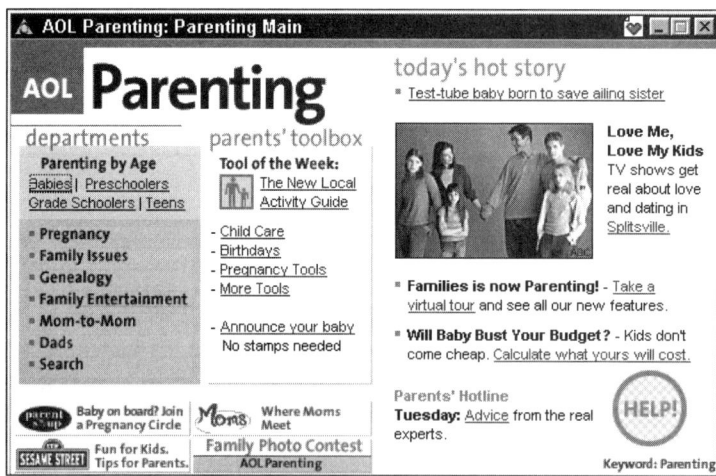

Figure 21-18. The Parenting Channel is the ultimate family room with something for everyone.

Parent Soup

Parent Soup is a heart-warming forum for parents, whether they are parents-to-be or parents of teens. Even those who hope to be parents will find a place here. Resources include news, articles, tips, databases, newsletters, message boards, chats — you name it, they probably have it. Visit the Pre-Pregnancy Community to learn how to predict ovulation. Expectant parents have an interactive pregnancy calendar. Parents of newborns can find names for their babies online. Parents of toddlers and preschoolers can commiserate together over potty-training troubles. Class is in session for parents of school-agers on summer break. Parents of teens can learn about adolescent sleep cycles and setting allowances. This is just a taste of Parent Soup — learn more by visiting the area through the link in the Parenting Channel window or at AOL Keyword: **PS** (see Figure 21-19).

Figure 21-19. Parent Soup is m-m-m good for parents.

Moms Online

Mom, mother, mama, or ma ... whatever we call her, she still has one of the most important jobs in the world. Support is near at hand with Moms Online, a community for moms-to-be, working moms, stay-at-home moms, and even Mr. Mom. This forum has rich, active message boards and ten different chat rooms offering regular chats on everything from differently-abled children to second marriages. We're particularly impressed with their Hot Tips, a huge collection of parenting tips in more than 60 categories. Moms and honorary moms can visit through the link in the Parenting Channel window or at AOL Keyword: **MO** (see Figure 21-20).

Figure 21-20. Network with other mothers at Moms Online.

The Genealogy Forum

We've met genealogists who became so bogged down in research that they either gave up the whole thing or ignored their living families. You can avoid both pitfalls with The Genealogy Forum, an incredible resource of helpful guides, surname and family history files and databases, and a supportive community of fellow genealogists. The forum has been around for a long time on AOL, so it's gathered an impressive collection of information and garnered a loyal following of family researchers. In fact, the forum itself has become a family of sorts, helping one another track down long lost relatives and forgotten family branches. If the genealogy bug hasn't yet bitten you, wear your bug repellent when you visit AOL Keyword: **Roots**. You can also click the Genealogy link on the main Parenting Channel window.

Kids Only Channel

As the sign says, this is a channel for kids only. Technically, parents and adults can sneak in while the kids aren't looking (more on that later), but the entire channel is really geared for the young ones. The magic word to get in is AOL Keyword: **Kids Only** or simply **KO** for short (see Figure 21-21).

Figure 21-21. Climb up to the Kids Only tree house.

Note

Have you noticed that the Kids Only Channel is almost like a children's version of the entire AOL service? That's no accident. When parents set their kids' accounts to "kids only" in Parental Controls, kids see the Kids Only Channel and nothing else. To learn more about Parental Controls, see Chapter 4.

When you open the Kids Only channel, move your mouse over each of the six big buttons (News+Sports, Art Studio, Clubs, TV-Movies-Music, Games, and Homework Help) for a peek at what you'll find under the button. News+Sports offers kid-oriented features and weather, just as up to date as the big kids' news. The Art Studio gives kids cool activity projects, drawing software, and a place to show off their creations. Clubs is really a kids' clubhouse with clubs for cartoons, jokes, recipes, stories, and more. TV-Movies-Music covers the hottest movies, videos, shows, and celebrities. Games offers a treasure chest of kid-oriented games like trivia, Donkey Boing (for keyboard coordination), and MapIt ZapIt (a geography game). Homework Help leads kids in finding solutions and researching issues for school with the help of experienced teachers and community leaders.

Adults in Kids Only?

Adults can enter Kids Only to participate and interact with the kids; however, Kids Only is intended for kids. The staff and community leaders work hard to make this a safe and comfortable place for kids, but parents also need to monitor their children's activities online. Encourage your kids to read the Safety Tips (at AOL Keyword: **KO Help**) and discuss them together. If you have a concern about anything in the Kids Only Channel, visit AOL Keyword: **KO Parent** to send feedback to the AOL staff. We also recommend that you visit the Parental Control message boards at AOL Keyword: **Parental Controls**.

Teens Channel

Teenagers have their own hangout at the Teens Channel, a collection of news, entertainment, fashion, and friends (see Figure 21-22). Features include Teen People (an online version of the magazine), a forum just for teen girls, and links to teen-related areas throughout AOL. Of particular interest are the teen chat rooms and message boards. Catch a wave to the Teens Channel at AOL Keyword: **Teens**.

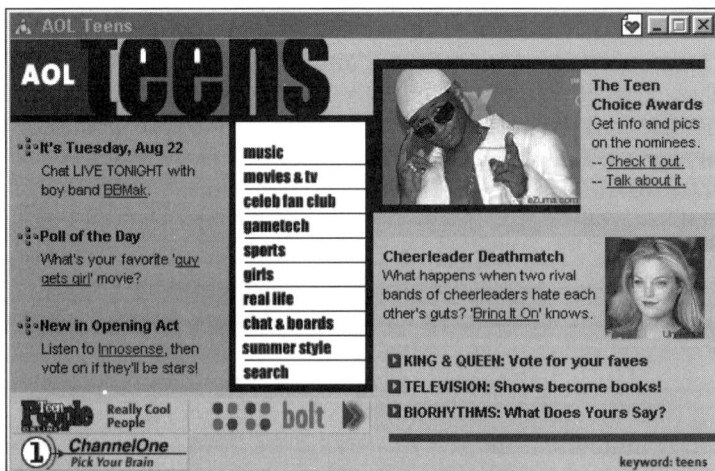

Figure 21-22. Teens Channel is the place for teens online.

People Connection

People Connection may not show up as a channel in your channels list, but it functions as one nonetheless. Sure, People Connection is the chat hub of AOL, but it's also the home to lifestyle forums, such as Ages & Stages and Gay & Lesbian. To reach the People Connection, choose People➪Chat (People Connection) from the AOL Toolbar or just use AOL Keyword: **People Connection**.

Ages & Stages

Whether you're 19 or 90, you'll find a home at Ages & Stages. Virtually every age and generation is covered here, from Generation X to the "Third Age." Click the Ages & Stages Communities button for a list of all available communities. Check out the Nerve Center if you're college-bound or college-stuck. If you've successfully made it out of college, visit Alumni Hall to find old college buddies. The Thirties Forum welcomes thirty-somethings. Baby Boomers is a gathering place for those born in the '50s and '60s. Folks 45 and up have a home at ThirdAge. And those of us approaching retirement age will appreciate the AARP (American Association of Retired Persons) forum. Use AOL Keyword: **Ages** to go directly to the Ages & Stages forum (see Figure 21-23).

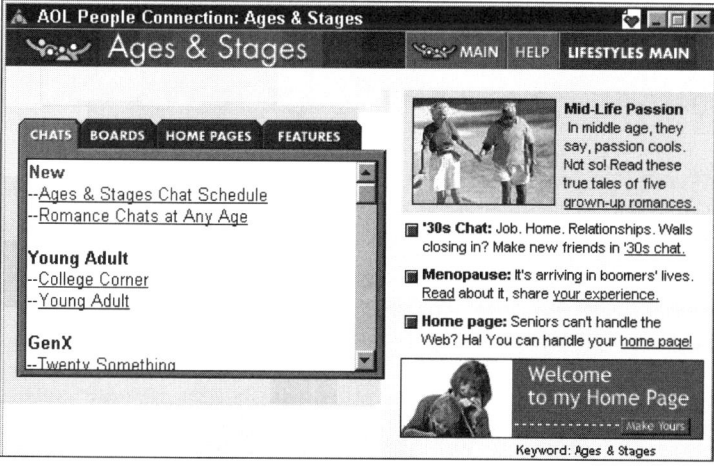

Figure 21-23. You don't need to hide your age at Ages & Stages.

Gay & Lesbian

The Gay & Lesbian scene online is not only a blessing for those who aren't yet "out," but also an incredibly rich and diverse resource for anyone searching for camaraderie, or understanding of a loved one's lifestyle. The forum offers active communities with message boards, chats, news, advice, experts, and articles. Use AOL Keyword: **Gay** (or **Lesbian** if you prefer) to get there quickly (see Figure 21-24).

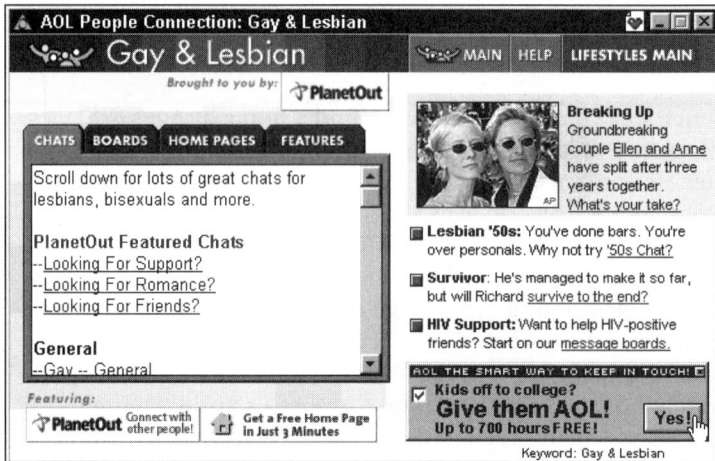

Figure 21-24. Come out online at Gay & Lesbian.

Putting Your Knowledge to Work

What a whirlwind tour of America Online's channels! We've only scratched the surface of the content available on AOL. Many more forums and areas are available in each of the channels we visited, and new content is being added daily. In fact, you can find out what's new at each channel by visiting AOL Keyword: **New**.

We encourage you to return to those spots that intrigue you the most and start exploring! Use the Search & Explore feature in each channel to home in on exactly what you want. We're always amazed at the depth of information we find online.

If all this content isn't enough, our next chapter gives you all the lowdown on all the benefits you get as an AOL member. Come along with us, and we'll show you your perks.

PART V

AOL MEMBER BENEFITS AND PREMIUM SERVICES

Chapter 22
AOL TV

Chapter 23
Long Distance and Paging

Chapter 24
Shopping and Reward Programs

CHAPTER

22

AOLTV

Quick Look

▶ **Find Out What's Playing** page 418

AOLTV℠ comes with an Electronic Program Guide that organizes TV shows into easy-to-browse categories, such as "News" or "Sports." To find the programs you want, just click through those categories or click the channel stations.

▶ **Favorite Places** page 419

Do you have a set of favorite TV stations? You can save each one as a Favorite Place for speedy access.

▶ **Chat While You Watch** page 419

Chat with friends while you're watching your favorite shows and movies. AOLTV's Picture-in-Picture (PIP) option lets you interact while viewing your show.

▶ **Demo AOLTV** page 422

AOLTV offers an interactive demo of the service at AOL Keyword: **AOLTV** on its Web site at www.aoltv.com.

Chapter 22
AOLTV

IN THIS CHAPTER

Navigating channels and TV programs with AOLTV

Checking e-mail, chatting, or getting stock quotes with AOLTV

Connecting to AOLTV services

As more and more people get online and make the Internet and online interactivity a part of their everyday lives, many are doing so while they watch TV. Therefore, AOL has introduced a new interactive service to make it easier to combine these two activities into one, creating an even more rewarding experience. The AOLTV service, part of the "AOL Anywhere"℠ initiative brings the most popular AOL features to your TV to enhance your viewing experience and to make TV more fun and entertaining.

What Is AOLTV?

AOLTV is the first interactive television service for mass-market consumers. AOLTV features a state-of-the-art Electronic Program Guide and other useful navigation features, which help you find what you want to watch faster and easier. In addition, AOLTV brings some of the most popular AOL features and services to the TV, enabling you to read and send e-mail, exchange instant messages, shop and chat online, and even access the Internet and browse the Web. You can also explore interesting online content about the program you're watching or its subject matter, set reminders and record your favorite TV shows, and more. With AOLTV, you're online, in tune, and in touch with the world like never before (see Figure 22-1).

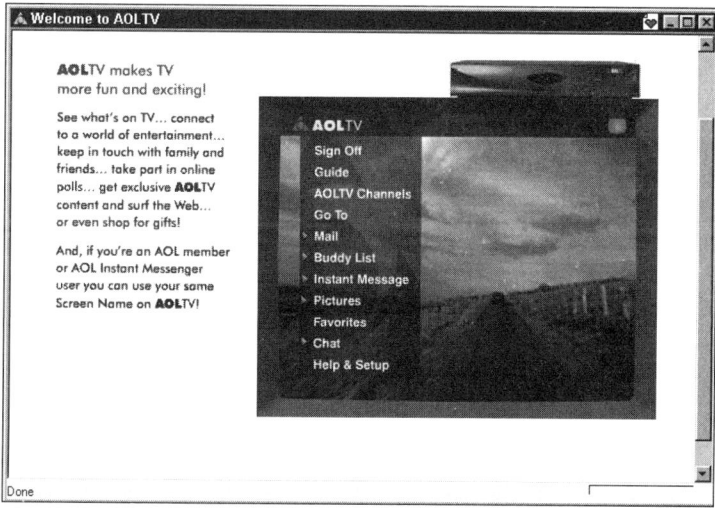

Figure 22-1. AOLTV combines your favorite AOL features with great TV.

AOLTV enhances your television viewing experience by giving you fast, easy access to your favorite AOL features and services while you're watching your favorite TV programs. Plus, you get the added convenience of being able to use the AOL service on the computer and AOLTV at the same time — so two members on one account can enjoy an interactive experience from different devices (a computer and a TV) at one time.

What You Can Do With AOLTV

Imagine this scenario that occurs in many homes every day: You sit down to watch television, begin scrolling up and down a list of channels, passively looking for something to watch, or surf endlessly through the whole channel line-up. Once you find a program you're interested in, you have to enter the channel number in order to see the program. Then you decide you want to watch something else, so you have to start scrolling, searching, and entering numbers all over again.

While watching a show you like, you think about how great it would be to talk to a friend, see how your stocks fared that day, get the score of a game, or check the weather forecast for the weekend. You also think about that one last e-mail you forgot to send or read. You want to do all these activities, but you also want to keep watching the show. With AOLTV, you can do everything at the same time. And you don't have to wait until a commercial break, miss one moment of a favorite program, or leave the comfort of the sofa.

Best of all, AOLTV gives you more control and makes navigating an array of TV channels simpler and easier — no scrolling through lists over and over. The AOLTV Main Menu gives you one-touch shortcuts to all the interactive features of the AOLTV service. Among its features is the Electronic Program Guide (shown in Figure 22-2), which simplifies navigation by organizing TV channels into 11 categories, called "MiniGuides."

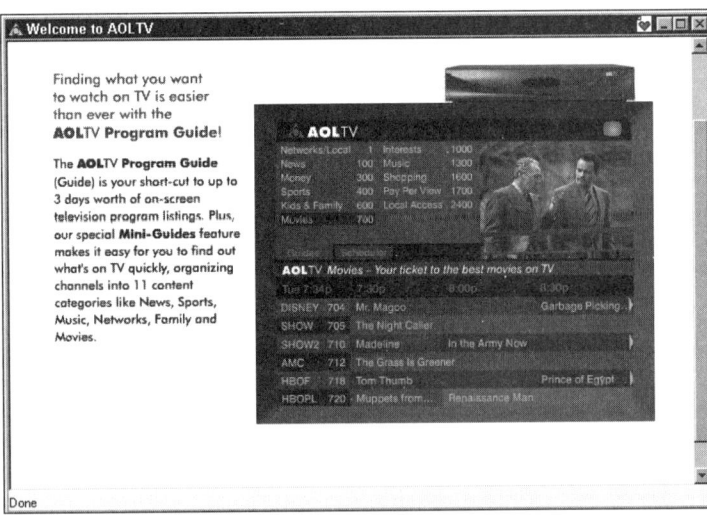

Figure 22-2. Finding what's on the tube is easy with AOLTV.

The Electronic Program Guide points you to networks, movies, news, kids and family, and other categories like money and sports — you can use the guide to find programs you want and change channels by clicking words and graphics. You can view program summaries up to three days ahead of the broadcast date and also customize a Favorite Places list of channels for quick access. And, to ensure that you never miss your favorite programs, AOLTV makes it easy to set reminders and will notify you on-screen when a selected show is about to begin. AOLTV even records shows to your VCR when you're away from your TV.

AOLTV is designed to allow for maximum enjoyment of both television programming and new interactive content. With its Picture-in-Picture (PIP) option, you can keep watching your favorite show while you check e-mail, get your stock quotes, and participate in a chat room discussion. At any time, you can go back to full picture viewing or simply sign off of the AOLTV service. A special Notification Bar displays unobtrusive alerts to indicate that you have new e-mail messages or are receiving an instant message, and with a single click, you can again maximize the TV program to full screen size. The Buddy List feature, shown in Figure 22-3, is translucent and fades or disappears when it's inactive. AOLTV's interactive features are always easily accessible whenever you want them with one touch on the lightweight wireless remote keyboard (described in the next section).

> **Tip**
>
> You can access the Electronic Program Guide regardless of whether or not you're signed on to the AOLTV service.

> **Tip**
>
> AOLTV offers simultaneous access to two screen names under one account. That means one person can be on the PC with one screen name, while another is on the TV with another screen name. You do need two phone lines, however: one for the PC and one for AOLTV.

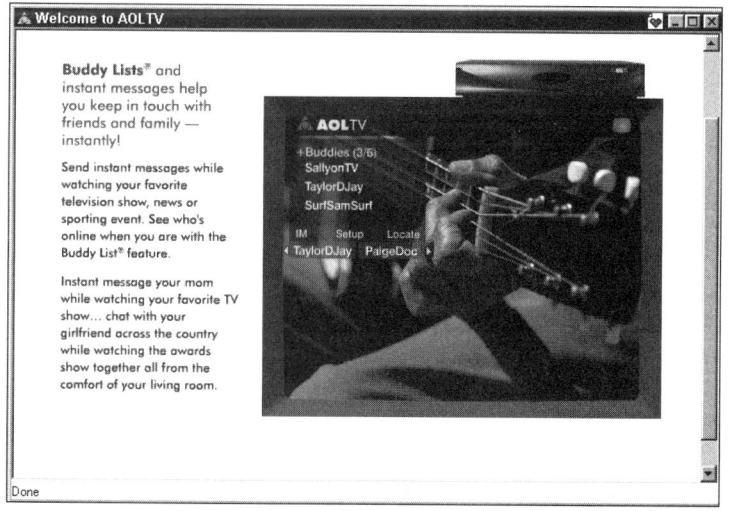

Figure 22-3. Your buddies won't get in the way of watching your favorite show.

AOLTV makes it easy for everyone in the family to get the most out of TV and have a personal, valuable interactive experience. AOLTV Channels offer interactive content and programming to complement TV shows. Sports fans watching a big game on TV, for example, can tune into the AOLTV Sports Channel to get immediate stats, scores, highlights, and additional coverage for other games and events. At any time, you can get instant weather forecasts for cities around the world, view local news updates, track stocks in your personal portfolio while watching business and market reports, or participate in online polls and vote on different issues while watching headline news.

Parents will appreciate a built-in Parental Controls feature, shown in Figure 22-4, which enables them to safeguard their children by limiting access to features such as chat, e-mail, instant messaging, and the Internet.

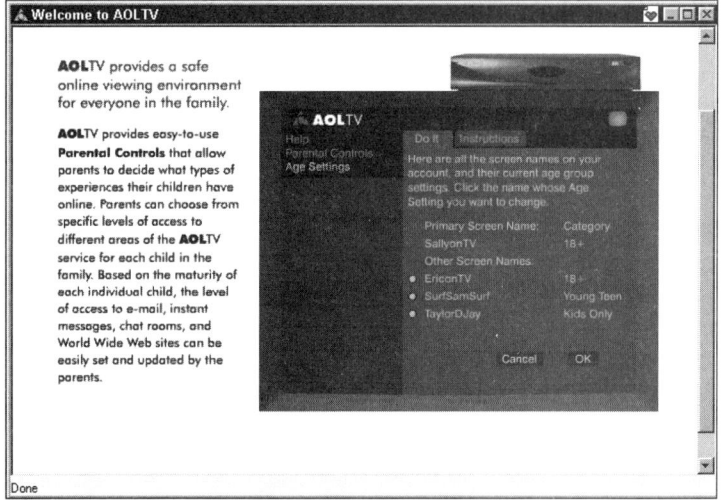

Figure 22-4. Control your kid's access with Parental Controls.

The "You've Got Pictures" service is perfect for get-togethers — you can view photos with family and friends — right on your TV. And Shop@AOL offers TV viewers the most convenient one-stop shopping resource available online.

What You Need For AOLTV

AOLTV is not a computer for the television. It's a new interactive service that delivers AOL's popular features, content, and services on the television through a small set-top box. The set-top box for the AOLTV service — which comes with a 56K modem and 5GB hard drive onboard — is easy to install and comes with a videotape explaining the setup process. The box plugs into the television through a cable port and connects online through a dial-up phone line.

You can watch your favorite TV shows and interact with the AOLTV service by using a specially designed wireless keyboard and universal remote control, which are configured with special shortcut keys that provide one-step access to the Electronic Program Guide, e-mail, or the Buddy List feature. This design makes multitasking with AOLTV easy — from chatting about a show and exchanging instant messages with a friend to checking e-mail and even viewing Web content.

All you need in order to operate AOLTV is a television and a phone line; everything else is provided with the service, including access to AOL and its global community of over 24 million people, and AOL's 24-hour customer service.

The Internet connection for AOLTV is presently based on AOL's nationwide dial-up network, but AOL is working with its manufacturing partners to support a number of high-speed options. In anticipation of such developments, all the AOLTV set-top boxes that are presently being manufactured come with a Universal Serial Bus (USB) port, which will allow for a Digital Subscriber Line (DSL), cable modem, or 56K-modem dial-up connection.

The AOLTV service is initially available with a Philips Electronics set-top box. A new platform also will soon be available through an AOLTV/DIRECTV set-top box manufactured by Hughes Network Systems that will combine AOLTV with digital television programming from DIRECTV. Additional platforms for accessing AOLTV are under development as well.

How much does all this cost? At the time of writing, the Philips receiver for the AOLTV service was retailing for about $249.95. For AOL Members, AOLTV also carries an additional $14.95 monthly charge over and above their standard membership fee. If you aren't an AOL member yet, you can join AOLTV for $24.95 a month, which includes unlimited access to AOLTV.

Your existing phone lines work with AOLTV; you don't need to install a special line.

If you're interested in getting AOLTV, visit the AOLTV site and sign up to be notified when AOLTV is available in your area.

Putting Your Knowledge to Work

You can learn more about AOLTV online at AOL Keyword: **AOLTV** or at the AOLTV Web site www.aoltv.com (see Figure 22-5). The Web site even offers a fun demo you can try!

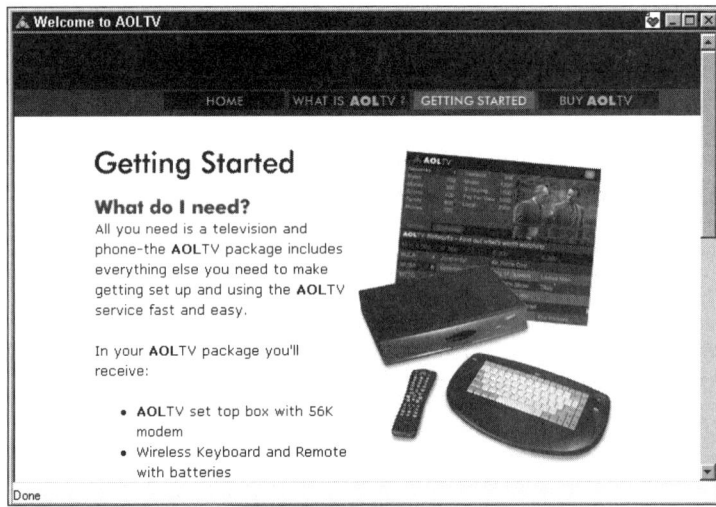

Figure 22-5. The AOLTV Web site offers help on getting started.

CHAPTER

23

LONG DISTANCE
AND PAGING

Quick Look

▶ AOL Long Distance Plan   page 424
AOL offers its members a low-cost, long-distance plan with calls for just 5 cents a minute, state to state. And, because it's AOL's plan, you can view your bill online at anytime. To learn more, see AOL Keyword: **Long Distance**.

▶ Send a Page   page 425
You can send a message to a Metrocall, MobileComm, or MCI WorldCom pager from the comfort of your AOL computer. Just go to AOL Keyword: **Send Page**, select the appropriate paging company, type the pager ID and message, and click Send.

▶ AOL Anywhere   page 426
The AOL Anywhere multi-platform strategy extends the benefits of the company's industry-leading brands as well as its popular features and services to members anywhere, anytime, and at any speed — on emerging interactive platforms beyond the PC.

▶ AOL Plus   page 429
Broadband users receive rich, multimedia content through AOL Plus, which is delivered when AOL detects a broadband connection. AOL even offers a broadband service for those who don't have it. Go to AOL Keyword: **AOL Plus**.

Chapter 23
Long Distance and Paging

IN THIS CHAPTER

Getting long-distance service at great rates

Sending messages to pagers through AOL

Accessing your favorite AOL features anytime, anywhere

Discovering enhanced content through AOL Plus

This isn't your father's AOL. Today, you can use AOL for more than just online communication and information. AOL provides long-distance phone service and a convenient way to send messages to pagers. Access your AOL e-mail, the Buddy List feature and other popular features on the AOL service from just about anywhere. And last but not least, AOL delivers enhanced content to broadband users (and even a broadband connection for those who don't have it yet).

AOL Long Distance

AOL offers its members a long-distance service for 5 cents a minute, state to state. The AOL Long Distance service costs $5.95 a month. The service fee also includes your calling card(s) (9 cents a minute per call, 75-cent surcharge per call) and extensive online reporting of your calls. You can sort your online reports in a variety of ways and even view the names (not just the numbers) of the people you call. AOL Long Distance also provides 24-hour customer service and a state-of-the-art telecommunications network.

For more information, go to AOL Keyword: **Long Distance** and click the More Information link. If you want to join, click the Click Here to Enroll button. As a member, the Member's Area at AOL Keyword: **LD Member** (see Figure 23-1) offers online tools for viewing your bill, managing your account, ordering calling cards, checking rates and fees, and getting answers to questions.

For an extra $3.95 a month, you can get great rates on international calls, too.

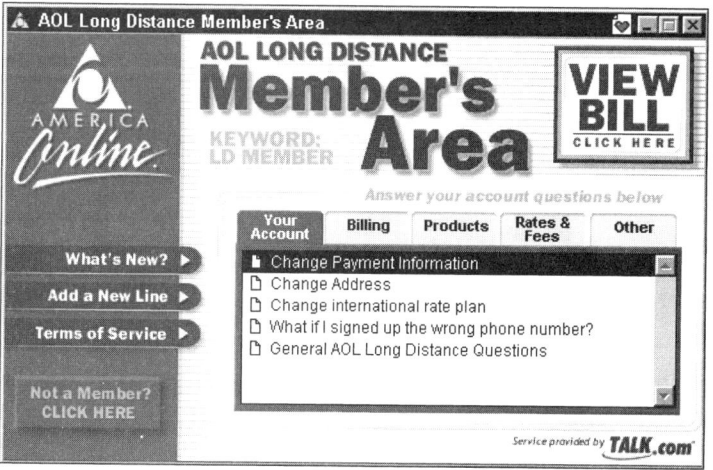

Figure 23-1. The AOL Long Distance Member's Area is always close at hand.

Paging

If you or someone you know has a Metrocall, MCI WorldCom, or MobileComm pager, you can use AOL to send text messages to it! Access is easy — just choose People⇨Send Message to Pager from the AOL toolbar (or use AOL Keyword: **Send Page**) and then click the appropriate paging company to get an online paging screen, as shown in Figure 23-2.

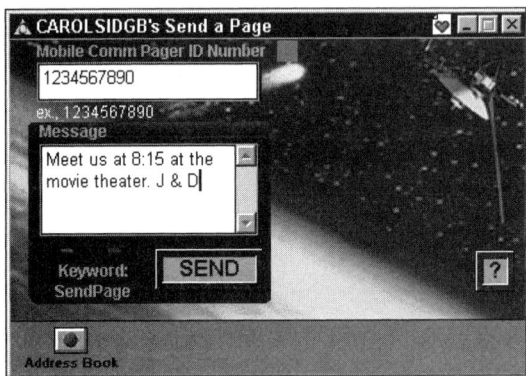

Figure 23-2. MobileComm's Send a Page window.

Some paging subscriber plans have character maximums for messages or charge extra fees for long messages. Unless you know exactly how many characters are allowed, keep your message short, out of consideration for the recipient.

You need to know the five- to ten-digit pager number, of course, and type that into the form. Follow that with a short message and then click the Send button. MobileComm's paging interface even offers a handy address book for remembering pager numbers.

AOL Anywhere

America Online Inc.'s (AOL's) AOL Anywhere multi-platform strategy extends the benefits of the company's industry-leading brands as well as its popular features and services to members anywhere, anytime, and at any speed — on emerging interactive platforms beyond the PC. Initially introduced in 1998 with the redesign of the AOL.COM Web site, the AOL Anywhere initiative has become a reality, with more ways than ever before for AOL members to access the easy-to-use and convenient services that have become a part of their everyday lives.

The AOL Household: Get "Connected" to Match Your Lifestyle

As the AOL service becomes more and more a part of your daily life, AOL has developed more and more ways for you to get the information you want whenever you want it. At home, members can access these services and much more:

- **On the Home Computer with the All-New AOL 6.0:** The AOL 6.0 software includes many new features that advance the "Anywhere" strategy. For example, the Address Book feature is now even easier to use and more accessible when you need to update it, when you're away from your own computer and signed on to AOL 6.0 as a Guest, and even when you're offline.

  In addition, the My Calendar service — a popular online calendar introduced with AOL 5.0 that helps members manage appointments, anniversaries, birthdays, or other personal events — is now even more useful and convenient. You can access it even when you're not signed on to the AOL service or from the Web at AOL.COM when you're at work or traveling. And soon, any updates you make will automatically synchronize with your online version — or with handheld devices and Personal Digital Assistants (PDAs).

  And, as with AOL 5.0, version 6.0 takes you to the next level of interactive experience no matter how you connect to the AOL service. AOL 6.0 offers full broadband support over DSL, cable, and satellite so that members who desire more speed are able to use the technology best suited and available to them.

- **In the Living Room with the AOLTV Service:** This exciting, new interactive service is designed to enhance the television viewing experience and make the TV more entertaining and useful. AOLTV makes it easy for everyone in your family to get the most out of your TV by offering some of the most popular AOL features and services such as e-mail, instant messages, chat rooms, and even the "You've Got Pictures" service.

AOL at Work or on the Road: Stay Connected to Fit Your Schedule

As part of their connected lifestyle, AOL members have said that they want a streamlined way to get to their e-mail, calendar, address book, local news, and other information by using one screen name and password — wherever they are, and especially at work. Now, there is a new AOL Anywhere site, which you can reach by going to AOL Keyword: **Anywhere**, or to AOL.COM. A new button on the toolbar of the AOL 6.0 service lets members go to the Anywhere site with just one click.

Beyond the PC, AOL has also developed new services and products that will offer a world of convenience whether you choose to connect via your PDA, cell phone, or regular telephone. Here are just some of the devices from which you can get your favorite AOL features and services:

- **Handheld Organizers — AOL for Palm and CE:** Since late 1999, AOL has made its popular e-mail service available to members on the go with handheld organizers and modems for the Palm Computing platform, as well as for Windows CE and Pocket PC devices. Members can download AOL's free AOL Mail software at AOL Keyword: **Anywhere**.

- **AOL Mobile Services on Internet-Ready Phones:** The new AOL Mobile services debuted in June 2000 on more than 15 models of Sprint PCS Web-enabled Phones nationwide. AOL Mobile gives AOL members across the country quick and easy access to their AOL e-mail, news, weather, and stock quotes, as well as content from some of AOL's other consumer-friendly brands, including Digital City and MovieFone. These services are also available to members using any of AT&T Wireless Internet-ready phones, where AOL will have top placement in the Portals channel of the AT&T Digital PocketNet service premium offer.

- **AOL by Phone — New Voice Service:** Soon, AOL will introduce a new companion service to enable you to access your AOL e-mail, stock quotes, weather forecasts, driving directions, dining guides, even AOL MovieFone by using your voice — from any telephone.

- **AOL Mail Alerts — New Alerts Service:** Soon, AOL will introduce a new companion service that can be used in conjunction with AOL Mail by Phone. AOL Mail Alerts offers you the convenience of never missing an important or urgent e-mail again. You can customize the alerts service to send a message to a cell phone or alphanumeric pager when a designated e-mail arrives in your AOL e-mail box. You can also customize AOL Mail Alerts to send alerts according to sender or by subject line.

Additionally, the new AOL Anywhere site not only offers the full spectrum of AOL features and services that are available to you wherever you are, but also lets you choose what type of information you want to receive on devices like pagers, cell phones, or PDAs.

AOL Plus

AOL Plus actually refers to two different components of AOL's broadband initiatives. First, AOL Plus refers to AOL's multimedia content offering. Secondly, AOL Plus refers to broadband connectivity to AOL and the rest of the Internet. The following few sections offer the details.

AOL Plus Broadband Services

AOL and its partners are working together to provide consumers with a "one-stop" shop for all their broadband needs, delivering complete services that include *both* the high-speed connection and the AOL Plus content. To learn more about broadband, and how to get a high-speed connection, you can visit AOL Keyword: **AOL Plus**.

AOL currently offers broadband DSL service for consumers who want faster connections to AOL and the rest of the Internet. AOL Plus DSL delivers high-speed connections over your existing telephone line, connecting you to AOL instantly without dialing. And yes, you can talk on the phone at the same time, using the same phone line. The AOL Plus service is $19.95/month over your standard AOL monthly membership fee. At the time of writing, AOL was also working with its partner Hughes Network Systems to deliver AOL Plus content via the DirecPC service.

AOL Plus Content

AOL Plus multimedia content delivers CD-quality audio, video highlights, high-speed downloads, and context-sensitive

Cross-Reference

Read more about AOL Plus and broadband in Appendix B.

Note

Just how fast is the AOL Plus DSL connection? Well, actual connection speeds depend upon your geographic location and your distance from the Regional Bell Operating Company's (RBOC) central office. In general, however, you can get speeds up to 50 times faster than a 28.8K modem.

Note

You need either AOL 5.0 or 6.0 for Windows software to receive AOL Plus content. At the time of writing, AOL Plus content for Macintosh computers is still in development.

information while you browse. Best of all, this content is completely free to all broadband users, regardless of whether you subscribe to the AOL Plus DSL service (described previously) or another high-speed connectivity provider. All AOL Plus content appears in the AOL Tower (see Figure 23-3), a small window that pops up in the lower right-hand corner of your screen when you're signed on with broadband access.

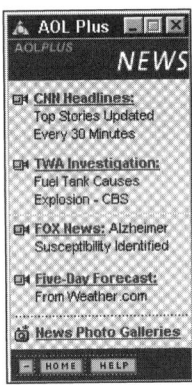

Figure 23-3. The AOL Plus Tower updates automatically as your browse the AOL service.

Tip

Look for a Getting Started link in the AOL Plus Tower (usually available immediately after you sign on) for an AOL Plus tutorial.

Just click one of the hyperlinks to get your high-speed audio and video streaming. The hyperlinks also change as you move through the AOL service. For example, you see travel highlights when you're in the Travel Channel and the latest news broadcasts when you're in the News Channel.

Putting Your Knowledge to Work

It has never been easier to access AOL. If you travel frequently or don't have AOL access at work, AOL Anywhere offers virtually everything you need. The only thing missing is a way to access AOL without any sort of computer or connected device, but AOL is probably working on that, too!

If that isn't enough, AOL offers even more benefits for its members. The next chapter discusses the various member rewards and perks available to you as an AOL member.

CHAPTER

24

SHOPPING AND REWARD PROGRAMS

Quick Look

▶ AOL Rewards   page 432
Would you like to get some free AOL time? With AOL Rewards, you can earn points for shopping and taking surveys, and then redeem those rewards for free time, merchandise, and travel. Go to AOL Keyword: **Rewards**.

▶ AOL Visa Card   page 433
Make purchases with the AOL Visa Card and earn points toward free time on AOL. The AOL Visa also offers a low introductory APR and online bill reports and payments. Go to AOL Keyword: **Visa**.

▶ AOL Insider Savings Club   page 434
Get a monthly e-mail of all the great deals AOL has cooked up for its members. Subscribe for free at AOL Keyword: **Insider Savings**.

▶ AOL Netmarket   page 435
Join an online warehouse club and get great discounts on merchandise. Best of all, you can shop 24/7! Go to AOL Keyword: **Netmarket**.

Chapter 24

Shopping and Reward Programs

IN THIS CHAPTER

Learning about the perks you receive for being an AOL member

Earning points by shopping and answering questions

Saving by joining the AOL member savings club

AOL offers its members many exclusive benefits, services, and rewards. And the deals and discounts are growing daily. We describe the most popular ones in this chapter, but by the time you read this, many more may be available. You can see the latest crop of member programs by choosing Favorites⇨Member Exclusives from the AOL toolbar. Also explore AOL Keyword: **Perks** for new programs and special offers.

AOL Rewards

Do you want your time online to count? With AOL Rewards, you can earn points for taking surveys and making purchases. These points can add up to free AOL service, merchandise like computer gear and clothing, and travel awards. To get started, use AOL Keyword: **Rewards**. The AOL Rewards window is shown in Figure 24-1.

Chapter 24 ▲ Shopping and Reward Programs

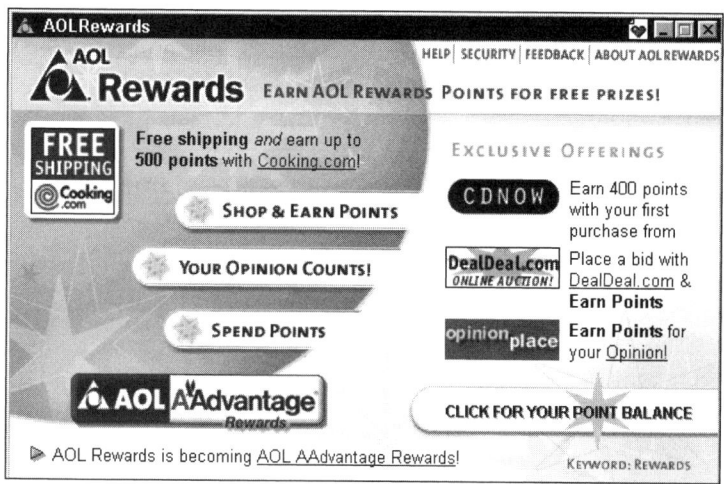

Figure 24-1. AOL Rewards gives you the opportunity to earn and spend points.

To get your reward point balance, just click the Click for Your Point Balance button in the lower right-hand corner of the AOL Rewards window — your balance is automatically updated and displayed. Don't have many points? You need at least 2,000 points to get free time on AOL. To start earning more points, click either the Shop & Earn Points button or the Your Opinion Counts Button in the AOL Rewards window. Now just make online purchases for things you need (see Chapters 15 and 19 for help on shopping online) or fill out surveys. Online purchase points vary, but most surveys earn you about 300 points each.

If you're not into making purchases or taking surveys, you can also earn points for winning contests. Love@AOL awards its chat game winners 400 AOL Reward points, for example.

AOL Visa

Yes, AOL offers an AOL Visa card to its members. What's the big deal? You can earn special points on your purchases and redeem your points for free AOL service. Specifically, you can earn . . .

▶ 1 point for every dollar spent on purchases and for every dollar transferred from other credit cards to your AOL Visa Card

- ▶ 2 points for every dollar billed to the Visa card for your monthly AOL membership fee and for premium services, including online games
- ▶ 5 points for every dollar spent on purchases from opening screen merchandise offers (those offers that appear when you first sign on to AOL) and from AOL Shop Direct
- ▶ 2,200 bonus points when you sign up and get approved for the AOL Visa card

You can redeem 200 points for an hour of AOL service, 1,000 points for one month of AOL (if you're on the $9.95/month plan), or 2,200 points for one month of AOL (if you're on the $21.95/month plan).

The AOL Visa card has a few other things going for it, too. At the time of writing, the AOL Visa card offers a 2.9 percent introductory APR (for the first six billing cycles), no annual fee, and the ability to get your account information and make payments online. If you're interested, visit AOL Keyword: **Visa** for more information and an application.

AOL Insider Savings Club

Tip

You don't have to subscribe to the AOL Insider Savings Club to find out about the discounts. Just visit the Insider Savings Club main window when you're in a shopping mood and find out about the latest deals.

If you're an online shopper, you'll want to join the AOL Insider Savings Club. In essence, it is a collection of great AOL member-only deals from the shops you know and love. Each month, AOL gathers together the deals it has made and sends an e-mail to you. To get this e-mail delivered monthly, just go to AOL Keyword: **Insider Savings** and click the Subscribe button.

AOL members have access to other savings clubs, too, such as AOL Netmarket (discount warehouse), AOL Credit Alert (credit reports), AOL Travelers Advantage (hotel discounts), and AOL AutoVantage (auto club) — we discuss all but AOL Credit Alert later in the chapter. AOL Credit Alert offers a way to get unlimited copies of your credit, driving, medical, and Social Security records. For more details on these savings clubs, go to AOL Keyword: **Savings Clubs**.

AOL Netmarket

AOL Netmarket is a discount warehouse club for AOL members, offering over 800,000 products at savings of 10 to 50 percent. Like most warehouse clubs, you must pay a membership fee for the privilege of shopping; in this case, it's a $19.95 annual fee, but you can try AOL Netmarket free for 30 days. When you become a member, you get a free electronic organizer just for joining. All purchases made through AOL Netmarket automatically receive two-year warranty protection for free. Perhaps, best of all, you can shop online 24 hours a day.

If you're interested in looking around AOL Netmarket before you join, just go to AOL Keyword: **Netmarket** and click the Go button (or go there directly with aol.netmarket.com). You can browse the store, or better yet, type the name of a product you're interested in buying into the search field near the top of the window and click Search. You'll get results, which you can further refine and sort — AOL Netmarket offers excellent search tools. Figure 24-2 shows an example of a search for videotapes.

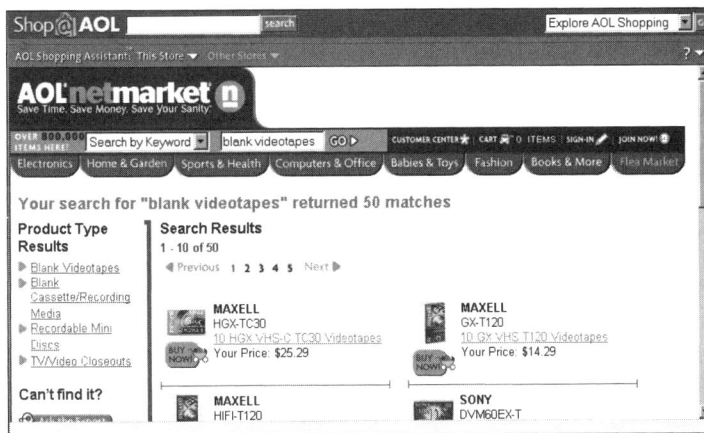

Figure 24-2. Searching for videotapes at AOL Netmarket.

AOL Travelers Advantage and AutoVantage

If you're a frequent traveler, you may want to check out AOL Travelers Advantage. This savings program offers its members 50 percent off at over 5,000 hotels, plus a low price guarantee on online car, hotel, and air purchases. To join AOL Travelers Advantage, you need to plunk down a $59.95 annual membership fee, but in return, you get a free hotel night, a 5-percent cash-back bonus on eligible travel bookings, savings of $20–$700 on American Airlines flights, last-minute deals, and member-only specials. You can try the program free for three months before that annual fee kicks in. To learn more, visit AOL Keyword: **Travelers Advantage**.

AOL AutoVantage is an auto club that offers 24-hour roadside assistance, car-care savings, travel discounts, and car-buying services. The annual fee is $79.95, but you can try the service for free for three months. Membership gets you 24-hour national emergency towing and lockout protection, auto-service savings at places like Jiffy Lube and Goodyear, hotel discounts, car-rental savings, and personalized car-buying services. Visit AOL Keyword: **AutoVantage**.

Blockbuster Movie

Blockbuster (AOL Keyword: **Blockbuster**) and AOL are teaming up to bring some great AOL member benefits your way. Blockbuster is the world's leading renter of videos and video games. Soon AOL members will be able to get special offers on rentals, personalized movie recommendations, pre-notification of new releases, and online reservations for new videos. One intriguing member benefit is AOL's Movie a Day program. For about $10 a month, you can get a movie from Blockbuster every day, at no extra charge.

Putting Your Knowledge to Work

There's a lot more to being an AOL member than just a great online service. AOL saves you money, offers rewards, and, through strategic alliances, creates a better service. In fact, we'd say congraulations are in order — congratulations on being a member of America Online and for making it to the end of this tour guide.

We hope you aren't too road-weary — you have an entire world ahead of you to explore on your own, after all. We're confident you'll find what you're seeking, too. If you reach a dead end, be persistent. Sometimes you need to come at it from several directions. Your reward is finding that elusive bit of information that can help you finish the paper, seal the deal, or find that long-lost friend.

PART VI

APPENDIXES

Appendix A
How to Get the Most Out of AOL

Appendix B
Broadband Opportunities

Appendix C: Glossary

Appendix A
How to Get the Most Out of AOL

Getting the most out of AOL begins with knowing what your computer needs in order to work with AOL. AOL's needs are fairly simple, and this appendix guides you through the process so that you can begin your adventures with AOL. We list the basic system requirements for AOL, show you how to gather what you need for AOL, and tell you how to upgrade the AOL software. For those of you who are using an older version of the AOL software, we explain how to upgrade your software to AOL version 6.0. Finally, we show all our travelers how to get online as a guest, away from your home computer, with the AOL software.

Basic System Requirements

AOL software version 6.0 for Windows is available for computers running Windows 95, Windows 98, Windows NT (with Service Pack 4 or higher), and Windows 2000. Here are the specific requirements for each of these operating systems:

AOL 6.0 for Windows 95

- Pentium-class PC
- 16MB of RAM or more
- 70MB of available hard drive space (you may need up to 170MB if Internet Explorer isn't already installed on your computer)
- VGA, SVGA or better monitor capable of displaying at least 256 colors at 640 x 480 resolution (optimized for 800 x 600)

Is your computer up to speed? If not, pay a visit to AOL Keyword: **Upgrade Shop** for AOL member deals on hardware.

- 14,400 bps or faster modem, or another Internet connection
- Internet Explorer 5.5 (included with AOL)

AOL 6.0 for Windows 98

- Pentium-class PC
- 16MB of RAM or more
- 80MB of available hard drive space (you may need up to 180MB if Internet Explorer isn't already installed on your computer)
- VGA, SVGA or better monitor capable of displaying at least 256 colors at 640 x 480 resolution (optimized for 800 x 600)
- 14,400 bps or faster modem, or another Internet connection
- Internet Explorer 5.5 (included with AOL)

AOL 6.0 for Windows NT/2000

- Pentium-class PC 166MHz or higher
- Remote Access Services (RAS) installed
- 64MB of RAM or more
- 80MB of available hard drive space (you may need up to 190MB if Internet Explorer isn't already installed on your computer)
- VGA, SVGA or better monitor capable of displaying at least 256 colors at 640 x 480 resolution (optimized for 800 x 600)
- 14,400 bps or faster modem, or another Internet connection
- Internet Explorer 5.5 (included with AOL)

Macintosh

At the time of writing, AOL 5.0 was just released for the Mac, and AOL 6.0 wasn't yet available. To find out if AOL 6.0 is now available, visit AOL Keyword: **Upgrade** with any version of AOL for the Mac.

The Software

After you have the computer, you need the software. The latest version of AOL software is version 6.0. If you don't have the software on a CD-ROM, don't worry — AOL distributes many CDs bearing the software. You may have gotten it in the mail. If not, the software may be installed (or ready to install) on your computer (if it's new); search your desktop icons on your computer or search your hard drive for *AOL*.

If you don't have the software handy, free copies of AOL sign-on kits are usually available at bookstores, video stores, home electronics stores, and even grocery stores. You may also find the software in magazines (though you need to purchase the magazine to get the software, naturally).

If you're unable to find the AOL software locally, you have several options. You can call AOL at 800-827-6364 and request a sign-on kit; delivery takes about a week. An even better solution may be to ask a friend who is already on AOL to go to AOL Keyword: **Friend** and request that a sign-on kit be sent to you in the mail. If you create a new account with the sign-on kit a friend orders for you and you stay online for at least 90 days, your friend earns $20 (or even $50, depending on the current promotion). Better yet, you may get more free time to use AOL in your first month if your friend orders a sign-on kit for you. Alternatively, if you're already on the Internet with another online service or ISP, point your Web browser to www.aol.com and download the software from AOL's Web site.

Definition

A *sign-on kit* is the free software, registration codes, and directions for creating a new AOL account. A sign-on kit generally comes on a CD and is packaged in a cardboard CD sleeve with printed codes and directions.

If you have an older version of AOL, you can use it to get the latest version. If the older software is already installed on your computer, skip to the section "Upgrading Your Software," later in this appendix. If you simply have an older version of the AOL software on a CD that hasn't yet been installed, it may be easier to order a CD with the latest version. If you can't wait that long, go ahead and install the older version and follow the on-screen directions. After you're online, refer to "Upgrading Your Software" later in this appendix.

The pricing plans are subject to change — use AOL Keyword: **Billing** when you're online to double-check the rates.

You can get a month of free AOL when you apply and receive the AOL Visa Card. See Chapter 25 for details.

None of the pricing plans include the use of premium areas (such as certain games), which carry additional charges.

If you're not sure what makes a good screen name, refer to Chapter 12.

The Money

Of course, you have to pay to use AOL. Thankfully, it's a lot of value for the money. At the time of writing, AOL offers five different pricing plans:

- The **Standard Unlimited Monthly plan** costs $21.95 a month and gives you unlimited usage of AOL.
- The **One Year plan** gives you the same benefits as the Standard Unlimited Monthly plan, but it's a bit cheaper because you pay a lump sum for the year upfront ($239.40, which is a savings of $24 over the monthly plan).
- If you plan to use AOL less frequently, the **Limited plan** is $9.95 a month and includes five hours; additional hours of usage are $2.95.
- If you really don't expect to use AOL often, try the **Light Usage plan** — $4.95 a month for three hours, with additional hours at $2.50.
- The **Bring Your Own Access plan** is for those of you who already have an Internet service provider (ISP) or other network connection that you can use to access AOL. This plan is $9.95 a month and includes unlimited usage.

After you decide on the plan that's right for you and your family, you need to figure out how to pay for it. AOL accepts credit cards (Visa, MasterCard, American Express, Discover/ Novus, and Diners Club). Automatic withdrawals from checking accounts are also accepted, though this carries an additional handling fee of $5 each month. Whichever method you opt to use, get the information ready and have it on hand during installation.

The Screen Name

AOL (and the rest of the world) needs to know how to address you when you're online. Thus, every AOL member has a unique screen name and can have up to seven total screen names per account, in fact. If you aren't yet a member, you should brainstorm several possible screen names *before* you actually begin the installation process. We recommend that you come up with at least a handful of possibilities — jot them down on a piece of paper.

Upgrading Your Software

Are you still using that old version of the AOL software? Although many of the older versions can continue to connect to AOL, they don't give you access to all the bells and whistles of AOL version 6.0 (which this book is based upon). Upgrading to AOL 6.0 is free of charge and easy to do. Here's how:

1. If you have an AOL 6.0 CD-ROM, you're home free! If not, sign on with your older AOL software and go to AOL Keyword: **Upgrade**.

   The Upgrade Center, shown in Figure A-1, not only lets you download the most recent version of AOL software, but also gives you a peek at the new features and offers help for installing and troubleshooting the software itself. If your computer isn't quite up to speed for AOL 6.0, the Upgrade Center even offers resources to upgrade your computer as well. Whether you have the installation disc or download the software, the AOL upgrade installation process begins automatically.

If you aren't yet an AOL member and are installing the AOL software for the first time, be sure to select the New Member option in that first screen (shown in Figure A-2) and follow the on-screen directions. Have your payment information and screen name choices ready, too.

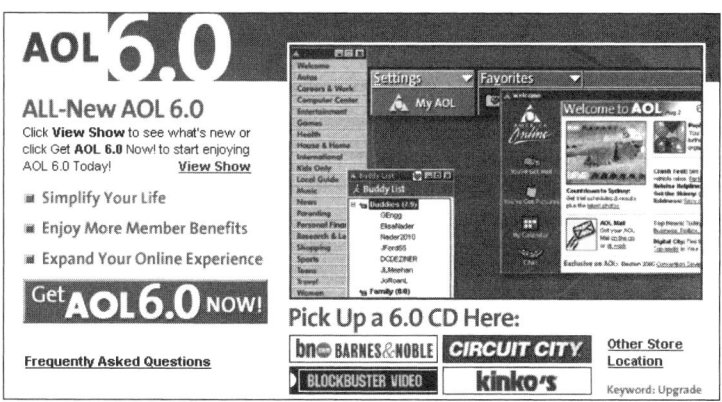

Figure A-1. The Upgrade Center offers free downloads of the latest AOL software.

2. In the next window (shown in Figure A-2), indicate that you are a current member rather than a new member (because you're upgrading to a newer version of AOL). Then click the Current Members button.

Note

Sometimes technical difficulties with your current installation of AOL 6.0 may require a "clean install" that ignores all the settings and information you accumulated in your current AOL software installation. Or, perhaps, you may not want your settings and e-mail copied. In either situation, you're better off not doing an upgrade. Instead, click the Back button, select the Adding Your Existing AOL Account to This Computer option, and continue with the installation process.

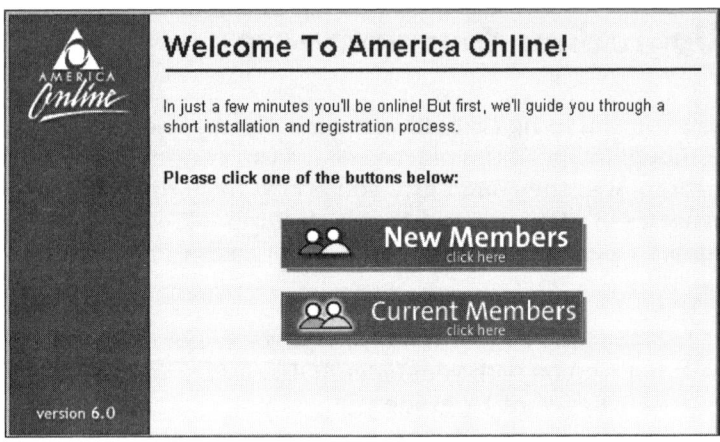

Figure A-2. Click the Current Members button if you want to upgrade your existing software rather than create a new account.

3. In the Current Member window (shown in Figure A-3), indicate whether you're upgrading to a new version of AOL, adding an existing AOL account to this particular computer, or creating a new AOL account on your computer. In most cases, you should do nothing; the default setting is to upgrade to a new version of AOL. Otherwise, select the appropriate radio button. Then click Next to continue.

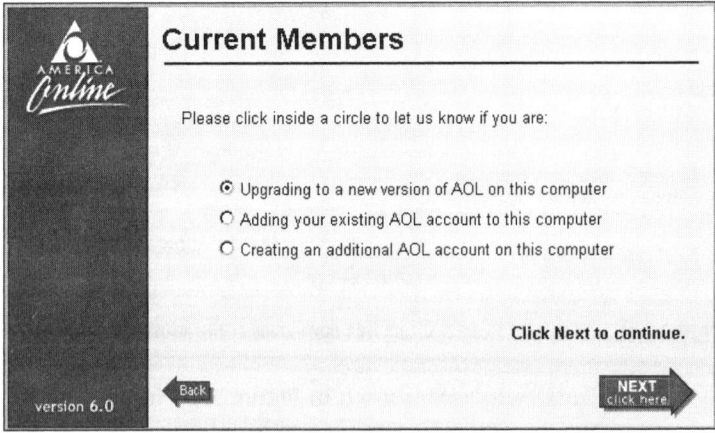

Figure A-3. Let AOL know whether you want to upgrade, add an existing AOL account, or create a new AOL account.

Upon clicking Next, AOL begins to search your computer for previous versions of AOL. Assuming you indicated that you want to upgrade to a new version, this is a crucial step in the installation process. Note that the search may take a while if you have a particularly large hard drive or many copies of AOL installed.

4. If AOL finds that you've already installed this version, it notifies you of this and asks you to confirm that you really do want to install it again. Otherwise, AOL displays all versions of the AOL software found on your computer and asks you to choose the one you want to upgrade (see Figure A-4). Choose (highlight) the AOL version you want to upgrade and click the Next button to continue.

AOL suggests, and so do we, that you upgrade the version you've been using most recently. This is important because it has your most recent settings and e-mail (if you save e-mail in your Filing Cabinet), and you will likely want to preserve these.

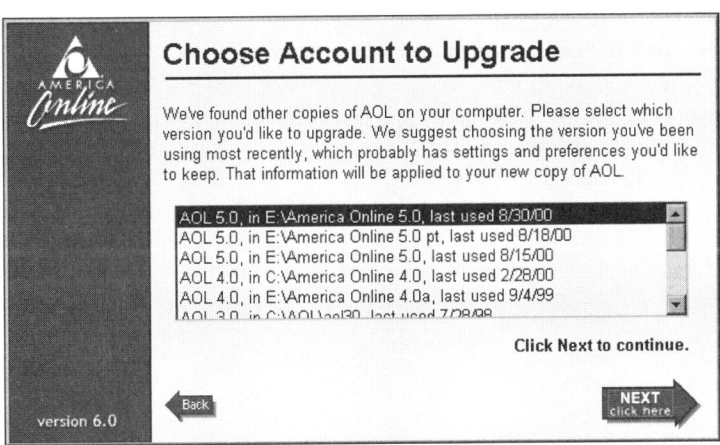

Figure A-4. Choose the version of installed software you want to update.

5. In the next window (shown in Figure A-5), indicate what AOL should do with your previously downloaded files in your previous version of AOL. If you previously downloaded files to the Download directory in your old AOL software, AOL asks you what to do with these. We recommend that you move them to your new software, which is the default. Note that only files that are

Note

If, at anytime, you need to cancel the upgrade process, just click the Cancel button. If the Cancel button isn't available, press the Esc key.

residing in your Download directory are affected by this; files downloaded (or later moved) to other locations on your hard drive will be untouched. Make your selection and click Next.

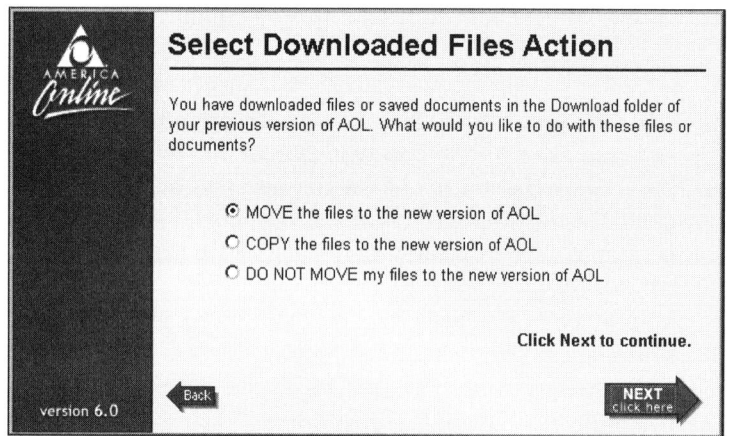

Figure A-5. AOL gives you the option to move, copy, or not move downloaded files.

6. In the Select Destination Directory window (shown in Figure A-6), confirm (or change) the destination directory for your AOL 6.0 software. Note that upgrading your software still entails adding new software into a new directory on your computer — it doesn't simply modify your existing software.

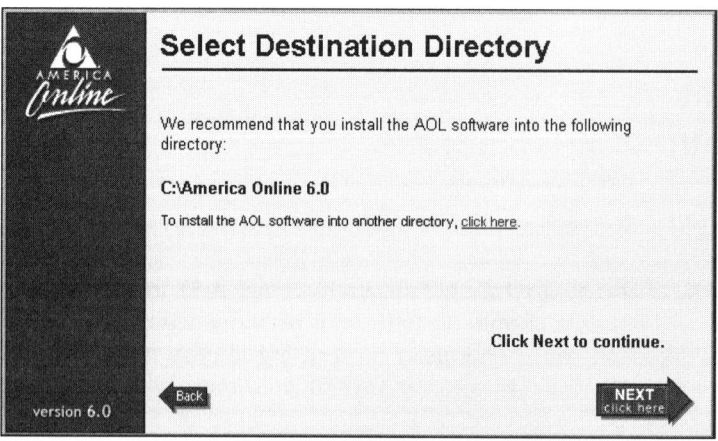

Figure A-6. Decide where you want AOL to install your new software.

If you want to change the directory, find the text that says To install the AOL software in another directory, click here and then click the link to open the Select Installation Directory window, shown in Figure A-7. You can either type your directory in the top field, or use the two lists below to navigate to the location in which you'd like to place your new software. Make your selection and click Next, and Next again.

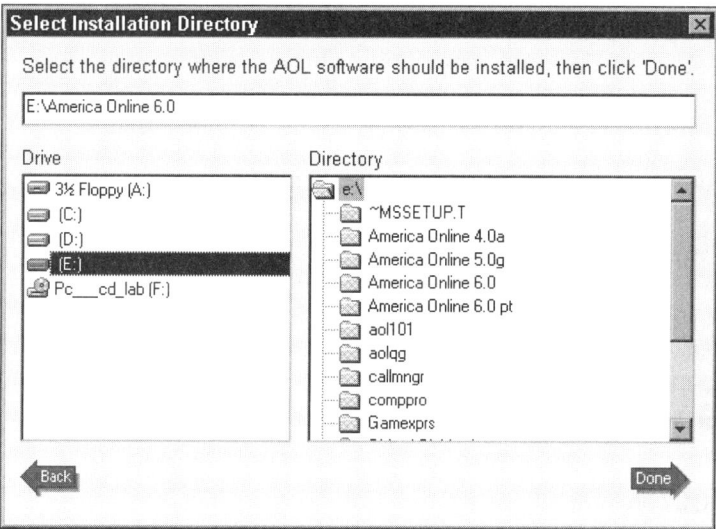

Figure A-7. Select a new location for your software if you don't like the default.

After you select your directory, AOL begins the installation process for you. It takes a few minutes to initialize and then displays a progress bar so you can watch the installation, as shown in Figure A-8.

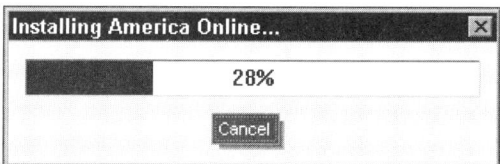

Figure A-8. The installation process is simple and quick.

Caution

Before you choose AOL as your default Internet application for Web pages, newsgroups, and e-mail, stop and be sure of your choice. If you already have (and plan to continue using) an account with another ISP (Internet service provider), or are connected to a LAN with e-mail and Web services, you may want to say, "No," to this option. By doing so, your current e-mail program, newsgroup reader and/or browser will no longer be automatically opened when you click hyperlinks.

7. After installation is complete, restart your computer.

8. After you restart your computer, you may be asked if you want this copy of AOL to be your default Internet application for Web pages, newsgroups, and e-mail. We recommend that you click Yes.

AOL then automatically starts the software and presents the Sign On screen, completely updated with your screen names and locations from the previous version of AOL. If you look closer, you see that AOL transferred your settings and information. Your address book, any offline mail in the Filing Cabinet, your list of files to be downloaded (and already downloaded) in your Download Manager, Favorite Places, shortcuts (Hot Keys), and toolbar icons should all be present.

You can now sign on as usual and begin exploring the new AOL 6.0 software. The Welcome to 6.0 window (refer to Chapter 3) appears for upgrades as well, and you may find it helpful for becoming acquainted with 6.0's new features.

Guest Access

AOL conveniently provides a way for your guests to access their AOL accounts from the installed software on your computer. Better yet, this means *you* can access your AOL account when you're visiting a friend or family member who also has AOL installed. And in case you're wondering, there's no extra charge for this service. How does it work? Follow these steps:

1. Begin by starting the AOL software. In the Sign On window, choose Guest from the Select Screen Name dropdown menu (see Figure A-9).

Appendix A ▲ How to Get the Most Out of AOL

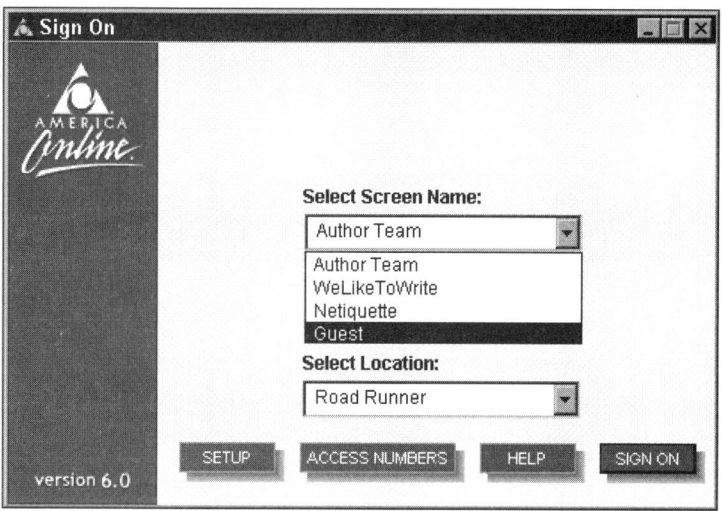

Figure A-9. Select the Guest screen name from the Sign On screen.

2. Click the Sign On button or just press Enter on your keyboard. AOL connects to the service as usual, and then asks for your screen name and password (see Figure A-10).

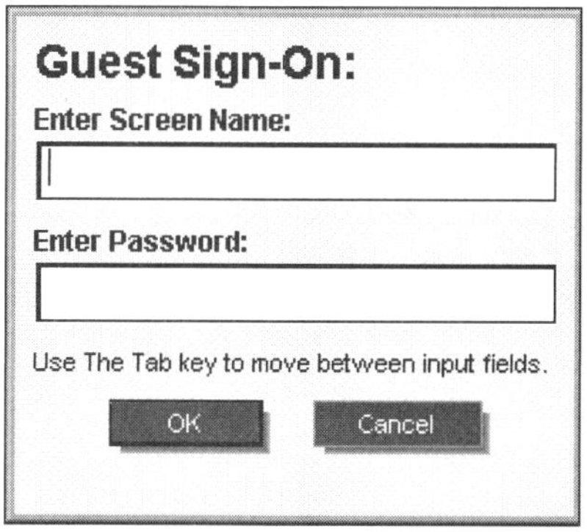

Figure A-10. Type your screen name and password carefully.

3. Enter your screen name and password in the Guest Sign On window.

   Pay close attention to this window. If you mistype either your screen name or your password, you won't be able to sign on. AOL gives you one more try, but if you make a second mistake, AOL automatically signs you off as a protective measure, and you have to repeat the process to try again.

After you're signed on as a Guest, you can use AOL much as you do on your own computer. There are a couple important differences, however. You cannot use the Switch Screen Names feature or Create New Screen Names option. Additionally, your preferences, Filing Cabinet, Download Manager, Favorite Places, e-mail signatures, shortcuts, and toolbar icons are inaccessible — these features are all running on your own computer's hard drive. However, your address book, Buddy List, mailboxes (New, Old, Sent, and Recently Deleted), "You've Got Pictures," preferences and signatures for message board and newsgroups, Parental Controls settings, My Calendar, stock portfolios, and news and interest profiles will all work fine.

Another use for the Guest option comes in handy for those with more than one AOL account. For example, you may have a corporate AOL account at work and a personal AOL account at home. If you want to access your personal account at work, you may not be able to install a new copy of the software with the personal account's screen names. But you can still access your personal account at work using the Guest option.

Appendix B
Broadband Opportunities

The vast majority of AOL's members connect to the service via conventional telephone lines plugged into their computer's modems. Although this means of connecting is very convenient (and often very economical), transmitting large chunks of information — such as graphics, sound, large computer programs, and video — can take a long time. Gradually, a new buzzword is making the rounds, *broadband*. All broadband means to the consumer is that the connection can carry far more information at one time. This is something like comparing a drinking straw to a water main. An AOL software upgrade can take over two hours using a conventional 56K modem but can take less than ten minutes with some broadband connections.

Although corporations have the budgets to connect directly to the Internet with special high-capacity connections, few consumers can afford that. However, over the past few years, the need for speed on the Internet has brought us more reasonably priced options. Today's high-speed options are *DSL (Digital Subscriber Line),* which is a system for increasing the speed of plain old telephone service; satellite, which requires a small dish antenna and special equipment; and cable, which uses the enormous capacity of the coaxial cable that carries your TV signal.

The field of broadband access is constantly changing, and availability is still limited in most areas. We suggest you visit AOL Keyword: **High Speed** regularly, to keep up-to-date.

Broadband service may cost more on the surface, but some hidden cost savings can make up for some or all of the extra cost:

▶ **You may be able to cancel the extra telephone line you've been using to connect to AOL.**
Whether you can do this depends on the kind of broadband connection you have. DSL and many cable systems offer two-way broadband access over a single connection, which means you don't need a dedicated modem line any more. Some older cable broadband systems and all satellite systems are one-way — you receive data from AOL at high speed, but you still need a conventional modem and telephone line to send data to AOL. Ask your service provider about this before you connect.

▶ **You can use AOL's Bring Your Own Access billing plan (BYOA) to reduce your monthly AOL bill.**
BYOA is intended for members who don't have to dial in to an AOL access number in order to connect to the Internet. BYOA currently costs $9.95 per month for unlimited use. What if you switch to BYOA and your broadband access fails, or you use a laptop computer when you travel? You can still use a conventional modem and dial in to AOL, but you'll be charged $2.50 per hour (in one-minute increments) for the connection. As always, any of AOL's charges for Premium Services (such as games) still apply. You can read more about BYOA (and change your billing plan) at AOL Keyword: **Billing**.

Configure AOL for TCP/IP Access

To use any broadband access option, you have to create a new access location in your AOL sign-on setup for TCP/IP (meaning your connection to AOL is via the Internet, rather than by direct connection to AOL). This process is no harder than adding a new AOL access number to your setup. These are the instructions for AOL 6.0:

1. Click the Setup button in the AOL 6.0 Sign On screen.

2. Click the Add Location button in the Edit America Online Setup window.

3. Type an appropriate name in the Name text box in the Add Location window.

4. Click the Select a Connection Using One of These Available Devices option in the Add Location window.

5. Select TCP/IP LAN or ISP (Internet Service Provider) from the drop-down list.

6. Click the Next button.

7. Select the new TCP/IP location from the Select Location list on the Sign On screen, and sign on as usual.

DSL

DSL (or Digital Subscriber Line) uses the same telephone wires that already come into your home. DSL can be more than ten times faster than a 56K modem, and you can make and receive regular phone calls at the same time you're connected to AOL. "Dialing" in to AOL via DSL is also speedy — you don't have to wait while the phone dials and connects — you're online in a matter of seconds.

This is what you need for a DSL connection to AOL:

- ▶ DSL service from your local telephone company (often offered as part of a package from a DSL service provider).
- ▶ DSL modem (external or internal) for your computer, compatible with the DSL technology used by your local telephone company (the external modem may require a USB [Universal Serial Bus] port connection on your computer — confirm in advance whether USB is needed and whether your computer has USB).
- ▶ Software for your DSL modem and computer operating system (this comes with the modem).
- ▶ Plug-in phone filters for every telephone or other device that shares the DSL line. (These filters prevent the digital data from interfering with the function of conventional analog telephone equipment.)
- ▶ AOL 4.0 software or greater (AOL 5.0 or 6.0 preferred).
- ▶ Configure your AOL software for TCP/IP access (see the "Configure AOL for TCP/IP Access" sidebar).

Note

The actual DSL connection speed is dependent on the distance to your local telephone company's central office.

You normally get everything you need from your telephone company or DSL service provider when you sign up for the service, but be sure to ask. AOL sells a wide range of DSL equipment and accessories at AOL Keyword: **DSL Store**.

Typically, your telephone company converts an existing telephone line to DSL, and because you can use the DSL line for both voice and data calls at the same time, you may be able to cancel service on that second modem line you've been using for AOL.

AOL Plus Broadband Service

You must have AOL 5.0 or 6.0 for Windows to enjoy AOL Plus broadband programming.

AOL offers a special AOL Plus broadband package in conjunction with several local telephone companies. You must be on AOL's Unlimited Pricing plan and pay an additional $19.95 per month for AOL Plus broadband service. At the time of writing, this package offer included a one-month free trial, all telephone company charges, free equipment, and free activation. After you order the service, your telephone company contacts you to schedule installation of the telephone service, and AOL ships you the equipment. You are responsible for installing the DSL modem and software. See AOL Keyword: **AOL Plus** for information on the current offer and availability in your area.

AOL Plus is also the name of AOL's broadband programming service, which you receive at no extra charge if you're an AOL member with a broadband connection and use AOL 5.0 or 6.0 for Windows. (AOL Plus programming is also in the works for Macintosh users.) You can read more about AOL Plus in Chapter 24.

If AOL Plus DSL service is not available in your area, you can use any other DSL Internet service to connect to AOL. You have to configure your AOL software for a TCP/IP connection (see the sidebar on TCP/IP earlier in this appendix). After you've set up your TCP/IP location in your AOL software, you just start AOL and sign on as usual (only a whole lot faster than before). You can learn how to connect using DSL at AOL Keyword: **High Speed**.

Satellite

AOL and Hughes Electronics will soon be offering high-speed Internet access via Hughes' DirecPC satellite-delivered Internet access service, a part of Hughes' DIRECTV digital satellite television system. Two options will be available: AOL Plus broadband service, providing conventional AOL access including AOL Plus broadband programming; and AOLTV, AOL's new interactive television programming service.

This is a one-way high-speed connection. You receive data from the satellite at speeds up to seven times the rate of a 56K modem. You send your data to AOL and the Internet over a conventional telephone line and modem at normal speeds (typically 28.8 or 56K). The big advantage of satellite service is that you can get high-speed downloads (and most of us download far more than we upload) in places where cable and DSL broadband services don't reach.

Here's what you need for satellite-delivered Internet access:

- DirecPC satellite dish and associated equipment — a small satellite dish, typically mounted on the side or roof of your home.
- DirecPC satellite receiver — external receivers and internal receiver cards should be available. The external receiver requires a USB port on your computer, and Windows 98.
- DirecPC software.
- Conventional 28.8K or better modem and telephone line.
- AOL 4.0 (or higher) software (AOL 5.0 or 6.0 is preferred).
- Configure your AOL software for TCP/IP access (see the "Configure AOL for TCP/IP Access" sidebar).

Additional details about the service and pricing weren't available at the time of this writing. Watch AOL Keyword: **High Speed Access** and AOL Keyword: **AOL Plus** for news about service offerings.

Cable

The coaxial cable that can carry so many television channels at one time can also be used for broadband Internet access. Cable access is often the fastest of the broadband access methods, offering download speeds measured in the millions of bits per second range (Mbps), and typical upload speeds (for two-way systems) of around 300 Kbps

You can connect to AOL using any cable-based Internet access system. Contact your local cable television provider to learn whether cable access is available in your city and what the charges and setup requirements are.

Cable access is available in one of two basic forms. One-way access uses the coaxial cable for high-speed downloads from AOL and the Internet, and a conventional telephone line and modem for uploads. Two-way access uses the coaxial cable in both directions, eliminating the need for a phone line and conventional modem.

AOL does not currently offer an AOL Plus cable access service package, but has various plans in development. However, after you can connect to the Internet, you can use your existing AOL software (4.0 and higher) to connect to AOL via the cable.

Many different equipment setups are possible for cable service, but the following equipment is typical:

- Cable "modem" installed by your cable television provider
- Internal Ethernet network card (installed by your cable TV provider if you don't already have one)

OR

- USB port connection (cable modems may be equipped for either Ethernet or USB)
- AOL 4.0 (or higher) software
- Configure your AOL software for TCP/IP access (see the "Configure AOL for TCP/IP Access" sidebar)
- Conventional telephone line and modem (only for one-way cable systems)

Your local cable service provider offers equipment and installation services.

Watch AOL Keyword: **High Speed** and AOL Keyword: **AOL Plus** for news and information about high-speed cable access.

Appendix C:
Glossary

800 and 888 numbers
America Online provides 800 and 888 numbers to U.S. and Canadian members who are without local access numbers; additional hourly charges apply. You can find additional information on these numbers at AOL Keyword: **Access.**

A

access number
A phone number (usually local) that your modem uses to access AOL. To find an access number online, go to AOL Keyword: **Access.**

address
(1) An e-mail address that allows you to send an e-mail to anyone on AOL or anywhere on the Internet. You can look up addresses for AOL members at AOL Keyword: **Members**, and addresses for Internet denizens at various places on the Web. More information is available in Chapters 5 and 6.

(2) A location address for information on AOL or the Web; better known as a URL (Universal Resource Locator). An example of an address on America Online is aol://1722:help, which takes you to Member Services when entered into the Keyword window. On the Web, the address www.aol.com takes you to AOL's Web site.

Address Book
An AOL software feature that allows you to store e-mail addresses for easy access. You can create, edit, or use the Address Book by clicking the Address Book icon, which is available when composing mail. You can also create or edit the address book with the Edit Address Book or Address Book option in the Mail menu on the AOL toolbar. See Chapter 5.

America Online, Inc. (AOL)
The nation's leading online service, headquartered in Virginia. Founded in 1985 and formerly known as Quantum Computer Services, America Online has grown rapidly in both size and scope. America Online has over 23 million members and hundreds of alliances with major companies. America Online's stock exchange symbol is *AOL*. To contact AOL headquarters, call 703-448-8700 or use 800-827-6364 to speak to a Member Services representative.

AOL
Abbreviation for America Online, Inc. Occasionally abbreviated as AO. See also *America Online, Inc.*

AOL Instant Messenger (AIM)

Software that allows people with Internet accounts to send and receive Instant Messages from AOL members. After a non-AOL member has downloaded, installed, and registered the AOL Instant Messenger software, America Online members can add that person to their Buddy Lists and send instant messages to him or her. More information is available online at AOL Keyword: **AIM**. See also *instant message*.

AOL Mail

(1) A new member of the AOL family that lets Palm organizer owners check their AOL e-mail. AOL Mail enables members to connect directly to AOL by using their regular screen names and passwords. Using AOL's global network of access numbers, AOL Mail allows members to connect with the service from just about anywhere. More information is available at AOL Keyword: **AOL Mail**. See also *PDA*.

(2) AOL's service for providing AOL members access to their AOL e-mail from any computer equipped with a browser and connected to the Internet, at aolmail/aol.com.

AOL Plus

(1) AOL's DSL service for AOL members. See AOL Keyword: **AOL Plus**. See also *broadband* and *DSL*.

(2) AOL's enhanced content via the AOL Plus Tower. AOL Plus content is available automatically to all broadband users accessing AOL. See Chapter 24 for more information.

AOL Search

AOL's exclusive Internet directory and search service available at www.aol.com or at AOL Keyword: **AOL Search**. See Chapters 17, 18, and 19 for more information.

AOL.COM

AOL's home page on the Web located at www.aol.com.

AOLNET

AOL's own packet-switching network that provides members with up to 56,600 bps local access numbers. For members who do not have a local access number, AOL has an 800 number that is more affordable than most long-distance fees. Another alternative is to sign on to America Online through an Internet or ISP (Internet service provider) connection. To find AOLNET local access numbers, go to AOL Keyword: **AOLNET**. See also *800 and 888 numbers, access number,* and *packet-switching network*.

archive

(1) A file that has been compressed with file compression software. See also *file, file compression,* and *WinZip*.

(2) A file that contains message board postings that may be of value, but have been removed from a message board due to their age, inactivity of topic, or lack of message board space. These messages are usually bundled into one document and placed in a file library for retrieval later. See also *file* and *library*.

Appendix C: Glossary

attached file
A file that hitches a ride with e-mail. Whether the file is text, sound, or pictures, it is said to be attached if it has been included with the e-mail for separate downloading by the recipient (whether addressed directly, carbon copied, or blind carbon copied). More information is available in Chapter 5. See also *archive, download, e-mail,* and *file.*

auditorium
Auditoriums are specially equipped online "rooms" that allow large groups of AOL members to meet in a structured setting. You can find more information on auditoriums at AOL Keyword: **AOL Live** or Chapter 9. Contrast with *chat room.*

Automatic AOL (Auto AOL)
An automated feature that can send and receive your e-mail and files, as well as receive newsgroup postings. You can set up Auto AOL to run at any time, including while you're online or away from home. It is accessible under the Mail menu on your AOL toolbar. More information is available in Chapters 6 and 10. See also *e-mail, file,* and *newsgroup.*

B

baud rate
A unit for measuring the speed of data transmission. Technically, baud rates refer to the number of times the communications line changes states each second. Strictly speaking, baud and bits per second (bps) are not identical measurements, but most nontechnical people use the terms interchangeably. See also *bps* and *V.90.*

blind courtesy copy (bcc)
A feature of the AOL e-mail system that allows you to send e-mail to a member or members without anyone other than you being aware of it. See Chapter 5 for more information. See also *e-mail;* contrast with *courtesy copy.*

board
An abbreviated reference to a message board or bulletin board service (BBS). See also *message board.*

Boolean search
A search that uses logical operators from Boolean algebra to narrow the number of matches. For example, a search in the classifieds for *car* would yield many matches, but not exactly what you want. A search for *car and brown and (Firebird or TransAm)* would help you find exactly what you're looking for. Most searches on America Online are Boolean searches and use the following Boolean operators: *and, or, not.*

bounce
Something that is returned, such as e-mail. For example, e-mail sent to recipients outside AOL may bounce and never make it to its intended destination, especially if it was not addressed correctly. Sometimes members who are disconnected refer to themselves as bounced. See also *e-mail.*

bps (bits per second)
A method of measuring data transmission speed. Currently, modem speeds up to 56,000 bps (56K) are supported on AOL (see AOL Keyword: **AOLNET** for more information). Much higher speeds are supported with broadband access. See also *baud, broadband, cable modem, DSL,* and *V.90.*

broadband

A type of data transmission medium capable of supporting a wide range of frequencies (channels). A broadband connection is much faster than a 56K modem connection because it is able to transmit several channels of data at once. Broadband users also get access to the AOL Plus Tower automatically, providing free multimedia content with streaming audio and video. You can find more information on AOL Plus in Chapter 23. See also *AOL Plus, cable modem,* and *DSL.*

browser

A component of your AOL software that allows you to access the Web. See also *Favorite Place, Internet, page,* and *World Wide Web.*

Buddy List

A special list that stores your *buddies* (screen names of friends, family members, coworkers, and so on) and informs you when they sign on or off AOL. You add (or remove) buddies yourself, as well as define several groups of buddies. See Chapter 8 for details. See also *invitation.*

bug

A problem or glitch in a product, be it software or hardware. A bug may be referred to jokingly as a "feature." You can report a problem with AOL software or services by going to AOL Keyword: **Help**.

C

cable modem

A type of modem that allows members to access the Internet (and AOL) via their cable television service. Cable modems can transfer data at 500 kbps or higher. Cable modem service is not available in all areas of the country yet. For more information, see AOL Keyword: **Cable Modem** or AOL Keyword: **AOL Plus**.

cache

A portion of a data storage device, RAM, or processor set aside to temporarily hold recently accessed or frequently accessed information. By saving the information locally, performance is improved because it is quicker to receive the information from the cache than from the original source.

channel

This is the broadest category of information into which AOL organizes its content. See AOL Keyword: **Channel** for a list or **Channel Guide** for listings of the areas within each channel. See Chapters 21 and 22 for a description of AOL's channels.

chat

To engage in real-time online communications with other members. AOL members that are online at the same time can chat with each other in a number of ways: instant messages, chat/conference rooms, and auditoriums. Chapter 9 has more information on chatting. See also *instant message, chat room,* and *auditorium;* contrast with *message board* and *e-mail.*

chat room

An online area where members can meet to communicate and interact with others. There are two kinds of chat areas: public and private. You can find public chat areas in the People Connection area (AOL Keywords: **People Connection** or **PC**) or in the many forums around AOL (go to AOL Keyword: **AOL Live** for schedules). See Chapter 9 for more information. See also *private room, chat, host, TOS,* and *People Connection;* contrast with *auditorium.*

chat sounds

Sounds played in chat areas. You can play and broadcast sounds to others in chat areas by typing {S <sound>} (<sound> refers to the name of the sound you want to play) and pressing Enter. For example, {S Welcome} plays AOL's "Welcome" sound in a chat area. See also *chat room* and *library.*

Community Leader

AOL members who volunteer in the various forums and areas online. They usually participate from their homes, not AOL headquarters. They serve as Guides, Hosts, Forum leaders/assistants/consultants, and so on. To learn more, see AOL Keyword: **Leaders**. See also *host.*

compression

See *file compression.*

CompuServe

A large established commercial online service now owned by America Online. See AOL Keyword: **CS**. Contrast with *America Online, Inc.*

courtesy copy (cc)

A feature of the AOL e-mail system that allows you to address e-mail to a member for whom the e-mail is not directly intended or is of secondary interest. The primary addressees are aware that the copy was made, similar to the carbon copy convention used in business correspondence. As such, the members copied are not usually expected to reply. See also *e-mail;* contrast with *blind courtesy copy.*

Customer Relations

The number for AOL's Customer Relations Hotline is 800-827-6364. The billing and technical assistance departments are open 24 hours a day. The Terms of Service, Community Action Team, and screen name departments are open 9 a.m. to 12 a.m. eastern time, seven days a week.

D

database

A collection of information, stored and organized for easy searching. A database can refer to something as simple as a well-sorted filing cabinet, but today most databases reside on computers because they offer better access. Databases are located all over AOL, with a prominent example being the People Directory (AOL Keyword: **Members**). See the AOL Research & Learn Channel (AOL Keyword: **Research**) for a large collection of databases. See also *AOL Search, Boolean search, People Directory,* and *searchable database.*

Delete

An AOL e-mail system feature that allows you to permanently remove an e-mail from any and all of your mailboxes. The Delete feature is useful for removing unneeded mail from your Old Mail box. Do not confuse this feature with the Unsend option, which removes mail you've sent from the recipient's mailbox (provided the recipient hasn't read it yet.). Chapter 5 contains more information. See also *e-mail* and *status*; contrast with *Unsend*.

domain

Used in Internet addresses and analogous to a city in a postal address. In e-mail addresses, usually everything to the right of the @ symbol is referred to as the domain. For example, the domain name for AOL member addresses is aol.com. See also *address, e-mail, e-mail address,* and *Internet*.

download

The transfer of information stored on a remote computer to a storage device on your personal computer. This information can come from AOL via its file libraries or from other AOL members via attached files in an e-mail. Usually, downloads are files intended for review when you're offline. More information on downloading is available in Chapter 10. See also *archive, attached file, Download Manager,* and *library*.

Download Manager

An AOL software feature that allows you to keep a queue of files to download at a later time. You can even set up your software to automatically sign off when your download session is complete. You can schedule your software to sign on and grab files listed in the queue at times you specify. See Chapter 10 for more information. See also *Automatic AOL, download, file,* and *Filing Cabinet*.

DSL

Short for Digital Subscriber Line. DSL is a family of digital telecommunications protocols designed to allow high-speed data communication over existing telephone lines. For more information, see AOL Keyword: DSL or AOL Keyword: **AOL Plus**.

E

e-mail

Short for electronic mail. One of the most popular features of online services, e-mail allows you to send private communications electronically from one person to another. E-mail is usually much faster and easier to send than ordinary mail; the shortcomings are that not everyone has an e-mail address to write to, and your mail resides in electronic form on a computer system. See AOL Keyword: **Mail Center** or Chapters 5 and 6 for more information. See also *attached file, blind courtesy copy, courtesy copy, Delete, e-mail address, Ignore, Keep As New, Filing Cabinet, return receipt,* and *status*; contrast with *message* and *instant message*.

Appendix C: Glossary

e-mail address

A cyberspace mailbox. On AOL, your e-mail address is simply your screen name; for folks outside AOL, your address is your screen name with `@aol.com` after it. See also *address, e-mail,* and *screen name.*

emoticon

Symbols consisting of characters found on any keyboard that are used to give and gain insight into emotional states. For example, the symbol :) is a smile — just tilt your head to the left, and you'll see the : (eyes) and the) (smile). The online community has invented countless variations to bring plain text to life, and emoticons are used everywhere from chat rooms to e-mail. Emoticons are more popular in "face-to-face" chat. Some people consider them unprofessional or overly cute in correspondence. Regardless, they are one of the best methods of effective communication online. Emoticons may also be referred to as *smileys* and collectively with other chat devices as *shorthands.*

encryption

The manipulation of data in order to prevent any but the intended recipient from reading that data. There are many types of data encryption, and they are the basis of network security.

ET (EST or EDT)

Abbreviation for eastern time. Most times are given in this format, because AOL is headquartered in the eastern time zone.

F

FAQ

Short for Frequently Asked Questions. FAQs may take the form of an informational file containing questions and answers to common concerns/issues. They are used to answer questions that are brought up often in message boards or discussions. These files may be stored online in an article or archived in a file library. See also *message board* and *library.*

Favorite Place

A feature that allows you to "mark" AOL and Web sites you'd like to return to later. These Favorite Places are stored in your Favorite Places list. Any Web site can be made a Favorite Place, as well as any AOL window with a heart icon in the upper-right corner of the window. See Chapter 14 for more details.

file

Any amount of information that is grouped together on a computer as one unit. On AOL, a file can be anything from text to sounds and can be transferred to and from your computer via AOL. Collections of files are available in libraries for downloading, and files can be attached to e-mail. See also *download* and *library.*

file compression

A programming technique by which files can be reduced in size without changing their content. Files are usually compressed so that they take up less storage space, can be transferred quicker, and/or can be bundled with others. Files must be decompressed before they can be used, but you can set up the AOL software to automatically decompress most files (check your Preferences). More information is available in Chapters 5 and 10. See also *file, download,* and *WinZip.*

file library

See *library*.

File Transfer Protocol

See *FTP*.

Filing Cabinet

A special feature of the AOL software that organizes your e-mail, as well as message board and newsgroup postings. Note that everything in your Filing Cabinet is stored on your hard drive. You can set your Filing Cabinet preferences by choosing SettingsPreferencesPersonal Filing Cabinet from the AOL toolbar. See Chapter 6 for more information. See also *e-mail, Favorite Place, file,* and *newsgroup*.

forum

A place online where members with similar interests can find valuable information, exchange ideas, share files, and get help on a particular area of interest. Forums (also known simply as areas or clubs) are found everywhere online, represent almost every interest under the sun, and usually offer message boards, articles, chat rooms, and libraries, all organized and accessible by a keyword. See also *keyword*.

FTP

Abbreviation for File Transfer Protocol. A method of transferring files to and from a computer that is connected to the Internet. America Online offers FTP access via AOL Keyword: **FTP**, as well as personal FTP sites at AOL Keyword: **My Place**. See also *Internet, World Wide Web,* and *home page;* contrast with *library*.

G

GIF (Graphic Interchange Format)

A type of graphic file that can be read by most platforms; the electronic version of photographs. GIFs can be viewed with your AOL software or with a GIF viewer utility, which is located at AOL Keyword: **Viewers**.

GPF

Abbreviation for General Protection Fault. If you get a GPF error, it means that Windows (or a Windows application) has attempted to access memory that has not been allocated for its use. If you experience a GPF while using Windows AOL software, write down the exact error message and then go to AOL Keyword: **GPF Help** for assistance. See also *bug*.

H

header

The information at the top (and/or bottom) of e-mail received from the Internet, which contains, among other things, the message originator, date, and time. Headers can also be found in newsgroup postings. See also *e-mail, Internet,* and *newsgroup*.

history trail

The last 25 places you visited online. You can find this history list by clicking the small arrow next to the Address box on the toolbar. You can clear your history list in your toolbar preferences, described in Chapter 12. More information on using the history list is available in Chapter 2. See also *toolbar*.

Appendix C: Glossary

home page

(1) The first page in a Web site.

(2) Your own page on the Web. All AOL members can now create their own home pages — go to AOL Keyword: **My Home Page**.

(3) The page you go to when you first enter the Web.

See also *browser, Favorite Place, page, URL,* and *World Wide Web.*

host

(1) The AOL computer system.

(2) An AOL Community Leader who facilitates discussion in chat rooms. These are usually chat-fluent, personable individuals with particular expertise on a topic. See also *chat room.*

html

Acronym for HyperText Markup Language. This is the language used in creating most Web pages and is interpreted by the AOL Web browser to display those pages.

http

Acronym for HyperText Transport Protocol, the data communications protocol used by the World Wide Web.

I

icon

A graphic image of a recognizable object or action that leads to somewhere or initiates a process. For example, the icons in the Write Mail window can lead you to the Address Book, allow you to attach a file, send the e-mail, or look up help. Click an icon to activate it; some icons can even be used with keyboard shortcuts. More information is available in Chapter 2. See also *keyboard shortcuts.*

Ignore

(1) A way of blocking a member's chat from your view in a chat/conference room window. Ignore is most useful when the chat of another member becomes disruptive in the chat room. Note that the Ignore button does not block or ignore instant messages from a member — it only blocks the text from your own view in a chat or conference room. For details, see Chapter 9.

(2) An AOL software e-mail system feature that allows you to ignore mail in your New Mail box, causing it to be moved to your Old Mail box without having to read it first. See also *e-mail* and *status.*

instant message

AOL's equivalent to passing notes to another person during a meeting, as opposed to speaking up in the room (chat) or writing out a letter or memo (e-mail). instant messages can be exchanged between two AOL members signed on at the same time and are useful for conducting conversations when a chat room isn't appropriate, available, or practical; for details, see Chapter 9. Internet users can also send and receive instant messages if they download and install the free AOL Instant Messenger program (go to AOL Keyword: **AIM**).

insertion point

The blinking vertical line in a document marking the place where text is being edited. You can navigate the insertion point through a document with either the mouse or the arrow keys. Also called a *cursor.*

Instant Messenger

See *AOL Instant Messenger.*

Internet

The mother of all networks is not an online service itself, but serves to interconnect worldwide computer systems and networks. The Internet, originally operated by the National Science Foundation (NSF), is now managed by private companies (one of which is America Online). AOL features the Internet Connection, which includes access to Usenet Newsgroups, Gopher & WAIS Databases, FTP, and the World Wide Web, plus help with understanding it all. To obtain more information about the Internet, use the AOL Keyword: **Internet**. See also *address, browser, domain, FTP, header, newsgroup, page,* and *URL.*

Internet Explorer

See *Microsoft Internet Explorer.*

invitation

A request by another member to join a chat, a service made possible by the Buddy List feature in your AOL software. For more information, see Chapter 8. See also *address, Buddy List,* and *URL.*

ISDN

Acronym for Integrated Services Digital Networks. ISDN is a type of network access that local telephone companies have offered for about ten years. You can use ISDN to connect to other networks at speeds as high as 64,000 bps (single channel). DSL and other broadband connectivity have largely replaced ISDN. See also *DSL* and *TCP/IP;* contrast with *packet-switching network.*

ISP

Acronym for Internet service provider. An ISP generally provides a point to which you can connect and access various Internet-based services such as Web sites, FTP, e-mail, and newsgroups. Some ISPs also provide more advanced services that range from hosting Web sites and servers to wide area networking. See also *FTP, newsgroup,* and *World Wide Web.*

Java

A computer language developed by Sun Microsystems. Java is similar to C++ and is used to develop platform-independent applications commonly known as applets. Java programs are safely downloaded to your computer through the Internet and immediately run without fear of viruses or other harm to your computer or files. You may encounter a *Javascript error* while browsing the Web; if you do, this simply means your browser was unable to successfully run the Java applet for one reason or another.

Keep As New

An AOL e-mail system feature that allows you to keep mail in your New Mail box, even after you've read or ignored it. See also *e-mail.*

Appendix C: Glossary

keyboard shortcuts

The AOL software provides you with keyboard command equivalents for menu selections. For example, rather than clicking the IM button on the AOL toolbar, you can press Ctrl+I (in Windows) to achieve the same results.

keyword

(1) A fast way to move around AOL. For example, you can go directly to the Games channel by using AOL Keyword: **Games**. An updated list of most public keywords is available online at AOL Keyword: **Keyword**. See Chapter 2 for more information on keywords.

(2) A single word you feel is likely to be included in any database on a particular subject. A keyword is usually a word that comes as close as possible to describing the topic or piece of information you're looking for. Several of America Online's software libraries, mainly those in the AOL Computing Channel, can be searched with keywords.

L

library

An area online in which files can be uploaded to and downloaded from. The files can be of any type: text, graphics, software, sounds, and so on. You can download these files from AOL's host computer to your personal computer's hard drive or floppy drive. See also *file, download, upload,* and *search;* contrast with *FTP.*

link

A pointer to another place that takes you there when you activate it (usually by clicking it). AOL probably has millions of links that criss-cross the service, but they can't compare to the billions of links on the Web (often called hyperlinks) that can cross continents without your knowing it. See also *address, browser, Favorite Place, page, URL,* and *World Wide Web.*

Mail Controls

A set of preferences that enable the master account holder to control who you receive mail from. Mail Controls can be set for one or all screen names on the account. The master account screen name can make changes at any time. To access controls, go to AOL Keyword: **Mail Controls**. You can also block junk mail from your e-mailbox at AOL Keyword: **Preferred Mail**.

mailing list

A group of e-mail addresses that receive e-mail on a regular basis about a topic in which they have a mutual interest. Mailing lists can be as simple as a few friends' addresses that you often e-mail, or as complex as a daily digest of news delivered to the e-mailboxes of millions of addresses. See also *address* and *e-mail.*

member

An AOL subscriber. The term *member* is embraced because AOL considers itself a member of the online community. AOL currently has over 23 million member accounts, each of which can have up to seven different screen names. See also *online community.*

member profile

A voluntary online information document that describes you. You can provide your name, address information, birthday, sex, marital status, hobbies, computers used, occupation, and a personal quote. Member profiles are located at AOL Keyword: **Members**. See also *member* and *Member Directory*.

message

A note posted on a message board or newsgroup for others to read. A message may also be referred to as a post. See also *message board*.

message board

An area where members can post messages to exchange information, ask a question, or reply to another message. Because messages are a popular means of communication online, message boards are organized by topic, wherein a number of messages on a specific subject *(threads)* are contained in sequential order. See Chapter 9 for more information. See also *message*.

Microsoft Internet Explorer

The Web browser software integrated in all America Online 3.0 and higher clients. AOL 6.0 uses Version 5.5 of Microsoft Internet Explorer. See also *Netscape Navigator*.

MSIE

See *Microsoft Internet Explorer*.

N

Net

Abbreviation for the Internet. See *Internet*.

netiquette

Net manners. Cyberspace is a subculture with norms and rules of conduct all its own; understanding these rules often makes your online life more enjoyable and allows you to move through it more smoothly. Online etiquette includes such things as proper capitalization (don't use all caps unless you mean to SHOUT). Basically, the most important rule to keep in mind is one we learned offline and in kindergarten of all places: Do unto others as you'd have them do unto you (a.k.a. The Golden Rule). See Chapter 4 for a primer in AOL etiquette.

Netscape Navigator

An Internet browser produced by the Netscape Corporation, which is owned by AOL. You can use Netscape Navigator in place of America Online's built-in browser with AOL software 3.0 or later. See also *Microsoft Internet Explorer*.

network

A data communications system that interconnects computer systems at various different sites. America Online could be considered a network.

newsgroup

The Internet's version of a public message board. Available on America Online at AOL Keyword: **Newsgroups**. See also *header* and *Internet;* contrast with *FTP* and *World Wide Web*.

O

online

The condition of a computer when it is connected to a network. Contrast with *offline,* the condition of a computer that is unconnected.

online community

A group of people bound together by their shared interest or characteristic of interacting with other computer users through online services, BBSs, or networks. Because of the pioneer aspects of an online community, established onliners welcome newcomers and educate them freely, in most cases. On AOL, elaborate conventions, legends, and etiquette systems have developed within the community.

P

packet-switching network (PSN)

The electronic networks that enable you to access a remote online service by dialing a local phone number. Information going to and from your computer is segmented into packets, which are given an address. The packets are then sent through the network to their destination, similar to the way a letter travels through the postal system, only much faster. AOL uses a variety of PSNs to supply local nodes (local telephone numbers) for members' access. See also *access number* and *AOLNET;* contrast with *ISDN.*

page

A document on the Web, presented in the browser window. Web pages can contain any combination of links, text, graphics, sounds, or videos. A set of pages is often referred to as a site. See also *browser, Favorite Place, home page, html, link, URL,* and *World Wide Web.*

palmtop

See *PDA.*

Parental Controls

Parental Controls enable the master account holder to restrict access to certain areas and features on AOL (such as blocking instant messages and chat rooms). They can be set for one or all screen names on the account. After Parental Controls are set for a particular screen name, they are active each time that screen name signs on. The master account holder can make changes at any time. To access these controls, go to AOL Keyword: **Parental Controls**. See Chapter 4 for more information.

password

The secret 6-to-8-character code word that you use to secure your account. Never reveal your password to anyone, even those claiming to be AOL employees. More information on passwords is available in Chapters 4 and 12.

PDA

Short for personal digital assistant. A handheld computer that performs a variety of tasks, including personal information management. PDAs are gaining in popularity and variety. A limited version of the AOL software, called AOL Mail, can be run on any Palm device with a Palm snap-on modem; go to AOL Keyword: **AOL Mail**. PDAs may also be referred to as palmtops. For more information, check out the PDA Forum at AOL Keyword: **PDA**. See also *AOL Mail.*

People Connection (PC)

The AOL channel dedicated to real-time chat. You can find many different rooms in this channel: AOL-created rooms, member-created rooms, and private rooms. You can access this area with AOL Keywords: **People Connection** or **PC**. You can find more information on the People Connection in Chapter 9. See also *channel* and *chat room*.

People Directory

The database of AOL member screen names that have profiles. To be included in this database, a member need only create a member profile. Note that profiles for deleted members are purged periodically; therefore, it's possible to have a member profile for a deleted screen name. You can search for any text string in a profile, as well as use wildcard characters and Boolean expressions in search strings. The Member Directory is located at AOL Keyword: **Members**. See also *member, member profile, database,* and *searchable database*.

Personal Filing Cabinet (PFC)

See *Filing Cabinet*.

post

(1) The act of putting something online, usually into a message board or newsgroup.

(2) A message in a message board or newsgroup. See also *message board* and *message;* contrast with *upload*.

postmaster

The person responsible for taking care of e-mail problems, answering queries from users, and doing other e-mail-related work at a site. You can reach AOL's postmaster at, you guessed it, screen name `Postmaster`. You can also reach other postmasters by simply adding the @ symbol and the domain name you want to reach — for example, `postmaster@msn.com`. See also *domain* and *e-mail*.

private room

A chat room that is created by a member via an option in People Connection where the name is not public knowledge. See Chapter 9 for information on creating private rooms. See also *chat room;* contrast with *auditorium*.

profile

AOL allows each screen name to have an informational file (a profile) attached to it. You can search profiles through the Member Directory. See also *member, Member Directory,* and *screen name*.

R

real time

Information received and processed (or displayed) as it happens. Conversations in instant messages and chat rooms happen in real time.

RealAudio

A streaming audio data format that allows Internet users and AOL members to listen to music and events in real time. The basic RealPlayer (which also plays RealVideo) is distributed with AOL 6.0.

return receipt

A feature available with the AOL software that returns an e-mail acknowledging that mail you sent to another AOL member (or members) has been received. Return receipts should be used sparingly because they can clutter up your mailbox. More information is available in Chapter 5. See also *e-mail, courtesy copy, blind courtesy copy,* and *status*.

S

satellite

(1) A smaller celestial object, natural or man-made, that orbits a larger celestial object. The moon is a satellite of planet Earth.

(2) Another method of obtaining a broadband connection to AOL. This method uses a small satellite dish and protocols that are designed to send and/or receive data at high speeds to your home. For more information, see AOL Keyword: **AOL Plus**. See also *Broadband*.

screen name

The name (actually pseudonyms more often than not) that identifies an AOL member online. To add, delete, or restore deleted screen names, sign on with a master screen name and go to AOL Keyword: **Names**. More information is available in Chapter 12. See also *address, e-mail address,* and *member*.

scroll

The movement of incoming text and other information on your computer screen. See also *scroll bar*.

scroll bar

The bar on the right-hand side of a window, which allows you to move the contents up and down, or the bar on the bottom of a window for moving things to the left or right. The area on the scroll bar between the up and down arrows is shaded if not all the information can fit in the window, or white if the entire content of the window is already visible. See also *scroll*.

search

Typically used in association with libraries and other searchable databases, the term refers to a specific exploration of files or entries themselves. More information is available in Chapters 17, 18, and 19. See also *searchable database, database, file,* and *library*.

searchable database

A collection of logically related records or database files, which serve as a single central reference; a searchable database accepts input and yields all matching entries containing that character string. The Member Directory is an example of a searchable database. See also *search, database,* and *Member Directory*.

self-extracting archive

A compressed file that contains instructions to automatically decompress itself when opened; the software that compressed it originally is not needed. Self-extracting archive files are often identified by an `.exe` extension as contrasted with `.zip` files, which generally require separate decompression software. See also *file compression*.

server

A computer on a network that functions as a provider of resources, such as a *file server*. AOL uses many different kinds of servers.

sig

Short for *signature*. A block of text that some folks include at the end of the newsgroup postings and/or e-mail. You can designate a sig for your e-mail, message board posts, and newsgroup posts through their respective preferences. More information on using signatures in e-mail is available in Chapter 6, and more information on message board and newsgroup signatures is in Chapter 9. See also *newsgroup* and *post*.

spam

To barrage a message board, newsgroup, or e-mail address with inappropriate, irrelevant, or simply numerous copies of the same post. Not only is this annoying, but it is also exceedingly bad netiquette. Members who spam often have their posts removed (in message boards), find their mailboxes full of e-mail from angry persons (if in a newsgroup), or even have their accounts terminated. See also *e-mail address, message board,* and *newsgroup*.

Spinner

A music plug-in that comes with AOL 6.0 and allows you to hear streaming digital music. A sound card and speakers are required for play. For more information, see www.spinner.com.

status (of e-mail)

An AOL software feature that allows you to check whether e-mail has been read and, if read, when. The status for an e-mail message may be (not yet read), (ignored), (deleted), or show the precise date and time when the mail was read. Status information includes recipients who were carbon copied (and even those who were blind carbon copied, if you were the sender). See Chapter 5 for more information. See also *e-mail, courtesy copy, blind courtesy copy,* and *return receipt*.

streaming

A method whereby information, usually in the form of audio or video, is delivered to your computer and becomes available for immediate playback. Information that is delivered through streaming technology differs from normal file downloads, because you don't have to wait for the entire file to download before it becomes usable. See also *download, RealAudio, Spinner,* and *Winamp*.

T

TCP/IP

Acronym for Transmission Control Protocol/Internet Protocol. The data communications protocol used by the Internet. Windows AOL version 2.5 and Mac AOL version 2.6 and higher allow you to sign on via TCP/IP. See also *Internet*.

timeout

(1) This happens when two computers are connected online and one gets tired of waiting for the other (that is, when the hourglass (PC) or beachball (Mac) cursor comes up and the "host fails to respond"). You can report problems with frequent timeouts at AOL Keyword: **System Response**.

(2) The result of remaining idle for a certain amount of time while signed on to AOL. This timeout time is about ten minutes or so but may vary at different times of the day. If your account remains inactive for an extended period, the AOL service automatically signs off your account.

toolbar

The row of menus and buttons in the AOL software, found at the top of your screen. Portions of the toolbar are customizable. See Chapter 1 for more information.

TOS

Short for AOL's Terms of Service — the rules everyone agrees to when registering for and becoming a member of America Online. These terms apply to all accounts on AOL. You can read these terms at AOL Keyword: **TOS**.

Trojan horse

A destructive program that is disguised within a seemingly useful program. A Trojan horse is only activated by running the program. If you receive a file attached to e-mail from a sender you're not familiar with, you're advised not to download it. If you ever receive a file you believe could cause problems, forward it to screen name `TOSEmail` and explain your concerns. Contrast with *virus*.

U

Unsend

An AOL e-mail system feature that allows you to retrieve mail that has been sent to other AOL members but has not yet been read. See Chapter 5.

upload

The transfer of information from a storage device on your computer to a remote computer, such as AOL's host computer. This information may be uploaded to one of AOL's file libraries, or it may be uploaded with an e-mail as an attached file. More information is available in Chapter 10. See also *file, file compression,* and *library;* contrast with *download*.

URL

An address for an online resource, such as a Web site or an AOL page. URL stands for Uniform Resource Locator, and the acronym is commonly pronounced as either "earl" or "U-R-L." You can enter a URL address directly into the Address box on the toolbar or in the Keyword window. There is no list of URL addresses because they are constantly changing and growing, but you can save your favorites by clicking the heart icon in the upper-right corner of a window. AOL's home page URL is www.aol.com. See also *address, browser, Favorite Place, page,* and *World Wide Web*.

V

V.90

The technical standard for 56K modems. If you have an older 56K modem that uses X2 or K56flex protocols, you should use a local access number that supports the V.90 standard and your modem's protocol. AOL has upgraded most of its network to take advantage of the V.90 standard. More information on V.90 connections is available at AOL Keyword: **V.90**. See also *baud* and *bps*.

virus

Computer software that has the capability to attach itself to other software or files, does so without the permission or knowledge of the user, and is generally designed with one intent — to propagate itself. A virus can also be intentionally destructive; however, not all virus damage is intentional. You can find virus prevention software and information at AOL Keyword: **Virus**. Contrast with *Trojan horse*.

W

Winamp

A music plug-in that comes with AOL 6.0 and allows you to hear streaming digital music. A sound card and speakers are required for play. For more information, choose File⇨Music Player from the AOL menu bar.

WinZip

A shareware compression utility for Windows. WinZip is used to compress one file or multiple files into a smaller file (called an archive). Compression makes for shorter uploading and downloading. AOL 6.0 can automatically decompress archives compressed with WinZip. For more information, go to www.winzip.com. See also *archive, download, file,* and *file compression.*

World Wide Web (WWW)

One of the more popular aspects of the Internet, the World Wide Web (or Web, for short) is actually an overarching term for the many hypertext documents that are displayed and linked together via a special protocol called HyperText Transfer Protocol (or HTTP). World Wide Web information is available on AOL, using URL addresses to get to various Web sites or pages, much like you use keywords on AOL. Chapters 17, 18, and 19 have several tips on searching the Web. See also *browser, Favorite Place, home page, Internet, page,* and *URL.*

Z

ZIP

See *WinZip.*

Index

Symbols & Numerics
* (asterisk), 169
... (ellipsis), 41
- (minus) button, 39
( ) (parentheses), 169
+ (plus sign), 169
@ symbol, 101
800 numbers, 459
888 numbers, 459

A
AARP channel, 409
Abort Incoming Text menu option, 35
access numbers
   changing, 278
   defined, 459
Add to Favorite Places menu option, 35
address, 459
Address Book. *See also* e-mail
   adding entries, 102–104
   adding sender, 91
   buttons, 104–105
   creating mailing lists, 104
   defined, 459
   deleting entries, 104
   editing entries, 104
   opening, 102
   printing entries, 104
Advanced Search feature, People Directory, 347
Advantix cameras, 226
Ages & Stages channel, 409
AIM (AOL Instant Messenger), 161, 460
allHealth.com channel, 402–403
Alumni Hall channel, 409
American Greeting online, 131–133
Ann Landers, 252
anniversaries
   invitations, 327–328
   reminder service, 305–307
Anti-Virus Center, 219, 380

antivirus programs, 219–220
AOL 6.0
   AOL Anywhere, 427
   Guest access, 450–452
   Macintosh, 442
   new features, 13–14, 49–50
   pricing plans, 444
   screen name requirements, 444
   software requirements, 443
   software upgrades, 445–450
   Windows 95, 441–442
   Windows 98, 442
   Windows NT/2000, 442
AOL (America Online, Inc.), 459
AOL Anywhere, 251–253, 426–429
AOL by Phone, 428
AOL for CE, 428
AOL for Palm, 428
AOL Help button, 51
AOL Hometown, 315–316. *See also* Web pages, creating
AOL Invitations, 327–328
AOL Keywords. *See* keywords
AOL Live auditorium events, 75, 183–185, 461
AOL Long Distance, 424–425
AOL Mail
   defined, 460
   Filing Cabinet and, 145
   limitations, 145
   reading/sending messages, 143–145
   software, free download, 428
AOL Mail Alerts, 428–429
AOL Member Directory, 344–347
AOL members, number of, 7, 62
AOL Mobile Services, 428
AOL News, 12
AOL Plus
   AOL Plus Broadband, 429
   AOL Plus Content, 429–430
   defined, 460
AOL Plus Tower, 429–430
AOL preferences. *See* preferences, setting
AOL Search, 460

AOL Search Results page, 334
AOL Search window, opening, 29
AOL Setup window, opening, 278
AOL software
    closing, 23
    signing off, 23
AOL Speaks, activating, 23
AOL.COM, 460
AOLNET, 460
AOLTV, 415–422, 427, 457
appointment book. *See* My Calendar service
archive, 460
arrow on screen changing shape, 32–33
Art Studio channel, 407
articles, saving to hard drive, 22
Ask The Staff button, 215
Ask-A-Teacher, 363, 382–383
AT&T Wireless Internet-ready phones, 428
attached file, 461
audio files, opening, 22
auditoriums, 75, 183–185, 461
Automatic AOL (Auto AOL), 261–263
    defined, 461
    Filing Cabinet and, 126
    message board preferences, 193
    Offline Newsgroups location, 23
Automatic AOL window, 222
automobiles
    AOL AutoVantage, 436
    Autos channel, 399–400
Autos channel, 399–400

B

Baby Boomers channel, 409
baud rate, 461
BBC News channel, 370
billing help options, 26
bill-paying reminder service, 305–307
birthdays
    invitations, 327–328
    reminder service, 305–307
Blind Copy button, Address Book, 105
blind courtesy copy (bcc), 461
boards, 461. *See also* message boards
bold text. *See* formatting text
bookmarks. *See* Favorite Places
Boolean operators, how to use, 337
Boolean search, defined, 461

bounce, 461
bps (bits per second), 461
broadband
    advantages of, 454
    AOL Plus Broadband, 429, 456
    cable, 457–458
    connection speeds, 429
    defined, 462
    DSL, 429, 455–456
    pricing plans, 454
    satellite, 456–457
    TCP/IP configuration instructions, 454–455
brokerage centers channel, 375
browsers
    defined, 462
    preferences, AOL Browser, 272–277
    preferences, History feature (for Web browsing), 273
    preferences, Web browser, 258, 272–277
Buddy List feature. *See also* instant messaging
    * (asterisk), 169
    ( ) (parentheses), 169
    + (plus sign), 169
    about, 9–10, 164
    adding buddies, 165–167
    adding groups, 167
    Away Message feature, 169–171
    Away Message icon, 169
    buddies, defined, 165
    Buddy Albums, 238
    defined, 462
    hiding group names, 169
    inviting buddies to private chats, 168
    locating buddies in chat rooms, 168
    maximum number of names, 166
    most recent sign off, 169
    most recent sign on, 169
    number of group members signed on, 169
    number per AOL account, 244
    numbers next to group names, 169
    preferences, setting, 256–258
    privacy preferences, setting, 256–258
    removing buddies, 167
    removing groups, 167
    renaming groups, 167
    right-clicking buddies, 168
    sending instant messages to buddies, 168
    yellow note icon, 169
Buddy List Setup window, opening, 166
Buddy List window, opening, 165

bug, 462
Build Better Pages link, 324–325
business news channel, 367
buttons
    defined, 35
    pressing without executing, 35–36

C

cable modem, 462
cache, 462
calendars. *See* Groups@AOL; My Calendar service
Career and Work channel, 376–377
Career resources, 377
cars
    AOL AutoVantage, 436
    Autos channel, 399–400
case sensitivity
    e-mail addresses, 102
    search tools, 337
Caution icons, 5
CBS News channel, 367
cell phone support, 428
Channel Bar, 364–366
channels. *See also individual channel names or topics*
    accessing, 364–366
    defined, 462
Channels window
    displaying, 28
    hiding, 28
chat sounds, 463
chats/chat rooms
    abbreviations used, 180
    adding Favorite Places to, 295
    adding hyperlinks to, 295
    AOL Live, 183–185
    auditoriums, 183–185
    The Bistro, 372
    blocking screen names from, 75–76
    contact Customer Service in chat, 54–55
    creating chat rooms, 180–181
    defined, 462–463
    finding communities, 175–177
    font preferences, 264–265
    global, 372
    graphics preferences, 265
    how it works, 177–179
    hyperlinks, blocking, 76
    logging chats, 182–183
    private (Groups@AOL), 326
    teens, 408
    text formatting preferences, 264–265
    violations, reporting to AOL, 66–68
    voice recognition software, 23
Check Spelling window, 130–131
Close menu option (Ctrl+F4), 34
CNET channel, 378
color styles, 321
comics, 252
Commentaries channel, 367
community, 9
    See also AOL live auditorium events
    See also Buddy List feature
    See also chats/chat rooms
    See also instant messaging
    See also message boards
Community Leaders, 58, 463
compression, 463
CompuServe, 463
Computer Center channel, 377–380
Computer Protection Center, 220
Computing Communities channel, 380
conference rooms, blocking screen names from, 76
connections, changing, 278
Copy menu option (Ctrl+C), 34
Copy To button, Address Book, 104
Country Information channel, 372
Courses Online, 383
courtesy copy (cc), 463
Cross-reference icons, 5
crossword puzzle, 252
cursor. *See* insertion point
Customer Relations, 463
customization options. *See* personalization options
customizing AOL software. *See* preferences, setting
Cut menu option (Ctrl+X), 34

D

database, 463
date book. *See* My Calendar service
Definition icons, 5
Delete, 464
Delete button, Address Book, 104
Desktop Publishing Company, 380
Destination Guides channel, 392
developing film. *See* "You've Got Pictures"
Dictionaries channel, 371, 381–382
Digital City, 384–385, 428
digital photographs. *See* "You've Got Pictures"
disposable cameras, 226
domains
    blocking e-mail from, 75
    defined, 75, 464
Download Center channel, 378–379
Download Later button, 214
Download Manager
    defined, 464
    Download button, 221
    Download Preferences button, 221
    Help button, 221
    Internet files and, 221
    Remove Item button, 221
    Select Destination button, 221
    Show Files Downloaded button, 221
    View Description button, 221
Download Manager window, 220
Download Now button, 214
downloading files
    antivirus programs, 220
    Automatic AOL, 222–223
    decompressing files automatically at sign off, 222
    defined, 98, 211, 464
    from Download Center, 216–218
    Download Manager feature, 220–221
    from file libraries, 214–215
    in Filing Cabinet, 221
    finding downloaded files, 213–214
    finding files to download, 216–218
    getting help, 212
    interrupted downloads, resuming, 221
    managing downloaded files, 220
    preferences, setting, 220
    steps to follow, 213
    Trojan horses, 98–99, 218–220, 475
    viruses, 98–99, 218–220
Downloading Files window, 212
downloading music, 396
Dr. Solomon's antivirus programs, 220
DSL, 429, 464

E

Edit button, Address Book, 104
Edit menu
    Capture Picture menu option, 24
    Copy menu option, 23–24
    Cut menu option, 23–24
    Dictionary menu option, 24
    Paste menu option, 23–24
    Spell Check menu option, 23–24
    Thesaurus menu option, 24
Editorials channel, 367
education online, 383
Education Resources channel, 383
electronic invitations, 327–328
Electronic Program Guide, AOLTV, 418–419
e-mail. *See also* Address Book; Filing Cabinet
    about, 9–10, 88–89
    Add Address button, 91
    adding entries to Address Book, 102–103
    adding Favorite Places to messages, 295
    adding hyperlinks to messages, 295
    adding sender to Address Book, 91
    aligning text, 136–137
    on any telephone, 428
    AOL Mail (WWW), 143–145
    attached files, downloading, 98–100
    attaching files to messages, 116–119
    Automatic AOL, 222–223
    banners, 132
    blind courtesy copies (bcc), 110–111
    blocking messages, 133–136
    blue border around messages, 90
    bold text, 136–137
    on cell phones, 428
    check mark icons, 92–93
    checking for new mail, 94, 143–145, 222–223
    checking status of sent mail, 114–115
    closing e-mail window, 92
    colors, 136–137
    copying text, 24
    courtesy copies (cc), 110
    date message was read, 93

Index

date message was sent, 93
defined, 88, 464
Delete button, 91
deleting messages, 91–92
downloading attached files, 98–100
E-mail Status window, 94
Find in Top Window menu option, 24
fonts, 136–137, 264–265
formatting, 91, 136–137
Forward button, 91
forwarding messages, 91, 113–114
graphics, adding to messages, 139–141
graphics preferences, 265
Groups@AOL, 326
headers, 91
Help button, 91
icon, 19
italic text, 136–137
junk mail, 95–97, 133–136
Keep As New button, 93
Mail Art, 133
Mail Center, 107
Mail Controls, 133–136
Mail menu, 105–106
marking messages as unread, 93
new mail notification, 19, 89
Next button, 91
number of mailboxes, 89
number of message per day on AOL, 9
Official AOL Mail, 90
Old Mail tab, 94–95
opening Filing Cabinet, 22
opening mailbox, 19, 89
opening next message, 91
pager alerts, 428–429
pasting text, 24
on PDAs, 428
pictures, adding to messages, 131–133, 139–141
pictures, finding, 142
printing, 92
private mailing lists (Groups@AOL), 326
quoting original message, 112–113
Read button, 90
Read Mail menu, accessing from AOL toolbar, 27
reading new messages, 89–93, 143–145
reading old messages, 94–95
red mail flag, 19
Reminder Service, 305–307
Reply All button, 91
Reply button, 91
replying to all recipients, 91
replying to messages, 91
replying to other than sender, 112
replying to sender, 111–113
retrieving deleted messages, 91
Save to Filing Cabinet button, 91
saving in Filing Cabinet, 22, 91–92
saving in Filing Cabinet automatically, 93
saving to hard drive, 22
sending messages, 107–109, 115–116, 143–145, 222–223
sending questions to AOL Customer Service, 53–54
signature files, 137–139, 245
smileys, 133
sorting mailbox, 97–98
sounds, adding to messages, 131–133
spam, 95–97
spell check, 24, 130–131
Status button, 93
styled text, 136–137
text formatting preferences, 264–265
underlined text, 136–137
unsending messages, 115–116
violations, reporting to AOL, 66–68
viruses, 64
voice recognition software, 23
Write mail, accessing from AOL toolbar, 27

e-mail addresses
@ symbol, 101
about, 101–102
blocking e-mail from, 75
case sensitivity, 102
defined, 465
finding, for AOL members, 344–347
finding, for non-AOL members, 351–353
Internet format, 101
yours, 101

emoticons, 465
Emotional Health channel, 404
encryption, 465
entertainment channel, 394–397
Entertainment News channel, 368
Esc key, to stop loading pages, 28
ET (EST or EDT), 465
Event Directory, 11–12, 281, 289
event invitations, 327–328

Exit Free Area menu option (Ctrl+E), 35
Exit menu option (Alt+F4), 34
Explore Shop@AOL, 310

F

Family News channel, 368
FAQ, defined, 465
Fares and Reservations channel, 392–393
Favorite Places
adding to Chats, 295
adding to e-mail, 295
adding to instant messages, 154, 295
adding to Welcome Screen, 299–300
defined, 465
Favorite Places list
adding items to, 293–295
adding top window to, 25
copying, 299
folders, creating new, 296–298
number per AOL account, 292
organizing, 296–298
renaming items, 298
saving with a new name, 299
as sign-on screen, 295
Favorite Places window, 295
file compression, 214, 465
file libraries, 78–79, 214–215
File menu
Download Manager menu option, 23
Exit menu option, 23
File Cabinet menu option, 22
Log Manager menu option, 23, 156
Music Player menu option, 23
New menu option, 22
Offline Newsgroups menu option, 23
Open menu option, 22
Open Picture Finder menu option, 22
Print menu option, 22
Print Setup menu option, 22
Save As menu option, 22
Save menu option, 22
Save to Filing Cabinet menu option, 22
Voice recognition menu option, 23
You've Got Picture menu option, 23

files. *See also* **Download Manager**
decompressing, 220
defined, 465
finding, 22, 214
opening, 22
printing, 22, 24
saving to hard drive, 22
Files You've Downloaded window, 221
Filing Cabinet. *See also* **Automatic AOL (Auto AOL); e-mail**
Add Folder button, 125
AOL Mail and, 145
Auto AOL button, 126
automatic retention, turning off, 128
automatically saving all e-mail, 123
backup preferences, 267–268
buttons, 125–126
compacting, 127
defined, 466
Delete button, 125
deleting items, 127
Find button, 126
folder, creating, 127–128
Help button, 126
Manage button, 126–127
number per AOL account, 244
offline mail, 128–129
Offline Newsgroups, 23
Open button, 125
opening, 22, 124
organizing, 127–128
reading messages, 125
rename button, 125
searching, 126–127
Send Later button, 128
Sort Folder By button, 125
film. *See* **"You've Got Pictures"**
financial centers channel, 375
Find Files feature, 214
Find It Online icons, 5
Find menu option, 35
finding image files, 22
formatting text, 136–137, 151, 154
forum, 187, 466
founder (Groups@AOL), 327
FTP (File Transfer Protocol)
defined, 466
storage per AOL account, 245

Index

G

Game Parlor channel, 398
Game Shows Online channel, 399
Games channel, 397–399, 407
Gay & Lesbian channel, 410
Genealogy Forum channel, 406
Generation X channel, 409
Get AOL Member Profile menu option, 35
GIF (Graphic Interchange Format), 466
gifts
    reminder service, 305–307
    suggestion area, 307
Global Gourmet channel, 371
Global Meeting Places channel, 372
glossary, 459–476
Go button, 28
Go to Keyword menu option, 35
Gossip channel, 368
GPF (General Protection Fault), 466
Grandstand channel, 390–391
graphic files
    Download Center, 216–218
    opening, 22
    saving to hard drive, 22
Great Gift Ideas area, 307
Greeting and Mail Extras window, 131–133
Groups@AOL, 325–327
Guest access, 450–452
guest lists online, 327–328
Guide screen names, 58

H

hand pointer, 35
handheld organizers, 428
hardware requirements, 2
headers, 466
Headline News channel, 369
Health channel, 402–404
Health News channel, 368
heart icon. *See* Favorite Places list
help classes, 57–58
Help menu
    AOL Access Phone Numbers menu option, 26
    AOL Help menu item, 51
    AOL Help menu option, 26
    Help With Keywords menu option, 26
    What's New in AOL 6.0 menu item, 50
Help menu option keyboard shortcut, 35
help resources offline
    books, 47, 49
    Help database (F1), 47–48
    Member Services, 49
    phone support (toll-free), 49
help resources online
    AOL Help, 51–54
    AOL Help Community, 55–57
    AOL Tips, 51
    Ask the Staff links, 53
    Best of AOL, 51
    chat with Computing help, 59
    chat with Customer Service, 54–55
    chat with other members, 57
    chat-room classes, 57–58
    classes, registering for, 57–58
    Computer Center Channel, 58–59
    Computer Service Center links, 53
    computing help, 58–59
    contact Customer Service in chat, 54–55
    Expert Live Help link, 59
    FastFacts, 51
    first-time users, 49–50
    Get Help Now window, 59
    guide for new members, 50–51
    Help Illustrated diagrams, 59
    help resources directory, 51
    How-To Tab (AOL Computing window), 59
    interactive classes, 57
    live chat with Computing help, 59
    live chat with Customer Service, 54–55
    live chat with other members, 57
    live chat-room classes, 57–58
    live one-on-one help, 54–55
    members, asking for help, 55–57
    message boards for posting questions, 55–57, 59
    More Help button, 51
    New Features button, 50
    new member guide, 50–51
    Quick Tour, 51
    QuickStart, 50–51
    searching AOL Help, 52–53
    sending e-mail to AOL Customer Service, 53–54
    Tell Me About AOL 6.0 button, 50

Continued

help resources online *(continued)*
   tips and tools, 51
   tutorial (basic AOL features), 51
   Welcome to AOL window, 49–50
   What's New in AOL 6.0 slide show, 50
high speed access. *See* **broadband**
History feature, Web browser, 273
History list, opening, 28
history trail, defined, 466
holidays
   invitations, 327–328
   reminder service, 305–307
home pages, about, 12–13
home pages, creating
   1-2-3 Publish, 316–320
   advanced authoring tools, 324–325
   Easy Designer, 320–324
   for events, 327–328
   for private groups, 325–327
home pages, defined, 467
Homework Help channel, 27, 382–383, 407
horoscopes, 252
host, 467
Host **screen names, 58**
House and Home channel, 400–401
How to Down load window, 212
HTML, defined, 467. *See also* **Web pages, creating**
HTML file, opening, 22
http, defined, 467
Hughes Network Systems DIRECTV set-top box, 421, 456–457
hyperlinks
   blocking from chat rooms, 76
   changing color, 36
   defined, 36
   determining destination before clicking, 36
   in junk mail, 95
   as underlined words, 36–37
hypertext links. *See* **hyperlinks**

I

icons
   Away Message (Buddy List), 169
   blue globe, 41
   book, 5

chat rooms, 41
check marks in e-mail window, 92–93
defined, 36, 467
Favorite Places, 37
file folder, 41
forums, 41
globe, 41
heart, 37
on menus, 41
mini-icons, 41
My Calendar, 283
people in profile, 41
sheet of paper, 41
swirling progress icon, 27
text articles, 41
triangle, 37
Web sites, 41
wrench (My Calendar), 283
yellow note (Buddy List Away Message), 169
icons, Welcome Screen
   AOL triangle, 20
   calender grid, 20
   Chat button, 20
   e-mail, 19
   film canister icon, 20
   My Calendar, 20
   picture links, 20
   What's New on AOL, 20
   You've Got Pictures, 19
Ignore, defined, 467
image files
   finding, 22
   viewing, 23–24
$im_off, 158
$im_on, 158
Independent traveler channel, 393–394
insertion mark, 42
insertion point, 467
instant messaging. *See also* **Buddy List feature**
   about, 9–10, 149
   adding Favorite Places to messages, 295
   adding hyperlinks to messages, 154, 295
   AIM, 161, 460
   Available button, 158
   Away messages, 159–160
   blocked messages, 151
   blocking screen names, 76–77
   credit card inquiries, 151

defined, 467
emoticons, adding to messages, 156
exchanging messages outside AOL, 161
font preferences, 264–265
formatting text, 151, 154
Get Profile button, 158
graphics preferences, 265
logging conversations, 156
multiple conversations, 153–154
Notify AOL button, 153
password inquiries, 151
personal icons, adding to messages, 156–157
privacy preferences, 159
private (Groups@AOL), 326
Profile button, 153
recipient not receiving, 151
replying to messages, 151–153
Respond button, 151–152
Send button, 153
sending messages, 150
smileys, adding to messages, 156
sounds, enabling/disabling, 270
spell checking, 154
starting a conversation, 149
text formatting preferences, 264–265
timestamping messages, 154–155
turning off/on, 157–159
unwanted messages, 149
violations, reporting to AOL, 66–68

Instant Messenger. *See* **AIM (AOL Instant Messenger)**
Interest Profile, number per AOL account, 245
International channel, 369–372
International News channel, 370
Internet
defined, 468
searching for phrases, 28–29
Internet connection requirements, AOLTV, 421
Internet Explorer. *See* **Microsoft Internet Explorer (MSIE)**
Internet newsgroups. *See* **newsgroups**
Internet-ready phones, 428
invitation, 468
ISDN, 468
ISP, 468
italic text. *See* **formatting text**

J

java, 468
Job Search channel, 376–377
junk mail, 95–97, 133–136
TOSSpam, 96

K

Keep As New, 468
keyboard shortcuts
about, 33–34
defined, 469
list of, 34–35
Keyword window, 29, 43, 340
Keywords
123 Publish, 317
AAC, 382
Access, 26, 459
Add2Cal, 287
Ages, 409
AH, 403
Anywhere, 428
AOL Book Shop, 325
AOL Plus, 429, 458
AOL Tips, 51
AOLTV, 422
Autos, 400
Best of AOL, 51
Billing, 444
Bistro, 372
Blockbuster, 436
Bookstore, 49
Buddy List, 166
BuddyView, 160, 165
Business News, 368
Calendar, 283
Call AOL, 49
CBS News, 367
CDN Smileys, 180
Channels, 365
Chic Simple, 360
Click and Go, 50
CNET, 378
Computer Center, 377
Computing Communities, 380

Continued

Keywords *(continued)*
  Courses, 383
  Customer Service, 53
  Daily Download, 213
  defined, 469
  Destinations, 392
  Dictionary, 381
  Digital City, 384
  Download Center, 216
  Download Manager, 220
  Easy Designer, 321
  Email Finder, 351
  Ent News, 368
  Entertainment, 394
  Family Net, 368
  FastFacts, 51
  File Search, 378
  Fools, 374
  Friend, 207, 443
  Game Shows, 399
  Games, 397
  Gay, 410
  Get Help Now, 379
  Global Meeting, 372
  going directly to, 28
  Groups@AOL, 326
  GS, 390
  GS Soccer, 187
  Guarantee, 301
  Hardware, 220
  Health, 402
  Help, 26, 51
  Help Class, 57
  Help Community, 186
  High Speed, 453
  Hometown, 315
  House & Home, 400
  How to Download, 211
  Insider Savings, 434
  Instant Messenger, 161, 207
  Intl Cultures, 371
  Intl News, 370
  Intl Travel, 372
  Invitations, 328
  Junk Mail, 95
  Keyword, 44, 341
  Kids Only, 407
  KO, 407
  KO Help, 408
  LD Member, 425
  Leaders, 58
  Lesbian, 410
  Life News, 368
  Live, 184
  Local Guide, 384
  Local News, 369
  Long Distance, 425
  Mail Controls, 133
  Member Opinions, 392
  Members, 345
  MNC, 374
  MO, 406
  Money Basics, 374
  Moviefone, 395
  Movies, 395
  Music, 23, 396
  My Boards, 207
  Neighborhood Watch, 63, 77
  Netmarket, 435
  New, 340, 410
  News Search, 336–367
  Newsgroup Scoop, 199
  Newsgroups, 198
  Notify AOL, 66
  number of, 44
  Online Learning, 379
  Oxygen, 402
  Parental Controls, 68
  Parenting, 404
  Parlor, 398
  Password, 250
  PC, 175
  People Connection, 175
  Petersons, 383
  Photo Developer, 227
  Photo News, 369
  Pictures, 227
  Politics, 368
  PS, 405
  Quick Checkout, 301
  QuickStart, 50
  Real Estate, 375
  Reminder, 301, 305
  Rewards, 432

Roots, 406
Savings Clubs, 434
Scoreboard, 389
Screen Names, 247
  searching for, 43–44
  searching list of, 341
Send Page, 425
Set My Places, 300
Shop Direct, 361
Shopping, 356
Shopping Customer Service, 308
SoftwareBuys, 217
Speak Out, 367
Teens, 408
Thrive, 404
Today in Health, 368
TOS, 64–66
Travel, 391
Travelers Advantage, 436
UCAOL, 383
Upgrade Shop, 441
US World, 367
Virus, 99, 219
Virus Info, 220
Visa, 434
Weather, 368
where to type, 43
Web Page, 325
White Pages, 350–351
Women, 401
Xtreme, 398
Yellow Pages, 348
YGP Help, 239
"You've Got Pictures," 23
  defined, 469
  going directly to, 28
  number of, 44
  searching for, 43–44
  searching list of, 341
Kids Only channel, 407–408
Kids Only chats, blocking screen names from, 76
Kodak film. *See* "You've Got Pictures"
Kodak pictures icon, 20

L

Ldrs screen names, 58
legal terms of AOL Membership, 65

library, 469
lifestyle forums, blocking screen names from, 75
link, defined, 469
List More Files button, 215
Listen to Online Radio, 396
Local Guides channel, 384–385
Local News channel, 369, 384–385
Local Weather channel, 368
Locate AOL Member Online menu option, 35
location, changing, 278
Log Manager
  Append Log button, 182
  Close Log button, 183
  logging instant message conversations, 156
  Open Log button, 182
long distance service, 424–425

M

Macintosh operating system
  AOL 6.0 requirements, 442
  keyboard shortcuts, 33–35
Mail Controls, 133–136, 469
Mail Controls window, 73–75
Mail menu, 105–106
  Recently Deleted menu option, 91
Mail Waiting to Be Sent window, 128–129. *See also* **Automatic AOL (Auto AOL)**
mailing list, defined, 469
Maps & Directions, 27
Market News Center, 374
master screen names and Online Timer, 74
McAfee's antivirus programs, 220
MCI WorldCom paging service, 425–426
meetings
  invitations, 327–328
  places to hold, global, 372
  reminder service, 305–307
member, defined, 469
Member Profile window, 347
member profiles
  defined, 470
  number per AOL account, 244
  searching, 344–347
member-created chat rooms, blocking screen names from, 76

menus
   . . . (ellipsis), 41
   Alt key shortcuts, 33–34
   arrow key shortcuts, 34
   closing with Esc key, 34
   Ctrl key shortcuts, 33–34
   drop-down lists, 42
   drop-down menus, 42
   Enter key shortcuts, 34
   Esc key shortcut, 34
   grayed-out menu items, 42
   list boxes, 41
   mini-icons, 41
   navigating with arrow keys, 42
   navigating with keyboard, 33–34
   navigating with Tab key, 42
   submenus, 41
   underlined letters, 34
   using keyboard instead of mouse, 33–34
message, 470. *See also* **e-mail**
message boards
   Auto AOL, 193, 222–223
   defined, 185–186, 470
   filtering preferences, setting, 194–195
   filters, creating, 195
   Find By menu, 189
   finding communities, 186–188
   finding messages, 191–192
   hiding message, 194–195
   List All button, 188
   List Unread button, 188
   Mark read button, 188
   members, asking for help, 55–57
   More button, 188
   Offline reading preferences, 193
   posting messages, 195–197, 222–223
   posting preferences, setting, 193
   preferences, setting, 192–195
   private (Groups@AOL), 326
   quoting message, 197
   reading messages, 188–190, 222–223
   replying to messages, 197–198
   signature file, 193, 195
   Subscribe button, 188
   teens, 408
   threading, defined, 193
   Travel Boards, 393–394
   viewing preferences, setting, 193–194
   violations, reporting to AOL, 66–68

meta tags, 322
Metrocall paging service, 425–426
Microsoft Internet Explorer (MSIE), 470
mini-icons, 41
35mm film, 226
MobileComm paging service, 425–426
modem, changing, 278
Moms Online channel, 405–406
Money Basics, 374
Monster.com channel, 376–377
The Motley Fool, 374
mouse. *See also* **keyboard shortcuts**
   buttons, 33
   context menus, 33
   double-clicking, 33
   double-headed arrow pointer, 40
   dragging and dropping, 33
   hand pointer, 35–36
   menus, 33
   on-screen arrow changing shape, 32–33
   right-clicking, 33
   single-clicking, 33
   using keyboard instead, 33–34
mouse pointer, changing shape, 32–33
mousepads with digital photos, ordering online, 238–239
Moviefone channel, 395–397
Moviefone support, 428
movies
   Blockbuster Movie, 436
   Movies channel, 384–385, 395–397, 407
MP3, 23
mugs with digital photos, ordering online, 238–239
multimedia
   Spinner plug-in, 396
   Winamp plug-in, 396
music, downloading, 396
Music channel, 395, 407
Music Player software, 23
My Calendar service. *See also* **AOL Anywhere**
   about, 11–12, 282
   accessing from AOL toolbar, 27
   AOL Anywhere synchronization, 252
   appointments, adding from Event Directory, 289
   appointments, adding from Idea List, 288
   appointments, adding new, 286–288
   appointments, viewing details, 284
   day start and stop times, specifying, 286

day view, 284
day view settings, 286
group scheduling (Groups@AOL), 326
horoscope settings, 286
location setting, 285
month view, 284
number per AOL account, 245
offline reading, 283
opening, 283
Options window, 285
preferences, setting, 285–286
recurring events, 287
Settings button, 285
time zone setting, 285
viewing from any computer, 290
weather forecast, turning off, 285
weather settings, 285
wrench icon, 283
zip code setting, 285

My Places
adding Favorites to Welcome Screen, 299–300
customizing, 20–21

My Portfolio, AOL Anywhere, 252
My Profile button, AOL Anywhere, 251

N

navigation bar
Address box, 28
AOL Hometown, 315–316
Back button, 28
Forward button, 28
Hide/Show Channels button, 28
History List, 28
Keyword button, 29
Reload button, 28
Search box, 28–29
Search button, 28–29
Stop button, 28

Nerve Center channel, 409
Net. *See* **Internet**
netiquette, 470
Netscape Navigator, 470
network, 470
New Contact button, Address Book, 104
New Group button, Address Book, 104
New Instant Message menu option, 35

New menu option (Ctrl+N), 34
News channel, 366–369, 407
News Profile, number per AOL account, 244
News Search channel, 367
News Ticker, 12, 369
newsgroups
Auto AOL, 222–223
blocking screen names from, 79–80
defined, 198, 470
downloading messages, 206–207, 222–223
filtering preferences, setting, 204–205
finding communities, 198–200
finding messages, 205
headers, setting preferences, 203
Offline Newsgroups location, 23
Offline Reading, 206–207
posting messages, 206, 222–223
posting preferences, setting, 204
preferences, setting, 203–205
reading messages, 201–202
spam, 204
subscribing to newsgroups, 200–201
viewing preferences, setting, 203

Newsgroups window
Add Newsgroups button, 201
Expert Add button, 201
Search All Newsgroups button, 200

Note icons, 5
Notification Bar, AOLTV, 419

O

offline reading, Auto AOL, 222–223
online, defined, 471
online calendar. *See* My Calendar service
Online Campus, 383
online community, 471
online dictionaries, 24, 371, 381–382
online film developing. *See* "You've Got Pictures"
Online Greetings, 27
online help, Kids Only category, 82
online invitations, 327–328
Online Learning Center channel, 379–380
online mailbox, number per AOL account, 244
Online Mailbox window, opening, 89
online pictures. *See* "You've Got Pictures"
Online Radio, listening to, 23

online safety. *See also* Parental Controls
  Community Action Team, 67
  community guidelines, 64–66
  Community Guidelines button, 65
  Computer Safety button, 64
  credit card inquiries, 64
  downloading files, 98–99
  E-mail Safety button, 63
  Index to Terms of Service button, 65
  Member Agreement button, 65
  Neighborhood Watch area, 62–63
  Notify AOL, 66–68
  Notify AOL button, 64
  Parental Controls button, 63
  password inquiries, 64
  password selection, 64
  Privacy Policy button, 65
  reporting problems to AOL, 66–68
  Shopping & Banking button, 64
  Suggested Safeguards button, 64
  Terms of Service (TOS), 64–66
  violations, reporting to AOL, 66–68
  viruses, 64
online thesaurus, 24
Online Timer, 74
Open menu option (Ctrl+O), 34
Other Stores button, AOL Shopping Assistant, 311
owner rights (Groups@AOL), 327

P

packet-switching network (PSN), 471
page, defined, 471
paging service, 425–426
Palm Computing platform, 428
Parent Soup channel, 405
Parental Controls
  about, 68
  age category, 69–72
  AOLTV, 420
  chat room controls, 75–76
  defined, 471
  download controls, 78–79
  editing existing controls, 71–72
  e-mail controls, 73–75
  file libraries, 78–79
  FTP site controls, 78–79
  General Access category, 69
  Groups@AOL, 327
  instant message controls, 76–77
  Internet access controls, 77–78
  Keyword: **Note to Parents**, 69, 83
  Kids Only category, 69, 81–82
  Mail Controls window, 73–75
  master screen names, additional, 78
  Mature Teen category, 69
  newsgroup controls, 78–79
  Online Timer, 72–73
  parental notification, 83
  personal information collection, 83
  Premium Services controls, 80
  privacy policy, 83
  screen names for children, creating, 68–69
  Set Parental Controls button, 71
  slideshow, viewing, 68
  software library controls, 78–79
  time limits, setting, 72–73
  Web access controls, 77–78
  Young Teen category, 69
Parenting channel, 404–406
party invitations, 327–328
password inquiries
  instant messaging, 151
  online safety, 64
passwords
  changing, 250
  defined, 471
  for Filing Cabinet, 255–256
  forgotten, 247, 304
  for screen name, 247, 250
  selection, 64
  for shopping, 304
  storage preferences, 255–256
  tricks for remembering, 247
Paste menu option (Ctrl+V), 34
path (Web), defined, 334
PDA support, 428
People Connection, defined, 472
People Connection channel, 409–410
People Connection chat areas, blocking screen names from, 75
People Directory, defined, 472
People menu
  Get Directory Listing menu option, 158
  Send Message to Pager menu option, 425–426
personal digital assistant (PDA), 471

Index

Personal Filing Cabinet (PFC). *See* Filing Cabinet
Personal Finance channel, 10–11, 373–375
personal reminder service, 305–307
personalization options, 27
Philips Electronics set-top box, 421
phone numbers for AOL, 26
Photo CDs with digital photos, ordering online, 238–239
photo collections, private (Groups@AOL), 326
photographs. *See* "You've Got Pictures"
photos channel, 369
Picture Finder, 142
Picture-in-Picture option, AOLTV, 419
Pocket PC devices, 428
political news channel, 368
post, defined, 472
postmaster, defined, 472
preferences, setting
   AOL access numbers, 278
   AOL Browser, 272–277
   application associations, 258
   associations (file types), 258
   AutoComplete (MSIE), 276–277
   Automatic AOL, 261–263
   Buddy List privacy, 256–258
   Certificates (MSIE), 276
   chat rooms, 266–267
   compressed Web Graphics, 277
   connection preferences, 278
   download preferences, 270–272
   e-mail, 123, 258–261, 267–268
   e-mail application, 258
   e-mail marketing, 255
   file type associations, 258
   Filing Cabinet, 123, 255–256, 267–268
   Filing Cabinet automatic retention of e-mail, 123
   Filing Cabinet password, 255–256
   fonts, 264–265
   grammar, 263–264
   graphics size, 265
   History feature (for Web browsing), 273
   history trial retention period, 269–270
   Home Page, 272
   instant message privacy, 256–258
   instant message sounds, 270
   Internet preference, 272–277
   mailing lists, removing name from, 254–255
   marketing preferences, 254–255
   Microsoft Internet Explorer, 272–277
   Microsoft Wallet, 276–277
   multimedia, automatic play, 277
   Netscape Navigator, 272
   newsgroups reader, 258
   password storage, 255–256
   pop-up online marketing, 255
   privacy options, 256–258
   punctuation, 263–264
   security (MSIE zones), 274–275
   setup preferences, 278
   shopping, Quick Checkout, 302–304
   shopping, Reminder Service, 305–307
   shopping, Shopping Assistant, 277, 309–311
   sounds, 270
   spell check, 263–264
   telephone marketing, 254
   text formatting, 264–265
   toolbar appearance, 268–270
   typing errors, 263–264
   Web browser, 258, 272–277
   Web preferences, 272–277
   Welcome Greeting sound, 270
Preferences window
   Association, 258
   Auto AOL, 261–263
   Chat, 266–267
   Download, 270–272
   Filing Cabinet, 267–268
   Font, Text, & Graphics, 264–265
   Internet Properties (WWW), 272–277
   Mail, 258–261
   Marketing, 254–255
   Multimedia, 277–278
   Passwords, 255–256
   Privacy, 256–258
   Spelling, 263–264
   Toolbar & Sound, 268–270
Preferences window, opening, 253
Print button, Address Book, 104
Print menu
   Print Central menu option, 24
   Print menu option, 24, 34
   Print Setup menu option, 24
   Printer Supplies menu option, 24
   Printing Service menu option, 24
Print menu option (Ctrl+P), 34
printer, setting up, 22, 24

private chat rooms, blocking screen names from, 76
private groups, 325–327
private room, defined, 472
profiles
   defined, 472
   violations, reporting to AOL, 66–68
puzzles with digital photos, ordering online, 238–239

Q

Quick Looks
   1-2-3 Publish, 313
   address book, 87
   AOL Anywhere, 243, 423
   AOL Help, 31
   AOL Hometown, 313
   AOL Insider Savings Club, 431
   AOL Instant Messenger, 121
   AOL Neighborhood Watch, 61
   AOL Netmarket, 431
   AOL Plus, 423
   AOL Rewards, 431
   AOL Search, 331
   AOL Shop Direct, 355
   AOL Shopping Guarantee, 301
   AOL Visa card, 431
   AOLTV, 415
   appointments, 281
   Ask-a-Teacher, 363
   attached files, 87
   broadband connections, 423
   business channels, 363
   Channel bar, 363
   channel searches, 331
   chat rooms, 173
   Chic Simple, 355
   communities, 387
   copying My Favorites, 291
   courtesy copies, 87
   customizing My Places, 291
   Download Manager, 209
   downloading files, 209
   downloading photos, 225
   Easy Designer, 313
   e-mail, 87, 121
   Email Finder, 343
   e-mail signatures, 121
   Event Directory, 281
   Favorite Places, 291
   Filling Cabinet, 121
   finding messages, 173
   games, 387
   gift reminder service, 301
   Groups@AOL, 313
   help, 31
   hyperlinks, 31
   information channels, 363, 387
   instant messages, 121
   Internet shopping, 355
   job search, 363
   junk mail, 87
   keyboard shortcuts, 31
   keyword searches, 331
   keywords, 31
   kids only AOL, 387
   local searches, 331
   long distance plan, 423
   mail center, 87
   message boards, 173
   My Calendar, 281
   My Places customization, 291
   navigation bar, 17
   newsgroups, 173
   Notify AOL, 61
   offline help, 31
   offline reading, 173
   online photo albums, 225
   online safety, 61
   organizing My Favorites, 291
   paging service, 423
   Parental Controls, 61
   passwords, 243
   People Directory, 343
   people search, 343
   personal enrichment channels, 387
   phone support, 31
   Photo Developer, 225
   picture-in-picture option, 415
   pictures in e-mail, 121
   preferences, 243
   private online area, 313
   Quick Checkout, 301
   QuickStart, 31

reading e-mail, 87
receiving instant messages, 121
reminder service, 301
reward programs, 431
screen names, 243
search tools, 331, 343
sending instant messages, 121
Shop@AOL, 355
shopping, 355, 431
shopping preferences, 301
spell checker, 121
television programs, 415
Terms of Service, 61
timestamping instant messages, 121
toolbar, 17
travel reservations, 387
viruses, 209
Visa card, 431
warehouse club, 431
weather, 363
Web pages (yours), 313
Welcome Screen, 17
White Pages, 343
Yellow Pages, 343
"You've Got Pictures," 225

Quick Search, People Directory, 345–346
Quit menu option (Alt+F4), 34

R

radio, listening online, 396
Read Description button, 215
Read Mail menu, accessing from AOL toolbar, 27
Read Mail menu option (Ctrl+R)
   keyboard shortcut, 35
Real Estate channel, 375, 384–385
real time
   defined, 472
RealAudio
   defined, 472
Reference Resources channel, 380–382
Related Files button, 215
Research and Learn channel, 380–383
return receipt
   defined, 472–473

S

satellite, defined, 473
Save menu option (Ctrl+S), 34
Save/replace button, Favorite Places list, 298
saving chats. *See* **Log manager**
Schedule Automatic AOL window, 223
Scoreboard channel, 389–390
screen names
   AOL Screen Names window, 247–249
   blocking from AOL Live auditorium events, 75
   blocking from chat rooms, 75
   blocking from conference rooms, 76
   blocking from instant message feature, 76–77
   blocking from Internet access, 77–78
   blocking from lifestyle forums, 75
   blocking from newsgroups, 79–80
   blocking from private chat rooms, 76
   blocking from the Web, 77–78
   choosing, 245–246
   creating, 247–249
   creating just for chatting, 77
   defined, 473
   deleting, 249–250
   determining current, 97
   downloading files, preventing, 78–79
   games (Premium Services), restricting access to, 80
   number per AOL account, 244
   password, changing, 250
   password, forgotten, 247
   password, tricks for remembering, 247
   restoring after deleting, 250
   violations, reporting to AOL, 66–68
scroll, defined, 473
scroll bar, defined, 473
search, defined, 473
Search box, leaving empty for more options, 29
search tools, content
   AOL Search, 332–336, 340–341
   Boolean operators, how to use, 337
   business, searching for, 336
   case sensitivity, 337
   channel-level searches, 338–339
   Classifieds search, 336
   Downloads search, 336
   Encyclopedia search, 336
   Government Guide search, 336

Continued

search tools, content *(continued)*
  Home Pages search, 336
  Internet content, 332–336
  Internet-only search tools, 338
  Job Search, 336
  keyword searches, 340–341
  Kids Only search, 336
  local searches, 339–340
  Maps search, 336
  Message Board Search, 336
  Monster.com, 336
  new additions to AOL, finding, 340
  News search, 336, 367
  Shopping Search, 335–336
  Stock Quotes search, 336
  tips and techniques for searching, 336–338
  Web content, 332–336
  White Pages search, 336
  Yellow Pages, 336
search tools, people
  businesses, 348–350
  E-Mail Finder, 351–353
  member profiles, 344–347
  non-AOL members, 351–353
  People Directory, 344–347
  Personals, 352
  privacy, 352
  White Pages, 350–351
  Yellow Pages, 348–350
searchable database, defined, 473
Select menu option (Ctrl+A), 34
self-extracting archive, 473
Send a Page window, 426
Send Instant Message window, 149
Send Mail menu option, 35
Send To button, Address Book, 104
server, defined, 473
settings, accessing from AOL toolbar, 27
Settings menu. *See* **preferences, setting**
set-top box, AOLTV, 421
Sexuality channel, 404
shareware files, finding, 216–218
Shop@AOL. *See also* **shopping**
  accessing from AOL toolbar, 27
  categories, 357–359
  stores, listing all, 358
Shop@AOL Search, 310

shopping
  AOL AutoVantage, 436
  AOL Insider Savings Club, 434
  AOL merchandise, 361
  AOL Netmarket, 435
  AOL Rewards, 432–433
  AOL Shop Direct, 361
  AOL Travelers Advantage, 436
  AOL Visa, 433–434
  Blockbuster Movie, 436
  Certified Merchants program, 307–308
  Chic Simple, 360
  comparison shopping service, 309–311
  credit card information, storing securely online, 302–304
  Customer Service contact information, 307–308
  Federal Trade Commission online tips, 312
  money-back guarantee, 308–309
  movies, 436
  online safety, 311–312
  Parental Controls, 304
  password, 304
  price comparisons, 309–311
  Quick Checkout, 302–304
  Reminder Service, 305–307
  reward programs, 432–434
  savings clubs, 434
  shipping information, storing securely online, 302–304
  Shopping Assistant, 309–311
  shopping cart, adding items to, 358–359
  shopping habits not tracked, 311
  Shopping Search, 359–360
  tips, 361–362
  Visa card, 433–434
  wardrobe advice, 360
  warehouse club, 435
Shopping Channel. *See* **Shop@AOL; shopping**
shortcuts, creating to top window, 25
Sign Off menu, 25
Sign On menu, 25
signatures
  defined, 473–474
  e-mail, 137–139, 245
  message boards, 193, 195
signing off AOL, 23
sign-on kit, requesting, 443

Index

software. *See also* downloading files
    Download Center, 216–218
    file libraries, 214–215
software, buying online, 217
software libraries. *See* file libraries
software requirements, 2, 9
Software Search window, 217
sounds
    Download Center, 216–218
    enabling/disabling, 270
spam, 95–97, 474. *See also* junk mail
Spell Check menu option (Ctrl+=), 34
Spinner plug-in, 396, 474
sports, 252, 388–391, 407
Sports News channel, 369
sports scores, 12, 27
Sprint PCS Web-enabled Phones, 428
SSL encryption, 304
status (e-mail), 474
Stock Market channel, 373–374
Stock Portfolio, 27
stocks, 252
storage space per screen name, 315
streaming, defined, 474
sweatshirts with digital photos, ordering online, 238–239
Switch Screen Name menu option, 25
Symantec's antivirus programs, 220

T

TCP/IP
    configuration instructions, 454–455
    defined, 474
Teens channel, 408
telephone
    AOL Long Distance, 424–425
    line requirements for AOLTV, 419, 421
telephone directories
    White Pages, 336, 343, 350–351
    Yellow Pages, 336, 343, 348–350
telephone numbers for AOL, 26
television
    AOLTV, 415–422
    Television channel, 395, 407

Terms of Service (TOS)
    accessing, 64–66
    defined, 475
    e-mail warning, receiving, 67–68
    violations, reporting to AOL, 66–68
text, 23–24
text boxes, 42–43
text files, opening, 22
text formatting. *See* formatting text
Theaters channel, 395–397
ThirdAge channel, 409
Thirties Forum channel, 409
This Store button, AOL Shopping Assistant, 310
threading, defined, 193
Thrive Online channel, 404
tile, defined, 321
timeout, defined, 474
Tip icons, 5
toolbar
    adding areas to, 295
    AOL Progress icon, 27
    AOL Service button, 27
    defined, 474
    favorites button, 27
    Mail button, 27
    People button, 27
    Settings button, 27
TOSSpam (for reporting junk mail), 96
Traffic channel, 384–385
travel
    AOL Travelers Advantage, 436
    fares and reservations channel, 392–393
    Travel Boards channel, 393–394
    Travel channel, 371, 391–394
    Travel Reservations, 27
    Travelocity channel, 393
Trojan horse, 98–99, 218–220, 475
T-shirts with digital photos, ordering online, 238–239

U

underlined text. *See* formatting text
Undo menu option (Ctrl+Z), 34
University of California Extension Online, 383
unsending, 115–116, 475
Upgrade Center, 445–450

upload, 475
Upload button, 215
URLs (Universal Resource Locators)
    defined, 459, 475
    entering in Address box, 44
    entering in Keyword window, 44
    going directly to, 28

V

V.90, 475
viruses
    Anti-Virus Center, 219, 380
    antivirus programs, 219–220
    defined, 475
    downloading files, 98–99, 218–220
    e-mail, 64
voice recognition software, 23

W

weather, 251, 368
Web addresses
    entering in Keyword window, 44
    going directly to, 28
Web browser preferences, setting, 272–277
Web home page, number per AOL account, 245
Web pages
    going directly to, 28
    navigating, 28
    opening, 28
    returning to with History list, 28
    returning to with with Back button, 28
    saving to hard drive, 22
    stop loading, 28
    viewing history list, 28
    violations, reporting to AOL, 66–68
    yours, 12–13
Web pages, creating
    1-2-3 Publish, 316–320
    advanced authoring tools, 324–325
    Easy Designer, 320–324
    for events, 327–328
    for private groups, 325–327
    storage space per screen name, 315
Welcome greeting, enabling/disabling, 270

Welcome Screen
    about, 8, 11
    adding items to, 299–300
    customizing, 20–21
    Edit menu, 23–24
    File menu, 21–23
    Have You Tried?, 20–21
    Help menu, 26
    icons, 19–20
    Kids Only category, 81–82
    links, 20–21
    minimizing, 19
    My Places, 20–21, 299–300
    navigation Bar, 27–29
    Print menu, 24
    screen name, finding, 19
    Sign Off menu, 25
    Toolbar, 26–27
    underlined words, 36–37
    Window menu, 24–25
    "You've Got Pictures," 227
What's new on AOL, 340
White Pages, 336, 343
Winamp plug-in, 396, 476
Window menu
    Add Top Window to Favorite Places menu
        option, 25
    Arrange Icons menu option, 25
    Cascade menu option, 25
    Close All Except Front menu option, 25
    Forget Window Size and Position menu option, 25
    Forget Window Size menu option, 25
    Remember Window Size and Position menu
        option, 25
    Remember Window Size menu option, 25
    Tile menu option, 25
windows
    - (minus) button, 39
    active, determining, 39
    adding to Favorite Places, 25
    AOL as, 37
    AOL icon, 37, 40
    arranging on screen, 25
    border, 37
    bringing to front, 25, 39
    Close button, 39
    closing, 39
    closing all except front, 25

Index

control boxes, 37, 39
control menu, 40
creating shortcuts to top window, 25
down arrow (scroll bar), 38
dragging and dropping, 40
frame, 37
icons, 37
left arrow (scroll bar), 38
listing all currently open, 25
making active, 39
Maximize button, 39
menu, 40
Minimize button, 39
minimizing and organizing, 25
moving, 25, 40
overlapping boxes, 39
parts of, 37–39
remembering position and size, 25, 40
resizing, 40
Restore button, 39
restoring, 39
ribbon (scroll bar), 38
right arrow (scroll bar), 38
scroll bars, 37–39
shrinking, 39
sizing, 25, 40
slider (scroll bar), 38
square button, 39
stop loading, 28
title bar, 37
title bar color, 39
up arrow (scroll bar), 38
X button, 39
Windows 95, 441–442
Windows 98, 442
Windows CE, 428
Windows NT/2000, 442
Windows operating system keyboard shortcuts, 33–35
WinZip, 476
wireless keyboard, AOLTV, 421
Women channel, 401–402
word processing, opening blank documents, 22
World News channel, 370
World Wide Web (WWW), 476
Write Mail menu option (Ctrl+M), 35
Write Mail window, 43, 131–133
writer's tools, 23–24

X

Xtreme Games channel, 398

Y

Yellow Pages, 336, 343, 348–350
"You've Got Pictures"
about, 226
albums, creating, 233–235
albums, image source restrictions, 233
albums, sharing, 238
albums, viewing restrictions, 233
Buddy Albums, 238
customer service, 232
downloading pictures, 235–237
e-mailing pictures, 237
expiration date for pictures, 229
filenames for downloaded pictures, 236
finding a missing roll, 231–232
local developers, where to find, 227
merchandise with digital photos, ordering online, 238–239
My Pictures page, 229
online safety, 239
Parental Controls, 239–240
Parental Controls and, 227
Picture Store, 238–239
prints, ordering online, 238–239
renaming rolls, 231
resolution options for downloading, 235–237
saving a roll on AOL, 232–233
saving individual pictures to hard drive, 235–237
time for processing, 227
TOS, 239
tutorial, 228
viewing a roll, 229–231

Z

.zip file extension, 213
zipped files
decompressing, 220, 222
defined, 214

Up-to-700-Hour Free Trial for One Month — Try AOL 6.0 Now!

Use the unique registration number and password below for your FREE trial.

6J-3194-7277
BRASS-SEDANS

CD-ROM Installation Instructions for Windows

1. Insert the AOL CD-ROM into your CD-Rom drive.
2. If installation does not begin immediately, click Start on the task bar and then select Run.
3. Type **D:\SETUP** (or **E:\SETUP**) and click OK. Follow the easy instructions and you'll be online in minutes!

CD-ROM Installation Instructions for Macintosh

1. Insert the AOL CD into your CD-ROM drive.
2. Double-click the Install icon.
3. Follow the easy instructions and you'll be online in minutes!

FREE UP-TO-700-HOUR TRIAL MUST BE USED WITHIN ONE MONTH OF INITIAL SIGN-ON. TO AVOID BEING CHARGED A MONTHLY FEE, SIMPLY CANCEL BEFORE TRIAL PERIOD ENDS. Premium services carry surcharges, and communication surcharges may apply in AK, even during trial time. Members may incur telephone charges on their phone bill, depending on their location and calling plan, even during trial time. Offer is available to new members in the US, age 18 or older, and a major credit card or checking account is required. 56K access available in many areas: actual connection speeds may vary. For information, go to AOL Keyword: **High Speed**. America Online, AOL, and the triangle logo are registered service marks of America Online, Inc. Windows and Internet Explorer are registered trademarks of Microsoft Corp. Other names are the property of their respective holders. Copyright ©2000 America Online, Inc. All rights reserved.

Availability may be limited, especially during peak times.

Minimum System Requirements for AOL 6.0 for Windows: Windows 95 32-bit or Windows 98 operating system, 16MB of RAM, Pentium-class processor, 38MB available hard disk space, 640x480 or 800x600 resolution, 256 color display, 14.4 Kbps modem.

Note: You may be given the opportunity to upgrade your Web browser to Internet Explorer 5.0 while you are upgrading your AOL software. If you choose to upgrade your browser at the same time, you will need 80 additional MB of available hard disk space.

Minimum System Requirements for AOL 6.0 for Macintosh: Power Macintosh with 8.1 operating system, 32MB of built-in RAM, Virtual Memory or RAM Doubler turned on. 30MB available hard disk space, 256 color display, 14.4 Kbps modem. *For optimal use:* G3 or faster processor with 64MB of built-in RAM (or 128MB without Virtual Memory or RAM Doubler turned on), 100MB hard disk space, millions of colors, and a 57.6 Kbps modem.

Need Help? Call us toll-free at **1-800-827-6364**

AOL Selects the Best!

Shop With Confidence At AOL Shop Direct!

1. Guaranteed Security
Millions of customers have shopped online safely with AOL and you can too! AOL uses advanced encryption technology to help insure the security, accuracy, and privacy of your AOL Shop Direct transaction. AOL protects you against liability for fraudulent charges if reported promptly to your credit card provider.

2. Guaranteed Satisfaction
AOL Buyers search the marketplace for today's best-quality products, and, with the purchasing power of our 20 million customers, AOL Shop Direct can bring them to you at terrific values. YOUR SATISFACTION IS GUARANTEED BY AOL Shop Direct. If you are not satisfied with your purchase, for any reason, return it within 30 days of receipt for a full refund, including original shipping and handling. How many other online companies offer that?

3. Guaranteed Service
We make every effort to provide a quick, trouble-free transaction and prompt delivery of your purchase. However, should you have a question or problem, you are entitled to quick and courteous assistance. Call us toll-free at 1-888-299-0329.

Keyword: AOL Shop Direct

So easy to use,
no wonder it's #1

AOL Selects the Best!

Just Say It And Send It!

- **Send Instant Messages Faster!**

- **Write E-mails by Simply Using Your Voice**

- **Create Word Documents at the Speed of Your Voice**

Use your voice to type!

AOL's Point & Speak lets you talk naturally and as you talk, your words are transcribed like magic onto your computer screen. It's fast, easy and fun - not to mention a snap to learn! It can handle up to 160 words per minute with a 99% accuracy rate, and will learn your speaking style-including dialects and accents.

- Uses same technology as award winning Dragon NaturallySpeaking!
- Works with AOL and Windows applications!
- Contains 30,000-word active vocabulary and 230,000-word total vocabulary.
- Great for creating reports, letters, documents, school projects and more!
- Comes with high quality microphone!

System Requirements
Windows 95, 98, 200 Millenium,or Windows NT4.0 (with SP-6 or greater)
266 Mhz Processor
150 MB free drive space
64 MB RAM
CD-ROM installation
Speakers
Noise-canceling headset (included)

Order Today!   1-888-299-0329

$39.95 (s&h $5.95)   #0017192N00013013

Please allow 1-3 weeks for delivery. Prices and availability are subject to change without notice.

So easy to use, no wonder it's #1

AOL Selects the Best!

Welcome to AOL Press and Software - resources to help AOL members enjoy a fun, easy and rewarding online experience. AOL is committed to developing quality products that are easy to use and affordable - and serve every aspect of your online life. We hope you enjoy the AOL Press titles and we welcome your feedback at AOL Keyword: **Contact Shop Direct**

Sharing Your Photos Online Has Never Been Easier!

Pictures Online

This easy to follow guide shows you how to get your pictures online and share them with family and friends. Loaded with expert advice on everything from taking better pictures to selecting the right hardware.

Digital Imaging Made Easy™

- Learn about digital imaging in minutes with multimedia videos.
- Receive, view and personalize your photos online with "You've Got Pictures".℠
- Share your online pictures in e-mail, web pages, photo albums and other online projects.

Create Your Own Web Page In Just Minutes!

Creating Web Pages

This easy-to-understand guide explains how to use the AOL Web design tools – and shows you step-by-step how to put together a great-looking page with all the bells and whistles. And, once your page is done, you'll get the scoop on setting up a Web address in *AOL Hometown* – and spreading the word about your page.

Web Pages Made Easy™

- Complete package offers step-by-step instructions for preparing, designing, jazzing up and publishing your web site.
- Create and publish your own personal or small business web site in minutes.
- Learn the simple "secrets" of good web page design, and find out how easy it is to make your web page exciting and original.

Get the Most Out of Your PC And The Internet!

America Online's Guide to
Powering Up The Internet

Today's Internet technologies blur the line between computers and consumer electronics – and let you do things you never thought possible. This unique guide takes you on a grand tour of cutting-edge Internet hardware, software, and services – and shows you step-by-step how to make the most of them.

America Online's
PowerSuite Deluxe™

- Fix most computer mistakes automatically.
- Save space and keep your computer running faster.
- Prevent system problems before they happen!
- "Preview" graphics and documents without having to download or launch any applications.

Maximize Your Online Enjoyment!

America Online's
Internet Guide™

America Online makes it easy to jump on the Internet. This comprehensive guide shows you how to find your way around with new browsers and search engines, get more out of popular Internet destinations, take advantage of all your communications options including broadband Internet access, AOL Anywhere, and more.

America Online's
Internet Accelerator™

- Customize your PC to automate hundreds of everyday tasks.
- Monitor, filter and block undesirable Internet materials to protect your children.
- Protect your computer with powerful anti-virus software and stop viruses before they infect your system.

Order Today!   1-888-299-0329

Item	Price	S&H	Order #
Pictures Online Book	$19.95	(s&h $4.95)	#0017197N00012705
Digital Imaging Made Easy CD	$29.95	(s&h $7.95)	#0017196N00012321
Creating Cool Web Pages Book	$19.95	(s&h $4.95)	#0017198N00011904
Web Pages Made Easy CD	$29.95	(s&h $5.95)	#0017199N00012320
Powering Up The Internet	$19.95	(s&h $4.95)	#0017200N00012364
PowerSuite Deluxe 2.0	$29.95	(s&h $5.95)	#0017201N00012312
Internet Guide Book	$24.95	(s&h $6.95)	#0017202N00013186
Internet Accelerator 2.0	$29.95	(s&h $5.95)	#0017203N00012342

Please allow 1-3 weeks for delivery. Prices and availability are subject to change without notice.

America Online®
So easy to use, no wonder it's #1

AOL Selects the Best!

Protect Your PC!
#1 Virus Detection And Removal Software

- Eradicates Viruses
- Quarantines Infected and Suspicious Files
- Destroys Internet Threats
- Attacks Infected E-mail
- Protects Your Data
- Easy To Install And Operate

System Requirements
Windows 95, 98, 200 or NT4
66 Mhz Pentium Processor
5 MB hard drive space
8 MB RAM

Order Today!   1-888-299-0329

$19.95 (s&h $5.95)   #0017195N00013255

Please allow 1-3 weeks for delivery. Prices and availability are subject to change without notice.

So easy to use, no wonder it's #1

AOL Selects the Best!

The Easiest way To Get Your Pictures Online!

AOL's
digiCam
DIGITAL CAMERA

Point,

Click,

& Connect!

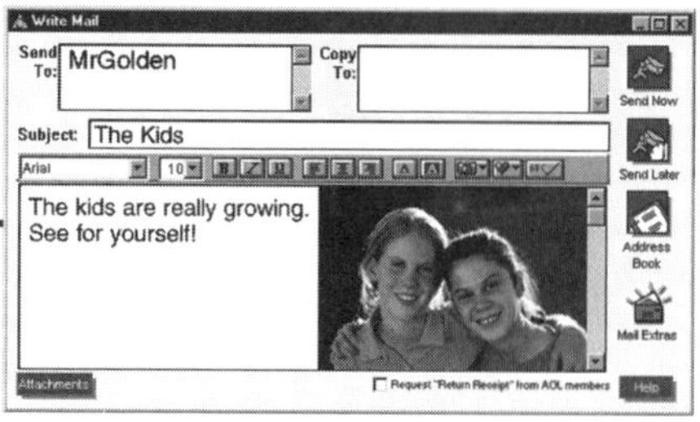

Everything you need in one great package to get you started with digital imaging. Just point, click, connect and send! Save money and time. There is no film or developing costs. It is easy to share your photos with family and friends through your e-mail or view pictures on your TV/VCR with the video output connector. AOL's PhotoCam includes an easy to use manual, MGI's PhotoSuite III SE, 8MB of built-in memory to shoot and store up to 128 pictures, beautiful black vinyl carrying case, 4AA batteries, USB and serial Connectors, and more. Available for PC.

System Requirements
- Pentium PC or higher • Windows 95/98 • PC Serial Connection
- 8 MB RAM • 70 MB hard drive space • CD-ROM Drive

Order Today!   1-888-299-0329

$59.95 (s&h $5.95)   **#0017193N00012815**

So easy to use,
no wonder it's #1

Please allow 1-3 weeks for delivery. Prices and availability are subject to change without notice.

AOL Selects the Best!

Learn Microsoft Office Programs The Easy, Interactive Way!

- Work faster and more efficiently with expert tools at your command
- Save hundreds, even thousands of dollars by teaching yourself!
- Learn at your own pace
- Increase your job skills

Word
Excel
Access
Outlook
Windows
PowerPoint

6 CD-Roms for one low price!

Six interactive training CD-ROMs covering each major module in the Microsoft Office 2000 suite. It's like having your own private tutor! LearnKey Experts are master trainers and know how to demonstrate and explain the many powerful features of this software. Our Experts will teach you the fundamentals you need to increase your productivity.

System Requirements
Windows 95, 98, 200 or NT4
66 Mhz Pentium Processor
5 MB hard drive space
8 MB RAM

Order Today!   1-888-299-0329

AOL's Office 2000 Training
$49.95 (s&h $5.95)   #0017191N00012905
Please allow 1-3 weeks for delivery. Prices and availability are subject to change without notice.

So easy to use, no wonder it's #1

AOL Selects the Best!

Keep It Clean With Window Washer
IMPROVE YOUR PC'S PERFORMANCE

Now Downloading
CDRIVE.psd

86%

■ Used space   □ Free space

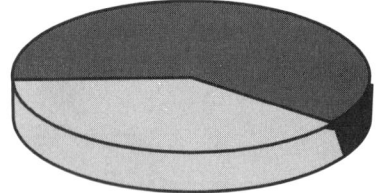

- Speed up your drive

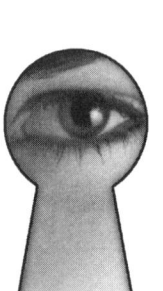

- Recover hard drive space

- Protect your privacy

A unique computer cleanup utility for Windows PCs that automatically cleans cache, cookies, history and other traces of computer and internet activity. Window Washer helps you keep your system clean and protects your privacy

System Requirements
Windows 95, 98, 2000 or NT4
66 Mhz Pentium Processor
5 MB hard drive space
8 MB RAM

Order Today!   **1-888-299-0329**

$29.95 (s&h $5.95)   #0017194N00013035

Please allow 1-3 weeks for delivery. Prices and availability are subject to change without notice.

So easy to use,
no wonder it's #1